Spanish

FOR

DUMMIES®

The CD files for this title can be found on the website
booksupport.wiley.com by entering the ISBN

9780470688151

Spanish
FOR
DUMMIES®

by Pedro Vázquez Bermejo and Susana Wald

WILEY

Spanish For Dummies®

Published by
John Wiley & Sons, Ltd
The Atrium
Southern Gate
Chichester
West Sussex
PO19 8SQ
England

E-mail (for orders and customer service enquires): cs-books@wiley.co.uk

Visit our Home Page on www.wiley.com

For general information on our other products and services, please contact our Customer Care Department within the U.S. at 877-762-2974, outside the U.S. at 317-572-3993, or fax 317-572-4002.

For technical support, please visit www.wiley.com/techsupport.

Wiley also publishes its books in a variety of electronic formats. Some content that appears in print may not be available in electronic books.

British Library Cataloguing in Publication Data: A catalogue record for this book is available from the British Library

ISBN: 978-0-470-68815-1

Printed and bound by CPI Group (UK) Ltd, Croydon, CR0 4YY

C9780470688151_291024

About the Authors

Pedro Vázquez Bermejo is a leading Spanish communicator, teacher, translator and interpreter living in London. He was born in the Spanish region of Extremadura (the land of the Conquistadores!) and grew up in Madrid, before settling down in London.

After studying sociology at Madrid's University Complutense in the late 1980s, Pedro developed a real passion for modern languages. He now specialises in teaching Spanish to all ages and levels of ability, from young multilingual children to retired enthusiastic academics. He holds both one-to-one and group sessions, including his innovative, absorbing and entertaining Spanish classes at the BBC headquarters in London.

The varied work Pedro has undertaken includes acting as a corporate interpreter and as a Spanish voiceover coordinator on educational interactive videos and multilingual historical role games. He is also a multilingual corporate image producer, and his work in this area has included producing some award-winning international corporate DVDs.

Pedro also holds a High Certificate in Foreign Commerce from the Chamber of Commerce of Madrid, and a masters degree in marketing and business administration.

Pedro is very personable and his excellent communication skills are imbued with warmth, humour and patience. He speaks in a standard Castilian Spanish accent, with pleasing and crystal-clear pronunciation. He also has a personal repertoire of *Spanglish* jokes and sayings, and is capable of 'talking the hind legs off a donkey' – try translating that into Spanish! He is never short of ideas for keeping the language (**lengua** in Spanish) rolling!

Susana Wald is a writer and a simultaneous and literary translator in Spanish, English, French and Hungarian. As a publisher, she has been working with books and authors for many years. She has been a teacher in Chile and Canada and has known the joy of learning from her students and their untiring enthusiasm and tolerance. She is also an artist and has had her work shown in many countries in North, Central and South America, and in Europe.

Authors' Acknowledgements

My thanks go to everyone who has helped to keep my blood pressure down throughout the time I've spent working on this book (excluding English tea and Spanish coffee)! I can now relax and acknowledge the following:

I thank my always-admired publishers, Wiley, and specifically my charming and professional commissioning editor, Wejdan Ismail, for finding and selecting me for the 'Spanish job' and for her great support; thanks also to my development editor, Steve Edwards, for always being so patient and encouraging.

Thanks, also, to all my pupils – especially the kids for their inspiration and laughter. Their passion for exploring language and communication makes all my efforts worthwhile!

I also thank my adorable Dee and my own family members – my dad Gregorio, mum Felisa, auntie Use and beloved super-sister Carlota. I acknowledge the support to the cerebral side of things provided by my bilingual friend, Fiona Campbell, and thank José Luís Ruíz-Calero García-Gil from Madrid for his enviable command of Spanish writing skills and for his friendship. Last but not least, thanks of course go to our favourite companions on our weekend walks in the forests of Kent – Chessie (a gorgeous border collie señorita) and Lily (the most enchanting miniature cocker spaniel niña), both of whom can now bark in a useful and fashionable Spanish!

Pedro Vázquez Bermejo

I would like to thank Wiley for the splendid idea of publishing these truly novel books. My thanks go as well to Jean Antonin Billard, greatest amongst the greatest translators. I must also mention that I owe Juergen Lorenz the structure of the text, as well as his friendly help with its first birthpangs.

And I thank from the heart the unflagging editorial help of Kathy Cox, at Wiley, who kept my spirit from sinking at all times, as well as Tammy Castleman, Patricia Pan, Billie Williams and Kathleen Dobie, who contributed their excellent copy editing skills. Thanks and excuses are also due to my lifetime partner, Ludwig Zeller, who for months saw mostly the back of my head while my face was glued to the monitor of my computer. May we all have a happy life.

Susana Wald

Publisher's Acknowledgements

We're proud of this book; please send us your comments through our Dummies online registration form located at www.dummies.com/register/.

Some of the people who helped bring this book to market include the following:

Commissioning, Editorial, and Media Development

Development Editor: Steve Edwards

Content Editor: Jo Theedom

Commissioning Editor: Wejdan Ismail

Assistant Editor: Jennifer Prytherch

Proofreader: Andy Finch

Technical Editor: Maria Violeta Millins Alarcón

Production Manager: Daniel Mersey

Cover Photos: © Gavin Hellier/JAI/Corbis

Cartoons: Ed McLachlan

Composition Services

Project Coordinator: Lynsey Stanford

Layout and Graphics: Claudia Bell, Carl Byers, Christine Williams

Proofreaders: Melissa Cossell, John Greenough

Indexer: Valerie Haynes Perry

Contents at a Glance

Table of Contents

Introduction

As society becomes more international in nature, knowing how to say at least a few words in other languages becomes increasingly useful: low-cost airfares are making travel abroad a more realistic option, global business environments necessitate overseas travel or you just may have friends and neighbours who speak other languages.

Whatever your reason for acquiring some Spanish, this book can help. *Spanish For Dummies* gives you the skills you need for basic communication in Spanish. We're not promising fluency here, but if you want to greet someone, purchase a ticket or order off a menu in Spanish, you need look no further than *Spanish For Dummies*.

What's Special about Spanish?

Spanish is one of the great European languages, rich in heritage from more than nine centuries of existence. This language comes from the central region of Spain called **Castilla** (*kahs-tee-y*ah) (Castile) and is also the language of much great literature.

The first European novel – as a matter of fact, the first novel in the modern sense – was written in Spanish by Miguel de Cervantes. You've probably heard about *Don Quixote*, the 'enthusiastic visionary'. His adventures have even become part of the English language: the word *quixotic* describes someone with an odd, eccentric or utterly-regardless-of-material-interests attitude.

Spanish is also the language of great poets. Many Nobel Prize winners in literature are Spanish-speaking, including the poets Gabriela Mistral and Pablo Neruda.

When **Cristobal Colón** (Christopher Columbus) and other Spanish explorers came to the New World of the Americas, Spanish became the language of all the peoples from Florida to Tierra del Fuego at the extreme tip of South America (with the exception of Brazil, where Portuguese is spoken).

When you go to places such as Spain, Argentina, Bolivia, Chile, Uruguay, Paraguay, Peru, Ecuador, Colombia, Venezuela, Mexico, Guatemala, Puerto Rico, Cuba, Costa Rica, Panama, Honduras or Nicaragua, you speak in or are spoken to in Spanish. If you visit cities such as Madrid, Barcelona, Valencia, Bilbao, Seville, Santiago de Chile, Montevideo, Asuncion, Buenos Aires, Lima, Caracas, Bogota, Mexico City, Quito, San Juan and many, many others, all the people you find speak Spanish.

So you have several reasons to embrace this beautiful language. You may want to understand the culture and the people and you may also want some future new Spanish friends to understand you, in their own language.

About This Book

Although you may think that 'Spanish is Spanish', things aren't quite that simple. The Spanish language carried to the New World by the **Conquistadores** *(kohn-kees-tah-doh-rehs)* (Spanish conquerors) developed over time in its own way, and at its own speed. Alternative words and conventions increased until the Spanish spoken in Latin American countries became, if not a different language, certainly one with a very different personality to the standard Spanish spoken in Spain.

This book concentrates on standard, contemporary Spanish – known as **Castellano** – meaning the Spanish spoken in Spain itself, even in regions such as the Basque Country or Cataluña where it may not be the language that people habitually use. By getting to grips with **Castellano**, you can be understood anywhere in the Spanish-speaking world, including Latin America.

This book isn't a class that you have to drag yourself to twice a week for a specified period of time. You can use *Spanish For Dummies* however you want to, whether your goal is to know some words and phrases to help you get around when you visit the Canaries, Balearics or mainland Spain, or you simply want to be able to say, 'Hello, how are you?' to a Spanish-speaking friend. This book can help you reach moments of true understanding in a different language. Use the text as a language and cultural guide for those moments when you really need to know how and why things are done.

Go through this book at your own pace, reading as much or as little at a time as you like. Also, you don't have to trudge through the chapters in order; just read the sections that interest you. The only way to know and love a language is to speak it. Throughout the book, we give you lots of words, phrases and dialogues, complete with pronunciations.

If you've never taken Spanish lessons before, you may want to read the chapters in Part I before tackling the later chapters. Part I gives you some of the basics that you need to know about the language, such as how to pronounce the various sounds.

Why We Wrote This Book

Language exposes you to every aspect of the human condition, allowing you to study the past, understand the present and ponder the future. Language sometimes changes the ways in which people express various emotions and conditions. People are connected through their ability to speak, but you can go one step further – to understanding – by being able to communicate in another language. Very few things are as exciting as that!

The best way to discover a new language is to immerse yourself in it. Listen to the way Spanish sounds, concentrate on the pronunciation and look at how it's written. By listening and repeating, you enter a new world of ideas and peoples. Acquiring Spanish through immersion really does feel like a sort of magic.

Conventions Used in This Book

To make this book easy for you to navigate, we set up a few conventions:

- ✔ Spanish terms are set in **boldface** to make them stand out.
- ✔ Pronunciations, set in brackets in *italics*, follow the Spanish terms.
- ✔ Verb conjugations (lists that show you the forms of a verb) are given in tables in this order: **yo**, the 'I' form; **tú**, the 'you' (singular) form, **él**, **ella**, **usted**, the 'he/she/it' form; **nosotros**, the 'we' form; **vosotros**, the 'you' (plural/formal) form; and **ellos**, **ellas**, the 'they' form. Pronunciations follow in the second column. Here's an example (of the verb **llevar**, meaning to take or carry):

Conjugation	*Pronunciation*
yo llevo	*yoh <u>yeh</u>-boh*
tú llevas	*too <u>yeh</u>-bahs*
él, ella, usted lleva	*ehl, <u>eh</u>-yah, oos-<u>tehd</u> yeh-bah*
nosotros llevamos	*noh-<u>soh</u>-trohs yeh-<u>bah</u>-mohs*
vosotros lleváis	*boh-<u>soh</u>-trohs yeh-<u>bah</u>-ees*
ellos, ellas llevan	*<u>eh</u>-yohs, <u>eh</u>-yahs <u>yeh</u>-bahn*

Studying a language is a peculiar beast, and so this book includes a few elements that other *For Dummies* books do not. Here are those new elements:

✔ **Talkin' the Talk dialogues:** The best way to improve with a language is to see and hear how it's used in conversation, and so we include dialogues throughout the book. The dialogues come under the heading 'Talkin' the Talk' and show you the Spanish words, the pronunciation and the English translation.

✔ **Words to Know blackboards:** Memorising key words and phrases is also important in language, and so we collect the important words that appear in a chapter (or section within a chapter) and write them on a 'blackboard', under the heading 'Words to Know'.

✔ **Fun & Games activities:** If you don't have Spanish speakers with whom to practise your new language skills, you can use the Fun & Games activities to reinforce what you're discovering. These word games are fun ways to gauge your progress.

Also, because each language has its own ways of expressing ideas, the English translations that we provide for the Spanish terms may not be literal. We want you to know the gist of what's being said, not just the words being said. For example, you can translate the Spanish phrase **de nada** *(deh nah-dah)* literally as 'of nothing', but the phrase really means 'you're welcome'. This book gives the 'you're welcome' translation.

Foolish Assumptions

To write this book, we had to make some assumptions about you and what you want from a book called *Spanish For Dummies*:

✔ You know no Spanish – or if you took Spanish in school, you don't remember a word of it.

✔ You're not looking for a book to make you fluent in Spanish; you just want to know some words, phrases and sentence constructions so that you can communicate basic information in Spanish.

✔ You don't want to have to memorise long lists of vocabulary words or a bunch of boring grammar rules.

✔ You want to have fun and discover a bit of Spanish at the same time.

If these statements apply to you, you've found the right book!

How This Book Is Organised

This book is divided by topic into parts, and then into chapters. The following sections tell you what types of information you can find in each part.

Part I: Getting Started

You get your feet wet in this part as we give you some Spanish basics: how to pronounce words, what the accents mean and so on. We even boost your confidence by reintroducing you to some Spanish words that you probably already know. In addition, we outline the basics of Spanish grammar that you may need to know when you work through more detailed chapters of the book.

Part II: Spanish in Action

In this part, you begin practising and using Spanish. Instead of focusing on grammar points, as many language textbooks do, this part focuses on every-day situations in which you may find yourself if you're living in a Spanish-speaking country or dealing with your Spanish-speaking friends. This part hones your small-talk skills and takes you on shopping and dining excursions. At the end of this part, you should be able to do some basic navigation in the Spanish language.

Part III: Spanish on the Go

This part provides the tools you need to take your Spanish on the road, whether you're going to a local Spanish restaurant or a museum in Madrid. These chapters help you to survive the Customs process, check into hotels and nab a cab, and have a great time doing it. Sprinkled throughout are cultural titbits that introduce you to people, places and things that are important in Spanish culture.

Part IV: The Part of Tens

If you're looking for small, easily digestible pieces of information about Spanish, this part is for you. Here, you can find ways to speak Spanish quickly, useful Spanish expressions to know and celebrations worth joining.

Part V: Appendixes

This part of the book includes important information that you can use for reference. We include verb tables that show you how to conjugate a regular verb, and then how to conjugate those verbs that stubbornly refuse to fit the pattern. We give you a mini-dictionary in both Spanish-to-English and English-to-Spanish formats and provide some brief facts about the Spanish language in the modern world.

Icons Used in This Book

You may be looking for particular information while reading this book. To make certain types of information easier for you to find, we place the following icons in the left-hand margins throughout the book:

We use this icon to indicate crucial pieces of information that you need to bear in mind.

This icon highlights tips that can make Spanish easier for you.

Languages are full of quirks that may trip you up if you're not prepared for them. This icon points to discussions of these weird grammatical rules.

If you're looking for information and advice about culture and travel, look for this icon.

Where to Go from Here

Discovering a new language is all about jumping in and giving it a try (no matter how bad your pronunciation is at first). So make the leap! Start at the beginning, or pick a chapter that interests you. Above all, make sure that you have fun!

Part I
Getting Started

In this part . . .

This part dips your feet gently into the water and gives you some Spanish basics: pronunciation, the meaning of accents and so on. We reintroduce you to some Spanish words that you probably already know and outline the basics of Spanish grammar.

Chapter 1

Realising that You Know a Little Spanish Already

In This Chapter

▶ Spotting the Spanish you know already

▶ Pronouncing words correctly

▶ Implying gestures

▶ Understanding typical expressions

*I*f you're familiar with the term 'Latin Lover', you may not be surprised to know that Spanish is called a Romance language. But the romance we're talking about here isn't exactly the Latin Lover type – unless you love to learn Latin.

Spanish (as well as other languages such as Italian, French, Romanian and Portuguese) is a Romance language because its origins reside in the Latin of ancient Rome. This common ancestry means that Romance languages have many similarities in grammar and the way they sound. (The fact that these languages all sound so romantic when spoken is purely a bonus!) For example, **casa** *(kah-sah)*, the word for 'house', is identical in look, meaning and sound whether you speak Portuguese, Italian, Romanian or Spanish.

The differences in the Romance languages aren't terribly difficult to overcome. For example, Spanish speakers can talk with Portuguese or Italian speakers and make themselves understood pretty well, even if the other person sounds a bit strange. Still, each Romance language is different from its sister languages.

Standard Spanish is a language that comes from a central region of Spain called Castilla. For that reason, some people call the language **castellano** *(kahs-teh-yah-noh)*, which simply means 'Castilian'. This book concentrates on standard, modern Spanish, and is based mostly on **castellano**: Spanish as good and crystal-clear as it comes.

A quick Spanish geography lesson

Spain consists of the Iberian mainland peninsula – except for Portugal and Gibraltar – the Islas Baleares (Balearic Islands), the Islas Canarias (Canary Islands) and two small areas in the North of Africa called Ceuta and Melilla. Outside of Spain, Spanish is most widely spoken in Latin America.

Thousands of miles away from the castellano-speaking Spanish mainland, however, the Spanish in Latin America developed in its own way to become a language still instantly recognisable as Spanish, but with its own words and pronunciations. For this reason, you may come across Americans who speak 'Spanish' but struggle to make themselves understood in Madrid, and Europeans who speak 'Spanish' but can't get a coffee in Cartagena!

This chapter is the foundation for the rest of the book and, among other things, discusses pronunciation and some of the conventions we use in subsequent chapters. We also give you a few quickie phrases to show Spanish speakers that you're part of the gang!

Recognising the Spanish You Know Already

The English language is like an ever-growing entity that, with great wisdom, absorbs what it needs from other cultures and languages. English is also a language that resembles a bouquet of flowers plucked from many different roots. One of these roots is Latin, which 2,000 years ago was spread all over Europe by the Romans and later by scholars of the Middle Ages.

Because all these live elements exist in the root of the language, you can find many similarities between English and Spanish in the words that come from both Latin and French roots. These words can cause both delight and embarrassment. The delight comes in the words where the coincident sounds give similar meanings. The embarrassment comes from words where the sounds and even the roots are the same, but the meanings are completely different.

Among the delightful discoveries of similarities between the languages are words such as **teléfono móvil** *(teh-leh-phoh-noh moh-beel)* (mobile telephone), **soprano** *(soh-prah-noh)* (soprano), **pronto** *(prohn-toh)* (right away; soon) and thousands of others that differ by just one or two letters, such as **conclusión** *(kohn-kloo-seeohn)* (conclusion), **composición** *(kohm-poh-see-thee-ohn)* (composition), **libertad** *(lee-behr-tahd)* (liberty), **economía** *(eh-koh-noh-meeah)* (economy), **invención** *(een-behn-theeohn)* (invention) and **presidente** *(preh-see-dehn-teh)* (president).

Watching out for false friends

The trouble begins in the world of words with what French linguists call false friends. Within the groups of false friends, you find words that look very similar and even have the same root, and yet mean completely different things. One that comes to mind is the word **actual**, which has very different meanings in English and Spanish. In English, you know that it means real, in reality or the very one. Not so in Spanish. **Actual** *(ahk-tooahl)* in Spanish means present, current, belonging to this moment, this day or this year.

So, for example, when you say the actual painting in English, you're referring to the real one, the very painting people are looking at or want to see. But when you say **la pintura actual** *(lah peen-too-rah ahk-tooahl)* in Spanish, you're referring to the painting that belongs to the current time, the one that follows present-day trends – a modern painting.

Another example is the adjective 'embarrassed', which in English means ashamed or encumbered. In Spanish, **embarazada** *(ehm-bah-rah-thah-dah)* is the adjective that comes from the same root as the English word, and yet its use nowadays almost exclusively means 'pregnant'. So you can say in English that you're a little embarrassed, but in Spanish you can't be just a little **embarazada**. Either you're pregnant or you're not!

Getting to know some crossover influences

Word trouble ends at the point where a word originating in English is absorbed into Spanish or vice versa. For instance, the proximity of the United States to Mexico produces a change in the Spanish spoken there: the result, for example, is that 'car' in Mexico is **carro** *(kah-rroh)*, but in South America people say **auto** *(ahoo-toh)* and in Spain **coche** *(koh-cheh)*.

Here are just a few examples of Spanish words that you know already because English uses them, too:

- You've may have been to a **fiesta** *(feeehs-tah)*.

- You've probably taken a **siesta** *(seeehs-tah)* or two.

- You probably know at least one **señorita** *(seh-nyoh-ree-tah)*, and you surely have an **amigo** *(ah-mee-goh)*.

- You know the names of places such as **Los Angeles** *(lohs ahn-Heh-lehs)* (the angels), **San Francisco** *(sahn frahn-thees-koh)* (Saint Francis), **Florida** *(floh-ree-dah)* (the blooming one) and **Puerto Rico** *(pooehr-toh ree-koh)* (rich harbour).

- You may have eaten a **tortilla** *(tohr-tee-yah)* or **paella** *(pah-eh-yah)*.

✔ You fancy the **tango** *(tahn-goh)* or the **rumba** *(room-bah)*, or you may dance the **flamenco** *(flah-men-koh)*.

✔ You have a friend named **María** *(Mah-ree-ah)* or **Ana** *(ah-nah)*.

Reciting Your ABCs

Correct pronunciation is vital to avoiding misunderstandings. The following sections present some basic guidelines for proper Spanish pronunciation.

Next to the Spanish words throughout this book, we show the pronunciation in parentheses, which we call pronunciation brackets. Within the pronunciation brackets, we separate the words that have more than one syllable with a hyphen, such as *(kah-sah)*. An underlined syllable within the pronunciation brackets tells you to accent, or stress, that syllable. We say much more about stress later in this chapter in the section 'Looking at Pronunciation and Stress'. In the meantime, don't let yourself get stressed out (pardon the pun). We explain each part of the language separately, and promise to ensure that the pieces fall quickly into place.

In the following sections we comment on some letters of the alphabet from the Spanish point of view. The aim is to help you to understand Spanish pronunciation. Here is the basic Spanish alphabet and its pronunciation:

a (ah)	**b** (beh)	**c** (theh)	**d** (deh)
e (eh)	**f** (eh-feh)	**g** (Heh)	**h** (ah-cheh)
i (ee)	**j** (Hoh-tah)	**k** (kah)	**l** (eh-leh)
m (eh-meh)	**n** (eh-neh)	**ñ** (eh-nyeh)	**o** (oh)
p (peh)	**q** (koo)	**r** (eh-reh)	**s** (eh-seh)
t (teh)	**u** (oo)	**v** (oo-beh)	**w** (doh-bleh oo-beh or oo-beh doh-bleh)
x (eh-kees)	**y** (ee gree eh-gah)	**z** (theh-tah)	

Spanish also includes some double letters in its alphabet: **ch** *(cheh)* and **ll** *(ye)*, and uses the **rr** *(a trilled r)* pairing.

We don't go through every letter of the alphabet in the sections that follow, only those that you use differently in Spanish than in English. The differences can lie in pronunciation, appearance, the fact that you seldom see the letters or that you don't pronounce the letters at all.

Checking out consonants

Consonants tend to sound the same in both English and Spanish. The following sections look more closely at the behaviour and pronunciation of the consonants that do differ.

Even within the Spanish-speaking world, some consonants are pronounced differently. For example, in standard Spain the consonant **z** is pronounced like the *th* in the English word *thesis*. Latin Americans, however, don't use this *th* sound; in those countries, **z** and **s** sound the same.

In the Spanish speaker's mind, a consonant is any sound that needs to have a vowel next to it when you pronounce it. For example, saying the letter **t** by itself may be difficult for a Spanish speaker. To the Spanish ear, pronouncing **t** sounds like **te** *(teh)*. Likewise, the Spanish speaker says **ese** *(eh-seh)* when pronouncing the letter **s**.

The letter K

In Spanish, the letter **k** is used only in words that have their origin in foreign or ancient languages. More often than not, this letter is seen in **kilo** *(kee-loh)*, meaning *thousand* in Greek, such as in **kilómetro** *(kee-loh-meh-troh)* (kilometre).

The letter H

In Spanish, the letter **h** is always mute. That's it!

Note, however, that the pronunciation brackets throughout this book do often include the letter *h*. These *h*s generally indicate certain vowel sounds, which we cover in the later section 'Finding Out About Vowels'. But the Spanish **h** itself doesn't appear within the pronunciation brackets, because the letter is mute.

Here are some examples of the Spanish **h**:

- **Huelva** *(ooh-ehl-ba)* (name of a city in Spain)
- **hueso** *(ooeh-soh)* (bone)
- **huevo** *(ooeh-boh)* (egg)

The letter J

The Spanish consonant **j** sounds like a guttural English letter h. Normally, in English, you say h quite softly, as though you're just breathing out. To pronounce the Spanish **j**, you say an h but gently raise the back of your tongue, as if you're saying the letter k. Push the air out really hard and you get the sound. Try it – you sound as if you're gargling, don't you?

To indicate that you need to make this sound, we use a capital letter *H* within the pronunciation brackets.

Now try the sound out on these words:

- **Cajon** *(kah-Hohn)* (big box)
- **Gijón** *(Hee-Hohn)* (the name of a city in Northern Spain)
- **jadeo** *(Hah-deh-oh)* (panting)
- **jota** *(Hoh-tah)* (the Spanish name for the letter **j**; also the name of a folk dance in Spain.)
- **tijera** *(tee-Heh-rah)* (scissors)

The letter C

The letter **c**, in front of the vowels **a**, **o** and **u**, sounds like the English letter k. We use the letter *k* in the pronunciation brackets to indicate this sound. Here are some examples:

- **acabar** *(ah-kah-bahr)* (to finish)
- **café** *(kah-feh)* (coffee)
- **casa** *(kah-sah)* (house)
- **ocaso** *(oh-kah-soh)* (sunset)

When the letter **c** is in front of the vowels **e** and **i**, it sounds like the English letters th in the word 'thanks'. In the pronunciation brackets, we indicate this sound as *th*. Check out these examples:

- **acero** *(ah-theh-roh)* (steel)
- **cero** *(theh-roh)* (zero)
- **cine** *(thee-neh)* (cinema)

The letters S and Z

In standard Spanish, the letter **z** is pronounced like the letters th in the English word 'bath'. We use *th* in the pronunciation brackets to indicate this sound. Following are some examples:

- **cerveza** *(ther-beh-thah)* (beer)
- **veloz** *(beh-loth)* (fast)
- **zarzuela** *(thahr-thoo-eh-lah)* (Spanish-style operetta)

The letters B and V

In Spanish, the letters **b** and **v** are pronounced the same, the sound being somewhere between the two letters. This in-between is a clear sound, closer to the English letter b than v. If you position your lips and teeth to make a v sound, and then try to make a b sound, you get it. To remind you to make this sound, we use *b* in our pronunciation brackets, for both **b** and **v**. Here are some examples:

- ✔ **cabeza** *(kah-beh-thah)* (head)
- ✔ **vida** *(bee-dah)* (life)
- ✔ **violín** *(beeoh-leen)* (violin)

The letter Q

Spanish doesn't use the letter **k** very much; when the language wants an English k sound in front of the vowels **e** and **i**, it unfolds the letter combination **qu** instead. So when you see the word **queso** *(keh-soh)* (cheese), you immediately know that you say the English k sound. Here are some examples of the Spanish letter **q**, which we indicate by *k* in the pronunciation brackets:

- ✔ **paquete** *(pah-keh-teh)* (package)
- ✔ **pequeño** *(peh-keh-nyoh)* (small)
- ✔ **química** *(keeh-meeh-kah)* (chemistry)
- ✔ **tequila** *(teh-kee-lah)* (Mexican liquor, spirits)

The letter G

In Spanish the letter **g** has a double personality, like the letter **c**. When you combine the letter **g** with a consonant or when you see it in front of the vowels **a**, **o** and **u**, it sounds like the English g in goose. Here are some examples:

- ✔ **begoñia** *(beh-goh-nyah)* (begonia)
- ✔ **gato** *(gah-toh)* (cat)
- ✔ **gracias** *(grah-theeahs)* (thank you)
- ✔ **pagado** *(pah-gah-doh)* (paid for)

The **g** changes personality in front of the vowels **e** and **i**. It sounds like the Spanish **j**, which we indicate with the capital *H* in our pronunciation brackets:

- ✔ **agenda** *(ah-Hehn-dah)* (agenda; date book)
- ✔ **gerente** *(Heh-rehn-teh)* (manager)

To hear the English sound g (as in goat) in front of the vowels **e** and **i**, you must insert a **u** in Spanish, making **gue** and **gui**. To remind you to make the goat sound (no, no, not *mmehehe*, but a hard g), we use *gh* in our pronunciation brackets:

- ✔ **guía** (*ghee*ah) (guide)
- ✔ **guiño** (*ghee*-nyoh) (wink)
- ✔ **guerra** (*gheh*-rrah) (war)

Double consonants

Spanish has two double consonants: **ll** and **rr**. These double consonants are considered to be a single letter, and each has a single sound. For this reason, they stick together when we separate syllables in the pronunciation brackets. For example, the word **calle** (*kah*-yeh) (street) appears as **ca-lle**. And **torre** (*toh*-rreh), (tower) separates into **to-rre**.

The letter LL

In standard Spanish, the **ll** consonant sounds like the letter y in the English word *yes*, and throughout this book in the pronunciation brackets, we use *y* to indicate this sound.

Try saying **ll**, using the *y* sound, in the following examples:

- ✔ **brillo** (*bree*-yoh) (shine)
- ✔ **llama** (*yah*-mah) (flame; also the name of an animal)
- ✔ **lluvia** (*yoo*-beeah) (rain)

Across the Atlantic, Argentineans and Uruguayans pronounce **ll** differently, as the sound that happens when you have your lips pursed to say **s** and then make the **z** sound through them. Try it. Fun, isn't it? But really, the sound isn't that difficult to make, because you can find the English equivalent in words like *measure* and *pleasure*. The way you say those English s sounds is exactly how **ll** is pronounced in Argentina and Uruguay.

The letters RR

The letters **rr** together sound like a strongly rolled **r**. In fact, every **r** is rolled in Spanish, but the double one is the real winner. To roll an **r**, curl your tongue against the roof of your mouth as you finish the **r** sound. It should trill.

An easy way to make this sound is to say the letter **r** as though you were pretending to sound like an outboard motor. There, you have it! Spanish speakers take special pleasure in rolling their **rrs**. One fun thing about **rr** is that no words begin with it. Isn't that a relief! In pronunciation brackets we simply indicate this sound as *rr*.

Play with these words:

- **carrera** *(kah-rreh-rah)* (race; profession)
- **correo** *(koh-rreh-oh)* (mail, post)
- **tierra** *(teeeh-rrah)* (land)

The letter Y

When falling at the start or in the middle of a word, the letter **y** in Spanish represents sounds that are very similar to those of **ll**, and we advise that you pronounce it as the English letter y in *yes* and *you*. In the pronunciation brackets, we indicate this sound as *y*:

- **playa** *(plah-yah)* (beach)
- **yema** *(yeh-mah)* (yolk; also finger tip)
- **yodo** *(yoh-doh)* (iodine)

In Spanish, the letter **y** is a consonant, but it sounds like the English vowel i when coming at the end of a word:

- **buey** *(boo-eh-eeh)* (ox)
- **ley** *(leh-eeh)* (law)
- **rey** *(reh-eeh)* (king)

The people of Argentina and Uruguay strongly pronounce this **y** sound – when it falls at the start or in the middle of a word – by keeping their tongue against their upper palate a little longer.

The letter Ñ

When you see a wiggly line on top of the letter **n** that looks like **ñ**, use the *ny* sound that you use for the English word *canyon*. The wiggly line is called a **tilde** *(teel-deh)*. In pronunciation brackets, we show this sound as *ny*. Try out the following examples:

- **cuñado** *(koo-nyah-doh)* (brother-in-law)
- **mañana** *(mah-nyah-nah)* (tomorrow)
- **niña** *(nee-nyah)* (girl)

Finding out about vowels

The biggest difference between English and Spanish is almost certainly in the way that people write and pronounce vowels, and so to sound like a native Spanish speaker you have to concentrate on them.

You may be well aware that one vowel in English can have more than one sound. Look, for instance, at *fat* and *fate*. Both words have the vowel a, but they're pronounced quite differently from one another. The good news is that in Spanish, you always say the vowels one way, and one way only.

The upcoming sections discuss the five vowels, which are the only vowel sounds in Spanish. These sounds are **a** *(ah)*, **e** *(eh)*, **i** *(ee)*, **o** *(oh)* and **u** *(oo)*. Spanish views each of these vowels as being by itself and combines the vowels into twos to make other sounds.

The vowel A

Almost all children sing their ABCs. In Spanish, the English letter a that starts off the song, is pronounced *ah*. The easiest way to remember how to pronounce the letter **a** in Spanish is to sing the chorus of the Christmas carol 'Deck the Halls' to yourself. You remember the chorus, don't you? *Fa la la la la, la la, la la*. We write this sound as *ah* in the pronunciation brackets.

Here are some sample words to practise. Remember that you pronounce each and every **a** exactly the same way:

- **Badajoz** *(Bah-dah-<u>Hohth</u>)* (a city in south-western Spain)
- **Guadalajara** *(gooah-dah-lah-<u>Hah</u>-rah)* (a city in Spain and also in Mexico)
- **mapa** *(<u>mah</u>-pah)* (map)

The vowel E

To get an idea of how the Spanish **e** sounds, smile gently, open your mouth a bit and say 'eh'. The sound should be like the letter e in the English word *pen*. In our pronunciation brackets, this vowel appears as *eh*.

Try these examples:

- **pelele** *(peh-<u>leh</u>-leh)* (rag doll; puppet)
- **pelo** *(<u>peh</u>-loh)* (hair)
- **seco** *(<u>seh</u>-koh)* (dry)

The vowel I

In Spanish the vowel **i** sounds like the English ee in 'seen', but just a touch shorter. To give you an example, when English speakers say 'feet' or 'street', Spanish speakers hear what sounds like almost two Spanish **is**.

We indicate this sound as *ee* in our pronunciation brackets. Here are a few examples:

 ✔ **irritar** *(ee-rree-tahr)* (to irritate)

 ✔ **piña** *(pee-nyah)* (pineapple)

 ✔ **pintar** *(peen-tahr)* (to paint)

The vowel O

To say **o**, the Spanish put their mouths in a rounded position, as if to breathe a kiss over a flower, and keep it in that position while saying **o**. The sound resembles the English o in floor, but a bit shorter. We indicate this sound as *oh* in the pronunciation brackets.

Try practising the sound on these words:

 ✔ **coco** *(koh-koh)* (coconut)

 ✔ **orilla** *(oh-ree-yah)* (a river bank)

 ✔ **oro** *(oh-roh)* (gold)

 ✔ **toro** *(toh-roh)* (bull)

The vowel U

The fifth and last vowel in Spanish is the **u**, and it sounds like the English letters oo in 'moon' or 'loon', but just a touch shorter. We write this sound as *oo* in the pronunciation brackets. Here are some examples of the Spanish **u** sound:

 ✔ **cuna** *(koo-nah)* (cradle)

 ✔ **cuñado** *(koo-nyah-doh)* (brother-in-law)

 ✔ **curioso** *(koo-reeoh-soh)* (curious)

 ✔ **fruta** *(froo-tah)* (fruit)

 ✔ **luna** *(loo-nah)* (moon)

 ✔ **tubo** *(too-boh)* (a tube)

Discovering diphthongs

Good grief, you say, what's that? Well, *diphthong* comes from Greek, where *di* means two and *thong* comes from a very similar word meaning sound or voice. (Don't worry, we had to look it up in the dictionary.) Very simply, it means *double sound*.

The Spanish word is **diptongo** *(deep-tohn-goh)*. From the Spanish-speaking point of view, **diptongos** are the combination of two vowels. For instance, **i** and **o** combine to make **io** as in **patio** *(pah-teeoh)* (courtyard or patio).

Joining the weak to the strong

Diptongos are always made up of a weak and a strong vowel. Calling vowels 'weak' or 'strong' is a Spanish language convention. The convention comes from the fact that the so-called strong vowel is always dominant in the diphthong. To the Spanish speaker, **i** and **u** are weak vowels, leaving **a**, **e** and **o** as strong ones.

To visualise this weak or strong concept, consider a piccolo flute and a bass horn. The sound of the piccolo is definitely more like the Spanish **i** and **u**, whereas the base horn sounds more like the Spanish **a**, **e** and especially **o**.

Any combination of one strong and one weak vowel is a **diptongo** *(deep-tohn-goh)*, which means that they belong together in the same syllable. In fact, they're not only together, they're stuck like superglue; you can't separate them.

In the **diptongo**, usually the stress falls on the strong vowel (we talk more about stress in the later section 'Looking at Pronunciation and Stress'). An accent mark – a little mark sitting above a vowel – alerts you when the stress falls on the weak vowel (turn to the later section 'Understanding accents in diphthongs' for more). In the combination of two weak vowels, the stress is on the second one.

Try these examples of diphthongs:

- **bueno** *(booeh-noh)* (good)
- **cuando** *(kooahn-doh)* (when)
- **fiar** *(feeahr)* (to sell on credit or to rely on someone or something)
- **fuera** *(fooeh-rah)* (out, outside)
- **suizo** *(sooee-thoh)* (Swiss)
- **viudo** *(beeoo-doh)* (widower)

Separating the strong from the strong

When you combine two strong vowels, they don't form a diphthong. Instead, the vowels retain their separate values, and so you must put them into separate syllables. Have a look at these examples:

- **aorta** *(ah-ohr-tah)* (aorta) (see, just as in English!)
- **feo** *(feh-oh)* (ugly)
- **marea** *(mah-reh-ah)* (tide)
- **mareo** *(mah-reh-oh)* (dizziness)

Did you notice in the previous list how changing one letter, in **marea** and **mareo** for example, can change the meaning of a word? This letter phenomenon occurs in Spanish, just as in English. Finding such words is fun. In the case of the previous list, at least the two words come from the same root **mar** *(mahr)* (sea). And, associating the tide to one's dizziness isn't all that difficult. But in other places you can have oceans of difference. Here are some more examples: **casa** *(kah-sah)* (house) and **cosa** *(koh-sah)* (thing), and **pito** *(pee-toh)* (whistle), **pato** *(pah-toh)* (duck) and **peto** *(peh-toh)* (bib or breastplate).

Looking at Pronunciation and Stress

In Spanish, you stress one syllable in every word. Stress is the accent that you put on a syllable as you speak it. One syllable always gets more stress than the other syllables in a word. Finding the stress is easy in single-syllable words, but many words have more than one syllable, and that's when the situation becomes stressful (geddit?).

Searching for stress, normally

Can you believe that you're searching for stress? In Spanish, the right stress at the right time is a good thing, and fortunately stress in Spanish is easy to control. If you have no written accent, you have two possibilities:

✔ The word is stressed next to the last syllable if it ends in a vowel, an **n** or an **s**. Here are some examples:

- **pollo** *(poh-yoh)* (chicken): the word ends in a vowel.

- **Carmen** *(kahr-mehn)* (Carmen, as in the female name): the word ends in an **n**.

- **mariposas** *(mah-ree-poh-sahs)* (butterflies): the word ends in an **s**.

✔ The word is stressed on the last syllable when it ends in a consonant other than **n** or **s**. Look at these examples:

- **cantar** *(kahn-tahr)* (to sing)

- **feliz** *(feh-leeth)* (happy)

Words not stressed in one of these two ways have an accent mark to indicate where you need to place the stress.

Spotting accented vowels

One good thing about having the accent mark on a vowel is that you can tell immediately where the stress is, just by looking at the word.

The accent mark doesn't affect how you pronounce the vowel, just which syllable you stress.

Here are some examples of words with accent marks on a vowel:

- **balcón** *(bahl-kohn)* (balcony)
- **carácter** *(kah-rahk-tehr)* (character, personality)
- **fotógrafo** *(foh-toh-grah-foh)* (photographer)
- **pájaro** *(pah-Hah-roh)* (bird)

Understanding accents in diphthongs

An accent within a diphthong (check out the earlier section 'Discovering diphthongs' for more about the doubled vowels) shows you which vowel to stress. Take a look at these examples:

- **¡Adiós!** *(ah-deeohs)* (Goodbye!)
- **¡Buenos días!** *(booeh-nohs deeahs)* (Good morning!)
- **¿Qué decías?** *(keh deh-theeahs)* (What were you saying?)
- **tía** *(teeah)* (aunt)

If the strange punctuation in some of the words in this list looks confusing, check out the following section, which explains all!

¡Punctuation Plus!

The unfamiliar punctuation in phrases such as **¡Buenos días!**, **¿Qué decía?** and **¡Adiós!** is a particularly Spanish attribute. The language indicates the mood (or tone) of what you're saying both at the beginning and at the end of the phrase that forms a question or an exclamation, as in **¿Qué decía?** *(deh-theeah)* (what were you saying?) or **¿me decías?** *(meh dehthee-ahs)* (what were you telling me?).

As far as we know, Spanish is the only language that provides this sort of punctuation, which is very useful when you have to read something aloud because you know beforehand how to modulate your voice when the phrase is coming up.

This punctuation is the verbal equivalent of making gestures, as the following examples demonstrate:

- ✔ **¿Dónde está?** *(dohn-deh ehs-tah)* (Where is it?)
- ✔ **¡Qué maravilla!** *(keh mah-rah-bee-yah)* (How wonderful!)

Some Basic Phrases to Know

The following phrases can get you through a number of awkward pauses while you think of the right word:

- ✔ **¡Olé!** *(oh-leh)* (Great!; Superb!; Keep going!): You often hear this Spanish expression during bullfights and at some rather passionate flamenco shows!
- ✔ **¿Qué pasa?** *(kee pah-sah)* (Hello, what's happening?): This expression is an informal, relaxed way to greet someone, or you can use it just to ask for an update on a situation.
- ✔ **¿De verdad?** *(deh behr-dahd)* (Really?): This phrase indicates slight disbelief.
- ✔ **¡No me digas!** *(noh meh dee-gahs)* (You don't say!): This phrase also conveys disbelief.

Fun & Games

Try to match these Spanish letters with the English letters they sound like. Draw a line from the Spanish letter to its English sounding equivalent and then provide a Spanish word that uses that sound.

Spanish Letter	English Letter	Spanish Word
ll	e	_____
j	H	_____
i	s	_____
z	k	_____
q	y	_____

Chapter 2

Getting Down to the Nitty-Gritty: Basic Spanish Grammar

Studying a language is similar to driving a car. After you get used to all the parts and gauges, driving becomes second nature, and fun, to boot. You don't really have to think about how you make your car go from A to B. Spanish is the same. You get used to the chatty parts and – without much thought – the language becomes second nature.

However, driving involves more than making a car move. You also have to incorporate the nitty-gritty elements of driving, such as obeying traffic rules. The nit-picky part of any language – the traffic rules, so to speak – is grammar.

To be honest, studying grammar isn't the most enjoyable part of discovering a language. Just keep in mind that what you get from the nitty-gritty of this grammar chapter is useful in other places, too. In addition, remember that you don't need to chew your way through this chapter at a single sitting. You can go to another part of the book, and when we want to draw your attention to something in this chapter, we tell you. (We provide cross-references throughout the book.)

Then again, you may be the kind of person who truly enjoys grammar, and all those little rules and structures. If so, you're in for a treat!

Constructing Simple Sentences

When you meet people, naturally, you want to talk to them. And how do you go about that? Using sentences, of course. You make a statement, or you ask a question. (When someone questions you, you answer, right? Most people do, and that's how conversations get started.) In Spanish, as in English, you form a sentence by combining a subject, a verb and perhaps further descriptive information. For example:

> **La casa es grande.** *(lah kah-sah ehs grahn-deh)* (The house is big.)

Here, **la casa** *(lah kah-sah)* (the house) is the subject of the sentence and comes first, before the verb **es** *(ehs)* (is) and the adjective **grande** *(grahn-deh)* (big), which describes the house. In Spanish, the three basic parts of a sentence go in this order.

Here are some more examples:

> ✔ **La mujer es bella.** *(lah moo-Hehr ehs beh-yah)* (The woman is beautiful.)
>
> ✔ **El hombre es bueno.** *(ehl ohm-breh ehs booeh-noh)* (The man is good.)
>
> ✔ **Las calles son largas.** *(lahs kah-yehs sohn lahr-gahs)* (The streets are long.)

Forming Questions

We have some good news for you: forming a question in Spanish is easy. All you have to do is reverse the order of the verb and the subject and add an extra inverted question mark at the beginning of your sentence. For example, where you say **Ésta es. . .** *(ehs-tah ehs)* in a regular sentence, for a question you say **¿Es ésta. . . ?** *(ehs ehs-tah)*. This arrangement works the same as in English, when you say 'This is. . .' and 'Is this. . . ?'. Easy!

Check out this example:

> **Esta es la puerta.** *(ehs-tah ehs lah poo-ehr-tah)* (This is the door.)
>
> **¿Es ésta la puerta?** *(ehs ehs-tah lah poo-ehr-tah)* (Is this the door?)

Now, suppose you want to answer in the negative. All you have to do is insert the word **no** before the verb (almost the way you do in English, but easier). Here's an example:

> **¿Es ese el coche?** *(ehs eh-seh ehl koh-cheh)* (Is that the car?)
>
> **No, ese no es el coche.** *(noh eh-seh noh ehs ehl koh-cheh)* (No, that isn't the car.)

English often includes the verb 'do' in questions, but Spanish makes things easier on you. In questions and negative statements in Spanish, the word 'do' is understood as part of the verb:

¿Vas al cine? *(bahs ahl thee-neh)* (Do you go to the cinema?)

Sí, voy. *(see bohy)* (Yes, I [do] go.)

In English, 'Yes, I do' can mean many things (going to the cinema, using your computer, making a phone call and so on). In Spanish you're a bit more specific:

¿Va tu padre al cine? *(bah too pah-dreh ahl thee-neh)* (Does your father go to the cinema?)

No, no va. *(noh noh bah)* (No, he doesn't go.)

Now we use some sentences to demonstrate the questioning (interrogative) and denying (negative) moods:

- ✔ **¿Es bella la mujer?** *(ehs beh-yah lah moo-Hehr)* (Is the woman beautiful?)
- ✔ **La mujer no es bella.** *(lah moo-Hehr noh ehs beh-yah)* (The woman isn't beautiful.)
- ✔ **¿Es bueno el hombre?** *(ehs booeh-noh ehl ohm-breh)* (Is the man good?)
- ✔ **El hombre no es bueno.** *(ehl ohm-breh noh ehs booeh-noh)* (The man isn't good.)
- ✔ **¿Son largas las calles?** *(sohn lahr-gahs lahs kah-yehs)* (Are the streets long?)
- ✔ **Las calles no son largas.** *(lahs kah-yehs noh sohn lahr-gahs)* (The streets aren't long.)

Introducing Regular and Irregular Verbs

Spanish verbs all end with one of three letter combinations: **-ar**, **-er** or **-ir**. You find both regular and irregular verbs with any one of these three endings. As you may guess, regular verbs all form different tenses (past, present, future and so on) and persons (I/we, you, he/she/they and so on) in the same way – a process called *conjugation*. So, if you know how to conjugate one regular verb, you can determine the conjugation of all regular verbs like it.

The form of irregular verbs, however, can change when you least expect it. Ultimately, you need to memorise the conjugation of each irregular verb to ensure that you use it correctly. (Don't worry, not many irregular verbs exist and if you make a mistake most Spanish speakers can figure out what you want to say, even if your verb ending isn't quite right.)

Regular verbs

In all regular verbs in Spanish, the first section of the word – its root – stays constant. For example, the verb **trabajar** *(trah-bah-Hahr)* (to work) is a regular verb ending in **-ar.** The root **trabaj-** stays the same throughout conjugation. The following table shows you how you conjugate this verb – and all other regular verbs ending with **-ar.**

Conjugation	*Pronunciation*
Present tense:	
yo trabaj*o*	*yoh trah-bah-Hoh*
tú trabaj*as*	*too trah-bah-Hahs*
él, ella, usted trabaj*a*	*ehl, eh-yah, oos-tehd trah-bah-Hah*
nosotros trabaj*amos*	*noh-soh-trohs trah-bah-Hah-mohs*
vosotros trabaj*áis*	*boh-soh-trohs trah-bah-Hahees*
ellos, ellas, ustedes trabaj*an*	*eh-yohs, eh-yahs, oos-teh-dehs trah-bah-Hahn*
Past tense:	
yo trabaj*é*	*yoh trah-bah-Heh*
tú trabaj*aste*	*too trah-bah-Hahs-teh*
él, ella, usted trabaj*ó*	*ehl, eh-yah, oos-tehd trah-bah-Hoh*
nosotros trabaj*amos*	*noh-soh-trohs trah-bah-Hah-mohs*
vosotros trabaj*ásteis*	*boh-soh-trohs trah-bah-Hahs-tehees*
ellos, ellas, ustedes trabaj*aron*	*eh-yohs, eh-yahs, oos-teh-dehs trah-bah-Hah-ron*
Future tense:	
yo trabaj*aré*	*yoh trah-bah-Hah-reh*
tú trabaj*arás*	*too trah-bah-Hah-rahs*
él, ella, usted trabaj*ará*	*ehl, eh-yah, oos-tehd trah-bah-Hah-rah*
nosotros trabaj*aremos*	*noh-soh-trohs trah-bah-Hah-reh-mohs*
vosotros trabaj*aréis*	*boh-soh-trohs trah-bah-Hah-rehees*
ellos, ellas, ustedes trabaj*arán*	*eh-yohs, eh-yahs, oos-teh-dehs trah-bah-Hah-ran*

Talkin' the Talk

Rosa is interested in Alejandro's job. It pays well, and Alejandro has a great deal of free time.

Rosa:	**¿Dónde trabajas?**
	dohn-deh trah-bah-Hahs
	Where do you work?
Alejandro:	**Trabajo en mi casa.**
	trah-bah-Hoh ehn mee kah-sa
	I work at home.
Rosa:	**¿Siempre trabajaste en tu casa?**
	see-ehm-preh trah-bah-Hahs-teh ehn too kah-sah
	Did you always work at home?
Alejandro:	**No, pero desde hoy trabajaré en mi casa.**
	noh peh-roh dehs-deh oy trah-bah-Hah-reh ehn mee kah-sah
	No, but from [today] now on, I'll be working at home.
Rosa:	**¿Juan y tú trabajaréis juntos?**
	Hooahn ee too trah-bah-Hah-rehees Hoon-tohs
	Will Juan and you work together?
Alejandro:	**Juan trabajará en su oficina y yo en casa.**
	Hooahn trah-bah-Hah-rah ehn soo oh-fee-thee-nah ee yoh ehn kah-sah
	Juan will work in his office, and I'll work at home.

Irregular verbs

In irregular verbs, the root and at times the endings of the verb keep changing, which complicates matters a little!

An example is the verb **tener** _(teh-nehr)_ (to have). As the following table shows, the root of the verb, **ten-**, changes into **teng-** and **tien-**. Look carefully at the endings though, and you can see that some things remain the same.

Conjugation	Pronunciation
Present tense:	
yo teng**o**	*yoh <u>tehn</u>-goh*
tú tien**es**	*too tee<u>eh</u>-nehs*
él, ella, usted tien**e**	*ehl, <u>eh</u>-yah, oos-<u>tehd</u> tee-<u>eh</u>-neh*
nosotros ten**emos**	*noh-<u>soh</u>-trohs teh-<u>neh</u>-mohs*
vosotros ten**éis**	*boh-<u>soh</u>-trohs teh-<u>neh</u>ees*
ellos, ellas, ustedes tien**en**	*<u>eh</u>-yohs, <u>eh</u>-yahs, oos-<u>teh</u>-dehs tee<u>eh</u>-nehn*
Past tense:	
yo tu**ve**	*yoh <u>too</u>-beh*
tú tuv**iste**	*too too-<u>bees</u>-teh*
él, ella, usted tuv**o**	*ehl, <u>eh</u>-yah, oos-<u>tehd</u> <u>too</u>-boh*
nosotros tuv**imos**	*noh-<u>soh</u>-trohs too-<u>bee</u>-mohs*
vosotros tuv**isteis**	*boh-<u>soh</u>-trohs too-<u>bees</u>-tehees*
ellos, ellas, ustedes tuv**ieron**	*<u>eh</u>-yohs, <u>eh</u>-yahs, oos-<u>teh</u>-dehs too-bee<u>eh</u>-rohn*
Future tense:	
yo ten**dré**	*yoh tehn-<u>dreh</u>*
tú ten**drás**	*too tehn-<u>drahs</u>*
él, ella, usted ten**drá**	*ehl, <u>eh</u>-yah, oos-<u>tehd</u> tehn-<u>drah</u>*
nosotros ten**dremos**	*noh-<u>soh</u>-trohs tehn-<u>dreh</u>-mohs*
vosotros ten**dréis**	*boh-<u>soh</u>-trohs tehn-<u>dreh</u>ees*
ellos, ellas, ustedes ten**drán**	*<u>eh</u>-yohs, <u>eh</u>-yahs, oos-<u>teh</u>-dehs tehn-<u>drahn</u>*

Haber *(ah-<u>behr</u>)* is another Spanish verb that means 'to have'. Although it means the same as **tener** – conjugated in the preceding table – **haber** is often used in the conjugation of other verbs – as is the case with the English verb 'to have', which can be used in such English conjugations as, 'He has written' or 'I have stopped'.

Talkin' the Talk

In the following conversation, Verónica tells Antonio about her new job, using several tenses of the verb **trabajar**.

Verónica: **¡Ya tengo trabajo!**
yah <u>tehn</u>-goh trah-<u>bah</u>-Hoh
I have a job already!

Antonio:	**¿Dónde tienes trabajo?** *dohn-deh teeeh-nehs trah-bah-Hoh* Where do you have a job?
Verónica:	**En una tienda.** *ehn oo-nah teeehn-dah* In a shop.
Antonio:	**¿En qué trabajas en la tienda?** *ehn keh trah-bah-Hahs ehn lah teeehn-dah* What do you do at the shop?
Verónica:	**Trabajo en ventas.** *trah-bah-Hoh ehn behn-tahs* I work in sales.
Antonio:	**¿Trabajaste en ventas antes?** *trah-bah-Hahs-teh ehn behn-tahs ahn-tehs* Did you work in sales before?
Verónica:	**Sí, tengo alguna experiencia en ventas.** *see tehn-goh ahl-goo-nah ehks-peh-reeehn-theeah* *ehn behn-tahs* Yes, I have some experience in sales.
Antonio:	**Ahora tendrás experiencias nuevas.** *ah-oh-rah tehn-drahs ehks-peh-reeehn-theeahs* *nooeh-bahs* Now you'll have new experiences.
Verónica:	**Sí, espero que tendré muchas experiencias.** *see ehs-peh-roh keh tehn-dreh moo-chahs* *ehks-peh-reeehn-theeahs* Yes, I hope I'll have many [new] experiences.

Hiding Pronouns: Él or Ella?

For the most part, the Spanish language stays quite regular and to the point, which makes discovering and speaking the language easy. However, Spanish often hides the pronouns he, she and it. The easy part with Spanish is that you don't have to say the pronoun – you can make a good guess about the intended pronoun simply from the ending of the verb form.

In English, you always use the pronoun before the verb. Not so in Spanish. Because each pronoun has its own verb form, Spanish generally leaves out the pronoun. Therefore, you say **Voy al cine**, for 'I go to the cinema'. Here are some other examples:

- ✔ **Están de vacaciones.** *(ehs-tahn deh bah-kah-theeoh-nehs)* (They are on holiday.)
- ✔ **No es el coche.** *(noh ehs ehl koh-cheh)* (It isn't the car.)
- ✔ **¿Tienes vino?** *(teeeh-nehs bee-noh)* (Do you have wine?)

Figuring out Spanish pronouns is much like playing hide-and-seek. For a language that gives every word a specific gender, Spanish still manages to hide the gender of the subject (the doer) of its verbs. In the sentence **Trabaja en ventas**, you know that someone or something is working in sales, but you don't know whether the doer is a woman, a man, a cat or a computer. In English you use he, she and it to indicate who (or what) performs the action, but because each pronoun has its own verb form, Spanish generally omits the pronoun. So, when you say to someone, **Voy al cine**, that person understands that you're saying '*I go to the cinema*', based on the form of the verb (**voy**).

Getting the Hang of that Whole Gender Thing

What Spanish lacks in pronouns, it makes up for by being very specific in other parts of a sentence. You see, in Spanish, not just people, but everything in creation has gender. Yes – everything!

When you refer to people and animals, understanding gender use in Spanish is easy because gender is a part of their essence – just as with flowers; everyone knows that flowers are pollinated, needing both genders to produce fruit and seeds. So why not refer to all things that grow with names that are marked by gender? And if things that grow have gender, why not give everything (and every word) that privilege? Many languages spread this gender thing into their universe.

English belongs to the group of languages that doesn't use genders for words.

A noun's gender conditions everything around it, just as your own gender conditions your lifestyle. For example, in English of course, the word 'piano' has no gender. In Spanish, however, the word **piano** *(peeah-noh)* ends in an **o**, and is therefore male, because **o** at the end of a word usually indicates masculine (although some exceptions do exist to this general rule). Consequently, **piano** has a male definite article before it, **el piano** *(ehl peeah-noh)* (the piano), or the male indefinite article, **un piano** *(oon peeah-noh)* (a piano).

Appreciating articles

In English, you use the articles 'the' and 'a' or 'an' without knowing the subject's gender, or even caring whether a plural or singular word follows – very comfortable, but also very vague. With Spanish articles, however, you can point out when you're referring to one or several specific beings or things, and in the same breath, you can specify their gender.

In Spanish, your reward for this precision is variety; a 'more is better' kind of policy. For instance, you have four different ways to say the word 'the': for example, 'the girl', 'the girls', 'the boy' and 'the boys', or any other subject you want to stick in!

- ✔ **el** *(ehl)* (male 'the', singular)
- ✔ **la** *(lah)* (female 'the', singular)
- ✔ **los** *(lohs)* (male 'the', plural)
- ✔ **las** *(lahs)* (female 'the', plural)

Also, you have four ways to say 'a' or 'an':

- ✔ **un** *(oon)* (the male 'a' or 'an')
- ✔ **una** *(oo-nah)* (the female 'a' or 'an')
- ✔ **unos** *(oo-nohs)* (the plural of **un**)
- ✔ **unas** *(oo-nahs)* (the plural of **una**)

So how do you know when to use which article? Easy, at least most of the time: when the noun ends in **o**, it's male and if a word ends in **a**, it's female.

Although some exceptions to this rule do exist, they're pretty easy to figure out because they follow another rule – the **ma**, **pa**, **ta** rule – which holds that words ending in **ma**, **pa** and **ta** are likely to be masculine even though **a** is the last letter.

The easy part to remember is that when you see the letter **s** at the end of a Spanish word, you know the word is plural. Here are some examples:

- ✔ **el niño** *(ehl nee-nyoh)* (the boy)
- ✔ **los niños** *(lohs nee-nyohs)* (the boys [or the children])
- ✔ **un niño** *(oon nee-nyoh)* (a boy)
- ✔ **unos niños** *(oo-nohs nee-nyohs)* (some boys [or children])
- ✔ **la niña** *(lah nee-nyah)* (the girl)

✔ **las niñas** *(lahs nee-nyahs)* (the girls)

✔ **una niña** *(oo-nah nee-nyah)* (a girl)

✔ **unas niñas** *(oo-nahs nee-nyahs)* (some girls)

Look at the **los niños** entry in the preceding list and notice that the translation is plural for both 'the boys' and 'the children'. When you have mixed company (in other words, when both the male and females genders are present), you use the male plural article. So **los niños** can mean 'the boys' or 'the boys and girls'. You follow the same pattern with **unos**.

Okay, so Spanish and English are both vague in places, you say. And Spanish speakers say, sorry, that's the way it is. Languages, like people, all reserve the right to be vague at times.

Spanish is a melodious language. It doesn't like to have two consonants at the end of a word, and so it inserts a vowel between them – as in **mujer, mujeres**. So when a noun ends in a consonant, before adding the letter **s** to turn it into a plural, Spanish inserts an **e**. Check out these examples:

✔ **la mujer** *(lah moo-Hehr)* (the woman)

✔ **una mujer** *(oo-nah moo-Hehr)* (a woman)

✔ **unas mujeres** *(oo-nahs moo-Heh-rehs)* (some women)

✔ **el pan** *(ehl pahn)* (the bread)

✔ **los panes** *(lohs pah-nehs)* (the breads)

✔ **un pan** *(oon pahn)* (a bread)

✔ **unos panes** *(oo-nohs pah-nehs)* (some breads)

✔ **el canal** *(ehl kah-nahl)* (the channel)

✔ **los canales** *(lohs kah-nah-lehs)* (the channels)

✔ **un canal** *(oon kah-nahl)* (a channel)

✔ **unos canales** *(oo-nohs kah-nah-lehs)* (some channels)

✔ **el doctor** *(ehl dohk-tohr)* (the doctor)

✔ **los doctores** *(lohs dohk-toh-rehs)* (the doctors)

✔ **un doctor** *(oon dohk-tohr)* (a doctor)

✔ **unos doctores** *(oo-nohs dohk-toh-rehs)* (some doctors)

You may not be aware, but you already know how to make plurals of some nouns: simply add the letter **-s** to both the article and to the noun. When a noun ends with a consonant, however, use **-es** instead of just **-s**.

A professional job

In Spanish, when a male word for a profession comes up, you form the female term by adding the letter **a** to the end of the word. Thus, 'doctor' becomes **doctora**. From this point, you know already how to find your articles:

✔ **la doctora** *(lah dohk-toh-rah)* (the female doctor)

✔ **una doctora** *(oo-nah dohk-toh-rah)* (a female doctor)

✔ **las doctoras** *(lahs dohk-toh-rahs)* (the female doctors)

✔ **unas doctoras** *(oo-nahs dohk-toh-rahs)* (some female doctors)

Not so tough, is it?

Words to Know

el camino	ehl kah-*mee*-noh	the road
el hombre	ehl *ohm*-breh	the man
el niño	ehl *nee*-nyoh	the boy
la mujer	lah moo-*Hehr*	the woman
la niña	lah *nee*-nyah	the girl
las casas	lahs *kah*-sahs	the houses
los coches	lohs *koh*-chehs	the cars
los vinos	lohs *bee*-nohs	the wines

Adding adjectives

A noun tells you what you're talking about and a pronoun tells whom you're talking about, but adjectives are more fun. They tell you what these things and people are like, describing things like shape, colour and size. Adjectives are the essence of gossip!

When you talk in Spanish, you're very specific about gender and number. In fact, even adjectives get to show their gender and number. Which form of the adjective you use depends upon whether the noun it modifies is masculine or feminine, singular or plural.

In Spanish, masculine adjectives normally end in **-o,** and the ones ending in **-a** are usually feminine. For example, suppose that you want to say, 'I have a white car'. In Spanish you say, **Tengo un libro blanco** (*tehn-goh oon lee-broh blahn-koh*). Remember that because the word **libro** ends in an **o,** it's masculine; a masculine noun gets a masculine adjective, in this case **blanco** (*blahn-koh*).

These adjectives can take on four different forms each, depending upon the noun they describe. If we take the adjective **bonito** (*boh-nee-toh*) (beautiful) as an example, we find it in these different forms:

- ✔ **el libro bonito** (*ehl lee-broh boh-nee-toh*) (the beautiful [masculine, singular] book)
- ✔ **los libros bonitos** (*lohs lee-brohs boh-nee-tohs*) (the beautiful [masculine, plural] books)
- ✔ **la chica bonita** (*lah chee-kah boh-nee-tah*) (the beautiful [feminine, singular] girl)
- ✔ **las chicas bonitas** (*lahs chee-kahs boh-nee-tahs*) (feminine, plural) (the beautiful [feminine, plural] girls)

Counting Numbers

You can get by in Spanish by asking for one thing, more than one thing or even some things . . . for a while. But eventually you're going to want to ask for a specific number of items, such as two things, ten things or more. When numbers are important, you need to know how to say them, and so now we show you how to count from one to ten in Spanish:

1. **uno** (*oo-noh*) (one)
2. **dos** (*dohs*) (two)
3. **tres** (*trehs*) (three)
4. **cuatro** (*kooah-troh*) (four)
5. **cinco** (*theen-koh*) (five)
6. **seis** (*sehees*) (six)
7. **siete** (*seeeh-teh*) (seven)
8. **ocho** (*oh-choh*) (eight)
9. **nueve** (*nooeh-beh*) (nine)
10. **diez** (*dee-eth*) (ten)

With adjectives (as with other Spanish words), you need to be very specific about gender and number. We discuss gender in the earlier section 'Getting the Hang of that Whole Gender Thing'; here's how to handle numbers.

When you talk about things in the plural, you add the letter **s** to the adjective to show that you're talking about more than one. Therefore, **blanco** (*blahn-koh*) becomes **blancos** (*blahn-kohs*), **alta** (*ahl-tah*) becomes **altas** (*ahl-tahs*) and so on. Here are some more examples:

- **Las dos mujeres son altas.** *(lahs dohs moo-Heh-rehs sohn ahl-tahs)* (The two women are tall.)

- **Ocho hombres altos van en un coche rojo.** *(oh-choh ohm-brehs ahl-tohs bahn ehn oon koh-cheh roh-Hoh)* (Eight tall men go in a red car.)

- **Las dos casas son grandes.** *(lahs dohs kah-sahs sohn grahn-dehs)* (The two houses are large.)

- **Los tres caminos son largos.** *(lohs trehs kah-mee-nohs sohn lahr-gohs)* (The three routes are long.)

Getting to Know You: The Tú/Usted Issue

Some relationships tend to be more formal in Spanish than in English. If you need to denote formality in English, you have to show it through your body movements, the stiffness of your upper lip or the tone of your voice. In Spanish, the distinction between **tú** *(too)* and **usted** *(oos-tehd)* allows you to introduce this formality right into the language.

In past years, English speakers said the informal 'thou' (for example, to their beloved) and the more formal 'you' (for example, to their beloved's parents). Anyone listening to such a conversation knew whether the speakers were intimate or had a more formal relationship. This habit was lost over time in English, but Spanish retains it. Spanish speakers use the informal **tú** *(too)* just as English speakers used to say 'thou', and they say **usted** *(oos-tehd)* to signify a more respectful way of talking to someone, such as a new acquaintance, an older person or someone they consider to be of higher rank.

Adults address children using the informal **tú**.

Human relations are rigged with feelings. Only you know when you want to be more personal with someone. The beauty of Spanish is that you have a verbal means to manifest these feelings.

At some point in a relationship between people who speak Spanish, a shift may occur from the formal **usted** to the more informal and intimate **tú**. Two people of the same age, rank or educational level, or people who want to express a certain intimacy, arrive at a point where they want to talk to each other in a more informal or intimate manner. At this point they start to use the word **tú** when addressing each other. In Spanish, this shift is known as **tutearse** *(too-teh<u>ahr</u>-seh)*, that is, 'to talk **tú**'. These formalities make relationships more graceful and more varied. Being graceful in your speech and your relationships is much appreciated in more traditional Spanish-speaking situations.

On the other hand, if you don't want to have a closer, more intimate relationship with someone, or if you want to keep the relationship more professional and less chummy, you can stick to calling that person **usted**. However, if you stick to the **usted** form forever, you may wait a long time for that person to invite you round for paella!

Here are some examples of sentences using **tú** and **usted**:

- ✔ **¿Cómo se llama usted?** *(<u>koh</u>-moh seh <u>yah</u>-mah oos-<u>tehd</u>)* (What's your name?) (Respectful)

- ✔ **¿Vas tú con Juan al cine?** *(bahs too kohn Hoo<u>ahn</u> ahl <u>thee</u>-neh)* (Are you going with Juan to the cinema?) (Friendly, intimate)

- ✔ **Va (usted) a su casa.** *(bah oos-<u>tehd</u> ah soo <u>kah</u>-sah)* (You [singular] are going home.) (Respectful)

When people in Spain want to address several persons, they use the word **vosotros** *(boh-<u>soh</u>-trohs)*, which is the informal 'you' in the plural and a very popular form of address.

One of the main differences between addressing several people in standard Spanish and in Latin American Spanish is that the latter say **ustedes** (meaning 'you' in the plural). **Ustedes** can be a formal way of addressing two or more people, or it can be very informal. The situation dictates the difference. Here are some examples:

- ✔ **¿Viajais en tren?** *(beeah-<u>Hah</u>-ees ehn trehn)* (Do you travel on the train?) (Informal, plural)

- ✔ **¿A ustedes les gusta el flamenco?** *(ah oos-<u>teh</u>-dehs lehs <u>goos</u>-tah ehl flah-<u>mehn</u>-koh)* (Do you like flamenco?) (Formal, plural)

In written texts you may find the words **usted** and **ustedes** in their abbreviated forms (**Ud** for **usted** and **Uds** for **ustedes**). When you read these abbreviations aloud, you say the whole word.

Congratulations, you're becoming a Spanish grammarian! Grammar may not be glamorous, but you can't beat it as a means of making sure that you understand, and are understood by, your Spanish-speaking friends.

Fun & Games

Suppose you want to say 'I have a white house'.

You already know how to say it! In Spanish you say, **'Tengo una casa blanca'** *(tehn-goh oo-nah kah-sah blahn-kah)*. You know **la casa** *(lah kah-sah)* is female, because it ends in the letter **a**. Therefore, the adjective, **blanca** *(blahn-kah)*, is also female.

The following examples further illustrate our point about the gender of adjectives. Just select the appropriate adjective from within the brackets to complete the sentence:

✔ **Tengo una caja (blanca, blanco).** I have a white box.

✔ **Mi coche no es (blanca, blanco).** My car isn't white.

✔ **La mujer es (alta, alto).** The woman is tall.

✔ **El hombre es (alta, alto).** The man is tall.

Part II
Spanish in Action

'Your Nigel's Spanish is certainly improving'

In this part . . .

In this part, you start using Spanish. We focus on everyday situations, as if you live in Spain or are dealing with Spanish-speaking people. We show you Spanish small-talk and take you shopping and out to dinner, and help you do basic navigation in the Spanish language.

Chapter 3

¡Hola! Hello! Greetings and Introductions

. . . .

In This Chapter

▶ Naming names and making introductions

▶ Speaking formally or informally

▶ Being you, **ser**, and being there, **estar**

▶ Mentioning cities, countries and nationalities

. . . .

Meeting and greeting go hand in hand! In Spain, how precisely you greet people doesn't matter a great deal, although Spanish people are respectful of each other and of strangers. So as a rule, when you greet someone for the first time say **¡Hola!** *(oh-lah!)* (Hello!) and smile! Spanish speakers tend to reply with a suitable response that fits the circumstances. In this chapter, we show you several ways in which greeting and introductions can take place.

Greeting Formally or Informally

When greeting someone in Spanish, deciding how formally or informally to speak should come naturally; just act as you do when speaking English. When you already know the person you're talking to, use the friendlier, informal phrases. However, with a customer in a business situation or with someone you need to respect, the conversation is always formal. These common-sense rules for greeting people are known as Spanish rocket science!

Be aware that speakers of Latin American Spanish don't use **tú** *(too)*, the informal version of 'you'. When addressing someone they always use **usted** *(oostehd)* (refer to Chapter 2 for more details) and always greet each other very formally on the first occasion they meet anyone. An overly friendly and informal person, however, may simply be trying to put you at ease. Don't worry . . . always follow your instincts!

Talkin' the Talk

Antonio Rivera and María Salinas (his boss) work in the same building. Here's how they may greet each other in the hallway, on a daily basis (you may notice that the boss only needs to address Sr. Rivera by his surname).

Sra. Salinas: **Buenos días, Rivera. ¿Cómo estás?**
            boo*eh*-nohs dee*eahs* ree-*beh*-rah *koh*-moh ehs-*tahs*
            Good morning, Rivera [familiar]. How are you?

Sr. Rivera: **Muy bien. ¿Y usted señora Salinas?**
            mooy *bee*ehn ee oos-*tehd* seh-*nyoh*-rah sah-*lee*-nahs
            Very well. And you Sra. Salinas [formal]?

Sra. Salinas: **Bien, gracias.**
            *bee*ehn *grah*-thee*ahs*
            Well, thank you.

Talkin' the Talk

Observe how Juan and Julia, two teenagers, greet each other informally.

Juan: **¡Hola! ¿Cómo te llamas?**
        oh-lah! *koh*-moh teh *yah*-mahs
        Hi! What's your name?

Julia: **Me llamo Julia. ¿Y tú?**
        meh *yah*-moh *Hoo*-lee*ah* ee too
        My name's Julia. And yours?

Juan: **Yo me llamo Juan.**
        yoh meh *yah*-moh Hoo-*ahn*
        My name's Juan.

Talkin' the Talk

Juan and Julia meet again by accident while on their way to school.

Juan: **Buenos días. ¿Qué tal?**
        boo*eh*-nohs dee*eahs* keh tahl
        Good morning. How are things?

Julia:	**¡Ah, hola, Juan! ¿Cómo estás?** *ah oh-lah Hoo-ahn koh-moh ehs-tahs* Ah, hello, Juan! How are you?
Juan:	**Bien. ¿Y tú?** *beeehn ee tooh* Well. And you?
Julia:	**Bien.** *beeehn* Well.

Using Names and Surnames

Spaniards are generally easy-going people who love to chat. In the Spanish-speaking world, waiting to be introduced to people before you talk to them isn't customary. An introduction as such isn't necessary, and so you can feel free to initiate contact with people, using the greetings we present in this chapter.

If you feel interest on your part and from the other person to keep the contact going, introduce yourself. If the other person doesn't give you his or her name, just ask what it is. In some specific situations, a third person introduces you to make your contact with the new acquaintance much faster, but usually Spanish people expect you to introduce yourself.

We need to clear up one little thing on the issue of names. When you meet people, they probably tell you just the name that they commonly use, or maybe only part of it – for example, **Carmen** (*kahr-mehn*) rather than **María del Carmen** (*mah-reeah dehl kahr-mehn*). But as you get to know people better, you find out their full names!

Discovering what's in a name

Suppose that you meet a woman named **María del Carmen Fernández Bustamante** (*mah-reeah dehl kahr-mehn fehr-nahn-dehth boos-tah-mahn-teh*). **María del Carmen** (*mah-reeah dehl kahr-mehn*) is her first name, **Fernández** (*fehr-nahn-dehth*) is her first surname, which comes from the father, and **Bustamante** (*boos-tah-mahn-teh*) is her second surname and comes (usually) from the mother.

CULTURAL WISDOM

Capitalising abbreviations

Spanish capitalises the abbreviated forms of
señor and **señora** just as English capitalises Mr
and Mrs:

señor	Sr.	Mister		Mr
señora	Sra.	Madam		Mrs
señorita	Srta.	(senorita)		Miss
usted	Ud.	you (singular, used in formal situations)		
ustedes	Uds.	you (plural, used in formal situations)		

So far, so good. But if Miss Fernández marries, she doesn't need to add on more names, but may do so. Imagine that she marries **señor** (*seh-nyohr*) (Mr) **Juan José García Díaz** (*Hooahn Hoh-seh gahr-theeah deeahth*). She is still called **Fernández Bustamante**, but she can change the position of her father's surname to insert her husband's first surname, which is **García**. If she does so, she becomes **señora María del Carmen de García Fernández Bustamante** (*mah-reeah dehl kahr-mehn deh gahr-theeah fehr-nahn-dehth boos-tah-mahn-teh*).

The effect of these conventions is that women keep their family names, which are considered very important and meaningful. Children's surnames indicate both their father and mother. **Señor García**, for example, has a child, **Mario**, by a previous marriage to a woman whose first surname is **Campo**. Because children carry the first surnames of both parents, **Mario** is called **Mario García Campo**.

Meeting the verb llamarse

Now is a good time to include the conjugation of the verb **llamarse** (*yah-mahr-seh*), the equivalent of 'name is', which you use when you introduce yourself.

GRAMMATICALLY SPEAKING

The verb **llamar** (*yah-mahr*) (to call) is a regular **-ar** verb; however, the **-se** at the end of **llamarse** (*yah-mahr-seh*) tells you that the verb is reflexive, which makes it irregular as well (that's grammar for you!). A *reflexive verb* is one that acts on the noun (or object) of the sentence. For instance, the sentence **yo me llamo** (*yoh meh yah-moh*) literally means 'I call myself'. In this case, 'I' is the subject of the sentence and 'call myself' reflects back to 'I'. Anytime you see the **se** at the end of a verb, you simply put the reflexive pronoun (**me** in the example sentence) in front of the verb. For more on reflexive pronouns, check out Chapter 16.

Take a look at the following table for the conjugation of **llamarse** in the present tense. Pay attention to the reflexive pronouns – they stay the same for all regular **-ar** verbs.

Conjugation	*Pronunciation*
yo me llamo	*yoh meh <u>yah</u>-moh*
tú te llamas	*too teh <u>yah</u>-mahs*
él, ella, usted se llama	*ehl, <u>eh</u>-yah, oos-<u>tehd</u> seh <u>yah</u>-mah*
nosotros nos llamamos	*noh-<u>soh</u>-trohs nohs yah-<u>mah</u>-mohs*
vosotros os llamáis	*boh-<u>soh</u>-trohs ohs yah-<u>mah</u>ees*
ellos, ellas, ustedes se llaman	*<u>eh</u>-yohs, <u>eh</u>-yahs, oos-<u>teh</u>-dehs seh <u>yah</u>-mahn*

Getting Introductions Right: Solemn and Social

Speaking Spanish involves joining in with social interactions where you're expected to introduce and say a few things about yourself and other people. The information you impart can include name, origin or nationality, occupation or interests, and so on. How to introduce yourself and other people, therefore, is one of the most important conversations to master when learning Spanish.

Some situations call for a certain level of solemnity, for example when you're being introduced to a very important or famous person. Just like in English, some specific Spanish phrases indicate this formality, as the following examples demonstrate:

- ✔ **¿Me permite presentarle a. . .?** (*meh pehr-<u>mee</u>-teh preh-sehn-<u>tahr</u>-leh ah*) (May I introduce. . .?)

- ✔ **Es un gusto conocerle.** (*ehs oon <u>goos</u>-toh koh-noh-<u>thehr</u>-leh*) (It's a pleasure to meet you.)

- ✔ **El gusto es mío, encantado [encantada** if a woman]. (*ehl <u>goos</u>-toh ehs <u>mee</u>oh ehn-kahn-<u>tah</u>-doh*) (The pleasure is mine, pleased to meet you.)

My name is Is, isn't it?

When, in English, you say, 'I introduce myself', you're using a reflexive form of the verb 'intro-duce', and so you say 'myself'. Likewise, when Pedro says '**me llamo Pedro**' (*meh yah-moh peh-droh*), the word **me** (*meh*) means 'myself'.

Often, beginners in Spanish say, '**Me llamo es**', using a mistakenly literal translation of 'my name is'. But **me** in Spanish means 'to me' or 'myself' – it never means 'I'. **Llamo** is the first person of the singular of a verb, and so **me llamo** can be translated as 'I call myself'. Even in English, you don't add 'is' to that, right?

Introducing yourself formally

Introducing yourself formally means that you don't talk in a familiar, informal way to a person with whom you have no relationship. You use the formal way of introducing yourself because you may want to keep a certain distance, just in case you decide later on that you don't want a closer relationship with this person.

Some Spanish people who don't know each other use **usted** (*oos-tehd*) – the formal form of 'you' – and its verbal form when addressing one another.

Talkin' the Talk

Here's an example of how Spanish people introduce themselves in a formal situation. Pedro García Fernández approaches a table at a café with a person already sitting there.

Pedro: **¿Me permite?**
meh pehr-mee-teh
May I?

Jane: **Sí, ¡adelante!**
see ah-deh-lahn-teh
Yes, [go] ahead!

Pedro: **Buenas tardes. Me llamo Pedro García Fernández.**
booeh-nahs tahr-dehs meh yah-moh peh-droh gahr-theeah fehr-nahn-dehth
Good afternoon. My name's Pedro García Fernández.

Jane: **Mucho gusto, señor García.**
moo-choh goos-toh seh-nyohr gahr-theeah
Nice to meet you, Mr García.

Pedro: **Y usted ¿cómo se llama?**
ee oos-tehd koh-moh seh yah-mah
And what's your name?

Jane: **Me llamo Jane Wells.**
meh yah-moh Jane Wells
My name's Jane Wells.

Pedro: **Mucho gusto.**
moo-choh goos-toh
A pleasure.

Talkin' the Talk

In this conversation, Pepe is formally introducing Lucía and Fernando to Mr Kendall.

Pepe: **Buenas tardes. ¿El señor Kendall?**
booeh-nahs tahr-dehs ehl seh-nyohr Kendall
Good afternoon. Are you Mr Kendall?

Mr Kendall: **Sí, me llamo Kendall.**
see meh yah-moh Kendall
Yes, my name's Kendall.

Pepe: **Permítame que le presente al señor Fernando Quintana Martínez.**
pehr-mee-tah-me keh leh preh-sehn-teh ahl seh-nyohr fehr-nahn-doh keen-tah-nah mahr-tee-neth
Allow me to introduce Mr Fernando Quintana Martínez.

Mr Kendall: **Mucho gusto.**
moo-choh goos-toh
A pleasure.

Pepe: **Esta es la señora de Kendall.**
ehs-tah ehs lah seh-nyoh-rah deh Kendall
This is Mrs Kendall.

Esta es la señora Lucía Sánchez de Quintana.
*ehs-tah ehs lah seh-nyoh-rah loo-theeah sahn-cheth
deh keen-tah-nah*
This is Mrs Lucía Sánchez de Quintana.

Mrs Kendall: **Mucho gusto, señora.**
moo-choh goos-toh seh-nyoh-rah
A pleasure, madam.

Some older adult speakers may be identified by the insertion of **don** (*dohn*)
(masculine form, a Spanish courtesy title for men that is prefixed to the fore-
name) or **doña** (*doh-nyah*) (feminine form, for women). Calling someone **don**
or **doña** can be a way of showing that you're addressing a very respected – or
very old – person. The use of **don/doña** is in decline, however.

Presenting yourself informally

A new acquaintance you've greeted for the first time will usually ask you for
your name. You may feel comfortable using **tú** *(too)* – the informal form of
'you' – when speaking with someone your age or younger. Sometimes you
can pick up cues from the person you're talking with: If someone starts the
conversation using **tú** *(too)* it'll probably be appropriate for you to use **tú** as
well.

Talkin' the Talk

Lisa and Oscar are two young students that, by chance, are watching the same photographic exhibition about different Spanish festivals and they're just about to introduce themselves to each other in
a casual way.

Lisa   **Hola, ¿te gustan estas fotos?**
oh-lah teh goos-tahn ehs-tahs foh-tohs
Hello, are you enjoying these photos?

Oscar   **Sí, mucho. Me interesa todo sobre la cultura popular.**
*see moo-choh meh een-teh-reh-sah toh-doh soh-breh
lah cool-too-rah poh-poo-lahr*
Yes, very much so. I'm very interested in popular
culture.

Lisa	**Yo también tengo el mismo interés. Perdona... ¿Cómo te llamas?**
	yoh tahm-bee-ehn tehn-goh ehl mees-moh een-teh-rehs pehr-doh-nah koh-moh teh yah-mahs
	I have the same interest too. Excuse me... What's your name?
Oscar	**Me llamo Oscar, ¿y tú?**
	meh yah-moh ohs-cahr ee too
	My name is Oscar, and yours is?
Lisa	**Me llamo Lisa. ¿De dónde eres, Oscar?**
	meh yah-moh lee-sah deh dohn-deh eh-rehs ohs-cahr
	My name is Lisa. Where are you from, Oscar?
Oscar	**Soy de Canarias. ¿Y tú, Lisa?**
	soh-ee deh cah-nah-reeahs ee too lee-sah
	I'm from the Canaries. And you, Lisa?
Lisa	**De Alcalá, un pueblo cerca de Madrid.**
	deh ahl-kah-lah oon poo-eh-bloh thehr-kah deh mah-dreed
	From Alcalá, a town close to Madrid.
Oscar	**¿Te gustan las fotos de las fiestas populares?**
	teh goos-tahn-lahs foh-tohs deh lahs feeehs-tahs poh-poo-lah-rehs
	Do you like photographs of popular festivals?
Lisa	**Sí, estudio sociología y me intersan las diferentes tradiciones.**
	See ehs-too-dee-oh soh-thee-oh-loh-Hee-ah ee meh een-teh-reh-sahn lahs dee-feh-rehn-tehs trah-dee-theeoh-nehs
	Yes, I'm studying sociology and I'm interested in the different traditions.

When you're talking to a child, you speak less formally, too. Note that people commonly describe children with diminutives. A *diminutive* is a suffix added to a word to convey the meaning 'small' or 'unimportant', and is often used for the purpose of expressing affection, as we explain in Chapter 2.

The most common Spanish diminutive suffixes are **-ito** and **-illo,** along with their feminine equivalents, **-ita** and **-illa**, as you can see in **chiquito** (*chee-kee-toh*) (kiddie) or **gatito** (*gah-tee-toh*) (kitten), for example. Although often translated using the English word 'little', diminutives more often indicate the speaker's feelings toward the person or object than to its size.

Feeling Free to Be the Way You Are

In Spanish, you have two ways to ask, 'to be or not to be'. You can say **Ser o no ser** (*sehr oh noh sehr*), when the state of being is unlikely to change (you're always going to be a person, for example), and you use **Estar o no estar** (*ehs-tahr o no ehs-tahr*) if the state of being is changeable (for example, you won't always be tired).

Being permanent: ser

Ser (*sehr*) (to be) refers to a kind of being that is permanent, like the fact that you are you. The word also refers to all things that are expected to be permanent, such as places, countries and certain conditions or states of being, such as shape, profession, nationality and place of origin. This permanent 'to be' in Spanish is **ser** (*sehr*):

- ✔ **Soy mujer.** *(sohy moo-Hehr)* (I'm a woman.)

- ✔ **Soy escocés.** *(sohy ehs-koh-thes)* (I'm Scottish.)

- ✔ **Soy de Madrid.** *(sohy deh mah-dreed)* (I'm from Madrid.)

- ✔ **Ellos son muy altos.** *(eh-yohs sohn mooy ahl-tohs)* (They're very tall.)

- ✔ **¿Ustedes son de Sevilla?** *(oos-teh-dehs sohn deh Seh-bee-yah)* (Are you [formal] from Seville?)

- ✔ **Ella es maestra.** *(eh-yah ehs mah-ehs-trah)* (She's a teacher.)

- ✔ **Eres muy bella.** *(eh-rehs mooy beh-yah)* (You're very beautiful.)

- ✔ **Eres muy simpático.** *(eh-rehs mooy seem-pah-teeh-koh)* (You're very pleasant.)

Conjugating ser (to be)

The verb **ser** (*sehr*) (to be) is the one most frequently used in Spanish. And, of course, just like the English 'to be', it's an irregular verb. (We discuss irregular verbs in Chapter 2.) The following table shows how to conjugate **ser**.

Conjugation	Pronunciation
yo soy	*yoh sohy*
tú eres	*too eh-rehs*
él, ella, usted es	*ehl, eh-yah, oos-tehd, ehs*
nosotros somos	*noh-soh-trohs soh-mohs*
vosotros sois	*boh-soh-trohs sohees*
ellos, ellas, ustedes son	*eh-yohs, eh-yahs, oos-teh-dehs sohn*

Spaniards all

You probably like to tell people where specifically you're from, and you like to know where the people you meet are from, too.

Almost everyone likes to talk about nationalities. And when you talk about nationalities with Spaniards, you're wise to remember one crucial point: Spaniards come from their very own

regions! So, to say just **español** *(ehs-pah-nyohl)* when you mean someone from Andalucía doesn't quite cover all the ground. You make yourself better understood if you say **andaluz** *(an-dah-looth)*, meaning 'a Spaniard from Andalucía'.

Talkin' the Talk

Now is a good time to practise the 'permanent' way to be, so that it becomes second nature. (You wouldn't want your being to flitter away, would you?) Imagine that you're in a café or a bar – the meeting places for socialising in most Spanish regions – and you overhear the following conversation at a nearby table.

Roberto: **¿Y tú Jane, de qué ciudad eres?**
ee tooh Jane deh keh theeoo-dahd eh-rehs
And you, Jane, what city are you from?

Jane: **Soy de Londres.**
sohy deh Lohn-drehs
I'm from London.

Roberto: **¿Es una ciudad grande?**
ehs oo-nah theeoo-dahd grahn-deh
Is that a very large city?

Jane: **Es una ciudad enorme, pero muy bonita.**
ehs oo-nah theeoo-dahd eh-nor-meh peh-roh mooy boh-nee-tah
It's a huge city, but very nice.

Roberto: **Bueno, esta es también una ciudad grande.**
booeh-noh ehs-tah ehs tahm-beeehn oo-nah theeoo-dahd grahn-deh
Well, this is also a big city.

Jane: **Es bastante grande.**
Ehs bahs-tahn-teh grahn-deh
It's pretty big.

Words to Know

bastante	bahs-_tahn_-teh	quite; enough
grande	_grahn_-deh	big; large
pequeño	peh-_keh_-nyo	little; small

Saying adios to pronouns

In an English sentence, you always use a noun or pronoun with a verb. You may already have noticed that Spanish doesn't use this convention. Because the verb form is different for each pronoun, Spanish frequently omits the pronoun.

Spanish verbs indicate the pronoun through their conjugation. English verbs don't. For example, in English, you say 'I sing', 'you sing' and 'we sing'. In Spanish, you say **canto** (_kahn_-toh) (I sing), **cantas** (_kahn_-tahs) (you sing) and **cantamos** (kahn-_tah_-mohs) (we sing). Therefore, Spanish-speakers can understand you clearly even if you use only the verb. Using the pronoun in Spanish isn't wrong, although leaving it off is more informal and conversational. However, especially as you start practising the language, using the pronoun may help you conjugate the verb correctly.

Talkin' the Talk

You hear this conversation from a table in a café. In this case, as the people are speaking in a colloquial style, the use of pronouns before the verbs is omitted.

Esperanza: **¿Es bueno el hotel Paraíso?**
ehs booeh-noh ehl oh-tehl pah-rah-ee-soh
Is the hotel Paraíso any good?

Esteban: **Sí, es un buen hotel.**
see ehs oon booehn oh-tehl
Yes, it's a good hotel.

Esperanza: **¿Es caro?**
ehs kah-roh
Is it expensive?

Esteban:	**Es un poco caro.**
	ehs oon poh-koh kah-roh
	It's a little expensive.

Esperanza:	**¿Es grande?**
	ehs grahn-deh
	Is it big?

Esteban:	**No, no es muy grande.**
	noh noh ehs mooy grahn-deh
	No, it's not very big.

Esperanza:	**¿Hay problema para reservar allí?**
	ahee proh-bleh-mah pah-rah reh-sehr-bar ah-yee
	Is there any problem reserving there?

Esteban:	**No, no hay ningún problema.**
	noh noh ahee neen-goon proh-bleh-mah
	No, no problem at all.

Words to Know

buen	*booehn*	good (male)
buena	*booeh-nah*	good (female)
bueno	*booeh-noh*	good (male)
caro	*kah-roh*	expensive
ningún	*neen-goon*	none
poco	*poh-koh*	a bit; small amount

Knowing a second 'be' for your bonnet: Estar

Spanish is a very precise language. In Spanish, you have two forms of 'to be', each with a different meaning, to supply more precision to your statements. Unlike in English, when you talk about 'being' in Spanish the verb you use removes any guesswork about your meaning.

When you speak of being someone or something *permanently* in Spanish, you use the verb **ser** *(sehr)*. But when you're talking about a state of being that is *not permanent* – such as being somewhere (you won't be there forever), or being some temporary way (being ill, for instance) – you use the verb **estar** *(ehs-tahr)*. So in Spanish, you don't say 'To be or not to be', but 'To be forever **(ser)** or not forever **(estar)**'.

So you know you can use one of two verbs to say 'to be'. We delve into the verb **ser** *(sehr)* in the earlier section 'Being permanent: **ser**'. The following table conjugates the present tense of the verb **estar**:

Conjugation	Pronunciation
yo estoy	*yoh ehs-<u>toh</u>ee*
tú estás	*too ehs-<u>tahs</u>*
él, ella, usted está	*ehl, <u>eh</u>-yah, oos-<u>tehd</u> ehs-<u>tah</u>*
nosotros estamos	*noh-<u>soh</u>-trohs ehs-<u>tah</u>-mohs*
vosotros estáis	*boh-<u>soh</u>-trohs ehs-<u>tah</u>ees*
ellos, ellas, ustedes están	*<u>eh</u>-yohs, <u>eh</u>-yahs, oos-<u>teh</u>-dehs ehs-<u>tahn</u>*

We use this verb many times in this book, and so we give you the simple past and future tenses as well. The following table provides conjugation of the simple past tense:

Conjugation	Pronunciation
yo estuve	*yoh ehs-<u>too</u>-beh*
tú estuviste	*too ehs-too-<u>bees</u>-teh*
él, ella, usted estuvo	*ehl, <u>eh</u>-yah, oos-<u>tehd</u> ehs-<u>too</u>-boh*
nosotros estuvimos	*noh-<u>soh</u>-trohs ehs-too-<u>bee</u>-mohs*
vosotros estuvisteis	*boh-<u>soh</u>-trohs ehs-too-<u>bees</u>-tehees*
ellos, ellas, ustedes estuvieron	*<u>eh</u>-yohs, <u>eh</u>-yahs, oos-<u>teh</u>-dehs ehs-too-bee<u>eh</u>-rohn*

Here's how you conjugate the future tense of **estar**:

Conjugation	Pronunciation
yo estaré	*yoh ehs-tah-<u>reh</u>*
tú estarás	*too ehs-tah-<u>rahs</u>*
él, ella, usted estará	*ehl, <u>eh</u>-yah, oos-<u>tehd</u> ehs-tah-<u>rah</u>*
nosotros estaremos	*noh-<u>soh</u>-trohs ehs-tah-<u>reh</u>-mohs*
vosotros estaréis	*boh-<u>soh</u>-trohs ehs-tah-<u>reh</u>ees*
ellos, ellas, ustedes estarán	*<u>eh</u>-yohs, <u>eh</u>-yahs, oos-<u>teh</u>-dehs ehs-tah-<u>rahn</u>*

Talkin' the Talk

Here's a dialogue to help you practise this new way of being, the one that isn't forever. You're in the same café as in the earlier section 'Saying adios to pronouns' – it's a popular place! – but you're listening to a different conversation.

Guillermo: **¿Cómo estás?**
koh-moh ehs-tahs
How are you?

Sra. Valdés: **Estoy muy bien, gracias.**
ehs-tohee mooy beeehn grah-theeahs
I'm very well, thank you.

Guillermo: **¿Estáis de compras?**
ehs-tahees deh kohm-prahs
Are you shopping?

Sra. Valdés: **Estoy de vacaciones.**
ehs-tohee deh bah-kah-theeoh-nehs
I'm on holiday.

Guillermo: **¿Estás contenta?**
ehs-tahs kohn-tehn-tah
Are you having a good time?

Sra. Valdés: **Estoy muy feliz.**
ehs-tohee mooy feh-leeth
We're very happy.

Guillermo: **¿Cómo está tu hija?**
koh-moh ehs-tah too ee-Hah
How's your daughter?

Sra. Valdés: **Más o menos, hoy no está muy feliz.**
mahs oh meh-nohs oeeh noh ehs-tah mooy feh-leeth
So-so, she's not very happy today.

Talkin' the Talk

Everyone, at one time or another, needs to ask where the toilet is. Here's a sample of how such a conversation may sound. You're again at the café, this time in the back, near the lavatories.

Carlota:	**¿Está libre el baño?** *ehs-tah lee-breh ehl bah-nyoh* Is the toilet free?
Elena:	**No, está ocupado.** *noh ehs-tah oh-koo-pah-doh* No, it's taken.
Carlota:	**¿Está libre el otro baño?** *ehs-tah lee-breh ehl oh-troh bah-nyoh* Is the other toilet free?
Elena:	**Sí, está libre.** *see ehs-tah lee-breh* Yes, it's free.

Words to Know

contento	kohn-_tehn_-toh	happy; satisfied
De compras	deh _kohm_-prahs	shopping
feliz	feh-_leeth_	happy
libre	_lee_-breh	free
ocupado	oh-koo-_pah_-doh	occupied; busy
otro	_oh_-troh	the other one

Speaking about Speaking: Hablar

To complete your conversations at the café, you need to know about the verb **hablar** *(ah-blahr)* (to speak; to talk). Fortunately, **hablar** is a regular verb, and so you don't need to memorise how it works. (We cover regular verbs in Chapter 2.) This verb is from the group that ends in **-ar**. The root of this verb is **habl-**, and the table that follows shows how to conjugate it in the present tense.

Conjugation	*Pronunciation*
yo hablo	*yoh <u>ah</u>-bloh*
tú hablas	*too <u>ah</u>-blahs*
él, ella, usted habla	*ehl, eh-yah, oos-<u>tehd</u> <u>ah</u>-blah*
nosotros hablamos	*noh-<u>soh</u>-trohs ah-<u>blah</u>-mohs*
vosotros habláis	*boh-<u>soh</u>-trohs ah-<u>blae</u>es*
ellos, ellas, ustedes hablan	*<u>eh</u>-yohs, <u>eh</u>-yahs, oos-<u>teh</u>-dehs <u>ah</u>-blahn*

Talkin' the Talk

In this conversation, Kathleen and Javier talk about talking.

Kathleen:	**¿María habla mucho?**
	mah-<u>ree</u>ah <u>ah</u>-blah <u>moo</u>-choh
	Does María talk a lot?
Javier:	**Sí, le encanta hablar.**
	see leh ehn-<u>kahn</u>-tah <u>ah</u>-blahr
	Yes, she loves to talk.
Kathleen:	**Yo hablo mal español.**
	yoh <u>ah</u>-bloh mahl ehs-pah-<u>nyohl</u>
	I speak Spanish badly.
Javier:	**¡Por el contrario, lo hablas muy bien!**
	pohr ehl kohn-<u>trah</u>-reeoh loh <u>ah</u>-blahs mooy bee<u>ehn</u>
	On the contrary, you speak it very well!

Words to Know

difícil	dee-<u>fee</u>-theel	difficult; hard
el idioma	ehl ee-dee-<u>oh</u>-mah	the language
fácil	<u>fah</u>-theel	easy
gustar	goos-<u>tahr</u>	to like
la lengua	lah <u>lehn</u>-gooah	the language [literally: the tongue]
mucho	<u>moo</u>-choh	a lot; much

Talkin' the Talk

At another table, you hear more talk about speaking.

Antonia: **¿Hablas español?**
ah-blahs ehs-pah-nyol
Do you speak Spanish?

Luís: **Sí. ¿Qué idiomas hablas?**
see keh ee-dee-oh-mahs ah-blahs
Yes. What languages do you speak?

Antonia: **Yo hablo inglés y francés.**
yoh ah-bloh een-glehs ee frahn-thehs
I speak English and French.

Luís: **Es muy difícil hablar inglés?**
ehs mooy dee-fee-theel ah-blahr een-glehs
Is it very difficult to speak English?

Antonia: **No, ¡es muy fácil!**
noh ehs mooy fah-theel
No, it's very easy!

Luís: **¿Y es difícil hablar francés?**
ee ehs dee-fee-theel ah-blahr frahn-thehs
And is it difficult to speak French?

Antonia: **No, no es en absoluto difícil.**
noh noh ehs ehn ahb-soh-loo-toh dee-fee-theel
No, it's not difficult all.

Luís: **A mí me gusta mucho hablar español.**
ah mee meh goos-tah moo-choh ah-blahr ehs-pah-nyohl
I like to speak Spanish.

Antonia: **A mí también.**
ah mee tahm-beeehn
So do I.

Words to Know

¿Cómo está usted?	_koh_-moh ehs-_tah_ oos-_tehd_	How are you? (formal)
¿Cómo estás?	_koh_-moh ehs-_tahs_	How are you? (informal)
¿Cómo te va?	_koh_-moh teh bah	How are you doing?
¿Cómo van las cosas?	_koh_-moh bahn lahs _koh_-sahs	How are things [going]?
Más o menos	mahs oh _meh_-nohs	So-so (Literally: more or less)
¿Qué pasa?	keh _pah_-sah	How are things? (Literally: what's happening?)
¿Qué tal?	keh tahl	How are things? (Literally: how such?)
Ser de aquí	sehr deh ah-_kee_	To belong to this place; to live here

Fun & Games

Translate the following English sentences into Spanish. All the statements are based on information in this chapter. Sit back, relax and marvel at how much Spanish you know.

Good afternoon! _____

My name is Kendall. _____

A pleasure, Mr Kendall. _____

My name is María Luisa. _____

Where are you from? _____

I'm from London. _____

What city are you from? _____

I'm from Madrid. _____

Is that a very large city? _____

Yes, it's a very large city. _____

We are on holidays. _____

Are you having a good time? _____

I'm very happy. _____

Chapter 4

Getting to Know You: Making Small Talk

Meeting and getting to know new people can be stressful, especially when you have to converse in a language that isn't your own. Small talk – discussing common, easily understood interests and concerns – is the universally recognised way of starting or carrying out a conversation in a new situation. This chapter helps you make small talk with Spanish-speaking people so that you can begin to achieve a solid, all-round understanding of how the people that you're getting to know live and go about their lives.

Using the Key Questions: Six Ws and Two Hs

You may have heard about 'The Five Ws', which represent the questions that you need to ask to cover the basic information about a situation (who, what, where, when and why). Well, we add three more questions to this group that you may find useful when first meeting someone. Here are the key questions:

✔ **¿Quién?** *(keeehn)* (Who?)

✔ **¿Qué?** *(keh)* (What?)

✔ **¿Dónde?** *(dohn-deh)* (Where?)

✔ **¿Cuándo?** *(kooahn-doh)* (When?)

✔ **¿Por qué?** *(pohr keh)* (Why?)

✔ **¿Cómo?** *(koh-moh)* (How?)

✔ **¿Cuánto?** *(kooahn-toh)* (How much/many?)

✔ **¿Cuál?** *(kooahl)* (Which?)

The following phrases show how to use these words:

✔ **¿Quién es él?** *(keeehn ehs ehl)* (Who is he?)

✔ **¿Qué hace usted?** *(keh ah-theh oos-tehd)* (What do you [singular] do?)

✔ **¿Dónde vives?** *(dohn-deh bee-bes)* (Where do you [singular] live?)

✔ **¿Cuándo llegásteis?** *(kooahn-doh yeh-gahs-tehees)* (When did you [plural] arrive?)

✔ **¿Por qué está ella aquí?** *(pohr keh ehs-tah eh-yah ah-kee)* (Why is she here?)

✔ **¿Cómo es la carretera?** *(koh-moh ehs lah kah-reh-teh-rah)* (What's the road like?)

✔ **¿Cuánto cuesta la habitación?** *(kooahn-toh kooehs-tah lah ah-bee-tah-thee-ohn)* (How much is the room?)

✔ **¿Qué hotel es mejor?** *(keh oh-tehl ehs meh-Hohr)* (Which hotel is better?)

You may notice that some of the vowels in these words feature accent marks over them. In questions and exclamations, these letters have an accent to help you, and readers of Spanish in general, distinguish how the word is being used. For example, you can use the word **quien** *(keeehn)* (who) in two different ways:

✔ **Quien** has no accent when you use it in a sentence to refer to someone who did this or that.

✔ **¡Quién!** or **¿quién?** carries an accent to call your attention to the fact that 'who' is being used as an exclamation or a question, such as 'who did it?'.

You use the same technique to indicate other words used to make a question or an exclamation, such as 'when?' **¿cuándo?** *(kooahn-doh)*; 'what!' **¡qué!** *(keh)*; 'where?' **¿dónde?** *(dohn-deh)*; 'why?' **¡por qué!** *(pohr keh)*; 'how?' **¿cómo?** *(koh-moh)*; and 'which?' **¿cuál?** *(kooahl)*.

The accents don't change the way the words sound; you use them only in written Spanish. When speaking, your inflection or tone of voice tells listeners how you're using the term in question.

Three useful sentences amid all the other talk

Sometimes you can't understand what someone's saying. Or you may bump into someone and want to apologise. The following courtesy phrases can come in handy:

✔ **No entiendo.** *(noh ehn-tee*ehn*-doh)* (I don't understand.)

✔ **Lo siento.** *(loh see-*ehn*-toh)* (I'm sorry.)

✔ **¡Perdone!** *(pehr-*doh*-neh)* (Excuse me!) Say this when you bump into someone.

Words to Know

la carretera	lah kah-rreh-*teh*-rah	the road
la habitación	lah ah-bee-tah-thee-*ohn*	the room
llegar	yeh-*gahr*	to arrive
vivir	bee-*beer*	to live

Talkin' the Talk

Carlos is on Flight Number 223, from Madrid to Barcelona. He introduced himself to his seatmates, and so he knows their names, but he wants to make small talk about himself. Here's how such a conversation may go.

Carlos: **Qué vuelo tan agradable!**
*keh boo*eh*-loh tahn ah-grah-*dah*-bleh*
Such a pleasant flight!

Juan: **Sí, es un viaje tranquilo.**
*see ehs oon bee*ah*-Heh trahn-*kee*-loh*
Yes, it's a quiet trip.

Carlos: **¿Viajas a menudo en avión?**
*bee*ah*-Has ah meh-*noo*-doh ehn ah-bee-*ohn*
Do you fly often?

Juan:	**No, éste es mi primer vuelo.** *noh <u>ehs</u>-teh ehs mee pree-<u>mehr</u> boo<u>eh</u>-loh* No, this is my first time flying.
Carlos:	**¿De dónde eres?** *deh <u>dohn</u>-deh <u>eh</u>-resh* Where are you from?
Juan:	**Soy de Barcelona. ¿Y tú?** *sohy deh bar-theh <u>loh</u>-nah ee too* I'm from Barcelona. And you?
Carlos:	**Yo soy de Londres . . . ¿cómo es Barcelona?** *yoh sohy deh <u>lohn</u>-drehs . . . <u>koh</u>-moh ehs bar-theh <u>loh</u>-nah* I'm from London. . . what's Barcelona like?
Juan:	**Es una ciudad grande y maravillosa.** *ehs <u>ooh</u>-nah theeoo-<u>dahd</u> <u>grahn</u>-deh ee mah-rah-bee-<u>yoh</u>-sah* It's a large, wonderful city.

Keeping an Eye on the Weather

Weather is an obsession in temperate countries where conditions vary a great deal, and where it often gets to be, as southern Spaniards like to say, **insoportable** *(een-soh-pohr-<u>tah</u>-bleh)* (unbearable). In warmer climates, such as Islas Canarias *(<u>ees</u>-lahs cah-<u>nah</u>-ree-ahs)* (the Canary Islands) weather is much less of an issue.

The tropics – including much of Central America – effectively have only two seasons: the rainy and dry seasons. When you travel to these countries, you may want to avoid the rainy season, which is also the time for hurricanes. Hurricanes are bothersome (if not downright dangerous!) on the coasts, and they bring a lot of rain into the highlands, where most of the cities are situated. In Mexico, the rainy season is from the end of May to November, really setting in by July and August.

South America has a region called The 'South Cone' that includes Uruguay, Argentina and Chile; the region is (you guessed it!) cone-shaped on the map. Here, the weather is temperate – that is to say, warm in summer and cold in winter. Very cold weather happens only in the far south in sparsely populated areas.

In mainland Spain, however, as you know, the 'rain falls mainly on the plain'. At least, it did for Eliza Doolittle in the musical *My Fair Lady*. Spain lies in the temperate zone, but just as the tropics have a rainy season and a dry season, Spain has a rainy country and a dry country. The rain that falls on the plains occurs in the north of Spain, in an area of cooler summers. The rest of the country is hot and dry, while the coastal areas, the Balearics and the Canary Islands are just about perfect any time of year.

Talkin' the Talk

Antonio has just returned from a six-month assignment in Valencia. Back in his home office, Antonio and his co-worker Ana talk about the weather there.

Ana: **¿Cómo es el clima de Valencia?**
koh-moh ehs ehl klee-mah deh bah-lehn-theeah
What's Valencia's climate like?

Antonio: **Es muy agradable y templado.**
ehs mooy ah-grah-dah-bleh ee tehm-plah-doh
It's very pleasant and temperate.

Ana: **¿Llueve mucho?**
yooeh-beh moo-choh
Does it rain a lot?

Antonio: **No, no llueve mucho.**
Noh, noh yooeh-beh moo-choh
No, there's not much rain.

Ana: **¿Y también hay sol?**
ee tahm-beeehn ah-ee sohl
And is it sunny?

Antonio: **Sí, hay sol casi todos los días.**
see ah-ee sohl kah-see toh-dohs lohs deeahs
Yes, it's sunny almost every day.

Ana: **¿No nieva nunca?**
noh neeeh-bah noon-kah
Does it ever snow?

Antonio: **No, en Valencia nunca nieva.**
noh ehn bah-lehn-theeah noon-kah neeeh-bah
No, in Valencia it never snows.

CULTURAL WISDOM

An understanding proverb

The following proverb comes in handy when you assume that the other person already knows about the issue you're discussing: it's the equivalent of a knowing wink:

A buen entendedor, pocas palabras. *(ah booehn ehn-tehn-deh-dohr poh-kahs pah-lah-brahs)* (Who knows, knows.) (Literally: to the one who understands, few words.)

Understanding the Verb Entender

Work and professions are always useful subjects for small talk. When discussing these topics, you use the irregular verb **entender** *(ehn-tehn-dehr)* (to understand; to know). (You can find more on the verb 'to work', **trabajar** *(trah-bah-Hahr)*, in Chapter 2.) **Entender** is an irregular verb, which you conjugate in the present tense as shown in the following table:

Conjugation	*Pronunciation*
yo entiendo	*yoh ehn-teeehn-doh*
tú entiendes	*too ehn-teeehn-dehs*
él, ella, usted entiende	*ehl, eh-yah, oos-tehd enh-teeehn-deh*
nosotros entendemos	*noh-soh-trohs ehn-tehn-deh-mohs*
vosotros entendéis	*boh-soh-trohs ehn-tehn-dehees*
ellos, ellas, ustedes entienden	*eh-yohs, eh-yahs, oos-teh-dehs ehn-teeehn-dehn*

Here are some examples to help you use the irregular verb **entender**:

- ✔ **Yo entiendo poco de enfermería.** *(yoh ehn-teeehn-doh poh-koh deh ehn-fehr-meh-reeah)* (I know a little bit about nursing.)

- ✔ **Francisco entiende de cocina.** *(frahn-thees-koh ehn-teeehn-deh deh koh-thee-nah)* (Francisco knows about cooking.)

- ✔ **Nosotros entendemos el problema.** *(noh-soh-trohs ehn-tehn-deh-mohs ehl proh-bleh-mah)* (We understand the problem.)

- ✔ **¡Pedro no entiende!** *(peh-droh noh ehn-teeehn-deh)* (Pedro doesn't understand!)

- ✔ **Ellos entienden lo que decimos.** *(eh-yohs ehn-teeehn-dehn loh keh deh-thee-mohs)* (They understand what we're saying.)

Talkin' the Talk

Observe Jane and Pedro in a café talking about their jobs.

Jane: **¿Dónde trabajas ?**
          dohn-deh trah-bah-Has
          Where do you work?

Pedro: **Trabajo en Bilbao, soy ingeniero.**
          trah-bah-Hoh ehn Beel-bah-oh sohy
          een-Heh-neeeh-roh
          I work in Bilbao, I'm an engineer.

Jane: **¿Para qué compañía trabajas?**
          pah-rah keh kohm-pah-nyeeah trah-bah-Hahs
          What company do you work for?

Pedro: **Soy empresario, promotor de viviendas.**
          sohy ehm-preh-sah-reeoh proh-moh-tohr deh
          bee-bee-ehn-dahs
          I'm a businessman – a housing developer.

Jane: **¿Cuántos empleados tienes?**
          kooahn-tohs ehm-pleh-ah-dohs teeeh-nehs
          How many employees do you have?

Pedro: **Tengo nueve empleados. ¿Tú entiendes algo de**
          construcción?
          tehn-goh nooeh-beh ehm-pleh-ah-dohs too ehn-tee-
          ehn-dehs ahl-goh deh cohns-trook-thee-ohn
          I have nine employees. Do you understand anything
          about building?

Jane: **No, yo soy dentista.**
          Noh yoh sohy dehn-tees-tah
          No, I'm a dentist.

Pedro: **¡Ah, bien¡ ¿Y dónde tienes tu clínica?**
          Ah beeehn ee dohn-deh teeeh-nehs too klee-nee-kah
          I see! And where's your clinic?

Jane: **En Palencia.**
          ehn Pah-lehn-theeah
          In Palencia.

Getting to Know People and Families

The individual is the basic element of many European societies. In Spain, however, the family is the basic unit. People often work, live and function in consonance with their families. When visiting your Spanish-speaking friends, therefore, you're going to be more comfortable if you pay attention to the way that they often stress the importance of family relationships.

Celebrations such as marriage and birthdays are carefully observed, with much energy and enthusiasm going into them. The first Sunday of May, Mother's Day, for example, is one of the most important days to keep in mind in Spain, as well as Christmas and Easter. (Travel to Chapter 19 for more about holidays).

The following list provides the basic names for family members:

- **padre** *(pah-dreh)* (father)
- **madre** *(mah-dreh)* (mother)
- **hijo** *(ee-Hoh)* (son)
- **hija** *(ee-Hah)* (daughter)
- **hermano** *(ehr-mah-noh)* (brother)
- **hermana** *(ehr-mah-nah)* (sister)
- **yerno** *(yehr-noh)* (son-in-law)
- **nuera** *(nooeh-rah)* (daughter-in-law)
- **cuñado** *(koo-nyah-doh)* (brother-in-law)
- **cuñada** *(koo-nyah-dah)* (sister-in-law)
- **primo** *(pree-moh)* (cousin [male])
- **prima** *(pree-mah)* (cousin [female])
- **padrino** *(pah-dree-noh)* (godfather)
- **madrina** *(mah-dree-nah)* (godmother)
- **tío** *(teeoh)* (uncle)
- **tía** *(teeah)* (aunt)
- **sobrino** *(soh-breeh-noh)* (nephew)
- **sobrina** *(soh-breeh-nah)* (niece)
- **abuelo** *(ah-booeh-loh)* (grandfather)
- **abuela** *(ah-booeh-lah)* (grandmother)
- **nieto** *(neeeh-toh)* (grandson)
- **nieta** *(neeeh-tah)* (granddaughter)

Talkin' the Talk

Shirley is visiting a family at their home for the first time. You may notice a certain amount of ceremony in the way people invite others into their homes.

Carlos: **Te invito a que conozcas mi casa.**
          teh een-bee-toh ah keh koh-noth-kahs mee kah-sah
          I'm inviting you to see my house.

Shirley: **Por favor, no quiero molestarte.**
          pohr fah-bohr noh keeeh-roh moh-lehs-tahr-teh
          Please, I don't want to bother you.

Carlos: **No es ninguna molestia, y así te presento mi familia.**
          noh ehs neen-goo-nah moh-lehs-teeah ee ah-see teh preh-sehn-toh mee fah-mee-leeah
          It's no bother, and this way I can introduce you to my family.

Shirley: **Pues si no te parece un poco abuso. . . .**
          pooehs see noh teh pah-reh-theh oon poh-coh ah-boo-soh
          Well, if you don't think I'm taking advantage [of your hospitality] . . .

Carlos: **No, para nada, te insisto.**
          noh pah-rah nah-dah teh een-sees-toh
          Not at all, I insist.

Talkin' the Talk

Shirley has been invited into a beautiful family house.

Carlos: **Bueno, ya llegamos a casa de mis padres.**
          booeh-noh yah yeh-gah-mohs ah kah-sah deh mees pah-drehs
          Well, we're at my parents' house.

Shirley: **¡Qué casa! Parece muy antigua.**
          keh kah-sah pah-reh-theh mooy ahn-tee-gooah
          What a great house! It looks very old.

Carlos:	**Sí, es una casa del siglo diecisiete.**
	see ehs <u>oo</u>-nah <u>kah</u>-sah dehl <u>see</u>-gloh deeeh-thee-see<u>eh</u>-teh
	Yes, it's a seventeenth century house.
Shirley:	**¡Qué patio tan bonito!**
	keh <u>pah</u>-teeoh tahn boh-<u>nee</u>-toh
	What a beautiful patio!
Carlos:	**Sí, el patio es muy tradicional.**
	see ehl <u>pah</u>-teeoh ehs mooy trah-dee-theeoh-<u>nahl</u>
	Yes, it's very traditional.

Living with Vivir: The Verb to Live

After you've been invited to someone's house, you naturally want to invite them back to yours. And 'where do you live?' is as frequent a question as 'where do you work' when making small talk. The verb **vivir** *(bee-<u>beer</u>)* (to live) is a regular verb and the following table shows you how to conjugate its present tense:

Conjugation	*Pronunciation*
yo vivo	*yoh <u>bee</u>-boh*
tú vives	*too <u>bee</u>-behs*
él, ella, usted vive	*ehl, <u>eh</u>-yah, oos-<u>tehd</u> <u>bee</u>-beh*
nosotros vivimos	*noh-<u>soh</u>-trohs bee-<u>bee</u>-mohs*
vosotros vivís	*boh-<u>soh</u>-trohs bee-<u>bees</u>*
ellos, ellas, ustedes viven	*<u>eh</u>-yohs, <u>eh</u>-yahs, oos-<u>teh</u>-dehs <u>bee</u>-behn*

Talkin' the Talk

Shirley has been introduced to Carlos' family. They want to know where she lives, and they invite her to visit again:

Family member:	**¿Dónde vives?**
	<u>dohn</u>-deh <u>bee</u>-behs
	Where do you live?

Shirley:	**Busco un apartamento pequeño.** *boos-koh oon ah-pahr-tah-mehn-toh* *peh-keh-nyoh* I'm looking for a small apartment.
Family member:	**A la vuelta, alquilan un apartamento.** *ah lah boo-ehl-tah al-keeh-lahn oon* *ah-pahr-tah-mehn-toh* Around the corner is an apartment for rent.
Shirley:	**Bueno, voy a verlo.** *booeh-noh boy ah behr-loh* Good, I'll go and see it.
Family member:	**Te va a gustar.** *teh bah ah goos-tahr* You'll like it.
Shirley:	**Bueno, no quiero molestar más, tengo** **que irme.** *booeh-noh noh keeeh-roh moh-lehs-tahr* *mahs tehn-goh keh eer-meh* Well, I don't want to bother you any more, I have to go.
Family member:	**Aquí tienes tu casa.** *ah-kee teeeh-nehs too kah-sah* Make yourself at home [literally: here you have your home.]
Shirley:	**Muchas gracias.** *moo-chahs grah-theeahs* Thanks very much.
Family member:	**Te invito a que vengas mañana a tomar un** **café con nosotros.** *teh een-bee-toh ah keh behn-gahs mah-nyah-* *nah ah toh-mahr oohn kah-feh kohn noh-soh-* *trohs* Come and have a coffee [with us] tomorrow.
Shirley:	**Con mucho gusto.** *kohn moo-choh goos-toh* I'd love to.

Discovering Diminutives

In English, when you want to say that something is small, you have to add an adjective such as 'small' or 'little' in front of the noun. Not in Spanish, however, where you add a few letters to the end of the noun in the form of a suffix. With that suffix, you create a diminutive, and people know that you're talking about something or someone small. The suffixes you add are the masculine **ito** *(ee-toh)* or feminine **ita** *(ee-tah)*. For example, a **niño** *(nee-nyoh)* (boy/child) becomes little when you add the suffix to form the word **niñito** *(nee-nyee-toh)* (little boy/child).

Talkin' the Talk

Throughout Spain, children are an important part of the family. See how Shirley takes this fact into consideration.

Flor: **Dime Shirley, tienes hijos?**
          dee-meh Shirley teeeh-nehs ee-Hohs
          Tell me Shirley, do you have children?

Shirley: **Tengo un hijo. Aquí está su foto.**
          tehn-goh oon ee-Hoh ah-kee ehs-tah soo foh-toh
          I have a son. Here's his photo.

Flor: **A ver . . . Un muchacho muy guapo.**
          ah behr . . . oon moo-chah-choh mooy guhah-poh
          Let's see . . . A good looking boy.

Shirley: **Sí. ¿Y tú?**
          see ee too
          Yes. And you?

Flor: **Yo tengo una hija y un hijo.**
          yoh tehn-goh oo-nah ee-Hah ee oon ee-Hoh
          I have a daughter and a son.

Shirley: **¿Cuántos años tienen?**
          kooahn-tohs ah-nyohs teeeh-nehn
          How old are they?

Flor: **Mi hija tiene seis años y mi hijo tres. Aquí viene mi hija.**
          mee ee-Hah teeeh-neh sehees ah-nyohs ee mee ee-Hoh trehs ah-kee beeeh-neh mee ee-Hah
          My daughter is six and my son three. Here comes my daughter.

Shirley:	**Hola, ¿cómo te llamas?**
	oh-lah koh-moh teh yah-mahs
	Hello, what's your name?
Rosita:	**Me llamo Rosita.**
	meh yah-moh roh-see-tah
	My name's Rosita.
Shirley:	**¡Qué bonito, me gusta mucho!**
	keh boh-nee-toh meh goos-tah moo-choh
	What a beautiful name, I really like it!

A little here and a little there

The following sets of words almost have identical meanings. Deciding which one to use is a question of personal taste:

✔ **allí** *(ah-yee)*   **allá** *(ah-yah)*   (there)

✔ **aquí** *(ah-kee)*   **acá** *(ah-kah)*   (here)

Allá is mostly used for 'over there' and acá is closer to 'over here' Both, however, are a little less precise than aquí and allí.

Fun & Games

You've been invited to attend a Spanish wedding. Both the bride and groom have very large families, and so you have several relationships to figure out. The night before the wedding, your host quizzes you on question words and family members. Unscramble the English word and then provide the Spanish translation.

✔ coinsu (female) _____

✔ chwih _____

✔ cleun _____

✔ draggundreath _____

✔ dreamthrong _____

✔ fatgodher _____

✔ franterdagh _____

✔ herfat _____

✔ hewn _____

✔ how _____

✔ hwy _____

✔ moodgreth _____

✔ nos _____

✔ ons-ni-awl _____

✔ owh _____

✔ redaught-ni-wal _____

✔ remoth _____

✔ resist _____

✔ robreth-ni-lwa _____

✔ sandgron _____

✔ sincou (male) _____

✔ strise-ni-wla _____

✔ thaw _____

✔ thredaug _____

Chapter 5

Dining Out and Going to Market

. . . .

In This Chapter

▶ Getting food and drink

▶ Asking simple questions at the restaurant

▶ Making reservations and paying the bill

▶ Eating tapas and other delicacies

▶ Comparing prices and having fun at the market

. . . .

*F*ood is an important element of any culture. Each area and region in Spain has its own, unique-tasting food, which makes restaurant-hopping and trying new dishes a wonderfully diverse experience. In every town, a variety of tasty dishes – such as fresh fish, mountain-cured ham, chorizo, paellas and an array of home-made treats – awaits you.

¡Buen Provecho! Enjoy Your Meal!

Spanish cuisine is blessed with a bounty of native ingredients and draws from a wide range of historical influences – Greek, Roman, Moorish, Italian, French and North African cultures have all contributed to Spanish food. Perhaps because of this enthralling diversity, people in Spain are incredibly interested in food. Spaniards are as devoted to their food as the French, Italians or Indians, and you can discover this fact even in very small places.

Spanish people have very fine palates and enjoy meals that range from delicate bites to truly fiery flavours. They also have an immense variety of ways to prepare food, such as paellas, Spanish stews, tapas and tortillas, which all make frequent appearances on Spanish dinner tables.

In Spain, one favourite dish is **la tortilla** *(lah tohr-<u>tee</u>-yah)* – round, flat, soft, succulent quiche-like savoury tarts made of two prime ingredients: potatoes and eggs. To these items you can add various foods such as onion, red peppers and even peas to make a dish called **tortilla campesina** *(tohr-<u>tee</u>-yah cahm-peh-<u>see</u>-nah)*. Also, Spaniards love to eat **tapas** *(<u>tah</u>-pahs)* – a mini-meal of appetisers – when out and about, any day of the week, and at any time of day!

Tapas bars serving these tempting treats are popular places to eat, where everyone tucks in from the same little dishes, though you can get your own **platos** (*plah-tohs*) (plate) if you ask for one.

Here are some popular dishes from various Spanish regions:

- Andalucía is home to the world-famous **gazpacho** (*gath-pah-choh*), a chilled soup made with fresh tomatoes, olive oil, onions, garlic and peppers, which is usually served with chopped vegetables and bread. **Ajo blanco** (*ah-Hoh blahn-coh*), a cold almond soup made with garlic, is another regional favourite. Be sure to investigate **cazuela** (*cah-thoo-eh-lah*) (the general word for stew, and used to refer to meat and fish stew) wherever you see it – it's particularly good with lamb, red wine, onions and vegetables.

- Cataluña and Levante are known across the world for their **paellas** (*pah-eh-yahs*) and other great specialities such as **arrós negre** (*ah-rohs neh-greh*) – squid cooked in its own ink with rice, peas, red peppers, garlic and onion. **Butifarra amb seques** (*buh-tee-fah-rah ahm seh-qehs*) – fried white sausages with white beans – is a more popular dish in Cataluña, as is **pa amb tomaquet** (*pah ahm toh-mah-qeh*) – bread drizzled with olive oil and rubbed with tomato and garlic – it's a wonderful regional speciality from this area now spreading across Spain as a tapas dish.

- Northern Spanish food is a more sophisticated sibling to its rustic but tantalising counterpart in the south, from the fresh salmon of the Atlantic Cantabrian shores to the wild boar of mountainous Navarre. **Fabada** (*fah-bah-dah*), for example, is an authentic dish from Asturia, and is a one-course meal served in huge quantities (which also goes for most other dishes of northern Spain). It consists of mild white beans called **fabes** (*fah-behs*) and cured and salted ham, bacon and **morcilla** (*mohr-thee-yeea*), a type of black pudding.

- The País Vasco (*pah-eehs bahs-koh*) (Basque Country) is known for its fish dishes. Cooks chop or slice fillets, serve them with complicated sauces, combine them with things you may not expect and sometimes even present the fish alongside a meat-based dish. Somehow, this mix usually works, and the resulting complex layers of flavour are one hallmark of Basque cuisine. Try the **pintxos** (*peehn-chohs*), which are like tapas, but better. Spaniards are very proud of their own regions, but even people from Andalucíia and Madrid admit that Basque pintxos are the best tapas in Spain!

- Madrid may not be especially well known for its native cuisine, but the variety of food on offer here may pleasantly surprise you. A good example is the winter stomach-heater, **cocido madrileño** (*coh-thee-doh mah-dree-leh-nyoh*), a meat and chickpea stew. Another tasty local meal to look out for is **cochinillo asado** (*coh-chee-nee-yeeo ah-sah-doh*) – a roasted sucking pig dish typical of nearby towns such as Segovia.

Eating around the clock

Desayuno *(deh-sah-yeeoo-noh)* in holiday areas is a light breakfast – what hotels call a 'Continental breakfast'. In big cities, a **desayuno** is even lighter, often just a cup of coffee or juice. In Madrid, around 10 a.m., people go down to a nearby bar or café to have a coffee or juice with a **bocadillo** *(boh-cah-dee-yoh)* (little sandwich) or **churros** *(choo-rohs)* (a savoury flour fritter eaten along with thick hot chocolate). People call this ritual **ir a desayunar** *(eer ah deh-sah-yeeoo-nahr)* (going out for breakfast).

In Spain, **almuerzo** *(alh-moo-erh-tho)* or **comida** *(coh-mee-dah)* is simply lunch, and is eaten around 2 or 3 p.m. Sometimes, lunch is a hearty affair – with appetisers such as soup, pasta or salad, and a main dish and dessert – which traditionally was followed by an immediate siesta. Sadly, the pace of modern life means that just a lucky few can still enjoy this day-breaking practice.

Cena *(theh-nah)* is supper, and is eaten late, between 9 and 10 p.m. In some regions, you have just a sandwich and fruit or dessert at this time, but some families do eat a main dish – again! – and dessert.

✔ In Galicia, you can find a variety of delectable crustaceans, fish and shellfish. The fan-shaped sea scallop, called **vieira** *(bee-ehee-rah)* (the pilgrim's shell) is a favourite. You can eat them straight from the water with a squeeze of lemon, or in their shells in a splash of local **Albariño** *(ahl-bah-ree-nyo)* wine. **Pulpo** *(pool-poh)* (octopus) is a very popular dish, cooked whole, cut into pieces after beating and seasoned with oil, paprika and salt. The **empanada** *(ehm-pah-nah-dah)* (crusted pie) is emblematic of Galicia. Cooks fill them with an endless variety of different meats and fishes as well as a lot of onion, which they place between two thin layers of oily saffron-coloured pastry. The most famous dish offered to visitors to Galicia, however, is **lacón con grelos** *(lah-kohn kohn greh-lohs)* (salted ham with turnip tops).

✔ Extremaduran *(ehks-treh-mah-doo-rah)* cuisine is at its best in the **cerdo iberico** *(thehr-doh ee-beh-ree-coh)* (the Iberian pig) and its top-quality, rare **pata negra** *(pah-tah neh-grah)* (literally, 'black leg') by-products, such as **jamón de pata negra** *(Hah-mohn deh pah-tah neh-grah)*. People from this area are enthusiastic carnivores and really know how to prepare meat so that it tastes superb. **Migas** *(mee-gahs)* is another great dish, and was originally created by shepherds and field workers. This simple but surprisingly tasty dish is based on breadcrumbs with dry or fried meat, vegetables such as roast red peppers, grilled sardines, fried garlic and a touch of Spanish olive oil.

Tackling table terms

You may find these phrases useful when you plan a meal:

- ✔ **¡A poner la mesa!** *(ah poh-nehr lah meh-sah)* (Set the table!)

- ✔ **Aquí están los platos y los vasos.** *(ah-kee ehs-tahn lohs plah-tohs ee lohs bah-sohs)* (Here are the dishes and glasses.)

- ✔ **¿Qué cubiertos?** *(keh koo-bee-ehr-tohs)* (What cutlery?)

- ✔ **Cuchara, cuchillo, tenedor, y cucharita.** *(koo-chah-rah koo-chee-yeeoh teh-neh-dohr ee koo-chah-ree-tah)* (Spoon, knife, fork and coffee spoon.)

- ✔ **Aquí están las servilletas.** *(ah-kee ehs-tahn lahs sehr-bee-yeh-tahs)* (Here are the napkins.)

- ✔ **Más sal en el salero.** *(mahs sahl ehn ehl sah-leh-roh)* (More salt in the salt shaker.)

Eating and drinking phrases

Here are some common terms connected with meals:

- ✔ **almuerzo** *(ahl-mooehr-thoh)* (mid-morning snack; lunch)

- ✔ **cena** *(theh-nah)* (supper)

- ✔ **comida** *(koh-mee-dah)* (lunch)

- ✔ **desayuno** *(deh-sah-yoo-noh)* (breakfast)

- ✔ **tengo sed** *(tehn-goh sehd)* (I'm thirsty)

- ✔ **tiene hambre** *(tee eh-neh ahm-breh)* (he/she's hungry)

You may hear the following phrases, or speak them yourself, when giving or receiving food and beverages:

- ✔ **¡Buen provecho!** *(booehn proh-beh-choh)* (Enjoy your meal! – the equivalent of the French Bon appetit!)

- ✔ **¿Con qué está servido?** *(kohn keh ehs-tah sehr-bee-doh)* (What does it come with?)

- ✔ **Está caliente.** *(ehs-tah kah-lee-ehn-teh)* (It's hot [temperature].)

- ✔ **Está frío.** *(ehs-tah freeoh)* (It's cold.)

- ✔ **Está picante.** *(ehs-tah pee-kahn-teh)* (It's hot [flavour/spicy].)

- ✔ **Es sabroso.** *(ehs sah-broh-soh)* (It's tasty.)

- ✔ **Lo lamento, no tenemos. . .** *(loh lah-mehn-toh noh teh-neh-mohs)* (Sorry, we don't have any. . .)

> ✔ **¿Qué ingredientes lleva?** *(keh een-greh-dee ehn-tehs yeh-bah)* (What are the ingredients?)
>
> ✔ **¿Qué más trae el plato?** *(keh mahs trah-eh ehl plah-toh)* (What else is in the dish?)

These words can help you when you're ordering something to drink:

> ✔ **Escoger un vino.** *(ehs-koh-Hehr oon bee-noh)* (Choose a wine.)
>
> ✔ **¡Salud!** *(sah-lood)* (Cheers!)
>
> ✔ **Tomar un refresco.** *(toh-mahr oon reh-frehs-koh)* (Drink a fizzy drink.)
>
> ✔ **Tomar una copa.** *(toh-mahr oo-nah ko-pah)* (Have a drink [alcoholic].)
>
> ✔ **Un vaso de agua.** *(oon bah-soh deh ah-gooah)* (A glass of water.)
>
> ✔ **Un vaso de leche.** *(oon bah-soh deh leh-cheh)* (A glass of milk.)

Using Three Verbs at the Table

When talking about drinking in Spanish, you can use two verbs. One is **tomar** *(toh-mahr)* and the other is **beber** *(beh-behr)*.

Taking and drinking: The verb tomar

Tomar *(toh-mahr)* means literally 'to take' and often means exactly that. But when you say **tomar un refresco** *(toh-mahr oon reh-frehs-koh)*, you're talking about drinking a soft drink, not literally taking one, and you know that's what you mean because **tomar** is followed by something you drink. So **tomar** is a verb with a certain imprecision.

Tomar is a regular verb of the **-ar** *(ahr)* group. The root of the verb is **tom-** *(tohm)*, as you can see from the table that follows:

Conjugation	Pronunciation
yo tomo	*yoh toh-moh*
tú tomas	*too toh-mahs*
él, ella, usted toma	*ehl, eh-yah, oos-tehd toh-mah*
nosotros tomamos	*noh-soh-trohs toh-mah-mohs*
vosotros tomáis	*boh-soh-trohs toh-mah-ees*
ellos, ellas, ustedes toman	*eh-yohs, eh-yahs, oos-teh-dehs toh-mahn*

Drinking only: The verb beber

In the case of the verb **beber**, you can have no doubts: this verb applies to drinking only.

Beber *(beh-behr)* is another regular verb and from the **-er** *(ehr)* group. The root of the verb is **beb-** *(behb)*, as the following table shows:

Conjugation	Pronunciation
yo bebo	*yoh beh-boh*
tú bebes	*too beh-behs*
él, **ella**, **usted bebe**	*ehl, eh-yah, oos-tehd beh-beh*
nosotros bebemos	*noh-soh-trohs beh-beh-mohs*
vosotros bebéis	*boh-soh-trohs beh-behees*
ellos, ellas, ustedes beben	*eh-yohs, eh-yahs, oos-teh-dehs beh-behn*

Tucking in: The verb comer

Comer *(koh-mehr)* means 'to eat'. A regular verb from the **-er** *(ehr)* group, the root of this verb is **com** *(kohm)*, as this table shows:

Conjugation	Pronunciation
yo como	*yoh koh-moh*
tú comes	*too koh-mehs*
él, **ella**, **usted come**	*ehl, eh-yah, oos-tehd koh-meh*
nosotros comemos	*noh-soh-trohs koh-meh-mohs*
vosotros coméis	*boh-soh-trohs koh-mehees*
ellos, ellas, ustedes comen	*eh-yohs, eh-yahs, oos-teh-dehs koh-mehn*

Eating Out: Trying Spanish Food at the Restaurant

A menu in a foreign language can be intimidating, but we don't want you to miss out on Spain's many tasty and colourful foods! Therefore, the following list identifies the most popular Spanish specialities:

- **Empanada** *(ehm-pah-<u>nah</u>-dah)* means 'in bread'. An empanada is a big, stuffed pastry made out of crunchy wheat dough, which is then stuffed with tuna, onion and tomato sauce, or mince and onion gravy or chorizo. Either way, they're delicious!

- **Filete de lomo** *(fee-<u>leh</u>-teh deh <u>loh</u>-moh)* in the southern regions is the tender cut of pork called sirloin in English. And yes, it comes with Spanish hand-cut chips!

- **Gazpacho** *(gath-<u>pah</u>-choh)* is a chilled tomato and vegetable soup from the south of Spain, flavoured with olive oil, garlic and vinegar, and a must during the scorching Spanish summer!

- **Jamón Serrano de pata negra** *(Hah-<u>mohn</u> seh-<u>rrah</u>-noh deh <u>pah</u>-tah <u>neh</u>-grah)*, top-quality salt-cured ham typical of the mountain regions, is the greatest delicacy where it comes from the rare black-legged pigs!

- **Paella** *(pah-<u>eh</u>-yah)*: This dish is a favourite throughout Spain and enjoyed all year around! **Paella** is made from chunks of poultry, pork, vegetables, fish, seafood and saffron rice.

- **Sangría** *(sahn-<u>gree</u>-ah)* literally means 'bloody', but it can also be a refreshing low-alcohol drink made with red wine, brandy, lemonade, brown sugar, orange juice and fresh fruits such as apple and peach. Sangría makes a refreshing drink with your meal. Watch out, though – it goes down faster that you can feel it!

- **Tortilla** *(tohr-<u>tee</u>-yah)* is a potato and egg omelette, usually with onion too, which is often served hot or at room temperature. **Tortilla** is delicious in a tapas bar with a Spanish wine or **caña** *(<u>cah</u>-nya)* (a small, cool glass of Spanish draught beer).

If you love fish and seafood, the places to go are to the Spanish coasts and to Madrid. With so much fish and seafood, some people say that Madrid is one of the best fish ports in the world!

One delight is **choco** *(choh-<u>koh</u>)*, a truly gigantic, chunky white fillet of calamari, generally grilled and served with **ali-oli** *(<u>ah</u>-lee <u>oh</u>-lee)*, a garlic and olive oil sauce, which is very popular in Cataluña but known throughout the whole of Spain.

You can also find **langosta** *(lahn-<u>gohs</u>-tah)* (lobster), **langostino** *(lahn-gohs-<u>tee</u>-noh)* (king prawn), **gambas** *(<u>gahm</u>-bahs)* (prawns or shrimps) and other delights to crowd your **sopa marinera** *(<u>soh</u>-pah mah-ree-<u>neh</u>-rah)* (fish soup).

Some people say that the truly special thing about many Spanish dishes is their sauces. This statement is especially true of the sauces served with meat and fish stews, which have a great variety of flavours and textures. Always have some rustic fresh bread handy to dunk in the sauces, which really are a delicacy on their own!

The famous Spanish tortilla, and other food facts

The famous Spanish omelette **la tortilla de patatas** *(lah tohr-tee-yah deh pah-tah-tahs)* is one example of how foods differ throughout the country. **Tortilla** may well be the national dish. At its most basic, a tortilla is an omelette made of eggs, potatoes, salt and olive oil. In Madrid *(mah-dreed)*, centre of many regional and international cultures, tortilla is served and eaten simply as it comes. But in other Spanish regions you find an extra ingredient, depending on the local growing traditions or the 'catch of the day', if you're in an area on the coast. Each area adds its own culinary identity to tortilla! For example, you can find **pimientos** *(pee-mee-ehn-tohs)* (peppers), **cebolla** *(theh-boh-yeeah)* (onion), **atún** *(ah-toon)* (tuna) or **calabacines** *(kah-lah-bah-thee-nehs)* (courgettes). In this way, what starts out as a simple and humble dish works as a cultural and geographical indicator!

In addition, you may find that the food in local eateries doesn't taste like the stuff you get in the cheap and cheerful restaurants that offer Spanish food in the more popular seaside resorts – or in tapas bars in the UK! Typically, local and home-made Spanish dishes are usually made fresh, and to the taste of the local residents.

Of course, at the inexpensive places the locals eat in, you're likely to find only the local fare. If you're like us, though, and eating out is your idea of fun, be adventurous and try eating where the Spaniards do: at their bars and local restaurants.

Look out for the following sauces:

- **Mayonesa** *(mah-yeeoh-neh-sah)* is a homemade Spanish mayonnaise simply made with olive oil, egg and a touch of lemon juice and used in many dishes, including **ensaladilla rusa** *(ehn-sah-lah-dee-yeea roo-sah)*, a very Spanish version of the Russian potato salad.

- **Mojos** *(moh-Hohs)* sauces are made with vinegar and oil and served cold, as an accompaniment to potatoes, meat and fish in the Canary Islands. These **mojos** can be red or green and sometimes spicy.

- **Romesco** *(roh-mehs-coh)* is a tasty sauce made of tomatoes, roasted almonds, olive oil and vinegar and served with fish, seafood – in Cataluña – with barbequed green onions.

- **Salsa brava** *(sahl-sah brah-bah)* is a spicy red sauce made with tomatoes and chilies. Hot!

- **Salsa marinera** *(sahl-sah mah-ree-neh-rah)* – also called **pescadora** *(pehs-kah-doh-rah)* – is based on fish stock and includes white wine, onions and touch of parsley. It forms part of many soups and stews in the Spanish kitchen, such as **almejas a la pescadora** *(ahl-meh-Hahs ah lah pehs-kah-doh-rah)*.

- **Sofrito** *(soh-free-toh)* is made from tomatoes, garlic, onions, peppers and olive oil and can accompany dishes such as **tortilla española** *(tohr-tee-yeeah ehs-pa-nyoh-lah)* or may be an ingredient within a dish.

- **Verde** *(behr-deh)* (literally 'green') owes its name and colour to the parsley that is the main ingredient and includes garlic, olive oil and white wine. Verde is used in many fish and shellfish dishes.

Getting What You Want: The Verb Querer

The verb **querer** *(keh-rehr)* is often used to mean 'to want' or 'to wish'.

Querer is an irregular verb. Notice that the root **quer-** *(kehr)* is transformed into **quier-** *(keeehr)* with some pronouns in the following table:

Conjugation	*Pronunciation*
yo quiero	*yoh keeeh-roh*
tú quieres	*too keeeh-rehs*
él, ella, usted quiere	*ehl, eh-yah, oos-tehd keeeh-reh*
nosotros queremos	*noh-soh-trohs keh-reh-mohs*
vosotros queréis	*boh-soh-trohs keh-rehees*
ellos, ellas, ustedes quieren	*eh-yohs, eh-yahs, oos-teh-dehs keeeh-rehn*

Talkin' the Talk

Señor Rivera wants to take his wife to a nice restaurant on her birthday. Observe how he calls the restaurant to make reservations.

Señor Rivera: **Quiero reservar una mesa para dos (personas).**
keeeh-roh reh-sehr-bahr oo-nah meh-sah pah-rah dohs pehr-soh-nahs
I want to reserve a table for two (people).

Waiter: **¡Como no señor! ¿Para qué hora?**
koh-moh noh seh-nyohr pah-rah keh oh-rah
Of course, Sir! At what time?

Señor Rivera: **Para las ocho de la noche.**
pah-rah lahs oh-choh deh lah noh-cheh
At eight in the evening.

Calling a waiter

In Spanish, most often you call a waiter **camarero** *(kah-mah-reh-roh)*. When a woman is serving you, call her simply **señorita** *(seh-nyoh-ree-tah)* (miss), no matter where you are.

You can get the attention of a waiter in several ways, but knowing which ways work best is useful. You may hear the old-fashioned term **mozo** *(moh-thoh)* (young man) being used to call a waiter, but calling anyone of any age **mozo** can be a little offensive and older waiters may not react. A better way to get a waiter's attention is to say **jóven** *(Hoh-behn)* (young) to the younger ones and simple **¡Por favor!** *(pohr fah-bohr)* to anyone else who may not be so young anymore!

Waiter:	**¿A nombre de quién?** *ah nohm-breh deh keeehn* Under what name?
Señor Rivera:	**Señor Rivera.** *seh-nyohr Rivera* Mr Rivera.
Waiter:	**Muy Bien, les esperamos.** *Moo-ee beeehn lehs ehs-peh-rah-mohs* Perfect, we'll be expecting you.
Señor Rivera:	**Muchas gracias.** *moo-chahs grah-theeahs* Many thanks.

Many restaurants in Spain don't require reservations; just walk in and enjoy!

Lots of Spanish people like to order an aperitif, or cocktail, before dinner. Most aperitifs served in Spanish restaurants are similar to those available in the UK. Exceptions are the local liquors such as **aguardientes** *(ah-gooahr-deeehn-tehs)*, which translates as 'fire waters'. These drinks can be made from grapes, herbs or fruits.

Talkin' the Talk

If you want to order a beverage to drink with your food, you may have a conversation similar to this one.

Waiter: **¿Quieren algo para beber?**
keeeh-rehn ahl-goh pah-rah beh-behr
Do you want anything to drink?

¿Les sirvo un aperitivo?
lehs seer-boh oon ah-peh-ree-tee-boh
Would you like me to bring you an aperitif?

Señora Rivera: **No, yo quiero un vaso de vino tinto.**
noh yoh keeeh-roh oon bah-soh deh bee-noh teen-toh
No, I'd like a glass of red wine.

Waiter: **Muy bien, ¿y usted?**
mooy beeehn ee oos-tehd
Very well, and you?

Señor Rivera: **Yo quiero una cerveza pequeña.**
yoh keeeh-roh oo-nah thehr-beh-thah peh-keh-nya
I'll have a small beer.

Waiter: **¿Botella o de barril?**
Boh-teh-yeeah oh deh bah-rreel
Bottled or draught?

Señor Rivera: **Prefiero de barril, una caña.**
preh-feeeh-roh deh bah-rreel oo-nah kah-nyah
I prefer draught, a small beer.

Talkin' the Talk

Now for some serious eating! You can use the following conversation as an example to order some soup or salad and ask about specials.

Waiter: **¿Están listos para pedir?**
ehs-tahn lees-tohs pah-rah peh-deer
Are you ready to order?

Señora Rivera: **Yo quiero una ensalada mixta.**
yoh keeeh-roh oo-nah ehn-sah-lah-dah meeks-tah
I'll have a mixed salad.

Señor Rivera: **Y para mí una sopa de mariscos.**
*ee pah-rah mee oo-nah soh-pah deh
mah-rees-kohs*
And for me, seafood soup.

Waiter: **¿Y de plato principal?**
ee deh plah-toh preen-thee-pahl
And as the main course?

Señor Rivera: **¿Qué nos recomienda?**
keh nohs reh-koh-meeehn-dah
What do you suggest?

Waiter: **Tenemos dos platos especiales: orejas de cerdo
picantes y bacalao con riñones a la riojana.**
*teh-neh-mohs dohs plah-tohs ehs-peh-theeah-lehs
oh-reh-Has deh thehr-doh pee-kahn-tehs ee bah-
kah-lah-oh koon ree-nyo-nehs ah lah
ree-oh-Hah-nah*
We have two specials: spicy pig ears and cod and
kidneys Riojana style.

Señora Rivera: **¿Qué es el bacalao a la riojana?**
keh ehs ehl bah-kah-lah-oh ah lah ree-oh-Hah-nah
What is cod Riojana style?

Waiter: **Es pescado blanco con tomates, pimentón y
cebolla.**
*ehs pehs-kah-doh blahn-koh kohn toh-mah-tehs
pee-mehn-tohn ee theh-boh-yah*
It's white fish with tomatoes, powdered red peppers and onions.

Señora Rivera: **¡Yo quiero pollo frito!**
yoh keeeeh-roh poh-yoh free-toh
I want fried chicken!

Waiter: **No tenemos pollo frito. Tenemos pollo asado en
salsa de ajo.**
*noh teh-neh-mohs poh-yoh free-toh teh-neh-mohs
poh-yoh ah-sah-doh ehn sahl-sah deh ah-Hoh*
We don't have fried chicken. We have roast
chicken with garlic sauce.

Señora Rivera: **¿Con qué está acompañado?**
kohn keh ehs-tah ah-kohm-pah-nyah-doh
What does it come with?

Waiter: **Con zanahorias frescas, y calabacines entomatados.**
kohn thah-nah-oh-reeahs frehs-kahs ee kah-lah-bah-theeh-nehs enh-toh-mah-tah-dohs
With fresh carrots, and cougettes in tomato sauce.

Señora Rivera: **Bueno, voy a probar este pollo.**
booeh-noh bohee ah proh-bahr ehs-teh poh-yoh
Good, I'll try the chicken.

Talkin' the Talk

You may have an exchange like the following as you pay your bill.

Señor Porter: **Jóven, ¿nos trae la cuenta por favor?**
Hoh-beh nohs trah-eh lah kooehn-tah pohr fah-bohr
Waiter, will you bring us the bill please?

Waiter: **¡Ya vuelvo con la cuenta, señor!**
yah boo-ehl-boh kohn lah koo-ehn-tah seh-nyohr
I'll be back with the bill, sir!

Señor Porter: **¿Aceptan tarjetas de crédito?**
ah-thehp-tahn tahr-Heh-tahs deh kreh-dee-toh
Do you accept credit cards?

Waiter: **No, lo lamento mucho, aquí no aceptamos tarjetas de crédito.**
noh loh lah-mehn-toh moo-choh ah-kee noh ah-thehp-tah-mohs tahr-Heh-tahs deh kreh-dee-toh
No, I'm very sorry; we don't take credit cards here.

Señora Porter [a bit later]: **¿Ya pagamos la cuenta?**
yah pah-gah-mohs lah koo-ehn-tah
Have we paid the bill?

Señor Porter: **Ya la pagué.**
yah lah pah-gheh
I already paid it.

Señora Porter: **¿Dejamos propina?**
deh-Hah-mohs proh-pee-nah
Did we leave a tip?

Señor Porter: **Sí dejé propina.**
see deh-Heh proh-pee-nah
Yes, I left a tip.

Taking a loo break

Inevitably, you want to wash your hands and freshen up before a meal and so require the use of a public toilet. In Spain, public toilets are very similar to those in the UK and elsewhere in Europe – the more expensive the restaurant, the more elegant the toilets. The following phrases can help you find the room you need:

✔ **¿Dónde está el servicio?** *(dohn-deh ehs-tah elh sehr-bee-thee-oh)* (Where's the toilet?)

✔ **Los baños están al fondo, a la derecha.** *(lohs bah-nyohs ehs-tahn ahl fohn-doh ah lah deh-reh-chah)* (The toilets are at the back, to the right.)

✔ **¿Es este el baño?** *(ehs ehs-teh ehl sehr-bee-thee-oh)* (Is this the toilet?)

✔ **No, este no es el baño. Es ese.** *(noh ehs-teh noh ehs ehl bah-nyoh ehs eh-se)* (No, that's not the toilet. It's that one [there].)

Using the Shopping Verb: Comprar

Comprar *(kohm-prahr)* means 'to shop', and **ir de compras** *(eer deh kohm-prahs)* means 'to go shopping'. **Comprar** is a regular verb of the **-ar** *(ahr)* group. The root of the verb is **compr-** *(kohmpr)*. Here's how you conjugate **comprar** in the present tense:

Conjugation	*Pronunciation*
yo compro	*yoh kohm-proh*
tú compras	*too kohm-prahs*
él, ella, usted compra	*ehl, eh-yah, oos-tehd kohm-prah*
nosotros compramos	*noh-soh-trohs kohm-prah-mohs*
vosotros compráis	*boh-soh-trohs kohm-prahees*
ellos, ellas, ustedes compran	*eh-yohs, eh-yahs, oos-teh-dehs kohm-prahn*

The following phrases, based on **ir de compras** *(eer deh kohm-prahs)* (to go shopping), can help you at the market:

✔ **Fue de compras.** *(fooeh deh kohm-prahs)* (She or he is out shopping.)

✔ **¡Voy de compras!** *(bohee deh kohm-prahs)* (I'm going shopping!)

✔ **¡Vamos de compras al mercado!** *(bah-mohs deh kohm-prahs ahl mehr-kah-do)* (Let's go shopping at the market!)

Shopping Around: At the Market

Shopping in Spanish markets, from road-side stalls and open-air markets to modern boutiques, supermarkets and department stores, is an enjoyable experience for many people, although it can be a little intimidating when coping with a different language at the same time. Don't be phased, though; a large part of the warmth of Spain is the attitude and friendliness of its people.

Here are some useful phrases to know when you're out shopping in a market:

- **Ahora no, gracias.** *(ah-oh-rah noh grah-theeahs)* (Not now, thank you.)
- **Ya tengo, gracias.** *(yah tehn-goh grah-theeahs)* (I already have some, thanks.)
- **Me interesa, gracias.** *(meh een-teh-reh-sah grah-theeahs)* (It does interest me, thank you.)
- **Más tarde, gracias.** *(mahs tahr-deh grah-theeahs)* (Later, thank you.)
- **No me gusta, gracias.** *(noh meh goos-tah grah-theeahs)* (I don't like it, thanks.)
- **No me moleste, ¡por favor!** *(noh meh moh-lehs-teh pohr fah-bohr)* (Don't bother [me], please!)

In markets, prices aren't usually displayed, although this practice varies from place to place. In some places, where prices aren't displayed, you may be able to negotiate a price by simply protesting that it's too high. The vendors are interested in selling, and so often allow some discount. (Flip to Chapter 6 for all about haggling in markets.)

When you go to the market, bringing your own shopping bags to carry away the stuff you buy is a good idea. Sellers may pack the stuff that you buy but don't always provide bags in which to carry it all away. Wherever this is the rule, you can find stalls that sell nice bags of all sizes that you may want to take home with you – many of them are quite trendy!

Purchasing fresh fruit

Here are the names of some fresh fruits you commonly find at Spanish markets:

- **la cereza** *(lah theh-reh-thah)* (the cherry)
- **la ciruela** *(lah thee-roo-eh-lah)* (the plum)
- **la fresa** *(la freh-sah)* (the strawberry)
- **el higo** *(ehl ee-goh)* (the fig)

CULTURAL WISDOM

Not open all hours

Shops and market sellers don't always open for business at the hours expected in other European countries. **Tiendas** *(tee-ehn-dahs)* (shops) and **supermercados** *(suh-pehr mehr-kah-dohs)* (supermarkets) don't open until 10 a.m. Also, although in some city centres more shops are starting to stay open during the afternoon, closing for the traditional afternoon **siesta** *(see-ehs-tah)* from 2 until 4 or 5 p.m. is more usual, particularly in the hotter regions.

Indoor markets usually follow the normal local shop trading hours. Most street markets take place in the morning, starting around 10 a.m. and finishing around 2 p.m.

Large department stores that offer a range of goods similar to any in London's Oxford Street, such as **El Corte Inglés** *(ehl kohr-teh een-glehs)*, are becoming more numerous in some larger towns and cities. At the other end of the scale, you can find many **mercado semanal** *(mehr-cah-doh seh-mah-nahl)* (literally: weekly market) or street markets in the towns of Spain. These markets sell a wide range of goods, some offering antiques and bric-a-brac while many offer the plants or fresh fruit and vegetable produce of their particular region.

- ✔ **el limón** *(ehl lee-mohn)* (the lemon)
- ✔ **la manzana** *(lah mahn-thah-nah)* (the apple)
- ✔ **el melocotón** *(ehl meh-loh-koh-tohn)* (the peach)
- ✔ **el melón** *(ehl meh-lohn)* (the melon)
- ✔ **la mora** *(lah moh-rah)* (the blackberry)
- ✔ **la naranja** *(lah nah-rahn-Hah)* (the orange)
- ✔ **la pera** *(lah peh-rah)* (the pear)
- ✔ **el plátano** *(ehl plah-tah-noh)* (the banana)
- ✔ **el pomelo** *(ehl poh-meh-loh)* (the grapefruit)
- ✔ **la sandía** *(lah sahn-deeah)* (the watermelon)
- ✔ **el tomate** *(elh too-mah-teh* (the tomato – yes, it's a fruit!)
- ✔ **la uva** *(lah oo-bah)* (the grape)

Buying vegetables

Fresh vegetables are always good. You can easily find the following in market-places:

- ✔ **las acelgas** *(lahs ah-thehl-gahs)* (the Swiss chard)
- ✔ **el aguacate** *(ehl ah-gooah-kah-teh)* (the avocado)
- ✔ **el ajo** *(ehl ah-Hoh)* (the garlic)
- ✔ **el brócoli** *(ehl broh-koh-lee)* (the broccoli)
- ✔ **el calabacín** *(elh kah-lah-bah-theen)* (the courgette)
- ✔ **la calabaza** *(lah kah-lah-bah-thah)* (the pumpkin)
- ✔ **la cebolla** *(lah theh-boh-yah)* (the onion)
- ✔ **la col** *(lah kohl)* (the cabbage)
- ✔ **la coliflor** *(lah koh-lee-flohr)* (the cauliflower)
- ✔ **las espinacas** *(lahs ehs-pee-nah-kahs)* (the spinach)
- ✔ **la guinda** *(lah geen-dah)* (the hot pepper)
- ✔ **la lechuga** *(lah leh-choo-gah)* (the lettuce)
- ✔ **la patata** *(lah pah-tah-tah)* (the potato)
- ✔ **el pimiento morrón** *(ehl pee-meeehn-toh moh-rrohn)* (the sweet pepper)
- ✔ **el pimentón** *(ehl pee-mehn-tohn)* (powdered sweet pepper)
- ✔ **el repollo** *(ehl reh-poh-yoh)* (the cabbage)
- ✔ **la zanahoria** *(lah thah-nah-oh-reeah)* (the carrot)

Shopping for fish

These terms can help you when you're selecting fish:

- ✔ **el bacalao** *(ehl bah-kah-lah-oh)* (cod)
- ✔ **las gambas** *(lash gahm-bahs)* (shrimps or prawns)
- ✔ **el langostino** *(ehl lahn-gohs-tee-noh)* (king prawn)
- ✔ **la lubina** *(lah loo-bee-nah)* (sea bass)
- ✔ **el marisco** *(ehl mah-rees-koh)* (seafood)
- ✔ **el pescado** *(ehl pehs-kah-doh)* (fish, as in fish for eating)
- ✔ **la trucha** *(lah troo-chah)* (trout)

Talkin' the Talk

Spaniards prepare fish and seafood in a variety of ways, all delicious. Here's how Ana shops for fish.

Ana:	**¿Cuánto cuesta este pescado?**
	Koo-ahn-toh kooehs-tah ehs-teh pehs-kah-doh
	How much is this fish?

Vendor:	**Cinco euros el kilo.**
	Theen-koh ehoo-rohs ehl kee-loh
	Five euros per kilo.

Ana:	**Lo quiero fileteado, sin espinas.**
	loh keeeh-roh fee-leh-teh-ah-doh seen ehs-pee-nahs
	I want it filleted, boneless.

Vendor:	**¿Se lleva la cabeza para la sopa?**
	seh yeh-bah lah kah-beh-thah pah-rah lah soh-pah
	Do you want the head for the soup?

Ana:	**Sí, aparte, por favor.**
	see ah-pahr-teh pohr fah-bohr
	Yes, separately, please.

Knowing the measures: Weight and volume

Like the UK, Spain uses the metric system, which means that understanding weights and measures isn't a problem for most people. But because some people still go by the old imperial measures, you may need some explanations, which we're happy to provide.

A **kilo** *(kee-loh)* is equivalent to just over than two pounds. **Kilo** comes from the word *kilogram*, which means one thousand grams. One gram is **un gramo** *(oon grah-moh)*. A **litro** *(lee-troh)* (litre) is equivalent to a quarter of a gallon. Here's a list of other quantities:

- **una docena** *(oo-nah doh-theh-nah)* (a dozen)
- **media docena** *(meh-deeah doh-theh-nah)* (a half dozen)
- **una centena** *(oo-nah thehn-teh-nah)* (100)
- **un millar** *(oon mee-yahr)* (1,000)

Talkin' the Talk

See how Ana asks a stallholder about the items at a fruit and vegetable market.

Ana: **¿A cuánto están las naranjas?**
ah koo_ahn_-toh ehs-_than_ lahs nah-_rahn_-Hahs
How much for the oranges?

Stallholder: **A seis euros las veinticinco.**
ah _seh_ees _eh_oo-rohs lahs beheen-tee-th_een_-koh
Six euros for 25.

Ana: **¿A cuánto los aguacates?**
ah koo_ahn_-toh lohs ah-gooah-_kah_-tehs
How much for the avocados?

Stallholder: **Cuatro euros el kilo.**
koo_ah_-troh _eh_oo-rohs ehl _kee_-loh
Four euros for one kilo.

Ana: **¡Es muy caro!**
ehs mooy _kah_-roh
That's very expensive.

Stallholder: **Está más barato que ayer.**
*Ehs-_tah_ mahs bah-_rah_-toh keh ah-_yehr_*
It's cheaper than yesterday.

Ana: **¿Tiene plátanos?**
tee_eh_-neh _plah_-tah-nohs
Do you have bananas?

Stallholder: **¿Sí, cuáles?**
see koo_ah_-lehs
Yes, which ones?

Ana: **De esos... ¿Cuánto cuestan?**
deh _eh_-sohs koo_ahn_-toh koo_ehs_-tahn
Those . . . how much?

Stallholder: **Tres euros el kilo.**
trehs _eh_oo-rohs ehl _kee_-loh
Three euros per kilo.

Ana: **Medio kilo, por favor. Los ajos, ¿a cuánto?**
*meh-deeoh kee-loh porh fah-bohr lohs ah-Hohs ah
kooahn-toh*
Half a kilo please. How much is the garlic?

Stallholder: **A cinco euros el ramillete.**
ah theen-koh ehoo-rohs ehl rah-mee-yeh-teh
Three euros per bunch [of heads].

Calling into the Supermercado

Of course, you can buy groceries at the **supermercado** *(soo-pehr-mehr-kah-doh)* (supermarket), where you proceed very much as you do in super-markets the world over. You may also find food to which you're more accustomed. Many Spanish supermarkets are good places to go for things such as fresh fish and local meats.

Here are some words and phrases to help you at the supermarket:

- **el arroz** *(ehl ah-rroth)* (the rice)

- **el atún** *(ehl ah-toon)* (the tuna)

- **la pasta** *(lah pahs-tah)* (the pasta)

- **los cereales** *(lohs theh-reh-ah-lehs)* (the cereals)

- **las galletas** *(lahs gah-yeh-tahs)* (the biscuits or crackers)

- **la leche** *(lah leh-cheh)* (the milk)

- **las sardinas** *(lahs sahr-dee-nahs)* (the sardines)

- **el vino** *(ehl bee-noh)* (the wine)

- **el pasillo** *(ehl pah-see-yoh)* (the aisle)

- **pagar** *(pah-gahr)* (to pay)

- **el cambio** *(ehl kahm-bee-oh)* (change [as in money back])

- **el tercer pasillo** *(ehl tehr-thehr pah-see-yoh)* (the third aisle)

- **al fondo** *(ahl fohn-doh)* (at the back)

- **Gracias, aquí está su vuelta.** *(grah-theeahs ah-kee ehs-tah soo booehl-tah)*
(Thanks, here's your change.)

Talkin' the Talk

A popular chicken dish in many Spanish homes is **arroz con pollo** *(ah-rroth kohn poh-yoh)* (rice with chicken). Ana has this conversation when she buys the chicken at a supermarket.

Ana:	**¿Cuánto cuesta el pollo?** *kooahn-toh kooehs-tah ehl poh-yoh* How much is the chicken?
Vendor:	**A cuatro euros el kilo.** *ah kooah-troh ehoo-rohs ehl kee-loh* Four euros per kilo.
Ana:	**Este, ¿cuánto es?** *ehs-teh kooahn-toh ehs* This one, how much?
Vendor:	**siete euros. ¿Lo quiere cortado?** *see-eh-teh ehoo-rohs loh keeeh-reh kohr-tah-doh* Seven euros. You want it in pieces?
Ana:	**Sí, lo quiero en pedazos, la pechuga aparte.** *see loh keeeh-roh ehn peh-dah-thohs lah peh-choo-gah ah-pahr-teh* Yes, I want it in pieces, the breast separate.
Vendor:	**¿La pechuga es para hacer filetes?** *lah peh-choo-gah ehs pah-rah ah-thehr fee-leh-tehs* Should I prepare the breast to make fillets?
Ana:	**No, mejor entera.** *noh meh-Hohr ehn-teh-rah* No, better in one piece.

Counting Numbers

You can't shop or do much of anything without running into a number sooner or later. The table that follows gives you list of numbers – for when it really counts:

From 1 to 10

uno	*oo-noh*	1
dos	*dohs*	2
tres	*trehs*	3
cuatro	*kooah-troh*	4
cinco	*theen-koh*	5
seis	*sehees*	6
siete	*see-eh-teh*	7
ocho	*oh-choh*	8
nueve	*nooeh-beh*	9
diez	*deeeth*	10

From 11 to 20

once	*ohn-theh*	11
doce	*doh-theh*	12
trece	*treh-theh*	13
catorce	*kah-tohr-theh*	14
quince	*keen-theh*	15
dieciséis	*deeeh-thee-sehees*	16
diecisiete	*deeeh-thee-seeeh-teh*	17
dieciocho	*deeeh-theeoh-choh*	18
diecinueve	*deeeh-thee-nooeh-beh*	19
veinte	*beheen-teh*	20

From 21 to 25

veintiuno	*beheen-teeoo-noh*	21
veintidos	*beheen-tee-dohs*	22
veintitres	*beheen-tee-trehs*	23
veinticuatro	*beheen-tee-kooah-troh*	24
veinticinco	*beheen-tee-theen-koh*	25

From 35 to 40

treinta y cinco	*treheen-tah ee theen-koh*	35
treinta y seis	*treheen-tah ee sehees*	36
treinta y siete	*treheen-tah ee seeeh-teh*	37
treinta y ocho	*treheen-tah ee oh-choh*	38
treinta y nueve	*treheen-tah ee nooeh-beh*	39
cuarenta	*kooah-rehn-tah*	40

From 10 to 100, in tens

diez	*dee<u>eth</u>*	10
veinte	*<u>beh</u>een-teh*	20
treinta	*<u>treh</u>een-tah*	30
cuarenta	*kooah-<u>rehn</u>-tah*	40
cincuenta	*theen-koo<u>ehn</u>-tah*	50
sesenta	*seh-<u>sehn</u>-tah*	60
setenta	*seh-<u>tehn</u>-tah*	70
ochenta	*oh-<u>chehn</u>-tah*	80
noventa	*noh-<u>behn</u>-tah*	90
cien	*the<u>ehn</u>*	100

Other numbers

trescientos	*trehs-thee<u>ehn</u>-tohs*	300
quinientos	*kee-nee<u>ehn</u>-tohs*	500
setecientos	*seh-teh-thee<u>ehn</u>-tohs*	600
ochocientos	*oh-choh-thee<u>ehn</u>-tohs*	800
mil	*meel*	1,000
dos mil	*dohs meel*	2,000
siete mil	*see<u>eh</u>-teh meel*	7,000
treinta mil	*tre<u>heen</u>-tah meel*	30,000
un millón	*oon mee-<u>yohn</u>*	1,000,000
diez millones	*dee<u>eth</u> mee-<u>yoh</u>-nehs*	10,000,000

Fun & Games

A Spanish friend has come to visit you in the UK. To celebrate, you take him to a fancy restaurant. Of course, the menu is in English, and your friend asks you to translate several items. Write the Spanish words in the blank following each menu item:

Beef _____

Coffee _____

Fried chicken _____

Brava sauce _____

Apples _____

Beer _____

Bananas _____

Your friend chooses his meal. Now translate his choices into English for the waiter:

Un vaso de agua _____

Un vaso de leche _____

Una ensalada mixta _____

Arroz con pollo _____

Calamares a la romana _____

Chapter 6
Shopping Made Easy

. . . .

In This Chapter

▶ Asking for help

▶ Trying things on

▶ Checking sizes, colours, materials and items

▶ Using the verbs **probar** and **llevar**

▶ Haggling at the market

. . . .

*E*ven experienced shoppers can find new ways to shop and new shops to explore in Spain. Shopping beyond the borders of the United Kingdom can be entertaining, and you can certainly find some great goods and bargains in Spain. Whether shopping is fun or hard work for you, in this chapter we explain how to go about it Spanish style!

In Spanish cities, you're likely to find that the shopping process resembles what you're used to at home. A worldwide trend seeks to make shopping faster and more abundant. In larger cities such as Madrid *(mah-drid)*, Barcelona *(bar-theh-loh-nah)* and Valencia *(bah-lehn-theeah)*, shops and markets may have clothes and objects in styles that are different from what you know and have already seen. If you like to shop in a familiar way, however, you usually find department stores and supermarkets that carry merchandise that feels unique and yet reassuringly familiar.

In smaller places, and in coastal areas where traditional goods are sold, you often find open-air markets. Here you enter a new kind of shopping world – one full of surprises. We call this fun time!

Hitting the Shops

If you're of the 'shop till you drop' variety, you may already be used to checking out the department stores whenever you travel. In larger cities, department stores are ideal places to see how and where the locals get their clothes and other necessities.

By contrast, if you want exotic items sold the old-fashioned way, a department store isn't the best place to go. Instead, you can find unique and stylish clothes and objects for sale in craft markets, where the whole shopping experience is different. We cover open-air markets in the later section 'Shopping in Open-Air Markets'.

In both Spanish department stores and specialist shops you can find items with some local flavour, and in all shops the prices are clearly posted and labelled.

These phrases can help you at a department store:

- **¿Dónde está la entrada?** (*dohn-deh ehs-tah lah ehn-trah-dah*) (Where's the entrance?)

- **¿Dónde está la salida?** (*dohn-deh ehs-tah lah sah-lee-dah*) (Where's the exit?)

- **empuje** (*ehm-poo-Heh*) (push)

- **tire** (*tee-reh*) (pull)

- **el ascensor** (*ehl ahs-thehn-sohr*) (the lift)

- **la escalera mecánica** (*lah ehs-kah-leh-rah meh-kah-nee-kah*) (the escalator)

- **el vendedor** (*ehl behn-deh-dohr*) or **la vendedora** (*lah behn-deh-doh-rah*) (the salesperson [male and female])

- **la caja** (*lah kah-Hah*) (the check out stand)

Suppose that you're planning your day and you want to know a shop's opening hours. Here's how to ask for that information:

- **¿A qué hora abren?** (*ah keh oh-rah ah-brehn*) (At what time do you [formal] open?)

- **¿A qué hora cierran?** (*ah keh oh-rah theeeh-rrahn*) (At what time do you [formal] close?)

In the UK, you're probably used to browsing and shopping by yourself. In some places in Spain, salespeople want to help you as soon as you enter the shop. If you find the person insistent, our advice is to let yourself be helped. The salespeople aren't trying to impose anything on you; quite the contrary, they can be very involved, charming and helpful. So let yourself feel like a celebrity, being pampered as you shop. On the other hand, if you want only to browse, be firm but polite about refusing help, but don't forget to smile!

Talkin' the Talk

Here's how to tell a salesperson that you want just to browse around the shop.

Salesperson: **¿Busca algo en especial?**
boos-kah ahl-goh ehn ehs-peh-theeahl
Looking for something special?

Silvia: **Sólo quiero mirar.**
soh-loh-keeeh-roh mee-rahr
I just want to browse.

Salesperson: **Me llama cuando me necesite.**
meh yah-mah kooahn-doh meh neh-theh-see-teh
Call me when you need me [formal].

Silvia: **Sí, le llamo, gracias.**
see leh yah-moh grah-theeahs
Yes, I'll call you, thanks.

Using the Verb Probar (To Try)

The verb **probar** *(proh-bahr)* (to try, to try on or to taste) is one that you may use quite a lot when shopping.

The root of **probar** changes from **pro-** *(proh)* to **prue-** *(prooeh)* in some tenses, because it's an irregular verb. Here's the conjugation:

Conjugation	*Pronunciation*
yo pruebo	*yoh prooeh-boh*
tú pruebas	*too prooeh-bahs*
él, ella, usted prueba	*ehl, eh-yah, oos-tehd prooeh-bah*
nosotros probamos	*noh-soh-trohs proh-bah-mohs*
vosotros probáis	*boh-soh-trohs proh-bahees*
ellos, ellas, ustedes prueban	*eh-yohs, eh-yahs, oos-teh-dehs prooeh-bahn*

When you know how to use **probar**, you can ask to try on anything before buying it, which is important when shopping in Spain. Different countries have different size cuts and so checking that an item looks good on you before making a purchase is vital.

Talkin' the Talk

You want to locate the section of the department store with the goods you're looking for. Here's how to ask.

Silvia: **¿Dónde están los vestidos de señora?**
dohn-deh ehs-tahn lohs behs-tee-dohs deh seh-nyoh-rah
Where are the ladies' clothes?

Salesperson: **En el quinto piso.**
ehn ehl keen-toh pee-soh
On the fifth floor.

Silvia: **¿Dónde está la ropa de hombre?**
dohn-deh ehs-tah lah roh-pah deh ohm-breh
Where are the men's clothes?

Salesperson: **En el cuarto piso.**
ehn ehl kooahr-toh pee-soh
On the fourth floor.

Silvia: **¿Dónde encuentro artículos de aseo?**
dohn-deh ehn-kooehn-troh ahr-tee-koo-lohs deh ah-seh-oh
Where do I find toiletries?

Salesperson: **Al fondo, a la izquierda.**
ahl fohn-doh ah lah eeth-keeehr-dah
At the back, to the left.

Silvia: **Busco la sección de ropa de cama.**
boos-koh lah sehk-theeohn deh roh-pah deh kah-mah
I'm looking for bed linen.

Salesperson: **Un piso más arriba.**
oon pee-soh mahs ah-rree-bah
One floor up.

Silvia: **¿Venden electrodomésticos?**
behn-dehn eh-lehk-troh-doh-mehs-tee-kohs
Do you sell electrical appliances?

Salesperson: **Sí, en el último piso.**
see ehn ehl ool-tee-moh pee-soh
Yes, on the top floor.

Creating a colourful you

Many colours in Spain are sun-warmed and vibrant. Shopping for clothes and other goods requires some familiarity with describing these colours so that you can select the best match for your needs and personality. Table 6-1 gives you a handle on the Spanish colour palette.

Table 6-1	Selecting Your Colours	
Colour	*Pronunciation*	*Translation*
blanco	_blahn_-koh	white
negro	_neh_-groh	black
gris	grees	grey
rojo	_roh_-Hoh	red
azul	ah-_thool_	blue
verde	_behr_-deh	green
morado	moh-_rah_-doh	purple
violeta	beeoh-_leh_-tah	violet, purple
marrón	mah-_rrohn_	brown
amarillo	ah-mah-_ree_-yoh	yellow
naranja	nah-_rahn_-Hah	orange
rosa	_roh_-sah	pink
celeste	theh-_lehs_-teh	sky blue
claro	_klah_-roh	light
oscuro	ohs-_koo_-roh	dark

Talkin' the Talk

María accidentally split her skirt bending down to pick up some boxes at work. She needs a new one quickly – one with pockets to hold the art supplies she uses as a graphic designer. She asks a salesperson for help.

María: **¿Me ayuda por favor?**
meh ah-_yoo_-dah porh fah-_bohr_
Can you help me, please?

Busco una falda, con bolsillos.
boos-koh _oo_-nah _fahl_-dah kohn bohl-_see_-yohs
I'm looking for a skirt, with pockets.

Salesperson:	**¿Qué talla tiene?**
	keh <u>tah</u>-yah tee<u>eh</u>-neh
	What size are you?
María:	**Talla doce inglesa.**
	<u>tah</u>-yah <u>doh</u>-theh een-<u>gleh</u>-sah
	Size 12, English size.
Salesperson:	**¿Me permite medirla, para estar seguras?**
	meh pehr-<u>mee</u>-teh meh-<u>deer</u>-lah <u>pah</u>-rah ehs-<u>tahr</u> seh-<u>goo</u>-rahs
	May I check your size so we can know for sure?
	Ah, su talla es la cuarenta.
	ah soo <u>tah</u>-yah ehs lah kooah-<u>rehn</u>-tah
	Ah, your size is 40.
	¿Qué color busca?
	keh koh-<u>lohr</u> <u>boos</u>-kah
	What colour are you looking for?
María:	**Rojo.**
	<u>roh</u>-Hoh
	Red.
Salesperson:	**La quiere con muchas flores?**
	lah kee<u>eh</u>-reh kohn <u>mooh</u>-chahs <u>floh</u>-rehs
	Do you want it in a floral design (literally 'with many flowers')?
María:	**No, lisa, por favor.**
	noh <u>lee</u>-sah pohr fah-<u>bohr</u>
	No, plain, please.

Shopping for shirts and trousers

A word of wisdom: men's shirts and trousers seem to come in the same sizes in Spain as they do in many other European countries. But just in case, checking their fit is a good idea.

In some areas, people are smaller and sizes vary; medium may be what you think of as small. Your best bet is to try on shirts and trousers before you leave the shop.

Words to Know

ayudar	ah-yoo-_dahr_	to help
el bolsillo	ehl bohl-_see_-yoh	the pocket
la falda	lah _fahl_-dah	the skirt
la talla	lah _tah_-yah	the size
liso	_lee_-soh	plain; flat
más	mahs	more
medir	meh-_deer_	to measure
menos	_meh_-nohs	less

Talkin' the Talk

Here's how you ask to try on trousers.

Claudio: **¿Puedo probarme este pantalón?**
po_oeh_-doh proh-_bahr_-meh _ehs_-teh pahn-tah-_lohn_
May I try on these trousers?

Salesperson: **Cómo no, por aquí.**
koh-moh no pohr ah-_kee_
Of course, this way.

Claudio: **Me queda grande.**
meh _keh_-dah _grahn_-deh
They're too big. (Literally: it fits me large.)

Salesperson: **Le busco otro.**
leh _boos_-koh _oh_-troh
I'll find you another [pair].

Claudio: **Este aprieta aquí.**
ehs-teh ah-pree_eh_-tah ah-_kee_
This pair is tight here.

Salesperson: **A ver este.**
ah behr _ehs_-teh
Let's try this one.

Claudio: **¿Lo tiene en verde?**
loh tee_eh_-neh ehn _behr_-deh
Do you have it in green?

Salesperson: **Este, ¿a ver?**
ehs-teh ah behr
This one? Let's see.

Claudio: **Queda muy bien.**
Keh-dah mooy bee_ehn_
It fits very well.

Words to Know

La camisa	lah kah-_mee_-sah	the shirt
Los pantalones	lohs pahn-tah-_loh_-nehs	the trousers
Queda bien	_keh_-dah bee_ehn_	the fit is just right
Queda grande	_keh_-dah _grahn_-deh	the fit is too big
Probar	proh-_bahr_	to try

Checking fibres and fabrics

You may notice that some street markets in poorer areas of Spain favour fabrics made with artificial fibres and that the prices for these fabrics are lower than for natural fibres. The following phrases help you to ask about the fibres (or fabrics) of which the garments are made:

- ✔ **¿Este pantalón es de lana?** *(ehs-teh pan-tah-lohn ehs de lah-nah)* (Are these trousers made of wool?)

- ✔ **No, es de lana con nylon.** *(noh ehs deh lah-nah kohn nah-ee-lohn)* (No, they're made of wool and nylon.)

- ✔ **¿La camisa es sólo algodón?** *(lah kah-mee-sah ehs soh-loh ahl-goh-dohn)* (Is the shirt made of pure cotton?)

- ✔ **No, es de algodón y poliéster.** *(noh, ehs deh ahl-goh-dohn ee poh-leeehs-tehr)* (No, it's made of cotton and polyester.)

- ✔ **¿Cuánto algodón tiene esta tela?** *(kooahn-toh ahl-goh-dohn teeeh-neh ehs-tah teh-lah)* (How much cotton is in this fabric?)

- ✔ **Tiene cuarenta por cicnto.** *(teeeh-neh kooah-rehn-tah pohr theeehn-toh)* (It has 40 per cent.)

- ✔ **Busco ropa de fibras naturales.** *(boos-koh roh-pah deh fee-brahs nah-too-rah-lehs)* (I'm looking for clothes in natural fibres.)

- ✔ **También tenemos.** *(tahm-beeehn teh-neh-mohs)* (We have them as well.)

Words to Know

el algodón	ehl ahl-goh-*dohn*	the cotton
la fibra	lah *fee*-brah	the fibre
la lana	lah *lah*-nah	the wool
por ciento	pohr thee*ehn*-toh	per cent; percentage
pura	*poo*-rah	pure

Wearing and Taking: The Verb Llevar

Whether you're wearing, taking or shopping, **llevar** *(yeh-bahr)* is a great verb to have around because it can mean 'to wear', 'to take with you' and 'to keep track of' (or 'to keep count of'). Good news! In addition, this verb is a regular one of the group ending in **-ar**; its root is **llev-** *(yehb)*:

Conjugation	Pronunciación
yo llevo	*yoh yeh-boh*
tú llevas	*too yeh-bahs*
él, ella, usted lleva	*ehl, eh-yah, oos-tehd yeh-bah*
nosotros llevamos	*noh-soh-trohs yeh-bah-mohs*
vosotros lleváis	*boh-soh-trohs yeh-baees*
ellos, ellas, ustedes llevan	*eh-yohs, eh-yahs, oos-teh-dehs yeh-bahn*

Vestir *(behs-teer)* (to dress) is another way to say 'to wear', and comes from the noun **vestido** *(bes-tee-doh)* (dress).

Count on the following examples to help you keep track of this dressing and tracking verb:

- **Me llevo esta camisa.** *(meh yeh-boh ehs-tah kah-mee-sah)* (I'll take this shirt.)

- **El vestido que llevas es precioso.** *(ehl behs-tee-doh keh yeh-bahs ehs preh-theeh-oh-soh)* (The dress you have on is very beautiful.)

- **Llevo un regalo para ti.** *(yeh-boh ooh reh-gah-loh pah-rah tee)* (I'm taking a present for you.)

- **Llevamos tres semanas sin vernos.** *(yeh-bah-mohs trehs seh-mah-nahs seen behr-nohs)* (It's been [literally: we're counting] three weeks without seeing each other.)

- **El lleva la cuenta de cuántos vestidos compraste.** *(ehl yeh-bah lah kooehn-tah deh kooahn-tohs behs-tee-dohs kohm-prahs-teh)* (He keeps track of the number of dresses you buy.)

- **Me lo llevo.** *(meh loh yeh-boh)* (I'll take it.)

Talkin' the Talk

You find a skirt that's the right colour and want to try it on to be on the safe side before making a final decision.

Salesperson: **Pase al probador, por favor.**
pah-seh ahl proh-bah-dohr pohr fah-bohr
Please go into the fitting room.

Silvia: **¿Dónde está?**
dohn-deh ehs-tah
Where is it?

Salesperson: **Por aquí.**
pohr ah-<u>kee</u>
This way.

¿Le queda bien?
leh <u>keh</u>-dah bee<u>ehn</u>
Does it fit?

Silvia: **No, está muy apretada.**
noh, ehs-<u>tah</u> mooy ah-preh-<u>tah</u>-dah
No, it's very tight.

¿Puede traer una talla más grande?
poo<u>eh</u>-deh trah-<u>ehr</u> <u>oo</u>-nah <u>tah</u>-yah mahs <u>grahn</u>-deh
Can you bring a larger size?

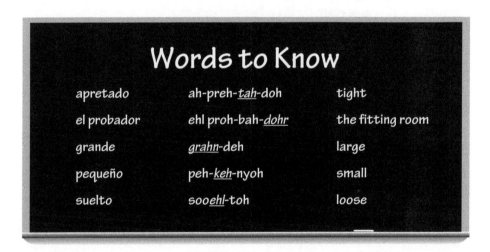

Words to Know

apretado	ah-preh-<u>tah</u>-doh	tight
el probador	ehl proh-bah-<u>dohr</u>	the fitting room
grande	<u>grahn</u>-deh	large
pequeño	peh-<u>keh</u>-nyoh	small
suelto	soo<u>ehl</u>-toh	loose

Making Comparisons: Good, Better, Best and More

When you compare one thing to another, you talk in comparatives (for between two items) and superlatives (for three or more items). In Spanish, most of the time you use the word **más** *(mahs)* (more) for comparisons and **el más** *(ehl mahs)* (literally, 'the most') for superlatives. One example is **grande** *(grahn-deh)* (large), **más grande** *(mahs grahn-deh)* (larger) and **el más grande** *(ehl mahs grahn-deh)* (the largest).

In English, you usually change the word's ending to form a comparative or superlative (as in 'large', 'larger' and 'largest'), but in Spanish you add **más** or **el más**. For long words, however, English does use a similar system of adding words in front to create comparatives and superlatives, such as 'expensive', where the comparative is 'more expensive' and the superlative 'most expensive' (and not 'expensiver' or 'expensivest'!).

Here are some examples of Spanish comparatives and superlatives:

- **grande** *(grahn-deh)* (big; large)
  más grande *(mahs grahn-deh)* (bigger; larger)
  el más grande *(ehl mahs grahn-deh)* (the biggest; the largest)

- **pequeño** *(peh-keh-nyoh)* (small)
  más pequeño *(mahs peh-keh-nyoh)* (smaller)
  el más pequeño *(ehl mahs peh-keh-nyoh)* (the smallest)

- **corto** *(cohr-toh)* (short)
  más corto *(mahs cohr-toh)* (shorter)
  el más corto *(ehl mahs cohr-toh)* (the shortest)

- **largo** *(lahr-goh)* (long)
  más lago *(mahs lahr-goh)* (longer)
  el más largo *(ehl mahs lahr-goh)* (the longest)

- **apretado** *(ah-preh-tah-doh)* (tight)
  más apretado *(mahs ah-preh-tah-doh)* (tighter)
  el más apretado *(ehl mahs ah-preh-tah-doh)* (the tightest)

- **suelto** *(sooehl-toh)* (loose)
  más suelto *(mahs sooehl-toh)* (looser)
  el más suelto *(ehl mahs sooehl-toh)* (the loosest)

- **caro** *(kah-roh)* (expensive)
  más caro *(mahs kah-roh)* (more expensive)
  el más caro *(ehl mahs kah-roh)* (the most expensive)

- **barato** *(bah-rah-toh)* (cheap)
  más barato *(mahs bah-rah-toh)* (cheaper)
  el más barato *(ehl mahs bah-rah-toh)* (the cheapest)

Just as in English, a few exceptions exist, in which the comparative form doesn't require the word **más**, such as:

- **bueno** *(booeh-noh)* (good)
  mejor *(meh-Hohr)* (better)
  el mejor *(ehl meh-Hohr)* (the best)

- **malo** *(mah-loh)* (bad)
  peor *(peh-ohr)* (worse)
  el peor *(ehl peh-ohr)* (the worst)

Notice that the English meanings are also exceptions to the English rules for forming comparatives and superlatives.

Exaggerating: When Superlatives Fail

Many Spanish speakers love to exaggerate. Whereas non-Spanish speakers may see this tendency as excessive, Spanish-speakers simply view it as adding a bit more emphasis.

Exaggeration is something you see everywhere, even in classical Spanish poetry. For example, Francisco de Quevedo y Villegas *(frahn-thees-koh deh keh-beh-doh ee bee-yeh-gahs)* – the Spanish poet of the Golden Century (who lived from 1580–1645) – uses the following phrase in his poem 'A una nariz' *(ah oo-nah nah-reeth)* (To a nose), which is addressed to a person with a very large one:

> **'muchísima nariz'** *(moo-chee-see-mah nah-reeth)* (a whole big nose).

So, in Spanish, you don't only compare things, but you can also express an exaggerated state.

To say that something is exaggeratedly this or that, you add **-ísimo** *(ee-see-moh)* or **-ísima** *(ee-see-mah)* to an adjective or an adverb. For example, to say that something is exaggeratedly good you use **bueno** *(booeh-noh)* and then you say **buenísimo** *(booeh-nee-see-moh)* (exceptionally good).

Here are some examples:

- ✔ **La película es buenísima.** *(lah peh-lee-koo-lah ehs booeh-nee-see-mah)* (The film is exceptionally good.)
- ✔ **La ciudad es grandísima.** *(lah theeoo-dahd ehs grahn-dee-see-mah)* (The city is huge.)
- ✔ **Los perros son bravísimos.** *(los peh-rrohs sohn brah-bee-see-mohs)* (The dogs are extremely fierce.)
- ✔ **El hotel es malísimo.** *(ehl oh-tehl ehs mah-lee-see-moh)* (The hotel is really bad.)
- ✔ **El postre está dulcísimo.** *(ehl pohs-treh ehs-tah dool-thee-see-moh)* (The dessert is sickeningly sweet.)
- ✔ **Los colores son vivísimos.** *(losh koh-loh-rehs sohn bee-bee-see-mohs)* (The colours are exceedingly bright.)
- ✔ **El autobús andaba lentísimo.** *(ehl ahoo-toh-boos ahn-dah-bah lehn-tee-see-moh)* (The bus advanced extremely slowly.)
- ✔ **La tienda era carísima.** *(lah teeehn-dah eh-rah kah-ree-see-mah)* (The shop was exorbitantly expensive.)

Shopping for Finer Objects

You may want to shop in the specialised shops or galleries located on the more elegant boulevards, streets and avenues of all major Spanish cities. Seeking the finest artistic, cultural or fashion items may include buying original art in Palma (*pahl-mah*) or shopping for paintings, sculpture, fine shoes, leather objects and exquisite collectibles in Madrid (*mah-drid*) and Valencia (*bah-lehn-thee-ah*).

You can use the following phrases when shopping at a specialised shop or gallery:

- **Busco grabados de Miró.** (*boos-koh grah-bah-dohs deh meeh-roh*) (I'm looking for engravings by Miró.)

- **¿Tiene broches de plata?** (*teeeh-neh broh-chehs deh plah-tah*) (Do you have silver brooches?)

- **¿Cuánto cuesta el collar que tiene en la ventana?** (*kooahn-toh kooehs-tah ehl koh-yahr keh teeeh-neh ehn la behn-tah-nah*) (How much is the necklace you have in the window?)

- **¿Y la pintura?** (*ee lah peen-too-rah*) (And the painting?)

- **¿Vende perlas?** (*behn-deh pehr-lahs*) (Do you sell pearls?)

- **¿De quién es la escultura en la vitrina?** (*deh keeehn ehs lah ehs-kool-too-rah ehn lah bee-tree-nah*) (Who made the sculpture in the display case?)

- **¿Lo embalamos y mandamos a su domicilio?** (*loh ehm-bah-lah-mohs ee mahn-dah-mohs a soo doh-mee-thee-leeoh*) (Shall we pack it and send it to your address?)

Words to Know

el collar	ehl koh-*yahr*	the necklace
el grabado	ehl grah-*bah*-doh	the engraving
la escultura	lah ehs-kool-*too*-rah	the sculpture
la perla	lah *pehr*-lah	the pearl
la pintura	lah peen-*too*-rah	the painting

Shopping in Open-Air Markets

You can find clothes and household objects in open-air Spanish markets, many of which are open one set day of the week, all year round. In these markets, you probably aren't going to find any labels stating the prices, because the prices aren't really fixed, and so be prepared to get involved in some bargaining and haggling.

Rooting out typical market items: An affordable treasure trove

As you travel around the many market-places of Spain – including the famous **El Rastro** *(ehl rash-troh)*, the 250 year-old open-air market in Madrid – you can look for a variety of souvenirs for yourself and your friends. Markets tend to open early in the morning around 8 a.m. and close at 3 p.m.

Spanish markets sell clothing, shoes, bags, leatherwear and all kinds of authentic gifts. If you bargain well you can end up with treasures such as the following:

- **Una lámpara de madera** *(oo-nah lahm-pah-rah deh mah-deh-rah)* (a table lamp, made from wood)

- **Un anillo hecho de concha marina** *(oon ah-nee-yeeoh eh-choh deh kohn-chah mah-reeh-nah)* (a ring made from sea shell)

- **Un collar de plata** *(oon koh-yahr deh plah-tah)* (a silver necklace)

- **Una chaqueta hecha de lana tejida a mano y bordada con seda** *(oo-nah chah-keh-tah eh-chah deh lah-nah teh-Hee-dah ah mah-noh ee bohr-dah-dah kohn seh-dah)* (a jacket made of handwoven wool and embroidered in silk)

In the markets, you find colour in the merchandise, in the conversation and in the shopping style. You also discover many handcrafted goods, made in the manner of pre-industrial times, in which the human hand leaves a mark that's unmatched in feeling by machine production. You find the informality that comes from the precariousness of open markets, and which also makes for displays of the goods in original ways – without display cases or marketing tricks.

Like the bazaars of *A Thousand and One Nights*, the **tiendas** *(tee-ehn-dahs)* (shops; literally: tents) of **El Rastro** *(el rahs-troh)* in Madrid are really magical and put you in touch with street life as it used to be for decades, and still is for many people in Spain.

Words to Know

el anillo	ehl ah-_neeh_-yoh	the ring
el collar	ehl koh-_yahr_	the necklace
la botella	lah boh-_teh_-yah	the bottle
la pintura	lah peen-_too_-rah	the painting
la pulsera	lah pul-_seh_-rah	the bracelet
rebajar	reh-bah-_Hahr_	to bring the price down

Bargaining at the open-air market

If you plan to shop in traditional markets, make sure that you arrive early. Many merchants feel that they must make a first sale to kick off their day. If you find yourself in such a situation, the merchant may not want you to leave without buying something and therefore be more willing to reduce the price to make a sale, and you can end up with a bargain.

The following phrases help you haggle in the market-place:

- ✔ **¿Cuánto cuesta?** _(koo_ahn_-toh koo_ehs_-tah)_ (How much is it?)
- ✔ **¿Cuánto vale?** _(koo_ahn_-toh _bah_-leh)_ (How much is it worth?)
- ✔ **¿A cuánto?** _(ah koo_ahn_-toh)_ (How much?)
- ✔ **Es barato.** _(ehs bah-_rah_-toh)_ (It's cheap/inexpensive.)
- ✔ **Es caro.** _(ehs _kah_-roh)_ (It's expensive.)

Use the following phrases to provide emphasis. You aren't going to be using these expressions very often, but they're fun to use and help you to express a certain level of emotion:

- ✔ **¡Una basura!** _(_oo_-nah bah-_soo_-rah)_ (Just rubbish!)
- ✔ **¡Una ganga!** _(_oo_-nah _gahn_-gah)_ (A bargain!)
- ✔ **¡Un robo!** _(oon _roh_-boh)_ (A robbery! [As in, that's 'daylight robbery!'])

Advice for the bargainer

In a traditional market or on the streets, when you're offered something you're interested in and price is mentioned, propose a better deal by offering a much lower amount. Of course, the merchant reacts to that suggestion with outrage. And thus a social game begins.

After the initial reaction to your first price, the merchant may state a sum slightly less than what was first requested. At this point you know the game is on. So you offer a bit more than your first amount. And the game goes on until you feel or believe that the merchant isn't going to go any further and the price is what you can afford.

Bargaining like this is a very satisfying activity for the seller and can be for the buyer as well. You establish a certain relationship while you bargain that shows your stamina and that of the seller in addition to your ability to follow a certain rhythm in the operation.

Talkin' the Talk

Bargaining is sometimes a little difficult in a shop, but at traditional open-air market-places in Spain, it's part of the deal. See how María haggles over a nice painting she's spotted at an outdoor market.

María: **Este cuadro, ¿cuánto cuesta?**
ehs-teh kooah-droh koo-ahn-toh kooehs-tah
How much is this picture?

Merchant: **Quince euros.**
keen-theh ehoo-rohs
15 euros.

María: **¿Tienes otro más barato?**
teeeh-nehs oh-troh mahs bah-rah-toh
Do you have a cheaper one?

Merchant: **Tengo este, más pequeño.**
tehn-goh ehs-teh mahs peh-keh-nyoh
I have this smaller one.

María: **No me gusta el dibujo.**
noh meh goos-tah ehl dee-boo-Hoh
I don't like the design.

Merchant: **Este en blanco y negro, a trece.**
ehs-teh ehn blahn-koh ee neh-groh ah treh-theh
This black and white one is 13 [euros].

María: **Me gusta. ¿A doce?**
            meh goos-tah ah doh-theh
            I like it. 12?

Merchant: **No puedo. Doce cincuenta. Ultimo precio.**
            noh pooeh-doh doh-thee-theen-kooehn-tah ool-tee-
            moh preh-theeoh
            I can't. 12.50. Last price.

María: **Bueno, me lo llevo.**
            booeh-noh meh loh yeh-boh
            Good. I'll take it.

Buying glass, ceramics, silver and wood

Spanish artisans are well known for their fine work in glass, silver, wood and ceramics; items made of these substances are highly sought after by collectors and lovers of their unique and original beauty.

Silver is beautiful and lasting. You can't resist these beautiful pieces . . . or the delicate, hand-blown glass . . . or the colourful but delicate ceramic ornaments. You see wooden carvings, and these intricately painted items aren't as fragile as glass or as heavy as the ceramic. What to buy?

These phrases can help you when you shop for these speciality items:

✔ **¿Dónde venden objetos de cerámica?** *(dohn-deh behn-dehn ohb-Heh-tohs deh theh-rah-mee-kah)* (Where do they sell ceramic objects?)

✔ **Busco objetos de vidrio soplado.** *(boos-koh ohb-Heh-tohs deh bee-dreeoh soh-plah-doh)* (I'm looking for hand-blown glass objects.)

✔ **Aquí hay cerámica hecha a mano.** *(ah-kee ah-ee theh-rah-mee-kah eh-chah ah mah-noh)* (Here are some handmade ceramics.)

Purchasing unique clothes

Who doesn't like owning a pretty, original piece of clothing? Well, in Spain, you can find some wonderful items designed by street market sellers themselves. Here are some phrases that can help you make a good selection:

✔ **¡Qué bonita es esta camiseta!** *(keh boh-nee-tah ehs-ehs-tah kah-mee-seh-tah)* (What a beautiful T-shirt!)

✔ **¿Tienes blusas con diseños originales para niña?** *(teeeh-nehs bloo-sahs kohn dee-seh-nyohs oh-ree-Hee-nah-lehs pah-rah nee-nyah)* (Do you have original design blouses for a girl?)

✔ **¿Tienes vestidos para mujer?** *(teeeh-nehs behs-tee-dohs pah-rah moo-Hehr)* (Do you have ladies' dresses?)

Words to Know

el vidrio	ehl *bee*-dreeoh	the glass
hecho a mano	*eh*-choh ah *mah*-noh	handmade
la cerámica	lah theh-*rah*-mee-kah	the ceramic
la plata	lah *plah*-tah	silver
soplado a mano	soh-*plah*-doh ah *mah*-noh	hand-blown

Searching out shoes and bags

When shopping, you can pack everything you buy in trendy, colourful bags and then use them at home. Because bags come in so many materials, shapes and sizes and are generally quite long-lasting, they make a beautiful addition to any home. You may also find yourself enjoying your shopping so much that you wear out your old shoes and need to buy a new pair! Never fear – the following sentences can help you purchase nice bags or Spanish shoes:

✔ **Estos son zapatos de cuero.** *(ehs-tohs sohn thah-pah-tohs deh koo-eh-roh)* (These are leather shoes.)

✔ **¿Tienes bolsos para la noche?** *(teeeh-nehs bol-sohs-pah-rah lah noh-cheh)* (Do you have any bags to go out in the evenings?)

✔ **Estos zapatos son de verano.** *(ehs-tohs thah-pah-tohs sohn de beh-rah-noh)* (These are summer shoes)

✔ **Estos bolsos son de piel.** *(ehs-tohs bol-sohs sohn deh peeh-ehl)* (These are leather bags)

If you need help with numbers and prices, check out Chapter 5.

Fun & Games

Your boss just gave you a huge, unexpected rise. With money burning a hole in your pocket, you decide to go on a shopping spree. You're going to a department store and to the open-air markets, allowing yourself five items from each of several shops. Use the chart below to help you plan your attack.

	Item	*Material*	*Colour*
Ropa	1.		
	2.		
	3.		
	4.		
	5.		
Objetos (de plata, vidrio o cerámica)	1.		
	2.		
	3.		
	4.		
	5.		
Bolsos, zapatos	1.		
	2.		
	3.		
	4.		
	5.		

Chapter 7

Organising a Night on the Town

In This Chapter
▶ Enjoying festivals, films, music and other entertainment
▶ Identifying times of the day and days of the week

S pain doesn't allow you much chance of getting bored. Whether you enjoy street festivals, music, films, theatre or dance – you name it – you have loads to see and experience.

Spaniards love culture, and they rejoice in turning their cultural activities into social events – gathering with old friends and new arrivals for festivals, concerts, shows and so on. Spanish events combine colour and costume, music and dance, artistry and passion. The people tend to be quite uninhibited and live life with great gusto. In fact, they invented the word *gusto*! (We show you how to conjugate the verb **gustar** (*goos-tahr*) (to like; to enjoy) in Chapter 8.)

The larger Spanish cities have more to see than any one person can handle. Even in the smallest village, someone may well decide to take a glass, call for a toast, treat you to a local tipple and entertain you – just for the joy of living! Even older people's parties can have live music, and when important events are celebrated with family and friends, people dance and sing into the wee small hours of the morning.

This chapter tells you all you need to know to enjoy yourself Spanish style.

Understanding that Timing Is Everything

If you can say and understand when an event is going to take place in Spanish, you need never miss a thing! Here are the days of the week in Spanish:

▶ **lunes** (*loo-nehs*) (Monday)

▶ **martes** (*mahr-tehs*) (Tuesday)

▶ **miércoles** (*meeehr-koh-lehs*) (Wednesday)

✔ **jueves** *(Hoo<u>eh</u>-behs)* (Thursday)

✔ **viernes** *(bee<u>ehr</u>-nehs)* (Friday)

✔ **sábado** *(<u>sah</u>-bah-doh)* (Saturday)

✔ **domingo** *(doh-<u>meen</u>-goh)* (Sunday)

Use the following phrases to practise the days of the week:

✔ **La clase va a ser el martes.** *(lah <u>klah</u>-seh bah a sehr ehl <u>mahr</u>-tehs)* (The class will be held on Tuesday.)

✔ **No puedo ir hasta el miércoles.** *(noh poo<u>eh</u>-doh eer <u>ahs</u>-tah ehl mee<u>ehr</u>-koh-lehs)* (I can't go until Wednesday.)

✔ **Ella va a llegar el viernes.** *(<u>eh</u>-yah bah ah yeh-<u>gahr</u> ehl bee<u>ehr</u>-nes)* (She's going to arrive on Friday.)

✔ **Me voy el domingo.** *(meh bohee ehl doh-<u>meen</u>-goh)* (I'm leaving on Sunday.)

Sometimes, you also need to state the approximate time, as in the following phrases:

✔ **la semana siguiente** *(lah seh-<u>mah</u>-nah see-<u>gheeehn</u>-teh)* (the next week [literally: the week entering].)

✔ **la semana próxima** *(lah seh-<u>mah</u>-nah <u>prohk</u>-see-mah)* (next week.)

✔ **la semana que viene** *(lah seh-<u>mah</u>-nah keh bee<u>eh</u>-neh)* (next week [literally: the week that comes].)

✔ **Es mediodía.** *(ehs meh-deeoh-<u>dee</u>-ah)* (It's noon.)

✔ **Es medianoche.** *(ehs meh-deeah-<u>noh</u>-cheh)* (It's midnight.)

✔ **Es tarde.** *(ehs <u>tahr</u>-deh)* (It's late.)

✔ **Es temprano.** *(ehs tehm-<u>prah</u>-noh)* (It's early.)

✔ **Voy tarde.** *(boh-ee <u>tahr</u>-deh)* (I'm late.)

The following phrases can help you practise saying the days of the week and approximate times:

✔ **Es un poco tarde; ya son las ocho.** *(ehs oon <u>poh</u>-coh <u>tahr</u>-deh; yah sohn lahs <u>oh</u>-choh)* (It's a bit late; it's already eight o'clock.)

✔ **A medianoche termina el baile.** *(ah <u>meh</u>-deeah-<u>noh</u>-cheh tehr-<u>mee</u>-nah ehl <u>bahee</u>-leh)* (The dance ends at midnight.)

✔ **Voy tarde; ya es mediodía.** *(boh-ee <u>tahr</u>-deh; yah ehs meh-deeoh-<u>dee</u>-ah)* (I'm late; it's already noon.)

✔ **Es el lunes, temprano por la mañana.** *(ehs ehl loo-nehs tehm-prah-noh porh lah mah-nyah-nah)* (It's on Monday, early in the morning.)

✔ **La semana próxima va a venir en avión.** *(lah seh-mah-nah prohk-see-mah bah ah beh-neer ehn ah-beeohn)* (She/He'll come by plane next week.)

✔ **La semana siguiente es buena fecha.** *(lah seh-mah-nah see-gheeehn-teh ehs boo-eh-nah feh-chah)* (The following week is a good date.)

Turn to Chapter 15 to discover the months in the year; for help with numbers, check out Chapter 5.

Having a Good Time

The pleasure that people take in cultural expression is universal. Everyone loves a good show, and most people love to sing (**cantar** *(kahn-tahr)*) and dance (**bailar** *(bahee-lahr)*) (and hear and see others do so as well). Through artistic expression, people share a piece of themselves; plus, singing and dancing are great for your health! (Take a look at the later sections, 'Singing For Your Supper: **Cantar**' and 'Dancing the Night Away: **Bailar**', for more on these all-singing, all-dancing verbs.)

Here are some phrases that Spanish speakers use to express their culture:

✔ **¡Bailar y cantar!** *(bahee-lahr ee kahn-tahr)* (Dance and sing!)

✔ **¡Esta es para ti!** *(ehs-tah ehs pah-rah tee!)* (This [song] is for you!)

The following phrases help you set the time and place when you're ready to go out on the town:

✔ **¿a qué hora?** *(ah keh oh-rah)* (at what time?)

✔ **¿cuándo comienza?** *(kooahn-doh koh-meeehn-thah)* (when does it start?)

✔ **¿hasta qué hora?** *(ahs-tah keh oh-rah)* (until what time?)

In the UK, social contacts can be explored and expanded in dinner parties. Such parties exist in Spain as well, but more often than not people get together during meals out or dances. Spanish people use their dining occasions and parties to meet and greet each other and to develop new social relationships.

Talkin' the Talk

In the following conversation, Raúl asks about the details of a party.

Consuelo: **¿A qué hora comienza la fiesta?**
ah keh oh-rah koh-meeehn-thah la feeehs-tah
What time does the party start?

Raúl: **A las diez de la noche.**
ah lahs deeeth deh lah noh-cheh
Ten at night.

Consuelo: **¿No será muy tarde?**
noh seh-rah mooy tahr-deh
Won't that be too late?

Raúl: **No, ¡simplemente duerme una buena siesta!**
noh seem-pleh-mehn-teh dooehr-meh ooh-nah booeh-nah seeehs-tah
Not at all, simply have a good siesta!

Consuelo: **¿A qué hora acaba la fiesta?**
ah keh oh-rah ah-kah-bah lah feeehs-tah
What time will the party end?

Raúl: **Dura hasta las dos de la mañana.**
doo-rah ahs-tah lahs dohs deh lah mah-nyah-nah
It lasts until two in the morning.

Consuelo: **¿Hasta esa hora?**
ahs-tah eh-sah oh-rah
Until then?

Raúl: **Sí, y luego vamos a tomar un buen chocolate caliente.**
see ee looeh-goh bah-mohs ah toh-mahr oon booehn choh-koh-lah-teh kah-lee-ehn-teh
Yes, and then we'll go and drink a good (cup of) hot chocolate.

Inviting and Being Invited: Invitar

When you visit Spain, you may well get invited to some parties or want to invite friends to your own parties. To do so, you need to be familiar with the verb 'to invite', which in Spanish is **invitar** *(een-bee-tahr)*. Fortunately, **Invitar** is a regular verb of the **-ar** variety, as you can see from the table that follows. The root of this verb is **invit-** *(een-beet)*.

Conjugation	*Pronunciation*
yo invito	*yoh een-bee-toh*
tú invitas	*too een-bee-tahs*
él, **ella**, **usted invita**	*ehl, eh-yah, oos-tehd een-bee-tah*
nosotros invitamos	*noh-soh-trohs een-bee-tah-mohs*
vosotros invitáis	*boh-soh-trohs een-bee-tahees*
ellos, **ellas**, **ustedes invitan**	*eh-yohs, eh-yahs, oos-teh-dehs een-bee-than*

Use the following phrases to help you give and receive invitations:

- ✔ **Te invito al teatro.** *(teh een-bee-toh ahl teh-ah-troh)* (I invite you to the theatre.)

- ✔ **Nos invitan al baile.** *(nohs een-bee-tahn ahl bah-ee-leh)* (We've been invited to the dance.)

- ✔ **Ellos invitan a todos a la fiesta.** *(eh-yohs een-bee-tahn ah toh-dohs ah lah feeehs-tah)* (They're inviting everybody to the fiesta.)

- ✔ **Tenemos que invitarles a casa.** *(teh-neh-mohs keh een-bee-tahr-lehs ah kah-sah)* (We have to invite them to our place [home].)

- ✔ **Voy a invitarla al concierto.** *(bohee ah een-bee-tahr-lah ahl kohn-theeehr-toh)* (I'm going to invite her to the concert.)

Notice the use of **al** *(ahl)* (to the) in phrases such as **al teatro** and **al baile**. **Teatro** and **baile** are masculine words that would normally take the article **el**. But **a el**, formed when you add the preposition **a** *(ah)* (to) to the mix, sounds unpleasant to the Spanish ear. Therefore, the language joins the two words into **al**, which sounds much smoother, don't you think?

Talkin' the Talk

Pedro decides to invite his new co-worker Julia to a party for two of their colleagues.

Pedro: **¿Quieres venir a una fiesta?**
Keeeh-rehs bee-neer ah oo-nah feeehs-tah
Do you want to come to a party?

Julia: **¿Cuándo?**
kooahn-doh
When?

Pedro: **El sábado a las ocho de la tarde.**
ehl sah-bah-doh ah lahs oh-choh deh lah tarh-deh
Saturday, at 8 p.m. (literally: Saturday, at eight in the evening.)

Julia: **Sí, puedo ir. ¿Qué fiesta es?**
see pooeh-doh eer keh feeehs-tah esh
Yes, I can go. What party is it?

Pedro: **Mario y Lucía se van de viaje y decidimos hacerles una fiesta informal.**
mah-reeoh ee loo-thee-ah seh bahn deh beeah-Heh ee deh-thee-dee-mohs ah-thehr-lehs oo-nah feeehs-tah een-fohr-mahl
Mario and Lucía are going on a trip . . . and we decided to throw them an informal party.

Julia: **Toda ocasión es buena para bailar. Claro que voy, con mucho gusto.**
toh-dah oh-kah-seeohn ehs booeh-nah pah-rah bahee-lahr klah-roh keh bohee kohn moo-choh goos-toh
Any chance to dance is great. Yes, I'll be glad to come.

Julia wants to know more about the party this Saturday and asks Pedro about it.

Julia: **¿Dónde va a ser la fiesta?**
dohn-deh bah ah sehr lah feeehs-tah
Where's the party going to be?

Pedro: **En el bar de Angel, mi amigo.**
ehn ehl barh deh ahn-Hehl mee ah-mee-goh
At my friend Angel's bar.

Julia: **¿Qué clase de música y bailes habrá?**
keh klah-seh deh moo-see-kah ee bah-ee-lehs ah-brah
What kind of dances will they have?

Pedro: **Habrá música moderna española, salsa, un poco de todo. ¡Va a ser la monda!**
ah-brah moo-see-kah moh-dehr-nah esh-pah-nyo-lah sahl-sah oon poh-koh deh toh-doh bah ah sehr lah mohn-dah
They'll have Spanish pop music, salsa, a bit of every-thing. It's going to be a riot!

Speaking in idioms

In Spanish the word for 'idiom' is **modismo** (*moh-dees-moh*). An idiom is a phrase that can't be translated literally. That is to say, translating it word-by-word doesn't give you the full meaning. So, when you translate idioms, you have to give an equivalent phrase. For example, when used in relation to a thing or an event, **¿A qué viene?** (*ah keh beeeh-neh*) – which literally translates as 'what does it come for?' – means 'what for?', 'why so?', 'what's the occasion?' or simply 'why?'.

When used with a pronoun or a person, **¿A qué viene él?** (*ah keh beeeh-neh ehl*) has the same meaning as its English translation, 'What does he come for?' (or **¿A qué viene ella?** (*ah keh beeeh-neh eh-yah*) 'What does she come for?').

Dancing the Night Away: Bailar

Bailar (*bahee-lahr*) (to dance) is a regularly beautiful verb, great to swing along to. The root of this verb is **bail-** (*bahee*). The conjugation of **bailar** in the present tense is as follows:

Conjugation	*Pronunciation*
yo bailo	*yoh bahee-loh*
tú bailas	*too bahee-lahs*
él, ella, usted baila	*ehl, eh-yah, oos-tehd bahee-lah*
nosotros bailamos	*noh-soh-trohs bahee-lah-mohs*
vosotros bailáis	*boh-soh-trohs bahee-lahees*
ellos, ellas, ustedes bailan	*eh-yohs, eh-yahs, oos-teh-dehs bahee-lahn*

These phrases can help you when you want to dance:

- ✔ **¡Este es un baile nuevo!** (*esh-teh ehs oon bahee-leh nooeh-boh*) (This is a new dance!)

- ✔ **Te invito a bailar.** (*teh een-bee-toh ah bahee-lahr*) (I invite you [informal] to dance.)

- ✔ **Bailamos toda la noche.** (*bahee-lah-mohs toh-dah lah noh-cheh*) (We danced all night.)

- ✔ **Bailan muy bien.** (*bahee-lahn mooy beeehn*) (They dance very well.)

- ✔ **Bailó hasta la mañana.** (*bahee-loh ahs-tah lah mah-nyah-nah*) (He/she danced until morning.)

Words to Know

el bar	ehl bahr	the bar
el gusto	ehl _goos_-toh	a pleasure (literally: the taste)
el viaje	ehl bee_ah_-Heh	the trip
la ocasión	lah oh-kah-see_ohn_	the occasion
la monda	lah-_mohn_-dah	to be extraordinarily good
la salsa	lah _sahl_-sah	an African-Cuban rhythm (literally: the sauce)

Enjoying Yourself at Shows and Events

The types of events and shows available in Spain vary depending on where they happen. In villages or small towns, usually the events are related to celebrations of important dates, both private and public. Occasionally a travelling show or circus may pass through a town. Larger cities offer bigger festivals, the latest films, theatres, concerts, literary presentations and readings, and exhibition openings. Some city neighbourhoods, however, also have celebrations like the kind you see in smaller towns.

Here are a couple of phrases to help when you're asking (or are asked) to attend an event:

✔ **Voy a buscarte a las ocho.** *(bohee a boos-kahr-teh ah lahs oh-choh)* (I'll pick you up at eight [literally: I'll go search you at eight].)

✔ **¡Qué pena, hoy no puedo!** *(keh peh-nah oh-ee noh pooeh-doh)* (What a pity, I can't [make it] today!)

Having a healthy battle

Spain is known the world over for its festivals, some of which are quite lively! One of the best-known and most modern Spanish street festivals is called **La Tomatina** *(lah toh-mah-tee-nah)* (the tomato fight), which takes place in **Buñol** *(boo-nyol)* in Valencia province annually on the last Wednesday in August. Being Spain, though, the partying starts earlier in the week! The highlight of the festival is the tomato fight: around 30,000 participants come from all over the world to fight in a harmless battle where more than one hundred metric tonnes of over-ripe tomatoes are thrown in the streets! In preparation for the mess that ensues, shop-keepers cover their windows to protect them from the tomato-carnage of this chaotic event.

The week-long festival features music, parades, dancing and fireworks. On the night before the tomato fight, participants of the festival compete in a **concurso de paellas** *(kohn-koor-soh deh pah-eh-yahs)* (a paella cooking contest).

The event has become one of the highlights of Spain's summer festivals calendar. So many people attend that **La Tomatina** is a victim of its own success. The huge numbers mean that getting anywhere near the central area where the tomato lorries arrive is difficult, and you may find yourself a few streets away from the main action. But never fear – plenty of people are always in the same boat and the street partying goes on no matter where you are.

Talkin' the Talk

María José is trying to get tickets to see Enrique Iglesias (she's been a fan for years).

María José: **Dos entradas para la tarde temprano, por favor.**
dohs ehn-trah-dahs pah-rah lah tahr-deh tehm-prah-noh pohr fah-bohr
Two tickets for the early evening show, please.

Box office attendant: **Las entradas para la tarde están agotadas.**
lahs ehn-trah-dahs pah-rah lah tahr-deh ehs-tahn ah-goh-tah-dahs
The tickets for the early evening show are sold out.

María José: **Dos para la noche, entonces.**
dohs pah-rah lah noh-cheh ehn-tohn-thehs
Two [tickets] for the late evening, then.

Talkin' the Talk

Imagine yourself in town with Carla and Lucas when a circus is playing.

Carla: **¡Dicen que este circo es muy divertido!**
           *dee-thehn keh esh-teh theer-koh ehs mooy
           dee-behr-tee-doh*
           They tell me the circus is really fun!

Lucas: **¡Sí, completamente nuevo!**
           see kohm-pleh-tah-mehn-teh nooeh-boh
           Yes, something completely new!

Carla: **¿Qué tiene de nuevo?**
           keh teeeh-neh deh nooeh-boh
           What's new about it?

Lucas: **Es un circo sólo con gente, no hay animales.**
           *ehs oon theer-koh soh-loh kohn Hehn-teh noh ahee
           ah-nee-mah-lehs*
           It's a circus with just people, no animals.

Carla: **¿Qué es tan especial?**
           keh ehs tahn ehs-peh-theeahl
           What special things does it have?

Lucas: **Trae los mejores magos y payasos.**
           trah-eh lohs meh-Hoh-rehs mah-gohs ee pah-yah-sohs
           It has the best magicians and clowns.

Carla: **¿Qué hacen estos payasos?**
           keh ah-thehn ehs-tohs pah-yah-sohs
           What do the clowns do?

Lucas: **Bromas sobre los políticos.**
           broh-mahs soh-breh lohs poh-lee-tee-kohs
           They joke about [make fun of] politicians.

Carla: **¿Y hay acróbatas?**
           ee ahy ah-kroh-bah-tahs
           And are there acrobats?

Lucas: **¡Los mejores! ¡Vamos!**
           lohs-meh-Hoh-rehs bah-mohs
           Really great ones! Let's go!

Words to Know

agotadas	ah-goh-_tah_-dahs	sold out (tickets)
divertido	dee-behr-_tee_-doh	amusing; funny
la broma	lah _broh_-mah	the joke
la gente	lah _Hehn_-teh	the people
la pena	lah _peh_-nah	sadness; regret
los mejores	lohs meh-_Hoh_-rehs	the best ones

Going to the cinema

Watching films on television is fine, but viewing them in an ultra-modern and well-equipped cinema is even better.

Spain has a great cinematic tradition and produces lots of rich and varied films, although too few make it into UK cinemas. One exception is the films of the director Pedro Almodóvar (_peh_-droh ahl-moh-_doh_-bahr). He had great success in the UK with his film **Hable con ella** (_ah_-bleh kohn _eh_-yah) (_Talk to Her_) and also won the Best Foreign Language Film Oscar award for **Todo sobre mi madre** (_toh_-doh _soh_-breh mee _mah_-dreh) (_All About My Mother_). He took the Best Original Screenplay Oscar for _Talk To Her_, several BAFTA awards and won a best director prize at the Cannes film festival.

Talkin' the Talk

Ana is a new girl in town and Juan wants to spend some time with her and make a good impression. Juan's a film buff, and has an idea.

Juan: **Si quieres, vamos al cine.**
see kee_eh_-rehs _bah_-mohs ahl th_ee_-neh
If you want, we can go to the cinema.

Ana: **¿Hay muchos cines en Valencia?**
ahy _moo_-chohs th_ee_-nehs ehn bah-_lehn_-theeah
Are there many cinemas in Valencia?

Juan:	**Sí, hay muchos cines.** _see ahee moo-chohs thee-nehs_ Yes, there are loads of cinemas.
Ana:	**¿Qué dan hoy?** _keh dahn oh-ee_ What's playing today?
Juan:	**Veamos la cartelera ¡Ah, mira, la versión original de Abrazos rotos!** _beh-ah-mohs lah kahr-teh-leh-rah ah mee-rah lah behr-seeohn oh-ree-Hee-nahl deh ah-brah-thos roh-tohs_ Let's check the listings. Look! The original version of Broken Embraces!
Ana:	**¡Esta película me gusta!** _ehs-tah peh-lee-koo-lah meh goos-tah_ I love that film!

Taking in a show

Researchers have found that people take on information more easily when that information is associated with emotions. And, because an opportunity to explore feelings is what lures people to films, shows and the theatre, these places are perfect for absorbing a new language.

Talkin' the Talk

Going to the theatre may involve a conversation similar to this one.

Marcos:	**¿Te gusta ir al teatro?** _teh goos-tah eer ahl teh-ah-troh_ Do you like going to the theatre?
Luisa:	**Sí, ¡dan la obra de un dramaturgo de Ibiza!** _see dahn lah oh-brah deh oon drah-mah-toor-goh deh ee-bee-thah_ Yes, they're doing a piece by a playwright from Ibiza.
Marcos:	**Tuvo muy buena crítica.** _too-boh mooy booeh-nah kree-tee-kah_ It got very good reviews.

Luisa: **Los actores son excelentes.**
lohs ahk-toh-rehs sohn ehks-theh-lehn-tehs
The actors are excellent.

Marcos: **El teatro es bastante pequeño.**
ehl teh-ah-troh ehs bahs-tahn-teh peh-keh-nyo
The theatre's quite small.

Luisa: **Tenemos que comprar las entradas pronto.**
*teh-neh-mohs keh kohm-prahr lahs ehn-trah-dahs
prohn-toh*
We better buy the tickets soon.

Marcos: **¿En qué fila te gusta?**
ehn keh fee-lah teh goos-tah
What row would you prefer?

Luisa: **Para el teatro prefiero estar adelante.**
*pah-rah ehl teh-ah-troh preh-feeeh-roh ehs-tahr
ah-deh-lahn-teh*
For a play, I prefer to be near the front.

Marcos: **Intentaré encontrar buenas butacas.**
*een-tehn-tah-reh ehn-kohn-trahr booeh-nahs
boo-tah-kahs*
I'll try to find good seats.

Words to Know

el actor	ehl ahk-tohr	the actor
la actriz	lah ahk-treeth	the actress
adelante	ah-deh-lahn-teh	in front; ahead
bastante	bahs-tahn-teh	quite; enough
las butacas	lahs boo-tah-kahs	the seats
la fila	lah fee-lah	the row; the line; the line-up
la obra	lah oh-brah	the play (literally: the work)
pronto	prohn-toh	soon

Visiting art galleries and museums

Numerous exhibitions by famous and up-and-coming Spanish artists appear all the time. In Spain, exhibitions take place in museums and in public and private art galleries. Great artists may be featured – people whose works sell for enormous amounts at art auctions. One such artist is the unique modern Valencian sculptor and architect Santiago Calatrava – one of the world's foremost structural engineers and designers.

Laughing at a comedy show

Comedy shows may be an idea imported from the UK and America, but good comedy is now enjoyed in every part of Spain. Going to see stand-up comedy is always a great opportunity for meeting up with friends. This lively form of entertainment is becoming ever more popular, and most Spanish cities now have comedy clubs.

Talkin' the Talk

In the following conversation, Raúl and Elena set a date to see stand-up comedians.

Raúl: **¿Te apetece ir a ver a los cómicos de moda, Gomaespuma?**
teh ah-peh-_teh_-theh eer ah behr ah lohs _koh_-mee-kohs deh _moh_-dah goh-mah-ehs-_poo_-mah
Would you like to come to watch the latest comedian: Gomaespuma?

Elena: **¿Cuándo?**
koo_ahn_-doh
When?

Raúl: **Hoy. En el Teatro Esfinge. Tengo dos entradas.**
ohee ehn ehl teh-_ah_-troh ehs-_feen_-Heh _tehn_-goh dohs ehn-_trah_-dahs
Today. At the Sphinx Theatre. I have two tickets.

Elena: **Me gusta la idea.**
meh _goos_-tah lah ee-_deh_-ah
Great idea [I like the idea].

Raúl: **Dicen que son muy buenos humoristas.**
dee-thehn keh sohn mooy _booeh_-nohs ooh-moh-_reehs_-tahs
They say they are great comedians.

Elena:	**Sí, y tienen muy buena reputación.**
	see ee teeeh-nehn mooy booeh-nah
	reh-poo-tah-theeohn
	Yes, and they've had very good reviews.

Raúl:	**Cuentan historias de sus vidas en Londres como españoles.**
	kooehn-tahn eehs-toh-ree-ahs deh oohs bee-dahs ehn lohn-drehs koo-moo ehs-pah-nyoh-lehs
	They are telling stories of their lives as Spanish guys in London.

Words to Know

buenos	*booeh-nohs*	good [masculine and plural]
las histórias	*lahs ees-toh-ree-ahs*	the stories/histories
hoy	*ohee*	today
reputación	*reh-poo-tah-theeohn*	reputation, reviews
sus vidas	*soos bee-dahs*	their lives

Launching a book

Book launches and readings draw attention to a recent publication and the public can often attend the latter for free.

Talkin' the Talk

The book mentioned in this discussion is a photography book by an author best known for having another role!

Leticia:	**En la biblioteca central van a presentar un nuevo libro.**
	ehn lah bee-bleeoh-teh-kah thehn-trahl bahn ah preh-sehn-tahr oon nooeh-boh lee-broh
	The central library is going to have a new book launching.

Mario:	**¿Qué libro es?**
	keh lee-broh ehs
	What book is it?

Leticia:	**Es un libro de fotos del Rey Don Juan Carlos.**
	ehs oon lee-broh deh foh-tohs dehl reh-ee dohn
	Hooahn kahr-lohs
	It's a book of photos about King Juan Carlos.

Mario:	**¿Cómo lo sabes?**
	koh-moh loh sah-behs
	How do you know?

Leticia:	**Lo ví en un cartel ayer. Es entrada libre**
	loh bee ehn oon kahr-tehl ah-yehr ehs ehn-trah-dah
	lee-breh
	I saw a poster yesterday. It's free admission.

Mario:	**¿De quién son las fotos?**
	deh keeehn sohn lahs foh-tohs
	Who took the photos?

Leticia:	**¡Del mismo rey!**
	dehl mees-moh reh-ee
	The king himself!

Mario:	**¡Maravilloso!**
	mah-rah-bee-yoh-soh
	Wonderful!

Words to Know

la biblioteca	lah bee-bleeoh-teh-kah	the library
el libro	ehl lee-broh	the book
libre	lee-breh	free of charge
maravilloso	mah-rah-bee-yoh-soh	wonderful

Singing For Your Supper: Cantar

Cantar *(kahn-tahr)* (to sing) is a regular verb (praise be!), and its root is **cant-**
(kahnt). Here's how to conjugate it in the present tense:

Conjugation	*Pronunciation*
yo canto	*yoh kahn-toh*
tú cantas	*too kahn-tahs*
él, **ella**, **usted canta**	*ehl, eh-yah, oos-tehd kahn-tah*
nosotros cantamos	*noh-soh-trohs kahn-tah-mohs*
vosotros cantáis	*boh-soh-trohs kahn-tahees*
ellos, **ellas**, **ustedes cantan**	*eh-yohs, eh-yahs, oos-teh-dehs kahn-than*

Talkin' the Talk

How exciting! Your favourite singer is coming to town in person.

Claudia: **¿Sabes si viene a cantar Enrique Iglesias?**
sah-behs see beeeh-neh ah kahn-tahr Ehn-rree-keh
ee-gleh-seeahs
Do you know if Enrique Iglesias is coming to sing?

Pedro: **Quizás. ¡Lo anuncian mucho!**
kee-thahs loh ah-noon-theeahn moo-choh
Maybe. They're advertising him a lot!

Claudia: **Sí, pero espero que no lo va a cancelar.**
see peh-roh ehs-peh-roh keh noh loh bah ah
kahn-theh-lahr
Yes, but I hope he's not going to cancel.

Talkin' the Talk

Sometimes you're lucky enough to know the people playing your
favourite music. In this case, Héctor and Edu are familiar with the
musicians giving a concert.

Héctor: **Sabes, mañana dan un concierto de violín y piano.**
sah-behs mah-nyah-nah dahn oon kohn-theeehr-toh
de bee-oh-leen ee peeah-noh

You know, tomorrow there's going to be a violin and piano concert.

Edu: **¿Quiénes tocan?**
keeeh-nehs toh-kahn
Who's playing?

Héctor: **Nuestros amigos: Luisa y Fernando.**
nooehs-trohs ah-mee-gohs looee-sah ee fehr-nahn-doh
Our friends Luisa and Fernando.

Edu: **¿Cuál es el programa?**
kooahl ehs ehl proh-grah-mah
What's the programme?

Héctor: **Unas piezas españolas de Andrés Segovia y de Manuel de Falla.**
oo-nahs pee-eh-thahs ehs-pah-nyo-lahs de ahn-drehs seh-goh-beeah ee deh mah-noohehl deh fah-yah
Some Spanish pieces by Andrés Segovia and by Manuel de Falla.

Edu: **¿Invitamos a María?**
een-bee-tah-mohs ah mah-ree-ah
Shall we invite Maria?

Héctor: **Claro, ella también toca el piano.**
klah-roh eh-yah tahm-beeehn toh-kah ehl peeah-noh
Sure, she plays the piano, too.

Words to Know

anunciar	ah-noon-theeahr	to advertise; to announce
cancelar	kahn-theh-lahr	to cancel
el cantante	ehl kahn-tahn-teh	the singer (a male one)
el programa	ehl proh-grah-mah	the programme
las piezas	lahs peeeh-thahs	the pieces (musical ones)

Fun & Games

· ·

We have good news and bad news for you. The good news is that you and several of your friends are leaving next week for a whirlwind vacation. The bad news is that you have to plan fun, group activities – in Spanish – for the entire week. Use the chart below to help organise your itinerary. For each day of the week, fill in what you're going to do and who you expect to meet. To keep your friends from complaining, try not to plan the same activity twice.

Day	What You're Going To Do	Who You Plan To See
lunes	_____	_____
martes	_____	_____
miércoles	_____	_____
jueves	_____	_____
viernes	_____	_____
sábado	_____	_____
domingo	_____	_____

· ·

Chapter 8

Enjoying Yourself: Recreation

In This Chapter

▶ Walking around the great outdoors

▶ Naming plants and animals

▶ Experiencing sports and other pastimes

▶ Doing what you like to do

*O*utdoor recreation is a large part of the Spanish lifestyle. You probably know many Spanish sporting figures such as Fernando Alonso from Formula One, the golfer Seve Ballesteros and **fútbol** *(foot-bohl)* (football) player Raúl.

As well as energising and inspiring you into action, being outdoors can also promote a quiet, contemplative feeling as you appreciate the beauty of nature. In this chapter, we deal with both the sporty and contemplative aspects of outdoor recreation as well as examining some less-energetic indoor pursuits.

Venturing Outdoors: The Good and the Bad

In Spanish, you can express the idea of going outdoors in two ways:

✔ **al aire libre** *(ahl ahee-reh lee-breh)* (in the open air). You use this phrase when you're talking about going out to the street – to bars and cafés – to the **parque** *(pahr-keh)* (public garden), fields or just **pasear** *(pah-seh-ahr)* (taking a walk). The phrase implies a feeling of openness and liberty.

✔ **a la intemperie** *(ah lah een-tehm-peh-reeeh)* (out of doors, a little 'less appealing', exposed to the elements [literally: in the unheated space]). This phrase implies that you're going to be without a roof nearby and therefore may suffer or enjoy whatever weather you find. **A la intemperie** gives a feeling of exposure and perhaps less safety.

The following examples can help you determine which phrase to use:

- ✔ **Voy a nadar en una piscina al aire libre.** *(bohee ah nah-dahr ehn oo-nah pees-thee-nah ahl ahee-reh lee-breh)* (I'm going to swim in an outdoor pool.)

- ✔ **No dejes las plantas a la intemperie.** *(noh deh-Hehs lahs plahn-tahs ah lah een-tehm-peh-reeeh)* (Don't leave the plants out in the open.)

Strolling Along: *Pasear*

In some Spanish towns or seaside resorts, **pasear** *(pah-seh-ahr)* (to walk; to stroll) is a national pastime.

The verb **pasear** has many applications, and usefully it's a regular verb. The root is **pase-** *(pah-seh)*. Here's how to conjugate its present tense:

Conjugation	*Pronunciation*
yo paseo	*yoh pah-seh-oh*
tú paseas	*too pah-seh-ahs*
él, ella, usted pasea	*ehl, eh-yah, oos-tehd pah-seh-ah*
nosotros paseamos	*noh-soh-trohs pah-seh-ah-mohs*
vosotros paseáis	*boh-soh-trohs pah-seh-ahees*
ellos, ellas, ustedes pasean	*eh-yohs, eh-yahs, oos-teh-dehs pah-seh-ahn*

Take the following phrases for a stroll:

- ✔ **Salimos a dar un paseo.** *(sah-lee-mohs ah dahr oon pah-seh-oh)* (We go for a walk.)

- ✔ **Mi abuela pasea todas las tardes.** *(mee ah-booeh-lah pah-seh-ah toh-dahs lahs tahr-dehs)* (My grandmother goes for a walk every afternoon.)

- ✔ **¿Quieres pasear conmigo?** *(keeeh-rehs pah-seh-ahr kohn-mee-goh)* (Would you go for a walk with me?)

- ✔ **Vivo en Alicante, aquí paseamos por el puerto.** *(bee-boh ehn ah-lee-kahn-teh ah-kee pah-sehah-mos pohr ehl pooehr-toh)* (I live in Alicante, where we like strolling along the port area.)

Talkin' the Talk

During a walk, Andrés and Luz talk about what they like to do.

Andrés: **De todos los paseos me gusta más el de montaña.**
*deh toh-dohs lohs pah-seh-ohs meh goos-tah mahs
ehl deh mohn-tah-nyah*
Of all kinds of walks, I prefer mountain ones.

Luz: **¿Eres alpinista?**
eh-rehs ahl-pee-nees-tah
Are you a mountaineer?

Andrés: **No, alpinista no, pero me gusta trepar.**
*noh ahl-pee-nees-tah noh peh-roh meh goos-tah
treh-pahr*
No, not a mountaineer, but I love to climb.

Appreciating Trees and Plants

Walking about in the open and enjoying the trees and plants go hand-in-hand. Following are some phrases you can use to describe such experiences:

- ✔ **Ayer paseamos por la alameda.** *(ah-yehr pah-seh-ah-mohs pohr lah ah-lah-meh-dah)* (Yesterday we walked along the poplar grove.)

- ✔ **Hay robles y cipreses.** *(ah-ee roh-blehs ee thee-preh-sehs)* (There are oaks and cypresses.)

- ✔ **Esa palmera da dátiles.** *(eh-sah pahl-meh-rah dah dah-tee-lehs)* (That palm tree produces dates.)

- ✔ **En Extremadura crecen muchos eucaliptos.** *(ehn ehks-treh-mah-dooh-rah kreh-thehn moo-chohs ehoo-kah-leep-tos)* (Many eucalyptus trees grow in Extremadura.)

Searching Out Animals

In this section, we talk about some Spanish animals, and the first that comes to mind is the black and brave **el toro** *(ehl toh-roh)* (the bull) and his partner **la vaca** *(lah bah-kah)* (the cow). These creatures come from the same family as cattle, and you see them mostly in the northern regions around the mountains – from Galicia to the País Vasco. If you're lucky, you may also spot

Iberian **linces** *(leen-thehs)* (lynxes) – wild mountain cats, very much in danger of extinction. **Linces** are beautiful to see in the wild, but please keep out of their way!

You're more likely, however, to see lovely **caballos españoles** *(kah-bah-yohs ehs-pah-nyoh-lehs)* (Spanish horses), a few **burros** *(boo-rrohs)* (donkeys) and **aves** *(ah-behs)* (birds) of all kinds – including the grand **águila** *(ah-gee-lah)* (eagle), the beautiful **cigüeña** *(thee-gooeh-nya)* (stork) and the voluptuous **vuitre negro** *(boo-eh-treh neh-groh)* (black vulture) – in the **Parque Nacional de Monfragüe** *(pahr-kee nah-thee-oh-nahl deh mohn-frah-gooeh)* (the forests of the national park of Monfragüe) in southwest Spain.

The Spanish islands of **Canarias** *(kah-nah-ree-ahs)* (the Canary Islands) and **Baleares** *(bah-leh-ah-rehs)* (the Balearics) retain their unique fauna and flora, the former in a volcanic environment and the latter of a Mediterranean kind. Also, **flamencos** *(flah-mehn-kohs)* (flamingos) stand and move around freely in **Coto de Doñana** *(koh-toh deh doh-nyah-nah)*, a stunning national park in the south of Andalucía, and you see **gatos** *(gah-tohs)* (cats) and **perros** *(peh-rrohs)* (dogs) everywhere, which are popular as pets.

The following phrases get you started talking about animals while you observe them:

- **En el paseo ví ardillas.** *(ehn ehl pah-seh-oh bee ahr-dee-yahs)* (During my walk I saw squirrels.)

- **Los toros están comiendo al aire libre.** *(lohs too-rohs ehs-tahn coh-meeehn-doh ahl ahee-reh lee-breh)* (The bulls are eating in the open field.)

- **En la playa vemos gaviotas.** *(ehn lah plah-yah beh-mohs gah-beeoh-tahs)* (At the beach, we see seagulls.)

- **En el centro hay muchas palomas.** *(ehn ehl thehn-troh ahy moo-chahs pah-loh-mahs)* (Many pigeons are in the centre of town.)

- **Los gorriones se ven en los pueblos.** *(lohs goh-rreeoh-nehs seh behn ehn lohs pooeh-blohs)* (Sparrows are seen in the villages.)

- **Voy a pasear los perros.** *(bohee ah pah-seh-ahr lohs peh-rrohs)* (I'm going to walk the dogs.)

- **Van a una carrera de caballos.** *(bahn ah oo-nah kah-rreh-rah deh kah-bah-yohs)* (They're going to a horse race.)

- **La burra del santuario tuvo un burrito.** *(lah boo-rrah dehl sahn-tuhah-reeoh too-boh oon boo-rree-toh)* (The sanctuary's [female] donkey had given birth to a little [baby] donkey.)

- **Hay conejos en casi todo el campo.** *(ah-ee koh-neh-Hohs ehn kah-see toh-doh ehl kahm-poh)* (Almost all the countryside has rabbits.)

We'd need a whole book to talk about animals in detail, but here are a few more examples:

- **El cerro estaba cubierto de mariposas.** *(ehl theh-rroh ehs-tah-bah koo-beeehr-toh deh mah-ree-poh-sahs)* (The hill was covered with butterflies.)

- **Paseando ví una manada de vacas.** *(pah-seh-ahn-doh bee oo-nah mah-nah-dah deh bah-kahs)* (While walking, I saw a herd of cows.)

- **Andamos con unos perros.** *(ahn-dah-mohs kohn oo-nohs peh-rrohs)* (We walk along with some dogs.)

- **Cuando pasé me perseguían unos gatos.** *(kooahn-doh pah-seh meh pehr-seh-gheeahn oo-nohs gah-tohs)* (As I went by, the cats chased me.)

- **En el lago vimos patos silvestres.** *(ehn ehl lah-goh bee-mohs pah-tohs seel-behs-trehs)* (We saw wild ducks in the lake.)

- **Una señora ¡paseaba un gato!** *(oo-nah seh-nyoh-rah pah-seh-ah-bah oon gah-toh)* (A lady was walking a [male] cat!)

- **La niña llevaba una gatita.** *(lah nee-nyah yeh-bah-bah oo-nah gah-tee-tah)* (The girl was carrying a [female] kitten.)

Words to Know

el aguila	ehl *ah*-gee-lah	the eagle
el lince	ehl *leen*-theh	the Iberian lynx [wild cat]
el toro	ehl *toh*-roh	the bull
la burra	lah *boo*-rrah	the [female] donkey
la gatatita	lah gah-*tee*-tah	the [female] kitten

Talkin' the Talk

The wonderful sport of horseback riding calls for harmony between horse and rider and allows the rider to enjoy the landscape, as Maria explains to Luz.

Maria: **Me encanta ir a caballo.**
meh ehn-kahn-tah eer ah kah-bah-yoh
I love riding a horse [literally: riding a horse enchants or delights me.]

Luz:	**¿Te preparas para algún torneo?**
	teh preh-pah-rahs pah-rah ahl-goon tohr-neh-oh
	Are you preparing for a competition?

Maria:	**No, simplemente me gusta el hecho de montar.**
	noh seem-pleh-mehn-teh meh goos-tah ehl eh-choh deh mohn-tahr
	No, I simply enjoy riding.

Luz:	**¿Tienes tu propio caballo?**
	teeeh-nehs too proh-pee-oh kah-bah-yoh
	Do you have your own horse?

Maria:	**Sí, tengo una yegua. Se llama Lirio.**
	see tehn-goh oo-nah yeh-gooah seh yah-mah lee-reeoh
	Yes, I have a mare. Her name is Lirio [Lilly].

Luz:	**¡Debe ser blanca!**
	deh-beh sehr blahn-kah
	She must be white!

Maria:	**Es blanca y tiene una mancha café en la frente.**
	ehs blahn-kah ee teeeh-neh oo-nah mahn-chah kah-feh ehn lah frehn-teh
	She's white and has a brown spot on her forehead.

Words to Know

el caballo	ehl kah-bah-yoh	the horse
encantar	ehn-kahn-tahr	to enchant; to be delighted by
gozar	goh-thahr	to enjoy
la mancha	lah mahn-chah	the stain; the spot
preparar	preh-pah-rahr	to prepare
propio	proh-peeoh	[one's] own
torneo	tohr-neh-oh	competition; tournament
la yegua	lah yeh-gooah	the mare

Saying What You Like: Gustar

When you talk about liking something in Spanish, you use the reflexive verb form. The action, in this case, is **gustar** *(goos-tahr)* (to like; to enjoy) – flip to Chapter 7 for more examples of using **gustar**).

Conjugation	Pronunciation
me gusta	*meh goos-tah*
te gusta	*teh goos-tah*
le gusta	*leh goos-tah*
nos gusta	*nohs goos-tah*
os gusta	*ohs goos-tah*
les gusta	*lehs goos-tah*

The following expressions can help you express what you like:

- **Me gusta pasear.** *(meh goos-tah pah-seh-ahr)* (I love to walk.)

- **Ven cuando gustes.** *(behn kooahn-doh goos-tehs)* (Come whenever you like.)

- **A él le gusta jugar con el gato.** *(ah ehl leh goos-tah Hoo-gahr kohn ehl gah-toh)* (He likes to play with the cat.)

- **¿Te gusta comer paella?** *(teh goos-tah koh-mehr pah-eh-yah)* (Do you enjoy eating paella?)

Becoming Active with Sport

Sport is a favourite recreational activity among the Spanish, and a great way of enjoying yourself and having fun. What's more, joining in and playing a game with other people can be a great way of practising and picking up more Spanish terms and phrases.

Playing with the verb jugar

Jugar *(Hoo-gahr)* (to play) is a slightly irregular verb, but a very playful and useful one, nonetheless – definitely worth the effort.

Conjugation	Pronunciation
yo juego	*yoh Hooeh-goh*
tú juegas	*too Hooeh-gahs*
él, **ella**, **usted juega**	*ehl*, *eh-yah*, *oos-tehd Hooeh-gah*
nosotros jugamos	*noh-soh-trohs Hoo-gah-mohs*
vosotros jugáis	*boh-soh-trohs Hoo-gah-ees*
ellos, **ellas**, **ustedes juegan**	*eh-yohs*, *eh-yahs*, *oos-teh-dehs Hooeh-gahn*

Practising your game a little is always worthwhile. Here are two phrases that can help when you play:

- ✔ **¿Jugamos baloncesto hoy?** *(Hoo-gah-mohs bah-lohn-thehs-toh ohee)* (Shall we play basketball today?)

- ✔ **¡Juegas mejor que hace un mes!** *(Hooeh-gahs meh-Hohr keh ah-theh oon mehs)* (You're playing better than a month ago!)

Enjoying the 'beautiful game': Fútbol

Fútbol *(foot-bohl)* (football) is one of the most popular sports in Spain and the talk of cafés, bars, offices and living rooms; its stars are national heroes and some coaches household names! We dare say that more talk takes place about **fútbol** in the workplaces of Spain than about anything else!

The quality of Spanish **fútbol** is recognised the world over. Even if you're not a fan of the game, escaping the lingo is nigh on impossible.

Talkin' the Talk

Carla and Pedro talk shop about their favourite sport, football.

Pedro: **Me divierte ver jugar al fútbol.**
meh dee-beeehr-teh behr Hoo-gahr ahl foot-bohl
I enjoy watching football [literally: it amuses me to see football being played].

Carla: **¿Adónde vas a verlo?**
ah-dohn-deh bahs a behr-loh
Where do you go to watch it?

Pedro: **Voy al estadio Bernabeu, donde juega el Real Madrid.**
bohee ahl ehs-tah-deeoh behr-nah-behoo dohn-deh
Hooeh-gah ehl reh-ahl mah-dreed
I go to the Bernabeu stadium, where Real Madrid
play.

Carla: **¿Eres hincha del Real Madrid?**
eh-rehs een-chah dehl reh-ahl mah-dreed
Are you a Real Madrid fan?

Pedro: **Sí, hace muchos años.**
see ah-theh moo-chohs ah-nyohs
Yes, for many years.

Carla: **¿Qué jugadores te gustan?**
keh Hoo-gah-doh-rehs teh goos-tahn
Which players do you like?

Pedro: **Siempre he preferido los de la defensa.**
seeehm-preh eh preh-feh-ree-doh lohs deh lah
deh-fehn-sah
I've always preferred those who play defence.

Carla: **¿Y no te gustan los centrodelanteros?**
ee noh teh goos-tahn lohs
thehn-troh-deh-lahn-teh-rohs
You don't like the centre-forwards?

Pedro: **Sí, pero creo que la defensa tiene un papel muy
especial.**
see peh-roh kreh-oh keh lah deh-fehn-sah teeeh-neh
oon pah-pehl mooy ehs-peh-theeahl
Yes, but I feel the defence has a very special role.

Words to Know

el campo	ehl _kahm_-poh	the playing field [literally 'the field']
el defensa	ehl deh-_fehn_-sah	the defence
los delanteros	lohs deh-lahn-_teh_-rohs	the forwards
divertir	dee-behr-_teer_	to amuse
el equipo	ehl eh-_kee_-poh	the team
el estadio	ehl ehs-_tah_-deeoh)	the stadium
ganar	gah-_nahr_	to win
el gol	ehl gohl	the goal
el hincha	ehl _een_-chah	the fan [hincha (een-_chahr_) means to inflate or bloat]
el jugador	ehl Hoo-gah-_dohr_	the player
el papel	ehl pah-_pehl_	the role [literally, the paper]
el portero	ehl pohr-_teh_-roh	the goalkeeper [puerta (_pooehr_-tah) means door]

Zoning in on basketball

El baloncesto _(ehl bah-lohn-thehs-toh)_ (basketball) is possibly the second most important ball game (after **fútbol**) in Spain. As with **fútbol**, Spain has an excellent track record at this sport, with some Spanish players even playing in the prestigious North American NBA (National Basketball Association).

Talkin' the Talk

In the following conversation, Emilio and Anabel, two avid fans, discuss a recent basketball match.

Emilio: **Ese chico corre y tira de maravilla.**
           *eh-seh chee-koh coh-rreh ee tee-rah deh
           mah-rah-bee-yah*
           That boy's a wonder at running and scoring.

Anabel: **Hizo una carrera estupenda a la canasta.**
           *ee-thoh oo-nah kah-rreh-rah ehs-too-pehn-dah ah lah
           kah-nahs-tah*
           He had an amazing run to the basket.

Emilio: **No podía creerlo cuando llegó a la canasta. . .**
           *noh poh-dee-ah kreh-ehr-loh kooahn-doh yeh-goh ah
           lah kah-nahs-tah*
           I couldn't believe when he made it to the basket. . .

           . . .¡y antes también tiró desde tan lejos!
           *ee ahn-tehs tahm-beeehn tee-roh dehs-deh tahn
           leh-Hohs*
           . . .and also, earlier he threw the ball [to the basket]
           from so far away!

Anabel: **¡Este jugador merece un fuerte aplauso!**
           *ehs-the hoo-gah-dohr meh-reh-theh oon fooehr-teh
           ah-plah-oo-soh*
           That player deserves a huge [round of] applause!

Words to Know

la canasta	lah kah-nahs-tah	the basket]
la carrera	lah kah-rreh-rah	the run, the race
tirar	tee-rahr	to throw [the ball]

Serving up tennis

Many young Spaniards have reached the top ranks of professional tennis. For example, the great **Rafa Nadal** (*rah-fah nah-dahl*) has won many titles and an Olympic gold medal. **Carlos Moya** (*kahr-lohs moh-yah*), **Juan Carlos Ferrero** (*Hoo-ahn kahr-lohs feh-rreh-roh*) and **Sergi Bruguera** (*sehr-gee broo-geh-rah*) are other famous Spanish tennis players.

Talkin' the Talk

In this conversation, Lola and Enrique arrange to play a game of tennis.

Lola:	**¡Mañana vamos a jugar al tenis!**
	mah-nyah-nah bah-mohs a Hoo-gahr ahl teh-nees
	Tomorrow we're going to play tennis!
Enrique:	**¿Juegas a menudo con otros?**
	Hooeh-gahs ah meh-noo-doh kohn oh-trohs
	Do you play with other [players] often?
Lola:	**Sí, practico todos los días.**
	see prahk-tee-koh toh-dohs lohs dee-ahs
	Yes, I practise every day.
Enrique:	**Compré una raqueta muy buena recientemente.**
	kohm-preh oo-nah rah-keh-tah mooy boo-eh-nah reh-thee-ehn-teh-mehn-teh
	I bought a very good racket recently.
Lola:	**¿Hacemos un juego de dos horas?**
	ah-theh-mohs oon Hooeh-goh deh dohs oh-rahs
	Shall we play a two-hour game?

Words to Know

juego	Hoo-eh-goh	the set
la pista	lah pees-tah	the court
la raqueta	lah rah-keh-tah	the racket

Getting on your bike

Spanish professional and competitive road cycling is currently enjoying a high profile. Taking **vacaciones de ciclismo** *(bah-cah-theeoh-nehs deh thee-clees-moh)* (cycling holidays) in Spain offers you the chance feel the freedom yourself , to get out there and explore the country. Being on a bike enables you to venture into areas off the beaten track that are only now being discovered by the tourist industry.

Talkin' the Talk

Fernando and Marta are discussing their friend Angel, who's training for the Tour de France bicycle race.

Fernando: **Angel practica el ciclismo.**
Ahn-Hehl prahk-tee-kah ehl thee-klees-moh
Angel [as a male name] goes cycling.

Mata: **¿Tiene una bicicleta de montaña?**
teeeh-neh oo-nah bee-thee-kleh-tah deh mohn-tah-nyah
Does he have a mountain bike?

Fernando: **No, usa una bicicleta de carreras.**
noh oo-sah oo-nah bee-thee-kleh-tah deh kah-rreh-rahs
No, he uses a racing bike.

Marta: **¿Participa en concursos?**
pahr-tee-thee-pah ehn kohn-koor-sohs
Does he take part in competitions?

Fernando: **Sí, la semana pasada estuvo en una carrera.**
see lah seh-mah-nah pah-sah-dah ehs-too-boh ehn oo-nah kah-rreh-rah
Yes, he was in a race last week.

Marta: **¿Qué posición obtuvo?**
keh poh-see-theeohn ohb-too-boh
How did he do?

Fernando: **Llegó segundo.**
yeh-goh seh-goon-doh
He came in second.

Words to Know

la bicicleta	lah bee-thee-_kleh_-tah	the bicycle
la carrera	lah kah-_rreh_-rah	the race
de carreras	deh kah-_rreh_-rahs	racing bicycle
el ciclismo	ehl thee-_klees_-moh	cycling
la montaña	lah mohn-_tah_-nyah	the mountain

Splashing About: Nadar

Water, water, everywhere – inviting you to jump right in. Before you do, how-ever, you need to know how to conjugate the verb **nadar** (_nah-dahr_) (to swim). Fortunately, **nadar** is a regular verb and therefore doing so is easy; its root is **nad-** (_nahd_).

Conjugation	Pronunciation
yo nado	_yoh nah-doh_
tú nadas	_too nah-dahs_
él, ella, usted nada	_ehl, eh-yah, oos-tehd nah-dah_
nosotros nadamos	_noh-soh-trohs nah-dah-mohs_
vosotros nadáis	_boh-soh-trohs nah-dahees_
ellos, ellas, ustedes nadan	_eh-yohs, eh-yahs, oos-teh-dehs nah-dahn_

The following phrases help you to practise your swimming, for just a couple of laps:

✔ **Carlos nada como un pez.** (_kahr-lohs nah-dah koh-moh oon pehth_) (Carlos swims like a fish.)

✔ **Yo no sé nadar.** (_yoh noh seh nah-dahr_) (I can't swim.)

Swimming pun

Take a look at the following Spanish pun:

¿No nada nada? *(noh nah-dah nah-dah)* (Aren't you swimming at all?)

No traje traje. *(noh trah-Heh trah-Heh)* (No, I didn't bring [my] swimsuit.)

This pun is based on the double play of the words **nada** *(nah-dah)* and **traje** *(trah-Heh)*. **Nada** means both the third person of the verb **nadar** *(nah-dahr)* (to swim) and 'nothing', and **traje** can be the past tense of the verb **traer** *(trah-ehr)* (to bring) as well as meaning 'suit'.

Talkin' the Talk

Luisa likes to swim, and she wants to compete against Antonio. But first she needs to find out how good a swimmer he is.

Luisa: **¿Cuándo vas a nadar?**
kooahn-doh bahs ah nah-dahr
When do you go swimming?

Antonio: **Los martes y los viernes.**
lohs mahr-tehs ee lohs beeehr-nehs
Tuesdays and Fridays.

Luisa: **¿Qué estilo nadas?**
keh ehs-tee-loh nah-dahs
What style do you swim?

Antonio: **Nado principalmente mariposa.**
nah-doh preen-thee-pahl-mehn-teh mah-ree-poh-sah
I swim mainly breaststroke style.

Luisa: **¿Sabes nadar crol?**
sah-behs nah-dahr krohl
Do you know how to swim the crawl?

Antonio: **Sí, y también de espalda.**
see ee tahm-beeehn deh ehs-pahl-dah
Yes, and the backstroke.

Luisa: **¿Cuánto nadas?**
kooahn-toh nah-dahs
How far do you swim?

Antonio:	**Nado un kilómetro cada vez.**
	nah-doh oon kee-_loh_-meh-troh _kah_-dah behth
	I swim one kilometre each time.
Luisa:	**¡Que bien!**
	_keh bee_ehn
	Very good!

Words to Know

el estilo	_ehl ehs-tee-loh_	the style
el estilo crol	_ehl ehs-tee-loh krohl_	the crawl
el estilo espalda	_ehl ehs-tee-loh ehs-pahl-dah_	the backstroke
el estilo mariposa	_ehl ehs-tee-loh mah-ree-poh-sah_	the breaststroke

Checking Out Chess

Chess can be a fascinating game to watch or play and has been popular in Spain since the Arab invasion way back in the year 711. In fact, some of the terms used in chess come from a combination of Arabic and Spanish words. 'Checkmate', for example, is derived from the Arabic word **sheik** (_sheek_) (king) and the Spanish word **matar** (_mah-tahr_) (to kill). That's why you say 'checkmate' when the king is captured at the end of the game.

Talkin' the Talk

In this conversation, Gaby and Carmela discuss a chess tournament in Spain.

Carmela:	**¿También juegas al ajedrez?**
	_tahm-bee_ehn _Hoo_eh_-gahs ahl ah-Heh-dreth_
	Do you also play chess?

Gaby: **Sí, ayer estuve en una competición.**
see ah-yehr ehs-too-beh ehn oo-nah
kohm-peh-tee-theeohn
Yes, I was in a contest yesterday.

Carmela: **¿Quién ganó?**
keeehn gah-noh
Who won?

Gaby: **Pedro. Dió jaquemate en sólo diez movidas.**
peh-droh deeoh Hah-keh-mah-teh ehn soh-loh
deeeth moh-bee-dahs
Pedro. He checkmated [his opponent] in only ten
moves.

Words to Know

el ajedrez	ehl ah-Heh-drehth	chess
el jaquemate	ehl Hah-keh-mah-teh	checkmate

Booking in Some Reading Time: Leer

Reading is a real pleasure. Here's how to conjugate the verb that helps you
talk about reading in Spanish – **leer** *(leh-ehr)* (to read):

Conjugation	Pronunciation
yo leo	*yoh leh-oh*
tú lees	*too leh-ehs*
él, ella, usted lee	*ehl, eh-yah, oos-tehd leh-eh*
nosotros leemos	*noh-soh-trohs leh-eh-mohs*
vosotros leéis	*boh-soh-trohs leh-ehees*
ellos, ellas, ustedes leen	*eh-yohs, eh-yahs, oos-teh-dehs leh-ehn*

Obviously you're a great reader, and so try out the following couple of ways to speak about reading:

- ✔ **Felipe lee todo el día.** *(feh-lee-peh leh-eh toh-doh ehl deeah)* (Felipe reads all day long.)

- ✔ **A mí me gusta leer revistas.** *(ah mee meh goos-tah leh-ehr reh-bees-tahs)* (I like to read magazines.)

Talkin' the Talk

Marisa and Ana are discussing reading material.

Marisa: **¿Qué vas a leer?**
keh bahs ah leh-ehr
What are you going to read?

Ana: **Yo . . . una novela.**
yoh oo-nah noh-beh-lah
Me . . . a novel.

Marisa: **Estoy entusiasmada con las biografías.**
ehs-tohee ehn-too-seeahs-mah-dah kohn lahs beeoh-grah-fee-ahs
I'm passionate about biographies.

Ana: **Hablando de biografías. . .**
ah-blahn-doh deh beeoh-grah-fee-ahs
Speaking of biographies. . .

. . .**¿sabes que va a salir un libro sobre Pedro Vázquez?**
sah-behs keh bah ah sah-leer oon lee-broh soh-breh peh-droh bath-kehth
. . .did you know that there's going to be a book about Pedro Vázquez?

Marisa: **¿Quién, el escritor español?**
keeehn ehl ehs-cree-torh ehs-pah-nyohl
Who, the Spanish writer?

Ana: **Sí, ¡dicen que es buenísimo!**
see dee-thehn keh ehs boo-eh-nee-see-moh
Yes, they say it's going to be exceptional!

Scribbling Away: Escribir

The writing verb **escribir** *(ehs-kree-beer)* (to write) is a regular one and its root is **escrib-** *(ehs-kreeb)*. Here's how you conjugate its present tense:

Conjugation	Pronunciation
yo escribo	*yoh ehs-kree-boh*
tú escribes	*too ehs-kree-behs*
él, ella, usted escribe	*ehl, eh-yah, oos-tehd ehs-kree-beh*
nosotros escribimos	*noh-soh-trohs ehs-kree-bee-mohs*
vosotros escribís	*boh-soh-trohs ehs-kree-bees*
ellos, ellas, ustedes escriben	*eh-yohs, eh-yahs, oos-teh-dehs ehs-kree-behn*

You can use these phrases to practise talking about writing:

- ✔ **Mi madre escribe poemas.** *(mee mah-dreh ehs-kree-beh poh-eh-mahs)* (My mother writes poems.)

- ✔ **Tú siempre escribes en tu diario.** *(too seeehm-preh ehs-kree-behs ehn too deeah-reeoh)* (You always write in your diary/journal.)

Talkin' the Talk

Carlota is about to send an email, as she explains to Adela.

Carlota: **Voy a escribir un correo electrónico a mi padre.**
boh-ee ah ehs-kree-beehr oon koh-rre-oh eh-lehk-troh-nee-koh ah mee pah-dreh
I'm going to write an email to my father.

Adela: **¿Le escribes regularmente?**
leh ehs-kree-behs reh-goo-lahr-mehn-teh
Do you write [email] him regularly?

Carlota: **Sí, por lo menos una vez al día.**
see pohr loh meh-nohs oo-nah beth ahl deeah
Yes, at least once a day.

Adela: **¿Le escribiste algo interesante ayer?**
leh ehs-kree-bees-teh ahl-goh een-teh-reh-sahn-teh ah-yehr
Did you write anything interesting to him yesterday?

Carlota:	**No, pero hoy...¡Voy a enviarle una foto nueva con el correo electrónico!**
	Noh peh-roh ohee bohee ah ehn-bee-arh-leh oo-nah foh-toh noo-eh-bah kohn ehl koh-rre-oh eh-lehk-troh-nee-koh
	No, but today...I'm going to send him a new picture attached to the email.

Words to Know

la biografía	lah beeoh-grah-feeah	the biography
el correo electrónico	ehl koh-rre-oh eh-lehk-troh-nee-koh	the email
la novela	lah noh-beh-lah	the novel
el poeta	ehl poh-eh-tah	the poet

Fun & Games

Here's your chance to let your animal magnetism show through. Match the Spanish animals on the left with their English counterparts on the right.

ardilla	butterfly
caballo	cat
cabra	cow
ganso	dog
gato	goose
gaviota	goat
gorrión	horse
mariposa	mare
perro	seagull
vaca	sparrow
yegua	squirrel

Chapter 9

Talking on the Telephone

· ·

In This Chapter

▶ Conversing by phone

▶ Using the alphabet

▶ Understanding simple past tense

· ·

*T*elephones are an indispensable part of life, with modern technology enabling us to talk on the phone almost anywhere. The Spanish are very social people, and so talking on **el teléfono** *(ehl teh-leh-foh-noh)* (the telephone) comes naturally to them. Not only are Spaniards intensely social but also they're very **afectuosos** *(ah-fehk-too-oh-sohs)* (affectionate). When a **llamada telefónica** *(yah-mah-dah teh-leh-foh-nee-kah)* (phone call) ends between two female friends, a male and a female friend or two family members, Spaniards often say **un beso** *(oon beh-soh)* (a kiss) or **un abrazo** *(oon ah-brah-thoh)* (a hug).

In this chapter, you discover the words and expressions that you need when using a telephone in Spain. You find out basic phone vocabulary and tips on how to start, conduct and conclude your telephone conversations.

Starting Out with Your Opening Line

After you dial a phone number, the first thing to do is say hello! To do so, you say **¡Sí . . . diga!** *(see dee-gah)* (Hello! [literally: yes . . . tell me]).

Most Latin American Spanish-speaking countries use **aló** *(a-loh)* (hello) to start a phone conversation.

The following phrases come in very handy when you're making a phone call:

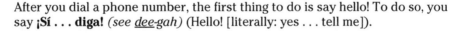

  ✔ **llamar por teléfono** *(yah-mahr pohr teh-leh-foh-noh)* (make a phone call)

  ✔ **marcar el número** *(mahr-kahr ehl noo-meh-roh)* (dial in the number)

✔ **colgar** *(kohl-__gahr__)* (hang up)

✔ **la línea está ocupada** *(lah __lee__-neh-ah ehs-__tah__ oh-koo-__pah__-dah)* (the line's busy)

Check out the later section, 'Calling on the Phone: **Llamar**', for more ways to use the verb **llamar** *(yah-__mahr__)* 'to call or phone'.

Words to Know

el número	ehl __noo__-meh-roh	the number
llamar	yah-__mahr__	to call; to phone
marcar	mahr-__kahr__	to mark; to dial; to punch in [the number]
la línea	lah __lee__-neh-ah	the line
ocupada	oh-koo-__pah__-dah	busy (female)
responder	rehs-pohn-__dehr__	to answer
colgar	kohl-__gahr__	to hang; to hang up

Dealing with 'Porridge' (When You Can't Make Out the Words)

When you're starting out with a new language, some people can talk too quickly for you to follow: perhaps you can't make out the words and everything seems mushy, like porridge. On the phone, fast talking is even more of a problem. You can't see the person, and therefore you don't have body language or facial expressions to help get the gist of the conversation.

Don't be too hard on yourself. Gently insist that the other person repeat the sentence more clearly. You're not being rude in the least; you simply didn't get the whole message, and you're asking for a repeat. No harm there. The person you're talking to may have similar difficulties understanding you, and so please just be as patient with other people as you want them to be with you.

Talkin' the Talk

Take a look at these handy phrases, which you can use when a phone conversation turns to 'porridge'.

Clara:	**¡Hola! ¿Eres Alberto?** *Oh-lah eh-rehs ahl-behr-toh* Hello! Is that Alberto?

(The voice on the other end of the phone is unintelligible.)

Clara:	**Perdone, no le escucho.** *pehr-doh-neh noh leh ehs-koo-choh* Excuse me, I can't hear you.

(Still the voice isn't intelligible.)

Clara:	**La cobertura es mala, ¿lo repite por favor?** *Lah koh-behr-tuh-rah ehs mah-lah loh reh-pee-teh pohr fah-bohr* The line is bad, will you please repeat what you said?
Voice on other side:	**En este momento [él] no está.** *ehn ehs-teh moh-mehn-toh [ehl] noh ehs-tah* He's not here at the moment.
Clara:	**Llamo más tarde, gracias.** *yah-moh mahs tahr-deh grah-theeahs* I'll call later, thanks.

Words to Know

escuchar	ehs-koo-*chahr*	to listen; to hear
hablar	ah-*blahr*	to talk
más tarde	mahs *tahr*-deh	later
por la tarde	pohr lah *tahr*-deh	in the afternoon

The word **tarde** *(tahr-deh)*, without the definite article **la** *(lah)* (the), means *late*. But when you hear the article **la** in front of it, as in **la tarde** *(lah tahr-deh)*, you know that the speaker is talking about *the afternoon*.

Thinking about 'Spelling Out'

English spelling is erratic, and so you may want to spell out your name or other information each time you give it out over the phone. Spanish has more regular spelling rules, however, and so generally no one asks to have a Spanish name such as Rodríguez *(rroh-dree-geth)* spelled out – the spelling is obvious. As a result, many Spanish speakers aren't used to spelling out information or taking down information that's being spelled out. Therefore, if asked to spell your name, try to do so veeeery slooowly so that people can absorb the unusual situation.

Talkin' the Talk

Use this conversation to help you practise spelling out names. (Chapter 1 contains the complete Spanish alphabet with pronunciation, and so head that way if you need to.)

Sheryl Lyons:	**Quiero dejar un mensaje.** *kee-eh-roh deh-Hahr oon mehn-sah-Heh* I'd like to leave a message.
	El mensaje es que la señora Lyons va a llegar hoy a las cinco de la tarde. *ehl mehn-sah-Heh ehs keh lah seh-nyoh-rah lah-ee-ohns bah ah yeh-gahr oh-ee ah lahs theen-koh deh lah tahr-deh* The message is that Mrs Lyons will arrive today at five in the afternoon.
Voice:	**¿Me puede repetir su apellido, por favor?** *meh pooeh-deh reh-peh-teer soo ah-peh-yee-doh pohr fah-bohr* Can you repeat your last name, please?
Sheryl Lyons:	**Me llamo Lyons.** *meh yah-moh lah-ee-ohns* My name is Lyons.
Voice:	**¿Cómo se escribe?** *koh-moh seh ehs-kree-beh* How do you spell it?

Sheryl Lyons:	**Ele, i griega, o, ene, ese.** *eh-leh ee greeeh-gah oh eh-neh eh-seh* L-Y-O-N-S.
Voice:	**Ah, Lyons. Gracias. ¿Cómo es su nombre?** *ah lah-ee-ohns grah-thee-ahs koh-moh ehs soo* *nohm-breh* Ah, Lyons, thank you. What's your [first] name?
Sheryl Lyons:	**Es Sheryl. Ese, hache, e, erre, i griega, ele.** *ehs Sheryl eh-seh ah-cheh eh eh-rreh ee greeeh-* *gah eh-leh* It's Sheryl. S-H-E-R-Y-L.
Voice:	**Ah, Sheryl, gracias. Diré que llamó la señora Sheryl Lyons, y va a llegar a las cinco de la tarde.** *ah sheh-reel grah-theeahs dee-reh keh yah-moh* *lah seh-nyoh-rah sheh-reel lah-ee-ohns ee keh bah* *a yeh-gahr ah lahs theen-koh deh lah tahr-deh* Ah, Sheryl, thanks. I'll say that Mrs Sheryl Lyons phoned, and that she'll arrive at 5 p.m.

For days, hours, months and other date and calendar words, check out Chapter 15. For numbers, take a look at Chapter 5.

Talkin' the Talk

Here's how you may discuss your weekend activities with a friend.

Jorge:	**Hola Felipe, ¿qué tal el fin de semana?** *oh-lah feh-lee-peh keh-tahl ehl feen deh seh-mah-nah* Hello, Felipe, how was your weekend?
Felipe:	**Muy bien. Ayer domingo fui a ver una nueva película de Almodóvar.** *mooy beeehn ah-yehr doh-meen-goh foo-ee ah behr* *oo-nah noo-eh-bah peh-lee-koo-lah deh* *ahl-moh-doh-bahr* Great. Yesterday I went to see a new Almodovar film.
Jorge:	**¿Una nueva? ¿Quién era el personaje principal esta vez?** *ooh-nah nooeh-bah keeehn eh-rah ehl pehr-soh-nah-* *Heh preen-thee-pahl ehs-tah behth* A new one? Who [played] the main character this time?

Felipe:	**¡Carlota Vázquez, la actriz favorita del director!** *Kahr-loh-tah bath-keth lah ahk-treeth fah-boh-ree-tah dehl dee-rehk-tohr* Carlota Vázquez, the director's favourite actress!
Jorge:	**¿Qué te pareció [ella]?** *keh teh pah-reh-theeoh [eh-yah]* What did you think of her?
Felipe:	**¡Que era muy creativa y apasionada!** *keh ee-rah moo-ee kreh-ah-tee-bah ee ah-pah-see-oh-nah-dah* She was very creative and passionate.
Jorge:	**¿Quién más estaba en la película?** *keeeehn mahs ehs-tah-bah ehn lah peh-lee-koo-lah* Who else was in the film?
Felipe:	**Un actor inglés . . . pero ahora no me acuerdo de su nombre.** *oon ahk-tohr een-glehs peh-roh ah-oh-rah noh meh ah-koo-ehr-doh deh suh nohm-breh* An English actor . . . but I can't remember his name right now.
Jorge:	**¡No tienes muy buena memoria, Felipe!** *noh-teeeh-nehs moo-ee boo-eh-nah meh-moh-reh-ah feh-lee-peh* Your memory isn't very good, Felipe!

Words to Know

ahora	ah-oh-rah	now
ayer	ah-yehr	yesterday
el fin de semana	ehl feen deh seh-mah-nah	the weekend
hoy	ohee	today
la película	lah peh-lee-kooh-lah	the film
apasionada	ah-pah-see-hoh-nah-dah	passionate [feminine]

| tienes | tee-_eh_-nehs | you have [singular] |
| ver | be_hr_ | to see; to watch |

Calling on the Phone: Llamar

The verb **llamar** *(yah-mahr)* means 'to call'. Why then, you ask, does that verb feature in Chapter 3, which covers names? Because when you ask Spanish people for their names, they respond with **me llamo** *(meh yah-moh)*, which literally means 'I call myself' or 'I give myself the name'.

In this section, however, we use the term in the sense of trying to reach someone with words and messages. We also talk about calling someone on the phone, because **llamar** also means 'to phone'.

Here are some examples:

- ✔ **Mañana te llamo por teléfono.** *(mah-nyah-nah teh yah-moh pohr teh-leh-foh-noh)* (I'll call you tomorrow.)

- ✔ **Hoy no llamó nadie.** *(ohee noh yah-moh nah-deeeh)* (Nobody called today.)

- ✔ **Ella llama a su madre todos los días.** *(eh-yah yah-mah ah soo mah-dreh toh-dohs lohs deeahs)* (She phones her mother every day.)

- ✔ **Llamamos para saber el horario.** *(yah-mah-mohs pah-rah sah-behr ehl oh-rah-reeoh)* (We're calling to ask about the timetable.)

Turn to Chapter 3 for more about using the verb **llamar**.

Spotting Phone-y Verbs: To Call, to Leave, and to Listen and Hear

Take a look at these three Spanish verbs: **llamar** *(yah-mahr)* (to call), **dejar** *(deh-Har)* (to leave) and **escuchar** *(ehs-koo-char)* (to listen; to hear). What do they have in common? All three are regular verbs (good news!), belonging to the **-ar** *(ahr)* group. If you take off the **-ar**, you get the root of each verb, and when you conjugate each one, the words end the same way for each pronoun. We give you the conjugation for **llamar** below, and you conjugate **dejar** and **escuchar** in the same way.

Conjugation	Pronunciation
yo llamo	*yoh yah-moh*
tú llamas	*too yah-mahs*
él, ella, usted llama	*ehl, eh yah, oos-tehd yah-mah*
nosotros llamamos	*noh-soh-trohs-yah-mah-mohs*
vosotros llamáis	*boh-soh-trohs yah-mah-ees*
ellos, ellas, ustedes llaman	*eh-yohs eh-yahs oos-teh-dehs yah-mahn*

Don't forget to try your own conjugation. Check the verb tables in Appendix B if you're stumped.

The next three sections show you how to use the past tenses of the three verbs **llamar**, **dejar** and **escuchar**, and because all three are regular verbs ending in **-ar**, again you simply add the same letters to each pronoun.

You called? The past tense of llamar

Use the root of **llamar** *(yah-mahr)*, which is **llam-**, to conjugate for the past tense.

Conjugation	Pronunciation
yo llamé	*yoh yah-meh*
tú llamaste	*too yah-mahs-teh*
él, ella, usted llamó	*ehl, eh-yah, oos-tehd yah-moh*
nosotros llamamos	*noh-soh-trohs yah-mah-mohs*
vosotros llamásteis	*boh-soh-trohs yah-mahs-tehees*
ellos, ellas, ustedes llamaron	*eh-yohs, eh-yahs, oos-teh-dehs yah-mah-rohn*

If you miss a call, you may hear the following:

✔ **Te llamaron por teléfono.** *(teh yah-mah-rohn pohr teh-leh-foh-noh)* (You had a phone call.)

✔ **Te llamé ayer.** *(teh yah-meh ah-yehr)* (I called you [informal] yesterday.)

✔ **Ayer no me llamaste.** *(ah-yehr noh meh yah-mahs-teh)* (Yesterday you [informal] didn't call me.)

✔ **Cuando te llamé me colgaron.** *(kooahn-doh teh yah-meh meh kohl-gah-rohn)* (When I called you [informal], they hung up on me.) (Literally: they hung me up!)

⊾ **Si hoy me llamaste, no me enteré.** *(see ohee meh yah-mahs-teh noh meh ehn-teh-reh)* (If you called me today, I didn't know about it.)

Did you leave a message? The past tense of dejar

Here is the past tense of **dejar** *(deh-Hahr)*, which means 'leaving' and 'allowing'. The root is **dej-** *(dehH)*.

Conjugation	Pronunciation
yo dejé	*yoh deh-Heh*
tú dejaste	*too deh-Hahs-teh*
él, ella, usted dejó	*ehl, eh-yah, oos-tehd deh-Hoh*
nosotros dejamos	*noh-soh-trohs deh-Hah-mohs*
vosotros dejásteis	*boh-soh-trohs deh-Hahs-tehees*
ellos, ellas, ustedes dejaron	*eh-yohs, eh-yahs, oos-teh-dehs deh-Hah-rohn*

The following sentences use forms of the verb **dejar**:

⊾ **Te dejé un recado.** *(teh deh-Heh oon reh-kah-doh)* (I left you a message.)

⊾ **¿Dejaste un mensaje largo?** *(deh-Hahs-teh oon mehn-sah-Heh lahr-goh)* (Did you leave a long message?)

⊾ **El mensaje que dejaron es breve.** *(ehl mehn-sah-Heh keh deh-Hah-rohn ehs breh-beh)* (The message they left is brief.)

⊾ **Dejamos tres mensajes.** *(deh-Hah-mohs trehs mehn-sah-Hehs)* (We left three messages.)

⊾ **Ella dejó el número de teléfono.** *(eh-yah deh-Hoh ehl noo-meh-roh deh teh-leh-foh-noh)* (She left the telephone number.)

Have you heard? The past tense of escuchar

The conjugation of the past tense of the verb **escuchar** *(ehs-koo-chahr)* (to listen or hear) follows the pattern of **llamar** and **dejar**. For **escuchar**, the root is **escuch-** *(ehs-kooch)*.

Conjugation	*Pronunciation*
yo escuché	*yoh ehs-koo-<u>cheh</u>*
tú escuchaste	*too ehs-koo-<u>chahs</u>-teh*
él, ella, usted escuchó	*ehl, <u>eh</u>-yah, oos-<u>tehd</u> ehs-koo-choh*
nosotros escuchamos	*noh-<u>soh</u>-trohs ehs-koo-<u>chah</u>-mohs*
vosotros escuchásteis	*boh-<u>soh</u>-trohs ehs-koo-<u>chahs</u>-tehees*
ellos, ellas, ustedes escucharon	*<u>eh</u>-yohs <u>eh</u>-yahs oos-<u>teh</u>-dehs ehs-koo-<u>chah</u>-rohn*

Test your verb-hearing abilities with the following phrases:

- ✔ **¿Me escuchas, Juan?** *(me ehs-<u>koo</u>-chahs Hoo<u>ahn</u>)* (Can you hear me, Juan?)

- ✔ **No te escucho nada.** *(noh teh ehs-<u>koo</u>-choh <u>nah</u>-dah)* (I can't hear anything.)

- ✔ **¿me escuchas bien?** *(meh ehs-<u>koo</u>-chahs bee<u>ehn</u>)* (Can you hear me clearly [well]?)

- ✔ **¡Ahora, te escucho un poco mejor!** *(ah-<u>oh</u>-rah teh ehs-<u>koo</u>-choh oon <u>poh</u>-koh meh-<u>Hohr</u>)* (Now [this way] I can hear you a little better.)

A popular book title that uses the verb **llamar** is Jack London's *The Call of the Wild,* which in Spanish reads ***La llamada de la selva*** *(lah yah-<u>mah</u>-dah deh lah <u>sehl</u>-bah).*

Fun & Games

Throughout this book (and particularly in Chapter 2), we show you how to conjugate regular Spanish verbs. You start with the root of the verb and add the same endings corresponding to the pronouns for each verb in that class: all regular **-ar** verbs conjugate the same way, as do all **-er** and **-ir** verbs.

We now ask you to complete the missing conjugation segments of the verb **dejar**. You can follow in the tracks of the verb **llamar**, which we conjugate for you in the earlier section 'Spotting Phone-y Verbs: To Call, to Leave, and to Listen and Hear'. The root of **llamar** is **llam-** *(yahm)*; the root of **dejar** *(deh-Hahr)* (to leave; to allow) is **dej-** *(dehH)*.

Are you ready to fly solo? Try filling in the gaps below. Go for it!

yo dej _____	I leave
tú dej _____	you leave
él dej _____	he leaves
nosotros dej _____	we leave
vosotros dej _____	you leave [plural]
ellos dej _____	they leave

You made it! For more practice, try another one. Here, the verb is **escuchar** *(ehs-koo-chahr)* (to listen; to hear). The root is **escuch-** *(ehs-kooch)*.

yo escuch _____	I listen; I hear
tú escuch _____	you listen; you hear
ella escuch _____	she listens; she hears
nosotros escuch _____	we listen; we hear
vosotros escuch _____	you listen; you hear [plural]
ellos escuch _____	they listen; they hear

Chapter 10

Looking Around the Home and Office

. . . .

In This Chapter

▶ Understanding work-related words

▶ Holding and attending meetings

▶ Renting properties

▶ Using vocabulary at home

. . . .

*E*verybody needs somewhere to live and most of us have to work (unfortunately!). Spanish architecture often provides very beautiful working and living environments, whether in the city or smaller towns. This chapter explores both work- and home-related Spanish vocabulary.

Talking at Work and About Work

In larger Spanish cities, people often work in high-rise buildings and office towers, as in certain parts of London. In smaller cities or towns, however, workplaces can be located in small and sometimes old buildings. Here are some words and phrases that you can use to describe work and office buildings:

- ✔ **edificio alto** *(eh-dee-fee-theeoh ahl-toh)* (tall building; high-rise)

- ✔ **edificio de muchos pisos** *(eh-dee-fee-theeoh deh moo-chohs pee-sohs)* (building with many floors; high-rise)

- ✔ **edificio de oficinas** *(eh-dee-fee-theeoh deh oh-fee-thee-nahs)* (office building; office block)

- ✔ **edificio de torre** *(eh-dee-fee-theeoh deh toh-rreh)* (tower block)

- ✔ **edificio de una planta** *(eh-dee-fee-theeoh deh oo-nah plahn-tah)* (one-storey building)

Considering the height of buildings

Practise the following phrases associated with buildings:

- **El edificio de Correos tiene siete pisos.** *(ehl eh-dee-fee-theeoh deh koh-rreh-ohs tee-eh-neh see-eh-teh pee-sohs)* (The postal building is seven stories high.)

- **La Torre del Banco tiene cincuenta y cinco pisos.** *(lah toh-rreh dehl bahn-koh teeeh-neh theen-kooehn-tah ee theen-koh pee-sohs)* (The Bank Tower is 55 stories high.)

- **La oficina está en un edificio de dos pisos.** *(lah oh-fee-thee-nah ehs-tah ehn oon eh-dee-fee-theeoh deh dohs pee-sohs)* (The office is in a two-storey building.)

- **Busco el edificio de oficinas municipales.** *(boos-koh ehl eh-dee-fee-theeoh deh oh-fee-thee-nahs moo-nee-thee-pah-lehs)* (I'm looking for the municipal offices.)

- **Vamos a un edificio muy alto.** *(bah-mohs a oon eh-dee-fee-theeoh moo-ee ahl-toh)* (We're going to a very tall building.)

- **En ese edificio sólo hay oficinas.** *(ehn eh-seh eh-dee-fee-theeoh soh-loh ah-ee oh-fee-thee-nahs)* (This building has only offices.)

- **Tres plantas de ese edificio son de la compañía.** *(trehs plahn-tahs deh eh-seh eh-dee-fee-theeoh sohn deh lah kohm-pah-nyee-ah)* (Three floors in that building belong to the company.)

 Some Spanish cities follow the UK convention of calling the street level floor **planta baja** *(planh-tah bah-Hah)* (ground floor [literally: low floor]), with the one immediately above it being the first floor. Other cities, however, refer to the ground floor as the first floor (as in American usage). Bear this information in mind when trying to find a specific address.

Words to Know

alto	ahl-toh	tall; high
el edificio	ehl eh-dee-fee-theeoh	the building
el piso	ehl pee-soh	the floor
la planta baja	lah plahn-tah bah-Hah	the floor at ground level

Conversing at work

Conversations about jobs, workplaces and offices don't differ much from one country to another. Here are some terms to help you talk about life at work:

- ✔ **antes** *(ahn-tehs)* (before)
- ✔ **el ascensor** *(ehl ahs-thehn-sohr)* (the lift)
- ✔ **el empleo** *(ehl ehm-pleh-oh)* (the job; employment)
- ✔ **el pasillo** *(ehl pah-see-yoh)* (the corridor; the aisle)
- ✔ **el personal** *(ehl pehr-soh-nahl)* (the staff; the personnel)
- ✔ **el secretario** *(ehl seh-kreh-tah-reeoh)* (the male secretary)
- ✔ **gerente** *(Heh-rehn-teh)* (manager)
- ✔ **la carta** *(lah kahr-tah)* (the letter)
- ✔ **la cita** *(lah thee-tah)* (the appointment; the date [as in going on a date with someone])
- ✔ **la compañía** *(lah kohm-pah-nyee-ah)* (the company; the firm)
- ✔ **la entrevista** *(lah ehn-treh-bees-tah)* (the interview)
- ✔ **la secretaria** *(lah seh-kreh-tah-reeah)* (the female secretary)
- ✔ **presentarse** *(preh-sehn-tahr-seh)* (to go to be present at some place; to introduce oneself)

Talkin' the Talk

Inés has been transferred to her company's Valencia office and now wants to move to a new department. Here's how she describes her work experience.

Manager: **¿Tiene experiencia con ordenadores?**
teeeh-neh ehks-peh-reeehn-theeah kohn ohr-deh-nah-doh-rehs
Do you have experience with computers?

Inés: **Sí tengo cinco años de experiencia.**
see tehn-goh theen-koh ah-nyohs deh ehks-peh-ree-ehn-theeah
Yes, I have five years' experience.

Manager: **¿Qué trabajo ha hecho con ordenadores?**
keh trah-bah-Hoh ah eh-choh kohn ohr-deh-nah-doh-rehs
What work did you do with computers?

Inés: **He trabajado con datos y también procesando textos.**
*eh trah-bah-Hah-doh kohn dah-tohs ee tahm-beeehn
proh-theh-sahn doh tehks-tohs*
I've done data processing, as well as word processing.

Manager: **¿Ha hecho algo de diseño?**
ah eh-choh ahl-goh deh dee-seh-nyoh
Have you done any design?

Inés: **Sí, el año pasado hice un curso especial de diseño.**
*see ehl ah-nyoh pah-sah-doh ee-theh oon koor-soh
ehs-peh-theeahl deh dee-seh-nyoh*
Yes, last year I took a special course.

Manager: **¿Usa usted normalmente correos electrónicos?**
*ooh-sah oos-tehd nohr-mahl-mehn-teh koh-rreh-ohs
eh-lehk-troh-nee-kohs*
Do you handle e-mails regularly?

Inés: **Sí. También manejo bien otros programas. Mi ante-
rior jefe era diseñador de programas.**
*see tahm-beeehn mah-neh-Hoh beeehn oh-trohs
proh-grah-mahs mee ahn-teh-ree-ohr Heh-feh eh-rah
dee-seh-nyah-dohr deh proh-grah-mahs*
Yes, and I have also worked with other programs. My
previous boss was a programmer.

Words to Know

el curso	ehl koor-soh	the course
el diseño	ehl dee-seh-nyoh	the design
el ordenador	ehl orh-deh-nah-dohr	the computer
el proceso de datos	ehl proh-theh-soh deh dah-tohs	data processing
el programa	ehl proh-grah-mah	the software
programar	proh-grah-mahr	to program (to make software)

manejar	mah-neh-_Hahr_	to handle
los textos	lohs _teks_-tohs	the texts (in computing: words)

Talkin' the Talk

No business is safe from meetings. Here, Sr. Alvarez, the general manager of the company, and his assistant Julia try quickly to set up a meeting to discuss new developments.

Sr. Alvarez: **Quiero organizar una reunión para el miércoles. Quiero que esté todo el personal de gerencia.**
keeeh-roh ohr-gah-nee-thahr oo-nah rehoo-nee-ohn pah-rah ehl mee-ehr-koh-lehs keeeh-roh keh ehs-teh toh-doh ehl pehr-soh-nahl deh Heh-rehn-theeah
I want to arrange a meeting for Wednesday with all the managerial staff.

Julia: **Usted tiene disponible . . . dos horas por la tarde.**
oos-tehd teeeh-neh dees-poh-nee-bleh dohs oh-rahs pohr lah tahr-deh
You have . . . two hours available in the afternoon.

Sr. Alvarez: **¡Bien! . . . en la sala de conferencias.**
beeehn ehn lah sah-lah deh kohn-feh-rehn-theeahs
Good! . . . [let's hold it] in the conference room.

Julia: **El miércoles, de cuatro a seis de la tarde en la sala de conferencias.**
ehl mee-ehr-koh-lehs deh kooah-troh ah sehees deh lah tahr-deh ehn lah sah-lah deh kohn-feh-rehn-theeahs
Wednesday, from four to six p.m. in the conference room.

Sr. Alvarez: **Avise por email a mi socio, por favor y recuérdemelo el día antes.**
ah-bee-seh pohr eeh-meh-eel ah mee soh-theeoh pohr fah-bohr ee reh-koo-ehr-deh-meh-loh ehl dee-ah ahn-tehs

Please let my partner know, via e-mail, and remind me the day before.

Julia: **Sin falta.**
seen fahl-tah
No problem, sir. [literally: without fail]

Words to Know

el archivo	ehl ahr-*chee*-boh	the file
el compromiso	ehl kohm-proh-*mee*-soh	the commitment; the engagement; plans
el informe	ehl een-*fohr*-meh	the report
el teclado	ehl teh-*klah*-doh	the keyboard
la base de datos	lah *bah*-seh de *dah*-tohs	the database
enviar	ehn-bee*ahr*	to send
imprimir	eem-pree-*meer*	to print
junto	*Hoon*-toh	together [masculine, singular]
quedarse	keh-*dahr*-seh	to stay
teclear	teh-kleh-*ahr*	to type

Talkin' the Talk

The meeting time arrives. All the managers – male and female – are together. (The plural for mixed company in Spanish is in the male form.) Sr. Alvarez, the General Manager, starts the meeting.

Sr. Alvarez: **Señores, ante todo agradezco su presencia. Estamos aquí por un asunto de importancia: estamos considerando este contrato. . .**

> *seh-nyoh-rehs ahn-teh toh-doh ah-grah-deth-koh soo preh-sehn-theah ehs-tah-mohs ah-kee-pohr oon ah-soon-toh deh eem-pohr-tahn-theeah ehs-tah-mohs kohn-see-deh-rahn-doh ehs-teh kohn-trah-toh*
> Ladies and gentlemen, I first want to thank you for coming. We're here for an important matter: to consider this contract. . .

Antonio Gutiérrez:
¿Se ha firmado algo ya?
seh ah feer-mah-doh ahl-goh yah
Has anything been signed yet?

Sr. Alvarez:
No, no hemos firmado nada. Quiero consultar con vosotros primero y también quiero consultar con nuestros abogados.
noh noh eh-mohs feer-mah-doh nah-dah kee-eh-roh kohn-sool-tahr kohn boh-soh-trohs pree-meh-roh ee tahm-bee-ehn kee-eh-roh kohn-sool-tahr kohn nooehs-trohs ah-boh-gah-dohs
No, we haven't signed anything. I want to consult with you first, and I also want to consult with our lawyers. [The grammar is informal, because the boss talking.]

Sr. Alvarez:
Julia, toma nota para las actas de la reunión.
Hoo-leeah toh-mah noh-tah pah-rah lahs ahk-tahs deh lah rehoo-nee-ohn
Julia, take minutes of the meeting. [Again, informal.]

Julia:
Lo estoy grabando.
loh ehs-toh-ee grah-bahn-doh
I'm recording it.

Words to Know

el abogado	ehl ah-boh-gah-doh	the lawyer [masculine]
el asunto	ehl ah-soon-toh	the matter
consultar	kohn-sool-tahr	to consult
firmar	feer-mahr	to sign
grabar	grah-bahr	to record

CULTURAL WISDOM

A proverb: Let them eat bread!

Here are a couple of Spanish proverbs for your amusement, which may be familiar:

✔ **A falta de pan buenas son tortas.** *(ah fahl-tah deh pahn booeh-nahs sohn tohr-tahs)* (Literally: if there's no bread, plain pastry will do.) The English proverb equivalent is: half a loaf is better than none.

✔ **Más vale pájaro en mano, que ciento volando.** *(mahs bah-leh pah-Hah-roh ehn mah-noh keh theeehn-toh boh-lahn-doh)* (Literally: a bird in your hand is worth more than 100 flying.) The English equivalent is: a bird in hand is worth two in the bush. (The Spanish version is more emphatic — some Spanish speakers love drama!)

Discovering Work-related Phrases and Idioms

In this section, we take a look at some really useful work-related words.

Getting down to business with 'Asunto'

The following sentences use the word **asunto** *(ah-soon-toh)* (subject; matter; business; that which concerns you):

✔ **Estoy hablando de asuntos de negocios.** *(ehs-tohee ah-blahn-doh deh ah-soon-tohs deh neh-goh-theeohs)* (I'm talking about business matters.)

✔ **¡No es asunto muy serio!** *(noh ehs ah-soon-toh moo-ee seh-ree-oh)* (It's not a very important matter.)

✔ **¡El asunto es que ya no tenemos más dinero!** *(ehl ah-soon-toh ehs keh yah noh teh-neh-mohs mahs dee-neh-roh)* (The thing is that we've already run out of money!)

GRAMMATICALLY SPEAKING

In Chapter 5, we show you how to conjugate the verb **tomar** *(toh-mahr)* (to take) and describe its meaning as 'to drink'. The primary meaning of **tomar**, however, is 'to take', as when a general manager urges a secretary to take notes at a meeting.

Employing the hiring verb: Emplear

Emplear *(ehm-pleh-<u>ahr</u>)* (to employ; to hire; to use) is a multifaceted, regular verb that uses the root **emple-** *(ehm-pleh)*. Here's how you conjugate **emplear**:

Conjugation	*Pronunciation*
yo empleo	*yoh ehm-<u>pleh</u>-oh*
tú empleas	*too ehm-<u>pleh</u>-ahs*
él, **ella**, **usted emplea**	*ehl, <u>eh</u>-yah, oos-<u>tehd</u> ehm-<u>pleh</u>-ah*
nosotros empleamos	*noh-<u>soh</u>-trohs ehm-pleh-<u>ah</u>-mohs*
vosotros empleáis	*boh-<u>soh</u>-trohs ehm-pleh-<u>ah</u>-ees*
ellos, **ellas**, **ustedes emplean**	*<u>eh</u>-yohs, <u>eh</u>-yahs, oos-<u>teh</u>-dehs ehm-<u>pleh</u>-ahn*

The following phrases show you how to use **emplear**:

- ✔ **La fábrica emplea cincuenta operarios.** *(lah <u>fah</u>-bree-kah ehm-<u>pleh</u>-ah theen-koo<u>ehn</u>-tah oh-peh-<u>rah</u>-reeohs)* (The factory employs 50 workers.)

- ✔ **Nosotros empleamos dos horas en ese trabajo.** *(noh-<u>soh</u>-trohs ehm-pleh-<u>ah</u>-mohs dohs <u>oh</u>-rahs ehn <u>eh</u>-seh trah-<u>bah</u>-Hoh)* (It took us two hours to do that work.)

- ✔ **Van a emplearlos en un taller.** *(bahn ah ehm-pleh-<u>ahr</u>-lohs ehn oon tah-<u>yehr</u>)* (They're going to give them a job in a workshop.)

- ✔ **Ese ordenador se emplea para diseñar.** *(<u>eh</u>-seh ohr-deh-nah-<u>dohr</u> seh ehm-<u>pleh</u>-ah <u>pah</u>-rah dee-seh-<u>nyahr</u>)* (That computer is used for designing work.)

- ✔ **Queremos emplear sólo personas responsables.** *(keh-<u>reh</u>-mohs ehm-pleh-<u>ahr</u> soh-loh pehr-<u>soh</u>-nahs rehs-pohn-<u>sah</u>-blehs)* (We want to employ only responsible people.)

- ✔ **Emplean sólo personas de confianza.** *(ehm-<u>pleh</u>-ahn soh-loh pehr-<u>soh</u>-nahs deh kohn-fee<u>ahn</u>-thah)* (They employ only reliable people.)

- ✔ **La emplean porque es una persona adecuada.** *(lah ehm-<u>pleh</u>-ahn pohr-keh ehs <u>ooh</u>-nah pehr-<u>soh</u>-nah a-deh-koo<u>hah</u>-da)* (They employ her because she's the right person for the job.)

Talkin' the Talk

Workers sometimes find their jobs through word of mouth. In the following dialogue, several positions in a furniture factory are vacant.

Carla: **En esa fábrica emplean gente nueva.**
ehn eh-sah fah-bree-kah ehm-pleh-ahn Hehn-the noo-eh-bah
That factory is hiring people now.

Marcos: **¿Qué producen?**
keh proh-doo-thehn
What do they make there?

Carla: **Es una fábrica de muebles.**
ehs oo-nah fah-bree-kah deh moo-eh-blehs
It's a furniture factory.

Marcos: **¿Qué empleos ofrecen?**
keh ehm-pleh-ohs oh-freh-thehn
What jobs do they have available?

Carla: **Un empleo en la oficina y otro en la planta.**
oon ehm-pleh-oh ehn lah oh-fee-thee-nah ee oh-troh ehn lah plahn-tah
There's an office job and another on the production line.

Marcos: **El de la planta me interesa. Yo tengo experiencia.**
ehl deh lah plahn-tah meh een-teh-reh-sah yoh tehn-goh ehks-peh-reeehn-theeah
I'm interested in the one on the floor [production line]. I have experience.

Carla: **¿Por qué no pides información?**
pohr keh noh pee-dehs een-fohr-mah-thee-ohn
Why don't you ask for information?

Marcos: **¡Muy bien, allí voy!**
Mooy beeehn ah-yeeh bohee
Right, I'm on my way!

Words to Know

el empleo	ehl ehm-_pleh_-oh	the employment; the job
el mueble	ehl moo_eh_-bleh	the furniture
la fábrica	lah _fah_-bree-kah	the factory
la planta	lah _plahn_-tah	the plant; the production line (as in a factory)
interesar	een-teh-reh-_sahr_	to interest; to have an interest in
ofrecer	oh-freh-_thehr_	to offer
pedir	peh-_deer_	to ask for
producir	proh-doo-_theer_	to produce; to make

Doing and making: Hacer

Like most of the verbs that you have to use frequently, **hacer** *(ah-thehr)* (to do; to make) is a highly irregular verb, changing its root from pronoun to pronoun and from tense to tense.

Hacer's root, **hac-**, transforms and deforms itself within the first person singular. Here's how you conjugate **hacer** in the present tense:

Conjugation	*Pronunciation*
yo hago	*yoh _ah_-goh*
tú haces	*too _ah_-thehs*
él, ella, usted hace	*ehl, _eh_-yah, oos-_tehd_ _ah_-theh*
nosotros hacemos	*noh-_soh_-trohs ah-_theh_-mohs*
vosotros hacéis	*boh-_soh_-trohs hah-_theh_ees*
ellos, ellas, ustedes hacen	*_eh_-yohs, _eh_-yahs, oos-_teh_-dehs _ah_-thehn*

Here are some phrases to help you practise the verb **hacer**:

- **Carlos hace muebles.** (*kahr-lohs ah-theh mooeh-blehs*) (Carlos makes furniture.)

- **Nosotros hacemos nuestro pan.** (*noh-soh-trohs ah-theh-mohs nooehs-troh pahn*) (We bake our own bread.)

- **Todos hacen cola.** (*toh-dohs ah-thehn koh-lah*) (They're all queuing. [literally: they all make a tail.])

- **¡Tú haces mucha comida!** (*too ah-thehs moo-chah koh-mee-dah*) (You make a lot of food!)

- **No tiene nada que hacer.** (*noh teeeh-neh nah-dah keh ah-thehr*) (He has nothing to do.)

- **No hacemos nada malo.** (*noh ah-theh-mohs nah-dah mah-loh*) (We're doing no harm [literally: no bad].)

- **Ignacio hace casas de madera.** (*eeg-nah-theeoh ah-theh kah-sahs deh mah-deh-rah*) (Ignacio makes wooden houses.)

- **Rosa hace jardines preciosos.** (*roh-sah ah-theh Har-dee-nehs preh-thee-oh-sohs*) (Rosa creates beautiful gardens.)

Speaking about Houses and Homes

Sometimes, the word **casa** (*kah-sah*) expresses what you call 'home' in English and in other situations **la casa** (*lah kah-sah*) can also express the actual building in which you make your home.

The Spanish word **el hogar** (*ehl-oh-gahr*) also means 'home' and is closest in meaning to 'the hearth' in English. **El hogar** invokes the idea of a fire in a shelter where warmth and food are offered: a place of warmth during cold days; a place to stay dry during rain and snow; a place of repose when you're tired; and a place of joy during the many happy events of your life.

Use the following phrases to discuss your house and home:

- **hogar dulce hogar** (*oh-gahr dool-theh oh-gahr*) (home sweet home)

- **especialidad de la casa** (*ehs-peh-theeah-lee-dahd deh lah kah-sah*) (speciality of the house)

- **un error como una casa** (*oon eh-rrohr koh-moh oo-nah kah-sah*) (an immense mistake [literally: a mistake the size of a house])

- **anda como Pedro por su casa** (*ahn-dah koh-moh peh-droh pohr soo kah-sah*) (acts like he owns the place [literally: goes about like Pedro in his house])

✔ **mudarse de casa** *(moo-dahr-seh deh kah-sah)* (to move [literally: to change houses [to move house yourself]])

Gaining rental wisdom

Almost everyone needs to search for a new home sooner or later. And with the world rapidly becoming one global village, you may find yourself living in Spain some day (or in close proximity to Spanish-speakers). This section covers the ins and outs of searching for a new place to live.

Make sure that you discover the rules for renting properties in Spain. For example, rental usually includes some basic appliances, unless you rent a totally unfurnished house or flat. The heating (**la calefacción**) *(lah kah-leh-fahk-theeohn)*, water (**el agua**) *(ehl ah-gooah)* supply and so on, however, aren't always included in the cost of rent. Therefore, when you rent, you need to think about the added cost of hooking up utilities.

In Spain, you may have no difficulty negotiating a lease that lasts for more than six months, unless the lease is for commercial use.

More likely than not, you're going to begin living on your own in a rented property, which can include several different kinds of housing. Use the following phrases to help with your search:

✔ **casa adosada** *(kah-sah ah-doh-sah-dah)* (semi-detached house)

✔ **casa de dos pisos** *(kah-sah deh dohs pee-sohs)* (two-storey house)

✔ **casa de una planta** *(kah-sah deh oo-nah plahn-tah)* (one-storey house)

✔ **edificio de apartamentos** *(eh-dee-fee-theeoh deh ah-pahr-tah-mehn-tohs)* (apartment building; block of flats)

✔ **piso compartido** *(pee-soh cohm-pahr-tee-doh)* (literally, shared flat)

✔ **piso en alquiler** *(pee-soh ehn ahl-kee-lehr)* (flat to let)

✔ **residencia** *(reh-see-dehn-theeah)* (residence; house used for residential purposes)

Estate agents are very useful. They charge, of course, but can save a great deal of footwork. Knowing your requirements, an estate agent can recommend spaces that fit your requirements. Use the following phrases to convey the urgency of your need for a dwelling to call your own:

✔ **Necesito un piso.** *(neh-theh-see-toh oon pee-soh)* (I need to rent a flat.)

✔ **Es urgente encontrar un piso.** *(ehs oor-Hehn-teh ehn-kohn-trahr oon pee-soh)* (We must find a flat urgently.)

✔ **Como tenemos niños, debemos encontrar una casa.** *(koh-moh teh-neh-mohs nee-nyohs deh-beh-mohs ehn-kohn-trahr oo-nah kah-sah)* (We have children and so must find a house.)

✔ **Hay que preguntar a los amigos.** *(ahy keh preh-goon-tahr ah lohs ah-mee-gohs)* (We must ask our friends [to help us find a place].)

✔ **Hay que ver los anuncios en Internet.** *(ahy keh behr lohs ah-nooh-theeohs ehn een-tehr-neht)* (We must look at the Internet ads.)

If you plan to buy a house or land, make sure that you first find out what kind of legal steps are necessary to give you ownership. The rules for house or land ownership can vary slightly between different **Regiones Autonómicas** *(rreh-Hee-oh-nehs ahoo-toh-noh-mee-kahs)* (Spanish administrative regions). Spain welcomes foreign buyers, and although you can get good deals, prices aren't quite as tantalising as they used to be! A **notario** *(noh-tah-reeoh)* (notary) is your best source for obtaining legal and cost information.

Words to Know

encontrar	ehn-kohn-_trahr_	to find
falta	_fahl_-tah	lack of something
urgente	oor-_Hehn_-teh	urgent

Talkin' the Talk

Jeff and Lydia have been hired as consultants to a company in Seville, and they need to find somewhere to live there, fast. They discover a promising flat advertised in the local paper, and they're checking it out.

Jeff and Lydia: **Vimos el anuncio en el diario y llamamos por lo del piso. ¿Está disponible aún?**
bee-mohs ehl ah-_noohn_-theeo ehn ehl _deeah_-reeoh ee yah-_mah_-mos pohr loh dehl _pee_-soh ehs-_tah_ dees-poh-_nee_-bleh ah-_oon_
We saw your ad in the paper, and we're calling about the flat. Is it still available?

Mónica: **No, ya está ocupado.**
noh yah ehs-<u>tah</u> oh-koo-<u>pah</u>-doh
No, it's already taken.

Jeff and Lydia: **Ah, qué lástima, gracias.**
ah keh <u>lahs</u>-tee-mah <u>grah</u>-theeahs
Oh, that's a shame. Thank you.

Mónica: **Os recomiendo otro piso.**
ohs reh-koh-<u>meeehn</u>-doh <u>oh</u>-troh <u>pee</u>-soh
I can recommend another flat.

Jeff and Lydia: **¿Cuándo podemos verlo?**
Koo-<u>ahn</u>-doh poh-<u>deh</u>-mohs <u>behr</u>-loh
When can we see it?

Mónica: **Mañana por la tarde se desocupa. Luego se va a pintar. El martes podéis verlo.**
mah-<u>nyah</u>-nah pohr lah <u>tahr</u>-deh seh deh-soh-koo-pah <u>looeh</u>-goh seh bah ah peen-<u>tahr</u> ehl <u>mahr</u>-tehs po-<u>deh</u>-ees <u>behr</u>-loh
It becomes vacant tomorrow afternoon. Then it'll be painted. You can see it on Tuesday.

Words to Know

desocupar	dehs-oh-koo-<u>pahr</u>	to vacate
disponible	dees-poh-<u>nee</u>-bleh	available
lástima	<u>lahs</u>-tee-mah	pity; shame
ocupar	oh-koo-<u>pahr</u>	to take up; to occupy
pintar	peen-<u>tahr</u>	to paint

Whose house?

In Spain, some people say **tu casa** *(too* kah-*sah)*, which literally translates as 'your house' or 'your home'. Spaniards use this phrase to express the generous implication that the house of the person speaking is also the house of the person invited (for example, 'treat my house is as house'). This phrase can lead to funny confusions. Susana, one of the authors, tells the following story:

When I first received an invitation in Murcia to visit someone, I was invited to dinner in the following manner:

¡Te esperamos para comer en tu casa! *(teh ehs-peh-*rah*-mohs pah-rah koh-*mehr *ehn*

too kah-*sah)* (literally: we're expecting you [informal] to have lunch at your house.)

My first and rather alarmed understanding of the invitation was that, somehow, these people expected to have the meal in my house, with me as the chef. However, the invitation meant no such thing. I discovered this the hard way though, because as I was waiting for them to come for a lunch I had managed to improvise, they phoned to tell me that they were still waiting for me, because the invitation was to *their* house. By using **tu casa**, they wanted me to feel as though I were in my own home.

Talkin' the Talk

In the following dialogue, Lola and Juan are looking at a flat that they know is vacant.

Lola y Juan:	**Venimos a ver el piso.**
	beh-*nee*-mohs ah behr ehl *pee*-soh
	We came to see the flat.

Lupe:	**Aquí está.**
	ah-*kee* ehs-*tah*
	Here it is.

Lola y Juan:	**¿Cuánto cuesta?**
	Koo-*ahn*-toh *kooehs*-tah
	How much does it cost?

Lupe:	**Mil euros al mes.**
	meel *ehoo*-rohs ahl mehs
	A 1,000 euros per month.

Lola y Juan:	**¿El gas y el agua están incluídos?**
	ehl gahs ee ehl *ah*-gooah ehs-*tahn* een-*klooee*-dohs
	Are gas and water included?

Lupe:	**No, el gas y el agua lo pagáis por separado. Aquí están los contadores.** *noh ehl gahs ee ehl ah-gooah loh pah-gah-ees pohr she-pah-rah-doh ah-kee ehs-tahn lohs kohn-tah-doh-rehs* No, you pay the gas and water separately. Here are the meters.
Lola y Juan:	**¿Necesitas un depósito?** *neh-theh-see-tahs oon deh-poh-see-toh* Do you require a deposit payment?
Lupe:	**Sí, necesito un depósito de mil euros, más el primer mes.** *see neh-theh-see-toh oon deh-poh-see-toh deh meel ehoo-rohs mahs ehl pree-mehr mehs* Yes, I need a down payment of 1,000 euros and the first month's rent.
Lola y Juan:	**Vamos a pensarlo, mañana volvemos.** *bah-mohs ah pehn-sahr-loh mah-nyah-nah bohl-beh-mohs* We're going to think about it. We'll come back tomorrow.

CULTURAL WISDOM

Four house-related proverbs

Although proverbs often contain wisdom, they can be fun as well. Here are four house-related proverbs that you may enjoy:

✔ **Echar la casa por la ventana.** *(eh-chahr lah kah-sah pohr lah behn-tah-nah)* (Literally: to throw the house out the window.) Use this proverb to express that you're doing things in a big way — when you're preparing a superb party, for example.

✔ **Empezar la casa por el tejado.** *(ehm-peh-thahr lah kah-sah pohr ehl teh-Hah-doh)*

(Literally: to start the house at the roof.) The English equivalent of this proverb is: to put the cart before the horse.

✔ **En casa de herrero, cuchillo de palo.** *(ehn kah-sah deh eh-rreh-roh koo-chee-yoh de pah-loh)* (Literally: tn the blacksmith's house, a knife of wood.) The English equivalent of this proverb is: the shoemaker's son always goes barefoot.

Three for one

Spanish has three words for 'room'. You can take your pick from any of them:

✔ **la habitación** *(lah ah-bee-tah-thee-<u>ohn</u>)*

✔ **el dormitorio** *(el dohr-mee-<u>toh</u>-ree-oh)* [usually a bedroom]

✔ **el cuarto** *(ehl koo<u>ah</u>r-toh)*

Renting a home: Alquilar

Spanish has two words for 'to rent': **alquilar** *(ahl-keeh-<u>lahr</u>)*, which is used most often, and **arrendar** *(ah-rrehn-<u>dahr</u>)*, which is more old-fashioned and rarely used. Here are some useful examples for using **alquilar**:

✔ **Alquilamos cohes.** *(ahl-kee-<u>lah</u>-mohs <u>koh</u>-chehs)* (Rental cars here.)

✔ **Necesito alquilar una casa.** *(neh-theh-<u>see</u>-toh ahl-kee-<u>lahr</u> <u>oo</u>-nah <u>kah</u>-sah)* (I need to rent a house.)

✔ **Aquí alquilan apartamentos.** *(ah-<u>kee</u> ahl-<u>kee</u>-lahn ah-pahr-tah-<u>mehn</u>-tohs)* (They rent apartments here.)

✔ **Emilia alquila su finca durante las vacaciones de verano.** *(eh-<u>mee</u>-leeah ahl-<u>kee</u>-lah soo <u>feen</u>-kah doo-<u>rahn</u>-teh lahs bah-kah-thee<u>oh</u>-nehs deh beh-<u>rah</u>-noh)* (Emilia rents her farm during summer holidays.)

✔ **Julio y María alquilan un piso.** *(<u>Hoo</u>-leeoh ee mah-<u>reeah</u> ahl-<u>Kee</u>-lahn oon <u>pee</u>-soh)* (Julio and María are renting a flat.)

✔ **Voy a alquilar un coche.** *(bohee ah ahl-kee-<u>lahr</u> oon <u>koh</u>-cheh)* (I'm going to rent a car.)

✔ **Tú alquilas una pequeña granja durante el verano.** *(too ahl-<u>kee</u>-lahs <u>oo</u>-nah peh-<u>keh</u>-nya <u>grahn</u>-Hah doo-<u>rahn</u>-the ehl beh-<u>rah</u>-noh)* (You're renting a small farm during summer.)

✔ **Nosotros alquilamos nuestra casa.** *(noh-<u>soh</u>-trohs ahl-ke-<u>lah</u>-mohs noo-ehs-trah <u>kah</u>-sah)* (We're renting our house.)

Talkin' the Talk

Use the following dialogue as a guideline for the conversation you may have when visiting an estate agent to look for a furnished flat. Carlos is looking for a flat in a high-rise building.

Carlos:	**Busco un piso amueblado.** *boos-koh oon pee-soh ah-mooeh-blah-doh* I'm looking for a furnished flat.
Estate agent:	**Tenemos uno en el noveno piso.** *teh-neh-mohs oo-noh ehn ehl noh-beh-noh pee-soh* We have one on the ninth floor.
Carlos:	**¿Está disponible?** *ehs-tah dees-poh-nee-bleh* Is it available?
Estate agent:	**Sí, está libre y disponible.** *see esh-tah lee-breh ee dees-poh-nee-bleh* Yes, it's vacant and available.
Carlos:	**Me gusta; lo voy a coger.** *meh goos-tah loh boh-ee ah koh-Hehr* I like it; I'll take it.

Words to Know

amueblado	ah-mooeh-blah-doh	furnished
el depósito	ehl deh-poh-see-toh	the deposit
incluido	een-klooee-doh	included
limpiar	leem-peeahr	to clean
pagar	pah-gahr	to pay
reembolsar	reh-ehm-bol-sahr	to refund

Talkin' the Talk

Instead of renting a flat, you may want to rent a house. Although renting a house may be a bit costlier and take more work, the trouble is worthwhile. Here, Victoria is discussing a house rental in Cádiz.

Victoria: **Esta casa ¿cuántos baños tiene?**
ehs-tah kah-sah kooahn-tohs bah-nyohs teeeh-neh
How many bathrooms does this house have?

Owner: **Hay dos baños: el baño principal y el baño de abajo**
ah-ee dohs bah-nyohs ehl bah-nyoh preen-thee-pahl ee ehl bah-nyoh deh ah-bah-Hoh
There are two bathrooms: the main bathroom and the downstairs bathroom.

Victoria: **¿Dónde está la cocina?**
dohn-deh ehs-tah lah koh-thee-nah
Where's the kitchen?

Owner: **Por aquí.**
pohr ah-kee
This way.

Victoria: **¿La cocina es a gas o eléctrica?**
Lah koh-thee-nah ehs ah gahs oh eh-lehk-tree-kah
Is there a gas or electric cooker?

Owner: **No, la cocina y el frigorífico los tiene que instalar usted.**
noh lah koh-thee-nah ee ehl free-goh-ree-fee-koh lohs teeeh-neh keh eens-tah-lahr oos-tehd
No, you have to have the cooker and fridge put in.

Victoria: **¿Cuántas habitaciones hay?**
kooahn-tahs ah-bee-tah-theeoh-nehs ah-ee
How many rooms are there?

Owner: **Está el salón, el comedor, dos dormitorios y uno de invitados.**
ehs-tah ehl sah-lohn ehl koh-meh-dohr dohs dohr-mee-toh-reeohs ee oo-noh deh eehn-beeh-tah-dohs
There's the living room, the dining room, two bedrooms and a guest room.

Words to Know

el comedor	ehl koh-meh-_dohr_	the dining room
el dormitorio	ehl dohr-mee-_toh_-reeoh	the bedroom
el salón	ehl sah-_lohn_	the living room
la sala	lah _sah_-lah	the living room (a smaller version)
la habitación	lah ah-bee-tah-thee-_ohn_	the room
la cocina	lah koh-_thee_-nah	the cooker; the kitchen [depending on the context]
los baños	lohs _bah_-nyohs	the bathrooms
el frigorífico	ehl free-goh-_ree_-fee-koh	the fridge

Talkin' the Talk

Jane is showing Juan her new house. Juan is especially impressed by the garden.

Juan: **Lo mejor de aquí es el jardín.**
loh meh-Hohr deh ah-kee ehs ehl Hahr-deen
The best [feature] here is the garden.

Jane: **Sí, los jardines dan mucho valor a una casa.**
see lohs Hahr-dee-nehs dahn moo-choh bah-lohr ah oo-nah kah-sah
Yes, gardens add a lot of value to a house.

Juan: **Este jardín está muy bien diseñado.**
ehs-teh Hahr-deen ehs-tah moo-ee beeehn dee-seh-nyah-doh
This garden is very well designed.

Jane: **Al fondo del jardín hay una piscina. Está pavimen-tado todo alrededor.**
ahl fohn-doh dehl Hahr-deen ah-ee oo-nah pees-thee-nah ehs-tah pah-bee-mehn-tah-doh toh-doh ahl-reh-deh-dohr
At the back of the garden there's a swimming pool. It's paved all around.

Juan: **El cesped del jardín está bien cuidado.**
ehl thehs-pehd dehl Hahr-deen ehs-tah beeehn kooee-dah-doh
The grass in the garden is well kept.

Jane: **¡Y las flores! . . . algunas son tropicales.**
ee lahs floh-rehs ahl-goo-nahs sohn troh-pee-kah-lehs
And the flowers! . . . some are tropical [flowers].

Juan: **Los árboles dan muy buena sombra.**
lohs ahr-boh-lehs dahn moo-ee booeh-nah sohm-brah
The trees are really good for shade.

Words to Know

la piscina	lah pees-_thee_-nah	the swimming pool
la sombra	lah _sohm_-brah	the shade; the shadow
pavimentado	pah-bee-mehn-_tah_-doh	paved

Words to Know

| el tamaño | ehl tah-_mah_-nyoh | the size |
| la vista | lah _bees_-tah | the view |

Fun & Games

Fernando, Claudia and their dog *Perro* have just moved into the house you see below. A solid line points to various rooms or items in the home. Please provide the Spanish word in each case. (If you really want to challenge yourself, look at the mini-dictionary in Appendix A or elsewhere in this book, and try to name several other items in the home as well.)

Part III
Spanish on the Go

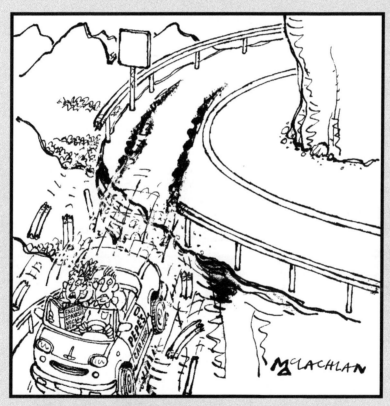

'Ah, yes– that sign said "Dangerous Bend –
Slow Down".'

In this part . . .

This part is devoted to the traveller in you and gives you all the tools you need to hit the road in Spain. We help you interact with and enjoy all the new experiences – from the moment of arrival to checking into hotels, hailing a taxi, exchanging your currency for euros and having a great time doing it all. In addition, we include loads of cultural information about important people, places and things from the diverse regional cultures of Spain.

Chapter 11

Money, Money, Money

. . . .

In This Chapter

▶ Changing money at the bank

▶ Using cash machines

▶ Identifying safe places to exchange currency

. . . .

*Y*ou work hard, you pay your dues and you earn your money. But you don't go through all that effort just for the money. You work because money gives you the means to get what you need and do what you want.

And yet you need to be able to get hold of your money easily so that you can provide for those needs and desires. Especially when you're away from home, you want to avoid any kind of frustration when out shopping or trying to access your cash. In this chapter, you discover all the money-handling knowledge that you need in Spain.

Cashing In With Some Basic Money Phrases

When travelling in Spain, you may feel that you can't (or shouldn't) use your money the same way you do at home. This chapter shows that this isn't completely true; financial transactions are a lot easier than you may suppose. Cash machines are easy to find all over Spain and often you can use them to withdraw funds directly from your home account. That's good news!

You can think about money as fun – when you have it – and as a problem – when you lose it. We talk about the losing bit in Chapter 16. Here, we roll out the red carpet treatment for the fun part.

Salary, a word you know in English, is **el salario** *(ehl sah-lah-reeoh)* in Spanish and comes from the word **sal** *(sahl)* (salt). In Roman times, some people were paid for their work with salt – valuable because you can't live without it.

Because you often need to carry some cash, here are a few cash-carrying terms:

- **dinero en efectivo** *(dee-neh-roh ehn eh-fehk-tee-boh)* (money in cash)
- **en billetes** *(ehn bee-yeh-tehs)* (in notes)
- **en monedas** *(ehn moh-neh-dahs)* (in coins)
- **los céntimos** *(lohs-then-tee-mohs)* (the cents [coins])
- **una moneda de euro** *(oo-nah moh-neh-dah deh ehoo-roh)* (a euro coin)

In addition, the following phrases may come in handy:

- **¿Traes algún dinero?** *(trah-ehs ahl-goon dee-neh-roh)* (Do you have any money?)
- **¿Tienes dinero en efectivo?** *(teeeh-nehs dee-neh-roh ehn eh-fehk-tee-boh)* (Do you have cash?)
- **¿Tienes una moneda de cincuenta céntimos?** *(teeeh-nehs oo-nah moh-neh-dah deh thee-kooehn-tah thehn-tee-mohs)* (Do you have a 50 cent coin?)
- **No tenemos monedas.** *(noh teh-neh-mohs moh-neh-dahs)* (We have no coins.)
- **El cambio es sólo una moneda de diez céntimos.** *(ehl kahm-bee-oh ehs soh-loh oo-nah moh-neh-dah deh deeeth thehn-tee-mohs)* (The change is just a ten cent coin.)
- **Pagamos con dos billetes de veinte euros.** *(pah-gah-mohs kohn dohs bee-yeh-tehs deh beheen-teh ehoo-rohs)* (We paid with two 20 euro notes.)
- **Aquí tiene un billete de cien.** *(ah-kee teeeh-neh oon bee-yeh-teh deh theeehn)* (Here you have a 100 [euro] note.)

Words to Know

algún	ahl-*goon*	some
el billete	ehl bee-*yeh*-teh	the note
el dinero	ehl dee-*neh*-roh	the money
la moneda	lah moh-*neh*-dah	the coin

Operating Cash Machines

Cash machines are available in cities and resorts all over the world and are the simplest and most discreet way to access your funds.

A cash machine is called **cajero** *(kah-<u>Heh</u>-roh)* and the person who exchanges money is also called **el cajero** *(ehl kah-<u>Heh</u>-roh)* (money changer).

When they're in working order – which is about 95 per cent of the time – you simply take your debit or credit card, punch in your personal identification number (PIN), get your cash in euros and away you go.

The exchange rate you get at cash machines is definitely the most favourable, because it's a bank exchange rate – between the other bank and yours – which is better than what you get at other currency-exchanging outlets.

On some occasions, a cash machine may not work or out of cash, or the computer systems of the banks involved can't communicate with each other (talk about not understanding a language!). When those situations happen, you can access your money only by using your credit card. For these moments, having some traveller's cheques comes in handy check out the later section 'Using Traveller's Cheques in Spain'.

We've seen some cash machines that display their messages in both Spanish and English. Just in case yours doesn't have the English display, here are the sentences you see in the order in which they appear:

- ✔ **Introduzca su tarjeta por favor.** *(een-troh-<u>dooth</u>-kah soo tahr-<u>Heh</u>-tah pohr-fah-<u>bohr</u>)* (Insert your card please.)

- ✔ **Por favor teclee su número personal.** *(pohr fah-<u>bohr</u> teh-<u>kleh</u>-eh soo <u>noo</u>-meh-roh pehr-soh-<u>nahl</u>)* (Please type your PIN.)

At this point, you have to press the button that reads: **continuar** *(kohn-tee-noo<u>ahr</u>)* (continue; keep going.) After you press the button, the following options appear:

- ✔ **Retirada en efectivo** *(reh-tee-<u>rah</u>-dah ehn eh-fehk-<u>tee</u>-boh)* (cash withdrawal)

    If you choose cash withdrawal, these other options come up:

    - • **tarjeta de crédito** *(tahr-<u>Heh</u>-tah deh <u>kreh</u>-dee-toh)* (credit card)
    - • **tarjeta de débito** *(tahr-<u>Heh</u>-tah deh <u>deh</u>-bee-toh)* (debit card)
    - • **cuenta corriente** *(koo-<u>ehn</u>-tah koh-rree-<u>ehn</u>-teh)* (current account)
    - • **cuenta de ahorro** *(koo-<u>ehn</u>-tah deh ah-<u>oh</u>-rroh)* (savings account)
    - • **consulta de saldo** *(kohn-<u>sool</u>-tah deh <u>sahl</u>-doh)* (checking your balance)

If you're slow about pressing those buttons, these messages may came up:

- **¿requiere más tiempo?** *(reh-kee__eh__-reh mahs tee-__ehm__-poh)* (do you need more time?)
- **sí/no** *(see/noh)* (yes/no.)

If you press **sí**, you go back to the previous screen. When this happens, choose your **tarjeta** or **cuenta**, which provide options for withdrawing cash:

- **5, 10, 20, 50, 100, 200 euros**
- **¿otra cantidad?** *(__oh__-trah kahn-tee-__dahd__)* (another amount?)

Press the key for the desired amount, and your money comes out. Then the following messages come up:

- **entregado** *(ehn-treh-__gah__-doh)* (delivered)
- **saldo** *(__sahl__-doh)* (balance)
- **por favor retire su dinero** *(pohr fah-__bohr__ reh-__tee__-reh soo dee-__neh__-roh)* (please take your money)

Keep all the receipts that cash machines deliver. If you get no receipt or if your trip to the cash machine is unsuccessful, write down the place, time and date. When you arrive home, check everything against your bank statement. Also, be sure to check that no amount was debited to you on those occasions when you received no money from a cash machine. Follow your bank's procedures for following up any discrepancies.

Words to Know

cantidad	kahn-tee-_dahd_	quantity; amount
cuenta	koo_ehn_-tah	account
débito	_deh_-bee-toh	debit
entregar	ehn-treh-_gahr_	to deliver
introducir	een-troh-doo-_theer_	insert
retirar	reh-tee-_rahr_	withdrawal
saldo	_sahl_-doh	balance

Wielding Your Credit Card

Credit cards are a safe, clean way of handling your money. Paying with your credit card has many advantages, including that you don't have to carry around cash and your expenses are registered in your account. Plus, you always have a valid receipt. Problems arise only when you come across a shop, hotel or restaurant that doesn't take your (or any type of) credit card.

Certain places that take credit cards are a bit pricier than ones that don't. You can eat at local restaurants that don't take credit cards and have excellent food and service for less money.

Talkin' the Talk

In this dialogue, Marcos wants to pay for his purchase in a clothes shop. Here's how he finds out whether the shop accepts his credit card.

Marcos:	**¿Aceptan tarjetas de crédito?** *ah-<u>thehp</u>-tahn tahr-<u>Heh</u>-tahs deh <u>kreh</u>-dee-toh* Do you take credit cards?
Storekeeper:	**Con mucho gusto.** *kohn <u>moo</u>-choh <u>goos</u>-toh* With pleasure.
Marcos:	**Aquí tiene mi tarjeta.** *ah-<u>kee</u> tee<u>eeh</u>-neh mee tahr-<u>Heh</u>-tah* Here's my card.
Storekeeper:	**Un momento señor . . . su recibo** *oon moh-<u>mehn</u>-toh seh-ny<u>ohr</u> soo reh-<u>thee</u>-boh* One moment sir . . . your receipt.
	Aquí tiene su tarjeta y su recibo. Gracias. *ah-<u>kee</u> tee<u>eeh</u>-neh soo tahr-<u>Heh</u>-tah ee soo reh-<u>thee</u>-boh <u>grah</u>-theeahs* Here's your card and your receipt. Thank you.

Words to Know

el recibo	ehl reh-_thee_-boh	the receipt
firmar	feer-_mahr_	to sign
la autorización	lah ahoo-toh-ree-thah-thee_ohn_	the authorisation
la identificación	lah ee-dehn-tee-fee-kah-thee_ohn_	the identification
la tarjeta	lah tahr-_Heh_-tah	the card
la ventanilla	lah behn-tah-_nee_-yah	the counter
servir	sehr-_beer_	to serve; to be of service

Using your card at a cash machine in Spain isn't very different from doing so at home. But if you want to get some cash directly from a bank cashier with your credit or debit card, you need to use a little bit of Spanish.

Using Traveller's Cheques in Spain

Traveller's cheques (**cheques de viaje**) (_cheh_-kehs deh bee-ah-_Heh_) are a safe way to carry your money. One inconvenience of traveller's cheques, though, is that you need to find the right place to use or cash them. Banks cash them, and so do many money exchange places. The better hotels also take traveller's cheques. Less expensive hotels, restaurants and most shops don't take traveller's cheques, however. Try to exchange them before you go on your buying forays, and take just moderate amounts of cash with you.

Talkin' the Talk

In the following dialogue, Ana is at a bank to cash in some traveller's cheques.

Ana: **¿A cuánto esta el euro en cheques de viaje?**
ah kooahn-toh ehs-tha ehl eh-oo-roh ehn cheh-kehs deh bee-ah-Heh
What's the exchange per euro for traveller's cheques?

Cashier: **A noventa con ocho.**
ah noo-behn-tah kohn oh-choh
At ninety eight.

Ana: **Quiero cambiar estos cheques de viaje.**
keeeh-roh kahm-beeahr ehs-tohs cheh-kehs deh bee-ah-Heh
I want to cash these traveller's cheques.

Cashier: **¿Tiene un documento de identidad, por favor?**
teeeh-neh oon doh-koo-mehn-toh deh ee-dehn-tee-dahd pohr fah-bohr
Do you have any identification please?

Ana: **Mi pasaporte.**
mee pah-sah-pohr-teh
My passport.

Cashier: **Muy bien. Ahora puede firmar sus cheques.**
mooy beeehn ah-oh-rah poo-eh-deh feer-mahr soos cheh-kehs
Very good. Now you may sign your cheques.

Words to Know

a cuánto	ah koo-ahn-toh	for how much
cambiar	kahm-bee-ahr	to change
el mostrador	ehl mohs-trah-dohr	the counter (literally: the place where you show)
el viajero	ehl beeah-Heh-roh	the traveller
los documentos	lohs doh-koo-mehn-tohs	identification (literally: documents)

Changing and Exchanging: Cambiar

In Spanish, to change and to exchange are expressed with the same verb, **cambiar** *(kahm-bee-ahr)*. **Cambiar** is a regular verb, and its root is **cambi-** *(kahm-bee)*. Here's how you conjugate its present tense:

Conjugation	Pronunciation
yo cambio	*yoh kahm-beeoh*
tú cambias	*too kahm-beeahs*
él, ella, usted cambia	*ehl, eh-yah, oos-tehd kahm-beeah*
nosotros cambiamos	*noh-soh-trohs kahm-beeah-mohs*
vosotros cambiáis	*boh-soh-trohs kahm-beeah-ees*
ellos, ellas, ustedes cambian	*eh-yohs, eh-yahs, oos-teh-dehs kahm-beeahn*

Try the following phrases to help practise using **cambiar**:

- ✔ **En esa ventanilla cambian moneda.** *(ehn eh-sah behn-tah-nee-yah kahm-beeahn moh-neh-dah)* (At that window, they change currency.)

- ✔ **Quiero cambiar libras por euros.** *(keeeh-roh kahm-beeahr lee-brahs-pohr ehoo-rohs)* (I want to exchange pounds for euros.)

- ✔ **En el banco cambian libras.** *(ehn ehl bahn-koh kahm-beeahn lee-brahs)* (At the bank you can exchange [your pounds].)

- ✔ **¡Es muy alta esta comisión de cambio!** *(ehs moo-ee ahl-tah ehs-tah koh-mee-see-ohn deh kahm-bee-oh)* (This commission charge [for the exchange] is too high!)

Exchanging Your Pounds for Euros

When you travel in Spain, you need to use euros (€) for all transactions. Don't use pounds sterling to buy goods or services because the exchange rate is very poor.

Banks and exchange bureaux charge a fee for their services; the fee is reflected in the way they chart their prices and so check those charts first. In some areas, the banks may be more expensive than the exchange bureaux because they charge an extra amount or commission; in other places, this situation can be reversed.

You may see signs such as the following:

British Pound (£)   We Buy £1 at €1.10   We Sell 1€ at £0.85

In this example, the official exchange rate is £1 = €1.15, which means that the company or bank buys your £1 for €1.10, and if you want to buy pounds back, they change €1 to you for £0.85. So they make a few cents on every pound they handle.

Exchange bureaux give you formal receipts, just as banks do; these receipts are the proofs of purchase that you need when you discover that something is amiss with your money. So instead of exchanging your money on the street, look for the sign that says **cambio** *(kahm-beeoh)* (exchange).

The following phrases come in handy when exchanging money:

- ✔ **¿Dónde puedo cambiar libras?** *(dohn-deh pooeh-doh kahm-beeahr lee-brahs)* (Where can I exchange pounds?)

- ✔ **A la derecha hay una agencia de cambio.** *(ah lah deh-reh-chah ah-ee oo-nah ah-Hehn-theeah deh kahm-bee-oh)* (To the right, there's an exchange bureau.)

- ✔ **Dónde encuentro una agencia de cambio?** *(dohn-deh ehn-kooehn-troh oo-nah ah-Hehn-theeah deh kahm-bee-oh)* (Where can I find a currency exchange bureau?)

Words to Know

derecha	deh-_reh_-chah	right
encontrar	ehn-kohn-_trahr_	to find
la agencia	ah-_Hehn_-theeah	the agency

Talkin' the Talk

In this conversation, José Manuel exchanges some currency.

José Manuel: **¿A cuánto está la libra?**
ah kooahn-toh ehs-tah lah leeh-brah
What's the exchange for the British pound?

Bureau attendant: **¿La compra o a la venta?**
lah kohm-prah oh ah lah behn-tah
Buying or selling?

José Manuel:	**La venta.** *lah behn-tah* Selling.
Bureau attendant:	**A uno con diez.** *ah oo-noh kohn-deeeth* At 1.10.
José Manuel:	**¿Y a la compra?** *ee ah lah kohm-prah* And buying?
Bureau attendant:	**A cero con ochenta y cinco.** *ah theh-roh-kohn oh-chehn-tah ee thehn-koh* At 0.85.
José Manuel:	**¿Me cambia cien libras, por favor?** *meh kahm-beeah theeehn lee-brahs poh fah-bohr* Will you exchange £100 for me, please?
Bureau attendant:	**Aquí tiene el recibo y...aquí el dinero.** *ah-kee-teeeh-neh ehl reh-thee-boh ee ah-kee ehl dee-neh-roh* Here's the receipt and . . . here's the money.

Fun & Games

A quick-change artist (aren't we punny?) has rearranged the letters in several Spanish words below. Unscramble the words and then match them with their English translation.

al promca	account
al tanev	balance
cibore	notes
damones	cash
dolsa	coins
entuac	credit card
ernoid	money
jetarat ed drotice	PIN number
le canob	receipt
ne votecife	the bank
romeun fendicclaon	the purchase
sibellet	the sale
tirearr	withdrawal

Chapter 12

Asking Directions: ¿Dónde Está? (Where Is It?)

. . . .

In This Chapter

▶ Locating restaurants, tapas bars, shops and museums

▶ Following directions

▶ Ordering ordinal numbers

▶ Going up and down

. . . .

'*L*et's go!' (**¡vamos!**) (*bah-mohs*) is a great motto for when you're walking or riding about or discovering places to visit. But to find out exactly where to go, you need to ask an important question. In Spanish, that question is **¿dónde?** (*dohn-deh*) (where?).

Asking the Question for Going Places: ¿Dónde?

Consider this question: **a dónde ir?** (*ah dohn-deh eer*) (where to go?)

'Where?' is one of the big questions, the wandering question, the question that answers your need to experience many new Spanish places, which provide a sense of wonder and discovery.

'Where' is the question of movement and concerns displacement. 'Where' is what you ask when you seek the unknown other place, the place that desire takes you. 'Where' encourages searchers to explore the planet and unravel its mysteries. For example, the question 'Where do we go for the sun?' has led seafarers to travel around the world, cross the oceans and discover that just around the corner from the UK, Spain has the answer.

Of course, usually asking 'where' simply helps you find what you're looking for, and takes you to somewhere quite ordinary but necessary. Where would you be without 'where'? The following sections help you to practise using this vital word in Spain.

Working Out Where to Go: ¿Dónde Vamos?

In Chapter 4, you find out about the Spanish verb that you most often associate with the question **¿dónde?** (*dohn-deh*) (where?). Now, looking for directions is a sign of movement – and because moving is an impermanent state of being – **dónde** is associated with **estar** (*ehs-tahr*), the verb that means 'to be' in a temporary state.

Sample the following sentences that use **¿dónde?** and **estar**:

- ✔ **¿Dónde está el Museo del Prado?** (*donh-deh ehs-tah ehl moo-seh-oh dehl prah-doh* (Where's the Prado Museum?)
- ✔ **¿Dónde estamos ahora?** (*dohn-deh ehs-tah-mohs ah-oh-rah*) (Where are we now?)
- ✔ **¿Dónde está el Hotel Avenida?** (*dohn-deh ehs-tah ehl oh-tehl ah-beh-nee-dah*) (Where's the Hotel Avenida?)
- ✔ **¿Dónde estuviste anoche?** (*dohn-deh ehs-too-bees-teh ah-noh-cheh*) (Where were you last night?)

Here's a sentence for the person who wants to know everything:

¡Quiero saber cómo, cuándo, y dónde! (*keeeh-roh sah-behr koh-moh kooahn-doh ee dohn-deh*) (I want to know how, when and where!)

You can use another line to express your determination to find that special place:

¡Donde esté, lo encontraremos! (*donh-deh ehs-teh loh ehn-kohn-trah-reh-mohs*) (Wherever it is, we're going to find it!)

Orienting the Space Around You

You can identify the space around your body in six ways:

✔ **delante** *(deh-lahn-teh)* (in front)

- **Paula camina delante de Clara.** *(pahoo-lah kah-mee-nah deh-lahn-teh deh klah-rah)* (Paula walks in front of Clara.)

✔ **detrás** *(deh-trahs)* (behind)

- **Clara va detrás de Paula.** *(klah-rah bah deh-trahs deh pahoo-lah)* (Clara goes behind Paula.)

✔ **a la derecha** *(ah-lah deh-reh-chah)* (to the right)

- **A la derecha de Paula está Pedro.** *(ah lah deh-reh-chah deh pahoo-lah ehs-tah peh-droh)* (To the right of Paula is Pedro.)

✔ **a la izquierda** *(ah lah eeth-keeehr-dah)* (to the left)

- **José se pone a la izquierda de Clara.** *(Hoh-seh seh poh-neh ah lah eeth-keeehr-dah deh klah-rah)* (José gets [literally: he puts himself] to the left of Clara.)

✔ **debajo** *(deh-bah-Hoh)* (beneath; under)

- **Hay barro debajo de los pies de José.** *(ah-ee bah-rroh deh-bah-Hoh deh lohs peeehs deh Hoh-seh)* (There's mud under Jose's feet.)

✔ **encima** *(ehn-thee-mah)* (above)

- **La rama está encima de la cabeza de Paula.** *(lah rah-mah ehs-tah ehn-thee-mah deh lah kah-beh-thah deh pahoo-lah)* (The branch is above Paula's head.)

Before you go any further, you need to understand the distinction between two very similar Spanish words: **derecho** *(deh-reh-choh)* (straight) and **derecha** *(deh-reh-chah)* (right).

What was that, you say? Look again. The only difference between the words is that one ends in the letter **o** and the other in the letter **a**, and the meaning is suddenly not the same!

✔ **derecho** *(deh-reh-choh)* (straight; straight ahead)

- **Siga derecho por esta calle.** *(see-gah deh-reh-choh pohr ehs-tah kah-yeh)* (Keep going straight on this street.)

✔ **derecha** *(deh-reh-chah)* (right)

- **En la esquina, a la derecha.** *(ehn lah ehs-kee-nah ah lah deh-reh-chah)* (At the corner, turn to the right.)

Talkin' the Talk

After checking in at her hotel, María asks the hotel receptionist for directions to the restaurant and the pool.

María: **¿Dónde está el restaurante?**
dohn-deh ehs-tah ehl rehs-tahoo-rahn-teh
Where's the restaurant?

Receptionist: **Está arriba, en el segundo piso.**
ehs-tah ah-rree-bah ehn ehl seh-goon-doh pee-soh
It's upstairs, on the second floor.

María: **¿En qué piso está la piscina?**
ehn keh pee-soh ehs-tah lah pees-thee-nah
On what floor is the pool?

Receptionist: **Está en el quinto piso.**
ehs-tah ehn ehl keen-toh pee-soh
It's on the fifth floor.
Puedes tomar el ascensor.
pooeh-dehs toh-mahr ehl ahs-thehn-sohr
You can take the lift.

María: **¿Y cómo llego al ascensor?**
ee koh-moh yeh-goh ahl ahs-thehn-sohr
How do I get to the lift?

Receptionist: **El ascensor está aquí, a la izquierda.**
ehl ahs-thehn-sohr ehs-tah ah-kee ah lah eeth-keeehr-dah
The lift is here, to the left.

Understanding Spatial Directions

You use words to tell where people or things are in relation to other people and things. The following terms describe such relationships:

- **al lado** *(ahl lah-doh)* (beside, next to, at the side of)
- **frente a** *(frehn-teh ah)* (in front of)

- **dentro** *(dehn-troh)* (inside)

- **adentro** *(ah-dehn-troh)* (inside; because **dentro** also means 'inside', **adentro** may express movement, as when someone or something moves toward an interior)

- **fuera** *(fooeh-rah)* (outside)

- **afuera** *(ah-fooeh-rah)* (outside; can express movement, as in the case of **adentro** – the fourth bullet point in this list)

- **bajo** *(bah-Hoh)* (under; below)

- **debajo** *(deh-bah-Hoh)* (underneath)

- **arriba** *(ah-ree-bah)* (above; up)

Practising these directions is sure to come in handy. The sentences that follow use these terms:

- **La pastelería está al lado del banco.** *(lah-pahs-teh-leh-reeah ehs-tah ahl lah-doh dehl bahn-koh)* (The pastry shop is next to the bank.)

- **Frente al banco hay una zapatería.** *(frehn-teh ahl bahn-koh ah-ee oo-nah thah-pah-teh-reeah)* (In front of the bank there's a shoe shop.)

- **Hay unos libros dentro de la caja.** *(ah-ee oo-nohs lee-brohs dehn-troh deh lah kah-Hah)* (There are some books inside the box.)

- **Cuando llueve ponen las mesas adentro.** *(kooahn-doh yooeh-beh poh-nehn lahs meh-sahs ah-dehn-troh)* (When it rains they put the tables inside.)

- **Las mesas de la cafetería están afuera.** *(lahs meh-sahs deh lah kah-feh-teh-ree-ah ehs-tahn ah-fooeh-rah)* (The cafeteria tables are outside.)

- **Hay agua bajo los pies de Carlos.** *(ah-ee ah-gooah bah-Hoh lohs peeehs deh kahr-lohs)* (There's water under Carlos's feet.)

- **Debajo de la calle está el metro.** *(deh-bah-Hoh deh lah kah-yeh ehs-tah ehl meh-troh)* (The tube runs under the street.)

- **Arriba hay cielo despejado.** *(ah-ree-bah ah-ee thee-eh-loh dehs-peh-Hah-doh)* (Above, the sky is clear.)

- **El nuevo supermercado está fuera del centro de la ciudad.** *(ehl-nooeh-boh soo-pehr-mehr-cah-doh ehs-tah fooeh-rah dehl thehn-troh deh lah thee-oo-dahd)* (The new supermarket is outside the city centre.)

- **Este ascensor va arriba.** *(ehs-teh ahs-thehn-sohr bah ah-rree-bah)* This lift goes up.)

Words to Know

despejado	dehs-peh-_Hah_-doh	uncluttered; clear
el barro	ehl b_ah_-rroh	the mud
encontrar	ehn-kohn-_trahr_	to find
la caja	lah _kah_-Hah	the box
la esquina	lah ehs-_kee_-nah	the corner
la gorra	lah _goh_-rrah	the cap
lejano	leh-_Hah_-noh	distant; far

Mapping the Place

Maps are key to getting around in Spain. The first thing to request at the car hire office, or the first thing to buy on arrival in a city, is a map. You can find your way around more easily using a map or if someone can show you on the map how to find the place you're looking for.

Some directions are universally used to explain how to get somewhere or find something by using the points on a compass. The following terms help you specify north from south and east from west:

- ✔ **el norte** _(ehl nohr-teh)_ (the north)
- ✔ **el sur** _(ehl soor)_ (the south)
- ✔ **el este** _(ehl ehs-teh)_ (the east)
- ✔ **oriente** _(oh-ree-ehn-teh)_ (the East, the Orient)
- ✔ **el oeste** _(ehl oh-ehs-teh)_ (the west)
- ✔ **poniente** _(poh-nee-ehn-teh)_ (westerly, from the west [literally: where the sun sets])

Here are some 'mapping' phrases to practise:

- ✔ **La avenida Venus está al este de aquí.** _(lah ah-beh-nee-dah beh-noos ehs-tah ahl ehs-teh deh ah-kee)_ (Venus Avenue is east of here.)

- ✔ **Al oeste está la calle Violetas.** *(ahl oh-__ehs__-teh ehs-__tah__ lah __kah__-yeh bee-oh-__leh__-tahs)* (To the west is Violeta's Street.)

- ✔ **El parque está al norte.** *(ehl __pahr__-keh ehs-__tah__ ahl __nohr__-teh)* (The park is to the north.)

- ✔ **Al sur se va hacia el río.** *(ahl soor seh bah ah-__thee__-ah ehl __ree__oh)* (To the south is [literally: one goes towards] the river.)

- ✔ **Oriente es donde el sol se levanta.** *(oh-ree__ehn__-teh ehs __dohn__-deh ehl sohl seh leh-__bahn__-tah)* (East is where the sun rises.)

- ✔ **Poniente es donde el sol se pone.** *(poh-nee__ehn__-teh ehs __dohn__-deh ehl sohl seh __poh__-neh)* (West is where the sun sets.)

- ✔ **Jordania está en el Cercano Oriente.** *(Hohr-__dah__-neeah ehs-__tah__ ehn ehl thehr-__kah__-noh oh-ree__ehn__-teh)* (Jordan is in the Near East.)

- ✔ **China está en el Lejano Oriente.** *(__chee__-nah ehs-__tah__ ehn ehl leh-__Hah__-noh oh-ree__ehn__-teh)* (China is in the Far East.)

- ✔ **Asia está al oriente de Europa.** *(__ah__-see-ah ehs-__tah__ ahl oh-ree-__ehn__-teh de eh-oo-__roh__-pah)* (Asia is east of Europe.)

- ✔ **América está en poniente.** *(ah-__meh__-ree-kah ehs-__tah__ ehn poh-nee-__ehn__-teh)* (America is to the west [of Spain].)

The following phrases are helpful when asking or giving general directions:

- ✔ **la calle** *(lah __kah__-yeh)* (the street)

- ✔ **la avenida** *(lah ah-beh-__nee__-dah)* (the avenue)

- ✔ **el bulevar** *(ehl boo-leh-__bahr__)* (the boulevard)

- ✔ **el río** *(ehl __ree__-oh)* (the river)

- ✔ **la plaza** *(lah __plah__-thah)* (the square)

- ✔ **el parque** *(ehl __pahr__-keh)* (the park)

- ✔ **el jardín** *(ehl Hahr-__deen__)* (the garden; sometimes a small park)

- ✔ **el barrio** *(ehl __bah__-rreeoh)* (the neighbourhood)

- ✔ **izquierda** *(eeth-kee-__ehr__-dah)* (left)

- ✔ **derecha** *(deh-__reh__-chah)* (right)

- ✔ **derecho** *(deh-__reh__-choh)* (straight)

- ✔ **doblar** *(doh-__blahr__)* (to turn)

- ✔ **seguir** *(seh-__gheer__)* (to keep going)

- ✔ **la manzana** *(lah mahn-thah-nah)* (the block)

Asking for directions is always a bit problematic. The people who answer your questions know the city and the answers seem so obvious to them! So to keep you going and to sharpen your ear, here are some phrases to practise:

✔ **En el barrio hay una avenida ancha.** *(ehn ehl bah-rree-oh ah-ee oo-nah ah-beh-nee-dah ahn-chah)* (In the neighbourhood, there's a wide avenue.)

✔ **Nuestra calle va de norte a sur.** *(noo-ehs-trah kah-yeh bah deh nohr-teh ah soor)* (Our street runs north to south.)

✔ **Mi tía vive en esta plaza.** *(mee tee-ah bee-beh ehn ehs-tah plah-thah)* (My aunt lives in this square.)

✔ **Junto al río hay un gran parque.** *(Hoon-toh ahl ree-oh ah-ee oon grahn pahr-keh)* (By the riverside is a large park.)

✔ **La plaza está en el centro de la ciudad.** *(lah plah-thah ehs-tah ehn ehl thehn-troh deh lah thee-oo-dahd)* (The square's in the centre of the city.)

✔ **En el jardín hay juegos para niños.** *(ehn ehl Hahr-deen ah-ee Hooeh-gohs pah-rah nee-nyohs)* (In the garden, they have a children's playground.)

✔ **El Zóco de Toledo es una plaza.** *(ehl thoh-koh deh toh-leh-doh ehs oo-nah plah-thah)* (The Zoco in Toledo is a square.)

✔ **Esa avenida se llama Alameda.** *(eh-sah ah-beh-nee-dah seh yah-mah ah-lah-meh-dah)* (The name of that avenue is Alameda [Poplar Grove].)

Talkin' the Talk

Ana is an artist who's anxious to visit the Reina Sofía Museum. She plans to walk there from her hotel so she can avoid the heavy traffic.

Ana: **Disculpe, ¿cómo voy al Museo Reina Sofía?**
dees-kool-peh koh-moh bohee ahl moo-seh-oh rreh-ee-nah so-phee-ah
Excuse me, how do I get to Reina Sofía Museum?

Receptionist: **Muy fácil. Está muy cerca.**
moo-ee fah-theel esh-tah moo-ee thehr-kah
Very easy. It's really close.

Sal del hotel.
sahl dehl oh-tehl
You go out of the hotel.

Ana: **¿Dónde está la salida?**
dohn-deh ehs-tah lah sah-lee-dah
Where's the exit?

Receptionist: **La salida está a tu derecha.**
lah sah-<u>lee</u>-dah ehs-<u>tah</u> ah tuh deh-<u>reh</u>-chah
The exit's to your right.

Al salir ve hacia la izquierda. . .
ahl sah-<u>leer</u> beh <u>ah</u>-theeah lah eeth-kee-<u>ehr</u>-dah
As you go out, turn to the left. . .

. . .camina hasta la segunda calle. . .
kah-<u>mee</u>-nah <u>ahs</u>-tah lah seh-<u>goon</u>-dah <u>kah</u>-yeh
. . .walk to the second street. . .

. . .da la vuelta a la derecha. . .
dah lah boo<u>ehl</u>-tah ah lah deh-<u>reh</u>-chah
. . .turn to the right. . .

. . .y llegas al museo.
ee <u>yeh</u>-gahs ahl moo-<u>seh</u>-oh
. . .and you arrive at the museum.

Ana: **Gracias por tu ayuda.**
<u>grah</u>-theeahs pohr too ah-<u>yoo</u>-dah
Thanks for your help.

Taking You Up: Subir

The following mini-table shows you how to conjugate the present tense of the verb **subir** *(soo-<u>beer</u>)* (to go up; to ascend) – a very useful regular verb when you want to go up! Its root is **sub-** *(soob)*.

Conjugation	*Pronunciation*
yo subo	*yoh <u>soo</u>-boh*
tú subes	*too <u>soo</u>-behs*
él, ella, usted sube	*ehl, <u>eh</u>-yah, oos-<u>tehd</u> <u>soo</u>-beh*
nosotros subimos	*noh-<u>soh</u>-trohs soo-<u>bee</u>-mohs*
vosotros subís	*boh-soh-trohs soo-<u>bees</u>*
ellos, ellas, ustedes suben	*<u>eh</u>-yohs, <u>eh</u>-yahs, oos-<u>teh</u>-dehs <u>soo</u>-behn*

Practising verb conjugations is essential so that they soon become second nature. But until they do become second nature, here are some phrases to help you:

✔ **Suben por la escalera.** (<u>soo</u>-behn pohr lah ehs-kah-<u>leh</u>-rah) (They go up the stairs.)

✔ **Subes por esa calle, a la izquierda.** (<u>soo</u>-behs pohr <u>eh</u>-sah <u>kah</u>-yeh ah lah eeth-kee-<u>ehr</u>-dah) (You go up on that street, to the left.)

✔ **Nosotros vamos a subir solos.** (noh-<u>soh</u>-trohs <u>bah</u>-mohs ah soo-<u>beer</u> <u>soh</u>-lohs) (We're going to go up alone.)

✔ **El ascensor de la derecha sube.** (ehl ahs-thehn-<u>sohr</u> deh lah deh-<u>reh</u>-chah <u>soo</u>-beh) (The lift to the right goes up.)

✔ **Yo subo allí todos los días.** (yoh <u>soo</u>-boh ah-<u>yee</u> <u>toh</u>-dohs lohs <u>deeahs</u>) (I go up there every day.)

Lowering You Down: Bajar

What goes up, must come down, right? The 'descending' verb is **bajar** (bah-<u>Hahr</u>) (to go down).

Bajar is a regular verb and its root is **baj-** (bahH). Here's how you conjugate **bajar** in the present tense:

Conjugation	Pronunciation
yo bajo	yoh <u>bah</u> Hoh
tú bajas	too <u>bah</u>-Hahs
él, ella, usted baja	ehl, <u>eh</u>-yah, oos-<u>tehd</u>, <u>bah</u>-Hah
nosotros bajamos	noh-<u>soh</u>-trohs bah-<u>Hah</u>-mohs
vosotros bajáis	boh-<u>soh</u>-trohs bah-<u>Hah</u>ees
ellos, ellas, ustedes bajan	<u>eh</u>-yohs, <u>eh</u>-yahs, oos-<u>teh</u>-dehs <u>bah</u>-Hahn

When you need to go down, for any reason, follow our examples and practice, practice, practice!

✔ **Ella baja por la escalera.** (<u>eh</u>-yah <u>bah</u>-Hah pohr lah ehs-kah-<u>leh</u>-rah) (She goes down the stairs.)

✔ **Bajamos por esta calle.** (bah-<u>Hah</u>-mohs pohr <u>ehs</u>-tah <u>kah</u>-yeh) (We go down this street.)

✔ **Tú bajas del coche con el perro.** (too <u>bah</u>-Hahs dehl <u>koh</u>-cheh kohn ehl <u>peh</u>-rroh) (You step out of [literally go down] the car with your dog.)

✔ **Dicen que van a bajar pronto.** (<u>dee</u>-thehn keh bahn a <u>bah</u>-Hahr <u>prohn</u>-toh) (They say they're going to go down [to the lobby or some other lower area] soon.)

✔ **Bajo a pasear al parque por la mañana.** (*bah-Hoh ah pah-seh-ahr ahl pahr-keh pohr lah mah-nyah-nah*) (I go for a walk down to the park in the morning.)

Heading Here, There and Everywhere

An old saying has confused people never knowing whether they're here or there. Well, in Spanish, whether you're here – **aquí** (*ah-kee*) – or there – **allí** (*ah-yee*) – doesn't matter, because the words are interchangeable: just choose which word you like and end the confusion.

Native Spanish speakers often interchange **aquí** or **allí**, with no distinction between the two words. Both these words are adverbs and so they always work in the vicinity of a verb and words that talk about space.

To show how you can use one of these words or the other, the following sentences enable you to practise situations in which you may be here or there:

✔ **Allí, en la esquina, está el banco.** (*ah-yee ehn lah ehs-kee-nah ehs-tah ehl ban-koh*) (There, on the corner, is the bank.)

✔ **Allí van los turistas ingleses.** (*ah-yee bahn lohs too-rees-tahs een-gleh-sehs*) (There they go, the English tourists.)

✔ **Aquí se come muy bien.** (*ah-kee seh koh-meh moo-ee beehn*) (Here one eats very well.)

✔ **Aquí está el museo.** (*ah-kee ehs-tah ehl moo-seh-oh*) (Here's the museum.)

✔ **¡Ven aquí!** (*behn ah-kee*) (Come here!)

✔ **¡Corre, allí!** (*koh-rreh ah-yee*) (Run, there! [in a particular direction])

Sometimes you need to talk about 'nowhere', 'everywhere' and perhaps 'anywhere'. You use the following phrases to express the idea of all places or no particular places in Spanish:

✔ **en todas partes** (*ehn toh-dahs pahr-tehs*) (everywhere)

✔ **en ninguna parte** (*ehn neen-goo-nah pahr-teh*) (nowhere, anywhere)

The following sentences can help you practise using these phrases:

✔ **En todas partes hay gente simpática.** (*ehn toh-dahs pahr-tehs ah-ee Hehn-teh seem-pah-tee-kah*) (There are pleasant people everywhere.)

✔ **Busqué las llaves por todas partes.** (*boos-keh lahs yah-behs pohr toh-dahs pahr-tehs*) (I searched for the keys everywhere.)

✔ **En ninguna parte encuentro mis llaves.** *(ehn neen-goo-nah pahr-teh ehn-kooehn-troh mees yah-behs)* (I can't find my keys anywhere.)

✔ **Ella mira por todas partes cuando busca algo.** *(eh-yah mee-rah pohr toh-dahs pahr-tehs kooahn-doh boos-kah ahl-goh)* (She looks everywhere when searching for something.

Counting Ordinal Numbers

You may find yourself telling people about your day by reciting what you did first, second, third and so on. These words – first, second and third – are ordinal numbers, and are different from one, two and three; they tell you order and sequence. (Check out Chapter 2 to see all the usual numbers in Spanish.)

When given directions, you hear a lot of phrases describing things such as the third street to the left or the fourth floor, and so ordinal numbers are extremely useful. Here are the first ten:

✔ **primero** *(pree-meh-roh)* (first)

✔ **segundo** *(seh-goon-doh)* (second)

✔ **tercero** *(tehr-theh-roh)* (third)

✔ **cuarto** *(kooahr-toh)* (fourth)

✔ **quinto** *(keen-toh)* (fifth)

✔ **sexto** *(sehks-toh)* (sixth)

✔ **séptimo** *(sehp-tee-moh)* (seventh)

✔ **octavo** *(ohk-tah-boh)* (eighth)

✔ **noveno** *(noh-beh-noh)* (ninth)

✔ **décimo** *(deh-thee-moh)* (tenth)

The following phrases help you practise using ordinal numbers:

✔ **Vivo en el octavo piso.** *(bee-boh ehn ehl ohk-tah-boh pee-soh)* (I live on the eighth floor.)

✔ **En la tercera esquina hay un museo.** *(ehn lah tehr-theh-rah esh-kee-nah ah-ee oon moo-seh-oh)* (At the third corner, there's a museum.)

✔ **Este es el cuarto bar que veo aquí.** *(ehs-teh ehs ehl koo<u>ahr</u>-toh bahr keh <u>beh</u>-oh <u>ah</u>-kee)* (This is the fourth bar I've seen here.)

✔ **En el primer piso hay un servicio.** *(ehn ehl pree-<u>mehr</u> <u>pee</u>-soh <u>ah</u>-ee <u>oon</u> sehr-<u>bee</u>-theeoh)* (On the first floor, there's a toilet.)

✔ **Voy a bajar al segundo piso.** *(bohee ah bah-<u>Hahr</u> ahl seh-<u>goon</u>-doh <u>pee</u>-soh)* (I'm going down to the second floor.)

✔ **La terraza está en el décimonoveno piso.** *(lah teh-<u>rrah</u>-thah ehs-<u>tah</u> ehn ehl <u>déh</u>-thee-moh-noh-beh-noh <u>pee</u>-soh)* (The terrace is on the 19th floor.)

Talkin' the Talk

Ana has just bought some postcards at a newsstand. But she also needs some stamps. She asks the news vendor for directions to the post office.

Ana: **¿Me puede decir dónde está la Oficina de Correos?**
meh <u>pooeh</u>-deh deh-<u>theer</u> <u>dohn</u>-deh ehs-<u>tah</u> lah oh-fee-<u>thee</u>-nah deh koh-<u>rreh</u>-ohs
Can you tell me where the Post Office is?

News
vendor: **Está a tres manzanas.**
ehs-<u>tah</u> a trehs mahn-<u>thah</u>-nahs
It's three blocks from here.

Ve derecho hasta la Catedral. . .
beh deh-<u>reh</u>-choh <u>ahs</u>-tah lah kah-teh-<u>drahl</u>
You go straight to the Cathedral. . .

. . .sigue derecho al lado de la Catedral. . .
<u>see</u>-gheh deh-<u>reh</u>-choh ahl <u>lah</u>-doh deh lah kah-teh-<u>drahl</u>
. . .keep going straight along side the Cathedral. . .

. . .cruza la plaza, siempre derecho. . .
<u>kroo</u>-thah lah <u>plah</u>-thah see<u>ehm</u>-preh deh-<u>reh</u>-choh
. . .cross the square, keeping straight ahead. . .

. . .y llegas a la Oficina de Correos.
ee <u>yeh</u>-gahs ah lah oh-fee-<u>thee</u>-nah deh koh-<u>rreh</u>-ohs
. . .and you get to the Post Office.

Ana:	**Muchas gracias.**
	moo-chahs _grah_-theeahs
	Thanks very much.

Knowing How Far To Go: Cerca and Lejos

In this section, you take a look at the words **cerca** _(thehr-kah)_ (near; close) and **lejos** _(leh-Hohs)_ (far). Use these two words when you want to discuss distance, and how much effort is going to be required to arrive at a specific place.

Talkin' the Talk

Ines is deciding how to spend her day. Should she attend the cinema, visit a museum or do both? First, she needs to find out how near these places are to her and to each other.

Ines:	**¿Está lejos el cine Paraíso?**
	ehs-_tah_ _leh_-Hohs ehl _thee_-neh pah-rah-_ee_-soh
	Is the Paraiso cinema far?

Martine:	**No, está muy cerca. . .**
	noh ehs-_tah_ _moo_-ee _thehr_-kah
	No, it's quite near. . .

	. . .a sólo dos calles.
	ah _soh_-loh dohs _kah_-yehs
	. . .only two streets away.

Ines:	**¿Y el Teatro de la Comedia?**
	ee ehl teh-_ah_-troh deh lah koh-_meh_-deeah
	And the Comedia Theatre?

Martine:	**El teatro de la Comedia está lejos. . .**
	ehl teh-_ah_-troh deh-lah koh-_meh_-deeah ehs-_tah_ _leh_-Hohs
	The Comedia Theatre is very far. . .

	. . .tienes que coger el metro.
	tee_eh_-nehs keh koh-_Her_ ehl _meh_-troh
	. . .you have to take the tube.

Words to Know

doblar	doh-_blahr_	to turn
el barrio	ehl _bah_-rree-oh	the neighborhood
el bloque	ehl _bloh_-keh	the block
el bulevar	ehl boo-leh-_bahr_	the boulevard
la avenida	lah ah-beh-_nee_-dah	the avenue
la calle	lah _kah_-yeh	the street
seguir	seh-_gheer_	to keep going

Fun & Games

Lucas and Gemma Ruíz, who speak very little English, are coming to your birthday party. You sent directions to everyone along with their invitations, but they are in English. Lucas asks you to translate your directions for them below:

Go to the square. _____

Go around the corner. _____

Go straight to Badajoz Ave. _____

Turn left. _____

Go north to Colón St. _____

Turn right. _____

Go two more blocks and turn left on Reina Victoria Blvd.
_____

My house is behind the old cathedral. _____

Chapter 13

Checking into a Hotel

. . . .

. . . .

Spanish hotels are often places of special pleasure. Here are a few types of accommodation you may come across:

- **casas rurales** *(kah-sahs roo-rah-lehs)* (country inns [literally: rural houses])

- **hostales** *(osh-tah-lehs)* (cheaper hotels)

- **paradores** *(pah-rah-doh-rehs)* (tourist hotels, high quality inns [literally: places to stop])

In warmer seasons, many hotels have open areas such as balconies, court-yards and patios for you to enjoy. More often than not, these areas are filled with flowers, plants and trees and, in some cases, birds. This chapter provides all the information you need to access accommodation anywhere in Spain.

Checking Out the Hotel Before You Check in

By the time you get to your chosen accommodation, you're likely to be tired from your travels. Nevertheless, seeing the rooms before you check in is still a good idea, because the facilities may differ from what you had in mind.

Size up the following aspects:

- ✔ Are the cupboards big enough?
- ✔ Does the bathroom have a bathtub?
- ✔ What do the windows look out on?

In addition, finding a place to park your car, if you have one, before you check in to your hotel is especially important when you visit places such as the beautiful but often cramped central areas of ancient Spanish cities. Often, an attendant is at the hotel door to help you, taking care of your vehicle while you go inside.

Knowing the following phrases before you arrive at your hotel can make getting a room much easier:

- ✔ **con baño** *(kohn bah-nyoh)* (with bathroom)
- ✔ **agua caliente** *(ah-gooah kah-leeehn-teh)* (hot water)
- ✔ **sólo con ducha** *(soh-loh kohn doo-chah)* (with shower only)
- ✔ **a la calle** *(ah lah kah-yeh)* (opening onto the street)
- ✔ **al interior** *(ahl een-teh-reeohr)* (opening onto the interior)
- ✔ **la piscina** *(lah pees-thee-nah)* (the swimming pool)

Sometimes, Spanish has two words for the same thing. For example, **la habitación** *(lah ah-bee-tah-theeohn)* and **el cuarto** *(ehl kooahr-toh)* both mean 'the room'.

Talkin' the Talk

Ana knows that finding a place to park her car is important when visiting the beautiful medieval downtown areas of Spanish cities, where few parking spaces are available except at the large hotels.

Ana Smith:	**Buenas tardes, ¿tiene aparcamiento para mi coche?**
	boo-eh-nahs tahr-dehs teeeh-neh ah-pahr-kah-mee-ehn-toh pah-rah mee koh-cheh
	Good afternoon, do you have parking for my car?

Receptionist:	**Sí. Hay aparcamiento. Está en la puerta de al lado. Ya van a abrirsela.**
	see ah-ee ah-pahr-kah-mee-ehn-toh ehs-tah ehn lah poo-ehr-tah deh ahl lah-doh yah bahn ah ah-breer-seh-lah
	Yes, there's parking. It's the next door. They're going to open it up for you now.

Ana Smith: **Gracias. Espero afuera.**
grah-theeahs ehs-peh-roh ah-fooeh-rah
Thanks. I'll wait outside.

Words to Know

abrir	ah-*breer*	to open
el parcamiento	ehl ah-pahr-kah-mee-*ehn*-toh	the parking
esperar	ehs-peh-*rahr*	to wait
la puerta	lah poo-*ehr*-tah	the door; the doorway

Check out the dialogue about table reservations in Chapter 5. Change the words of the dialogue from tables to rooms and much of the remaining conversation stays the same.

Talkin' the Talk

Ana has just arrived in town and she's at the front desk of a large hotel. She asks for a room for the night.

Ana Smith: **Necesito una habitación, con baño.**
neh-theh-see-toh oo-nah ah-bee-tah-thee-ohn kohn bah-nyoh
I need a room, with a bath.

Receptionist: **¿Le gusta hacia la calle o hacia el patio?**
leh goos-tah ah-theeah lah kah-yeh oh ah-theeah ehl pah-teeoh
Do you prefer a room [facing] towards the street or the patio?

Ana Smith: **Prefiero hacia el patio.**
preh-feeeh-roh ah-theeah ehl pah-teeoh
I prefer it facing the patio.

Receptionist:	**Las del patio son muy tranquilas. Las habitaciones hacia el patio cuestan sesenta euros, sin desayuno.**
	lahs dehl pah-teeoh sohn moo-ee trahn-kee-lahs lahs ah-bee-tah-theeoh-nehs ah-theeah ehl pah-teeoh kooehs-tahn seh-sehn-tah ehoo-rohs seen deh-sah-yoo-noh
	The patio rooms are very quiet. The rooms facing the patio cost 60 euros, without breakfast.
Ana Smith:	**¿En el primer piso?**
	ehn ehl pree-mehr pee-soh
	On the first floor?
Receptionist:	**No, las del segundo piso. Las del primero son a cincuenta euros.**
	noh lahs dehl seh-goon-doh pee-soh lahs dehl pree-meh-roh sohn a theen-kooehn-tah ehoo-rohs
	No, the second floor ones. The first floor rooms are priced at 50 euros.
Ana Smith:	**Prefiero una en el primer piso.**
	preh-feeeh-roh oo-nah ehn ehl pree-mehr pee-soh
	I prefer one on the first floor.
Receptionist:	**Muy bien**
	mooy beeehn
	Very well.

Words to Know

el baño	ehl *bah*-nyoh	the bath; the bathroom
el piso	ehl *pee*-soh	the floor
hacia	*ah*-theeah	towards
preferir	preh-feh-*reer*	to prefer
primer; primero	pree-*mehr*; pree-*meh*-roh	first
tranquila	trahn-*kee*-lah	quiet

Talkin' the Talk

Hotels can have diverse accommodation and you may well have a choice of which sort you prefer. The receptionist checks with Ana to see what type of room she wants.

Receptionist: **¿Prefiere con cama de matrimonio o con dos camas?**
preh-feeeh-reh kohn kah-mah deh mah-tree-moh-nee-oh oh kohn dohs kah-mahs
Do you prefer a double bed or two [single] beds?

Ana Smith: **Prefiero con dos camas.**
preh-feeeh-roh kohn dohs kah-mahs
I prefer [a room with] two beds.

Receptionist: **Tenemos disponible en el primer piso la habitación número ciento diecinueve. ¿Quiere verla?**
the-neh-mohs dees-poh-nee-bleh ehn ehl pree-mehr pee-soh lah ah-bee-tah-thee-ohn noo-meh-roh theeehn-toh-deeeh-thee-nooeh-beh keeeh-reh behr-lah
Room 119 is available on the first floor. Do you want to see it?

Ana Smith: **Sí, quiero verla.**
see keeeh-roh behr-lah
Yes, I do.

Receptionist: **Pedro, acompañe a la señora a la habitación ciento diecinueve. Aquí está la llave.**
peh-droh ah-kohm-pah-nyeh ah lah seh-nyoh-rah ah lah ah-bee-tah-thee-ohn theeehn-toh-deeeh-thee-nooeh-beh ah-kee ehs-tah lah yah-beh
Pedro, take the lady to room 119. Here's the key.

Words to Know

acompañar	ah-kohm-pah-ny<u>ahr</u>	to go with; to accompany
de matrimonio	deh mah-tree-<u>moh</u>-nee-oh	double (literally: for married people)

disponible	dees-poh-_nee_-bleh	available
la cama	lah _kah_-mah	the bed
la llave	lah _yah_-beh	the key
ver	behr	to see

Talkin' the Talk

Ana wants to be able to relax in her room. A bubble bath sounds good. But first, she needs to make sure that the room has a private bathroom and a bathtub. Otherwise, she may need to change her plans.

Pedro: **La ciento diecinueve está en el segundo patio. Es una habitación preciosa.**
lah _theeehn_-toh-deeeh-thee-_nooeh_-beh ehs-_tah_ ehn ehl seh-_goon_-doh _pah_-teeoh ehs _oo_-nah ah-bee-tah-thee-_ohn_ preh-_theeoh_-sah
119 is on the second patio. It's a beautiful room.

Ana Smith: **¿Tiene baño?**
teeeh-neh _bah_-nyoh
Does it have a [private] bath?

Pedro: **Sí. Pase, por aquí está el baño.**
see _pah_-seh pohr ah-_kee_ ehs-_tah_ ehl _bah_-nyoh
Yes. The bathroom is this way.

Ana Smith: **¿El baño no tiene bañera?**
ehl _bah_-nyoh noh teeeh-neh bah-nyeh-rah
The bathroom doesn't have a bathtub?

Pedro: **No. Como hace calor, aquí la gente prefiere ducharse.**
noh _koh_-moh _ah_-theh kah-_lohr_ ah-_kee_ lah _Hehn_-teh preh-_feeeh_-reh doo-_chahr_-seh
No. Because it's hot, people here prefer to have a shower.

Pedro: **. . .pero esta ducha tiene hidromasaje incorporado.**
peh-roh ehs-tah doo-chah teeeh-neh ee-droh-mah-sah-Heh een-kohr-poh-rah-doh
. . .but this shower does have a hydro-massage [device] built in.

Words to Know

caliente	kah-lee-*ehn*-teh	hot
ducharse	doo-*chahr*-seh	to take a shower
la bañera	lah bah-ny*eh*-rah	the bathtub
la ducha	lah *doo*-chah	the shower
fría	*free*ah	cold (female)
preciosa	preh-thee*oh*-sah	gorgeous; beautiful; lovely

Talkin' the Talk

Ana resigns herself to doing without her bubble bath and plans to watch satellite TV to relax instead. Of course, if she doesn't check to make sure that the room has a TV, she may have to change her plans again.

Ana Smith: **¿La habitación tiene television por satélite?**
lah ah-bee-tah-thee-ohn teeeh-neh teh-leh-bee-see-ohn pohr sah-teh-lee-teh
Does the room have satellite TV?

Pedro: **Sí, tiene satélite y . . . ¡una excelente pantalla plana! Está dentro de este mueble. Aquí está el control remoto.**
see teeeh-neh sah-tee-lee-teh ee oo-nah ehks-theh-lehn-teh pahn-tah-yeeah plah-nah ehs-tah dehn-troh dehl mooeh-bleh ah-kee ehs-tah ehl kohn-trohl reh-moh-toh
Yes, it has satellite and . . . an excellent flat screen TV! It's inside this cabinet. Here's the remote control.

Ana Smith:	**¿Se pueden ver canales en inglés?**
	seh poo<u>eh</u>-dehn behr kah-<u>nah</u>-lehs ehn een-<u>glehs</u>
	Can you get channels in English?
Pedro:	**Sí, hay muchos canales en inglés y también en español.**
	see <u>ah</u>-ee <u>moo</u>-chohs kah-<u>nah</u>-lehs ehn een-<u>glehs</u> ee tahm-bee<u>ehn</u> ehn ehs-pah-<u>nyohl</u>
	Yes, there are lots of channels in English and in Spanish.

Words to Know

el canal	ehl kah-<u>nahl</u>	the channel
el mueble	ehl moo<u>eh</u>-bleh	the cabinet
la pantalla	lah pahn-<u>tah</u>-yah	the screen

Talkin' the Talk

Ana likes the hotel. She had to give up her bubble bath, but the room's really nice and the TV has plenty of programmes. Now she needs to take care of the arrangements and check in at the reception desk.

Ana Smith:	**Me gusta la habitación ciento diecinueve. La voy a coger.**
	meh <u>goos</u>-tah lah ah-bee-tah-thee<u>ohn</u> thee<u>ehn</u>-toh-dee<u>eeh</u>-thee-noo<u>eh</u>-beh lah <u>boh</u>-ee ah koh-<u>Hehr</u>
	I like room 119. I'm going to take it.
Receptionist:	**¿Cuántos días desea quedarse?**
	koo-<u>ahn</u>-tohs <u>dee</u>-ahs deh-<u>seh</u>-ah keh-<u>dahr</u>-seh
	How many days do you want to stay?
Ana Smith:	**Me quedo tres dias.**
	meh <u>keh</u>-doh trehs <u>dee</u>-ahs
	I'm staying three days.

Receptionist: **Por favor, puede registrarse. El desayuno no está incluído en el precio. ¿Va a hacer un depósito por la primera noche?**
pohr fah-bohr poo-eh-deh reh-Hees-trahr-seh ehl deh-sah-yoo-noh noh ehs-tah een-klooee-doh ehn ehl preh-theeoh bah ah ah-thehr oon deh-poh-see-toh pohr lah pree-meh-rah noh-cheh
Can I please check you in? Breakfast isn't included in the price. Are you going to leave [literally: make] a deposit for the first night?

Ana Smith: **Sí, lo voy a hacer. ¿Con tarjeta de crédito o efectivo?**
see loh bohee ah ah-thehr kohn tahr-Heh-tah deh kreh-dee-toh oh eh-fehk-tee-boh
Yes, I'll leave one. Cash or credit card?

Receptionist: **Como usted guste.**
koh-moh oos-tehd goos-teh
Whichever you like.

Ana Smith: **¿Me pueden despertar a las siete de la mañana?**
meh pooeh-dehn dehs-pehr-tahr ah lahs seeeh-teh deh lah mah-nyah-nah
Can you wake me up at seven in the morning?

Receptionist: **Claro. Que pase buena noche.**
klah-roh keh pah-seh booeh-nah noh-cheh
Of course. Have a good night.

Words to Know

¿cuántos?	koo-ahn-tohs	how many
despertar	dehs-pehr-tahr	to awaken
en efectivo	ehn eh-fehk-tee-boh	in cash
incluído	een-kloo-ee-doh	included
la tarjeta	lah tahr-Heh-tah	the card
precio	ehl preh-theeoh	the price

quedarse	keh-_dahr_-seh	to stay
registrarse	reh-Hees-_trahr_-seh	to check in

Here are some useful terms to know when filling out your hotel registration form:

- **dirección permanente** _(dee-rehk-thee-ohn pehr-mah-nehn-teh)_ (permanent address)

- **calle, ciudad, provincia** _(kah-yeh thee-oo-dahd proh-been-theeah)_ (street, city, province)

- **país, código postal, teléfono** _(pah-ees koh-dee-goh pohs-tahl teh-leh-foh-noh)_ (country, post code, telephone [number])

- **número de pasaporte** _(noo-meh-roh deh pah-sah-pohr-teh)_ (passport number)

- **si viene con vehículo. . .** _(see beeeh-neh kohn beh-ee-koo-loh)_ (If coming by vehicle. . .)

- **número de la matrícula** _(noo-meh-roh deh lah mah-tree-koo-lah)_ (number plate)

- **fecha en que vence** _(feh-chah ehn keh behn-theh)_ (expiry date)

Words to Know

llenar	yeh-_nahr_	to fill in
la ciudad	lah thee-oo-_dahd_	the city
la provincia	lah proh-_been_-theeah	the province
el código postal	ehl _koh_-dee-goh pohs-_tahl_	the post code
el vehículo	ehl beh-_ee_-koo-loh	the vehicle
la matricula	lah mah-_tree_-koo-lah	the license plate
vencer	behn-th_ehr_	to expire

Wondering About the Water

Although the tap water in Spain is safe to drink, some people prefer to drink bottled water. Here are some phrases that can help you when you're thirsty:

- ✔ **¿Es buena el agua del grifo del hotel?** *(ehs booeh-nah ehl ah-gooah dehl gree-foh dehl oh-tehl)* (Is the hotel's tap water good to drink [as in having a hard or chlorine taste]?)

- ✔ **Sí, muy fina . . . también tenemos agua embotellada.** *(see moo-ee fee-nah tahm-beeehn teh-neh-mohs ah-gooah ehm-boh-teh-yah-dah)* (Yes, it's fine [in taste] . . . and we also have bottled water.)

- ✔ **¿Dónde encuentro el agua mineral?** *(dohn-deh ehn-kooehn-troh ehl ah-gooah mee-neh-rahl)* (Where do I find the mineral water [bottles]?)

- ✔ **Las botellas están en el minibar de su habitación.** *(lahs boh-teh-yahs ehs-tahn ehn ehl mee-nee-bahr deh soo ah-bee-tah-thee-ohn)* (The bottles are inside the mini-bar in your room.)

Words to Know

embotellada	ehm-boh-teh-yah-dah	bottled
fina	fee-nah	fine [as in very drinkable]

Sleeping Soundly: Dormir

After a long day, the sweet hour when you can finally rest and go to sleep comes. In Spanish, the verb **dormir** *(dohr-meer)* (to sleep) is a bit irregular, much like a really tired person!

In the following conjugation of the present tense of **dormir**, notice the differences between the singular and plural first person verb forms:

Conjugation	*Pronunciation*
yo duermo	*yoh dooehr-moh*
tú duermes	*too dooehr-mehs*
él, ella, usted duerme	*ehl, eh-yah, oos-tehd dooehr-meh*
nosotros dormimos	*noh-soh-trohs dohr-mee-mohs*
vosotros dormís	*boh-soh-trohs dohr-mees*
ellos, ellas, ustedes duermen	*eh-yohs, eh-yahs, oos-teh-dehs dooehr-mehn*

Here are some phrases to help you practise using **dormir**:

✔ **Yo duermo todos los días ocho horas.** *(yoh dooehr-moh toh-dohs lohs deeahs oh-choh oh-rahs)* (I sleep eight hours every day.)

✔ **Camila duerme en su cama.** *(kah-mee-lah dooehr-meh ehn soo kah-mah)* (Camila sleeps in his bed.)

✔ **Dormimos en nuestra casa.** *(dohr-mee-mohs ehn nooehs-trah kah-sah)* (We sleep at home.)

✔ **Los invitados duermen en tu habitación.** *(lohs een-bee-tah-dohs dooehr-mehn ehn too ah-bee-tah-thee-ohn)* (The guests sleep in your bedroom)

✔ **En mi cama duermen dos gatos.** *(ehn mee kah-mah dooehr-mehn dohs gah-tohs)* (Two cats sleep in my bed.)

✔ **Tú duermes con un osito.** *(too dooehr-mehs kohn oon oh-see-toh)* (You sleep with a teddy bear.)

✔ **Los pájaros también duermen.** *(lohs pah-Hah-rohs tahm-beeehn dooehr-mehn)* (The birds are sleeping as well.)

Waking Up: Despertar

You use the verb **despertar** *(dehs-pehr-tahr)* (to awaken) after a good night's sleep. You can tell that this verb is irregular when you see in the following table that the root of the verb in the first person singular is different from that of the first person plural:

Conjugation	*Pronunciation*
yo despierto	*yoh dehs-peeehr-toh*
tú despiertas	*too dehs-peeehr-tahs*
él, ella, usted despierta	*ehl, eh-yah, oos-tehd dehs-peeehr-tah*
nosotros despertamos	*noh-soh-trohs dehs-pehr-tah-mohs*
vosotros despertáis	*boh-soh-trohs dehs-pehr-tahees*
ellos, ellas, ustedes despiertan	*eh-yohs, eh-yahs, oos-teh-dehs dehs-peeehr-tahn*

Perhaps you understand the previous conjugations, but are wondering how to use **despertar** in practice. Well, the following examples show you:

- ✔ **Yo me despierto temprano por la mañana.** *(yoh meh dehs-pee<u>ehr</u>-toh tehm-<u>prah</u>-noh pohr lah mah-<u>nyah</u>-nah)* (I wake up early in the morning.)

- ✔ **Despertáis juntos.** *(dehs-pehr-<u>tah</u>-ees <u>Hoon</u>-tohs)* (You [plural] wake up together.)

- ✔ **Ellos no se despiertan de noche.** *(<u>eh</u>-yohs noh seh dehs-pee<u>ehr</u>-tahn deh <u>noh</u>-cheh)* (They don't wake up at night.)

- ✔ **Despierta con el canto de los pájaros.** *(dehs-pee<u>ehr</u>-tah kohn ehl <u>kahn</u>-toh deh lohs <u>pah</u>-Hah-rohs)* (He/she wakes with the dawn chorus [literally: the birds' singing].)

Being Possessive

In Spanish, you can use the words that indicate possession in the singular or plural form, depending on the number of things to which you're referring. For example, you say **mi llave** *(mee <u>yah</u>-beh)* (my key), when referring to one key. More often than not, however, you say **mis llaves** *(mees <u>yah</u>-behs)* (my keys), because you probably possess more than one key.

You follow the same rules when you say **esta llave es mía** *(<u>ehs</u>-tah <u>yah</u>-beh ehs <u>meeah</u>)* (this key is mine), or in the case of several keys, **estas llaves son mías** *(<u>ehs</u>-tahs <u>yah</u>-behs sohn <u>mee</u>-ahs)* (these keys are mine).

Notice that because **llave** is feminine, you use **mía,** the female-gender possessive. This rule sounds more complicated than it actually is. Just use the number (singular or plural) and the gender (male of female) of the things you talk about.

Possessive adjectives

The following list shows you all the possibilities of possessive adjectives:

- ✔ **mi/mis** *(mee/mees)* (my)
- ✔ **tu/tus** *(too/toos)* (your)
- ✔ **su/sus** *(soo/soos)* (his, her, its)
- ✔ **nuestro/nuestros** *(noo<u>ehs</u>-troh/noo<u>ehs</u>-trohs)* (our [when the possessed person, animal or object is masculine])
- ✔ **nuestra/nuestras** *(noo<u>ehs</u>-trah/noo<u>ehs</u>-trahs)* (our [when the possessed person, animal or object is feminine])

✔ **vuestro/vuestros** *(booehs-troh/booehs-trohs)* (your [when the possessed person, animal or object is masculine])

✔ **vuestra/vuestras** *(booehs-trah/booehs-trahs)* (your [when the possessed person, animal or object is feminine])

✔ **su/sus** *(soo/soos)* (their)

Here are some examples of how to use possessive adjectives:

✔ **Esta es mi habitación.** *(ehs-tah ehs mee ah-bee-tah-thee-ohn)* (This is my room.)

✔ **Tus llaves están en la mesa.** *(toos yah-behs ehs-tahn ehn lah meh-sah)* (Your keys are on the table.)

✔ **Sus llaves se las llevó la camarera.** *(soos yah-behs seh lahs yeh-boh lah kah-mah-reh-rah)* (The maid took his/her keys.)

✔ **Ese es nuestro hotel.** *(eh-seh ehs nooehs-troh oh-tehl)* (That is our hotel.)

✔ **Vinieron en su coche.** *(bee-neeeh-rohn ehn soo koh-cheh)* (They came in their car.)

✔ **Tus toallas están secas.** *(toos toh-ah-yahs ehs-tahn seh-kahs)* (Your towels are dry.)

✔ **Esas son mis maletas.** *(eh-sahs sohn mees mah-leh-tahs)* (Those are my suitcases.)

✔ **Nuestras sábanas están limpias.** *(nooehs-trahs sah-bah-nahs ehs-tahn leem-peeahs)* (Our sheets are clean.)

✔ **Mis zapatos están en tu habitación.** *(mees thah-pah-tohs ehs-tahn ehn too ah-bee-tah-thee-ohn)* (My shoes are in your bedroom.)

✔ **Tu pasaporte está en la recepción.** *(too pah-sah-pohr-teh ehs-tah ehn lah reh-thehp-thee-ohn)* (Your passport is at the reception [desk].)

Possessive pronouns

The following list shows you the basic possessive pronouns:

✔ **el mío/los míos** *(ehl meeoh/lohs meeohs)* (mine [when the possessed person, animal or object is masculine])

✔ **la mía/las mías** *(lah meeah/lahs meeahs)* (mine [when the possessed person, animal or object is feminine])

✔ **el tuyo/los tuyos** *(ehl too-yoh/lohs too-yohs)* (yours [when the possessed person, animal or object is masculine])

✔ **la tuya/las tuyas** *(lah too-yah/lahs too-yahs)* (yours [when the possessed person, animal or object is feminine])

✔ **el suyo/los suyos** *(ehl soo-yoh/lohs soo-yohs)* (his, hers, its [when the possessed person, animal or object is masculine])

✔ **la suya/las suyas** *(lah soo-yah/lahs soo-yahs)* (his, hers, its [when the possessed person, animal or object is feminine])

✔ **el nuestro/los nuestros** *(ehl nooehs-troh/lohs nooehs-trohs)* (ours [when the possessed person, animal or object is masculine])

✔ **la nuestra/las nuestras** *(lah nooehs-trah/lahs nooehs-trahs)* (ours [when the possessed person, animal or object is feminine])

✔ **el vuestro/los vuestros** *(ehl booehs-troh/lohs booehs-trohs)* (yours [when the possessed person, animal or object is masculine])

✔ **la vuestra/las vuestras** *(lah booehs-trah/lahs booehs-trahs)* (yours [when the possessed person, animal or object is feminine])

✔ **el suyo/los suyos** *(ehl soo-yoh/lohs soo-yohs)* (theirs [when the possessed person, animal or object is masculine])

✔ **la suya/las suyas** *(lah soo-yah/lahs soo-yahs)* (theirs [when the possessed person, animal or object is feminine])

Here are some examples of possessive pronouns for you to practise:

✔ **Esa cama es mía.** *(eh-sah kah-mah ehs mee-ah)* (That bed is mine.)

✔ **Las camas que están en el otro cuarto son suyas.** *(lahs kah-mahs keh ehs-tahn ehn ehl oh-troh koo-ahr-toh sohn soo-yahs)* (The beds in the other room are yours [formal plural].)

✔ **Esa maleta es la tuya.** *(eh-sah mah-leh-tah ehs lah too-yah)* (That suitcase is yours.)

✔ **El otro hotel es el suyo.** *(ehl oh-troh oh-tehl ehs ehl soo-yoh)* (That other hotel is his/hers.)

✔ **Esos pasaportes son los nuestros.** *(eh-sohs pah-sah-pohr-tehs sohn lohs nooehs-trohs)* (Those passports are ours.)

✔ **La maleta que es tuya está en la recepción.** *(lah mah-leh-tah keh ehs too-yah ehs-tah ehn lah reh-thehp-thee-ohn)* (Your suitcase is at the reception desk.)

✔ **Los calcetines son míos.** *(lohs kahl-theh-tee-nehs sohn mee-ohs)* (The socks are mine.)

✔ **Ese vaso es suyo.** *(eh-seh bah-soh ehs soo-yoh)* (That glass is his/hers.)

✔ **La cuenta del restaurante es nuestra.** *(lah koo-ehn-tah dehl rehs-tah-oo-rahn-teh ehs nooehs-trah)* (The restaurant bill is ours.)

✔ **¿Son suyas las almohadas?** *(sohn soo-yahs lahs ahl-moh-ah-dahs)* (Are the pillows his/hers/theirs?)

Fun & Games

The following word search contains several Spanish words that we introduce in this chapter. The English translations are listed below. Find the Spanish equivalent and circle it. (See Appendix C for the answer key.)

Word Search

R	Y	L	D	N	E	I	R	F	B	D
O	A	O	T	N	A	U	C	A	I	E
D	C	M	P	G	M	K	Ñ	R	Q	R
I	V	A	A	C	Y	O	E	O	U	I
U	C	V	L	C	X	C	W	I	E	R
L	U	L	W	I	C	M	F	C	D	E
C	H	F	A	I	E	Z	O	E	A	F
N	E	I	O	M	M	N	H	R	R	E
I	R	N	Z	L	B	G	T	P	S	R
F	N	I	A	T	P	A	C	E	E	P
I	C	X	E	S	R	A	H	C	U	D

address	hot	to prefer
bathroom	how much	to stay
bed	included	to take a shower
cold	price	

Chapter 14

Getting Around: Planes, Trains, Taxis and More

In This Chapter

▶ Getting through the airport and customs

▶ Hiring a car

▶ Navigating public transport

▶ Being early/late/on time

Getting where you want to go is, of course, a vital concern. As you travel around Spain and ask Spanish speakers to help you navigate, you're going to encounter all kinds of situations. This chapter gives you an idea of what to expect and shows you how to deal with the various circumstances that can arise.

Arriving in Spain

After you land at a Spanish airport, the airport staff can show you where to go to get through the various departments. While your luggage is being unloaded from the plane, you first have your identity checked. Here are some phrases that you may hear during this process:

✔ **Pase a Control de Pasaportes.** (*pah-seh a kohn-trohl deh pah-sah-pohr-tehs*) (Go to Passport Control.)

✔ **Pase a Inmigración.** (*pah-seh a een-mee-grah-thee-ohn*) (Go to Immigration.)

✔ **Pase por aquí, con su pasaporte en la mano.** (*pah-seh pohr ah-kee kohn soo pah-sah-pohr-teh ehn lah mah-noh*) (Go this way with your passport ready [literally: in your hand].)

While waiting in line at Passport Control or **Control de Policía** *(kohn-trol deh poh-lee-thee-ah)* (Police Control [booth]), you can prepare answers to some of the following questions that the officer may ask you:

- ✔ **¿Me permite su pasaporte?** *(meh pehr-mee-teh soo pah-sah-pohr-teh)* (May I have your passport?)

- ✔ **¿De dónde viene?** *(deh dohn-deh beeeh-neh)* (Where do you come from?)

- ✔ **¿En qué vuelo llegó?** *(ehn keh booeh-loh yeh-goh)* (What flight did you come on?)

- ✔ **¿A dónde va?** *(ah dohn-deh bah)* (Where are you going?)

- ✔ **¿Cuánto tiempo quiere quedarse en el país?** *(kooahn-toh teeehm-poh keeeh-reh keh-dahr-seh ehn ehl pah-ees)* (How long do you want to stay in the country?)

- ✔ **¡Que tenga una feliz estancia!** *(keh tehn-gah oo-nah feh-leeth ehs-tahn-theea)* (Have a pleasant stay!)

- ✔ **¡Que lo pase bien!** *(keh loh pah-seh beeehn)* (Have a good time!)

- ✔ **Pase a la Aduana, por favor.** *(pah-seh ah lah ah-dooah-nah pohr fah-bohr)* (Go to customs, please.)

Words to Know

el dinero	ehl dee-neh-roh	the money
el documento	ehl doh-koo-mehn-toh	the document; valid identification
el pasaporte	ehl pah-sah-pohr-teh	the passport
inmigración	een-mee-grah-thee-ohn	immigration
la estancia	lah ehs-tahn-theeah	the stay
quedar	keh-dahr	to stay

Dealing with the customs office

When you travel to Spain, make sure that you know the current customs regulations, because these can – and do – change from time to time. Take care not to carry any items that may be prohibited by law, such as anything that may present an in-flight security hazard.

Customs officers in Spain are often more concerned with things such as potential weapons and drugs than cigarettes or alcoholic beverage allowances. Declare (write on the form or verbally acknowledge) anything you have that may be subject to duties or anything you're unsure about. In most cases, for example, when things are for your personal use, you can take them into Spain without paying duties. The customs officials ultimately decide whether you owe any duties.

Here are some handy phrases for dealing with customs:

- ¿**Este objeto paga derechos?** *(ehs-teh ohb-Heh-toh pah-gah deh-reh-chohs)* (Do I have to pay duty on this item? [literally: does this item pay any duties?])

- ¿**Cuánto se paga por este objeto?** *(koo_ahn_-toh se pah-gah pohr ehs-teh ohb-Heh toh)* (How much duty does one pay for this item?)

- **Debe pagar impuestos.** *(deh-beh pah-gahr eem-pooehs-tohs)* (Duty must be paid [for it].)

- **Está libre de impuestos.** *(ehs-tah lee-breh de eem-pooehs-tohs)* (It's duty free.)

Customs officers aren't out to get you. They're simply being paid to see that people don't bring illegal or banned items into Spain.

Never attempt to joke around with customs officers. Unusually for Spaniards, they have to control their sense of humour because their job is serious business.

Talkin' the Talk

Here, Carlos meets with a customs officer.

Customs officer:	**¿Tiene algo que declarar?** *teeeh-neh ahl-goh keh deh-klah-rahr* Do you have anything to declare?
Carlos:	**No, no tengo nada que declarar.** *noh noh tehn-goh nah-dah keh deh-klah-rahr* No, I have nothing to declare.

Customs officer:	**¿Lleva algún material peligroso?** _Yeh-bah ahl-goon mah-teh-reeahl peh-lee-groh-soh_ Are you carrying any potentially dangerous items?
	¿Trae bebidas alcohólicas? _trah-eh beh-bee-dahs ahl-koh-oh-lee-kahs_ Are you bringing in any alcoholic beverages?
	¿Trae algún aparato electrónico? _trah-eh ahl-goon ah-pah-rah-toh_ _eh-lehk-troh-nee-koh_ Are you carrying any electronic devices?
Carlos:	**Sólo mi ordenador portátil . . . para uso personal.** _soh-loh mee orh-deh-nah-dohr porh-tah-teel pah-rah_ _oo-soh pehr-soh-nahl_ Only my laptop . . . for personal use.
Customs officer:	**Muy bien, pase. Que disfrute su estancia.** _moo-ee beeehn pah-seh keh dees-froo-teh soo_ _ehs-tanh-thee-ah_ Very good, go [this way] [formal]. Enjoy your stay.

Talkin' the Talk

The customs officer needs to see the contents of Pedro's luggage.

Customs officer:	**Necesitamos revisar sus maletas.** _neh-theh-see-tah-mohs reh-bee-sahr soos_ _mah-leh-tahs_ We need to see your suitcases.
	¿Cúantas tiene? _kooahn-tahs teeeh-neh_ How many [pieces] do you have?
Pedro:	**Tengo dos maletas.** _tehn-go dohs mah-leh-tahs_ I have two suitcases.
Customs officer:	**Póngalas aquí, por favor.** _pohn-gah-lahs ah-kee pohr fah-bohr_ Put them here, please.

Pedro:	**Aquí están.** *ah-kee ehs-tahn* Here they are.
Customs officer:	**Por favor, abra esta maleta.** *pohr fah-bohr ah-brah ehs-tah mah-leh-tah* Please, open this suitcase.
Pedro:	**En seguida.** *enh seh-gee-dah* Certainly [literally: right away].
Customs officer:	**¿Esto qué es, señor?** *ehs-toh keh ehs seh-nyohr* What's this, sir?
Pedro:	**Es mi máquina de afeitar eléctrica.** *ehs mee mah-kee-nah deh ah-feh-ee-tahr* *eh-lehk-tree-kah* It's my electric shaver.
Customs officer:	**¿Tiene alguna cámara digital fotográfica?** *teeeh-neh ahl-goo-nah kah-mah-rah dee-Hee-tahl* *foh-toh-grah-fee-kah* Do you have a digital camera? **¿Tiene cámara de video?** *teeeh-neh kah-mah-rah deh bee-deh-oh* Do you have a video camera?
Pedro:	**Aquí la tengo.** *ah-kee lah tehn-goh* I have it here.
Customs officer:	**¿Trae ordenador portátil?** *tra-eh orh-deh-nah-dohr pohr-tah-teel* Did you bring a laptop?
Pedro:	**Aquí está.** *ah-kee ehs-tah* Here it is.
Customs officer:	**Por favor pase a la oficina 'A'.** *porh fah-bohr pah-seh la oh-fee-thee-nah ah* Please go [with your equipment] to office 'A'.

Words to Know

abrir	ah-_breer_	to open
afeitar	ah-feh-ee-_tahr_	to shave
el aparato	ehl ah-pah-_rah_-toh	the machine; the appliance
el ordenador portátil	ehl ohr-deh-nah-_dohr_ pohr-_tah_-teel	the laptop [computer]
la aduana	lah ah-doo-_ah_-nah	customs
la cámara de video	lah _kah_-mah-rah deh _bee_-deh-oh	the video camera
las maletas	lahs mah-_leh_-tahs	the suitcases
revisar	reh-bee-_sahr_	to go through
salir	sah-_leer_	to exit; to get out
uso personal	_oo_-soh pehr-soh-_nahl_	personal use

Registering your camera, computer and other expensive equipment

Sometimes, registering the serial numbers of your digital camera, video camera or laptop computer can be a good idea. Come to think of it, you also benefit from knowing the details of everything that you take with you into the country in the unlikely event that any of these items go missing.

When registering goods, you generally have to take details of the objects to your Consulate (the office of a government representative from your own country) or to the police. Then, if anything happens to your goods you can pass those details on as a claim for your insurer, ideally before you leave the country.

Here are some phrases you may need to know when registering your electronic equipment:

✔ **Por favor, rellene este formulario.** *(pohr fah-bohr reh-yeh-neh ehs-teh foh-moo-lah-reeoh)* (Please, fill in this form.)

✔ **¿Cuáles son los aparatos que puedo registrar?** *(kooah-lehs sohn lohs ah-pah-rah-tohs keh pooeh-doh reh-Hees-trahr)* (Which [electronic] devices can I register?)

✔ **Si es necesario . . . presente este formulario.** *(see ehs neh-theh-sah-ree-oh preh-sehn-teh ehs-teh fohr-moo-lah-reeoh)* (If necessary . . . show this form [to whom it may concern].)

Finding a Train Station

Here are some phrases to help when you're trying to find a train station:

✔ **¿Dónde está la estación de tren?** *(dohn-deh ehs-tah lah ehs-tah-thee-ohn-deh trehn)* (Where's the train station?)

✔ **¿Cómo llego a la Estación Central?** *(koh-moh yeh-goh ah lah ehs-tah-thee-ohn thehn-trahl)* (How do I get to the Central Station?)

✔ **Lléveme por favor a la estación de tren.** *(yeh-beh-meh pohr fah-bohr ah lah ehs-tah-thee-ohn deh trehn)* (Please take me to the train station.)

Talkin' the Talk

Jane has decided to travel on an **AVE** *(ah-beh)* – an **Alta Velocidad Española** *(ahl-tah beh-loh-theeh-dahd ehs-pah-nyo-lah)* high-speed train – to Córdoba, in Andalucía. She's at **Madrid** *(mah-dreed)* train station and wants to buy her ticket.

Jane: **Un billete para Córdoba en el próximo AVE, por favor.**
oon bee-yeh-teh pah-rah kohr-doh-bah ehn ehl prohk-see-moh ah-beh pohr fah-bohr
One [single] ticket for Córdoba on the next *AVE*, please.

Salesperson: **¿Primera o, segunda clase?**
pree-meh-rah oh she-goohn-dah klah-she
First or second class?

Jane:	**Primera clase, por favor.**
	pree-meh-rah klah-she pohr fah-bohr
	First class, please.

Salesperson:	**Son cuarenta euros, por favor.**
	sohn koo-ah-renh-tah ehoo-rohs pohr fah-bohr
	That's 40 euros, please.

Jane:	**Aquí tiene. ¿A qué hora sale el tren?**
	ah-kee teeeh-neh ah keh oh-rah sah-leh ehl trehn
	Here [is the money]. What time does the train leave?

Salesperson:	**Sale dos minutos atrasado, a las 12:15.**
	sah-leh dohs mee-noo-tohs ah-trah-sah-doh ah lahs
	doh-theh keen-theh
	It leaves two minutes late, at 12:15.

Jane:	**¿De qué andén sale?**
	deh keh ahn-dehn sah-leh
	What platform does it leave from?

Salesperson:	**Del andén número dos de la zona AVE.**
	dehl ahn-dehn noo-meh-roh dohs deh lah thoh-nah
	ah-beh
	From Platform Two at the AVE zone.

Jane:	**Muchas gracias.**
	moo-chahs grah-theeahs
	Thank you very much.

Salesperson:	**De nada. ¡Que tenga un buen viaje!**
	deh nah-dah keh tehn-gah oon booehn beeah-Heh
	You're welcome. Have a good trip!

After you board the train, the ticket collector or the conductor may come along and says such things as the following:

✔ **¿Me permiten su billete por favor?** *(meh pehr-mee-tehn soo bee-yeh-teh pohr fah-bohr)* (May I have your ticket, please?)

✔ **Me llevo su billete un momentito, por favor.** *(meh yeh-boh soo bee-yeh-teh oon moh-mehn-tee-toh pohr fah-bohr)* (I'll take your ticket for just a moment, please.)

✔ **Aquí lo tiene de vuelta.** *(ah-kee loh teeeh-nehn deh booehl-tah)* (Here's your ticket back.)

Words to Know

de vuelta	deh boo*ehl*-tah	return ticket
el asiento	ehl ah-*seeehn*-toh	the seat
el billete	ehl bee-y*eh*-teh	the ticket
el tren	ehl trehn	the train
la estación	lah ehs-tah-thee-*ohn*	the station
primera clase	pree-*meh*-rah *klah*-seh	first class
segunda clase	seh-goon-dah *klah*-seh	second class

Bringing and Carrying: Traer

Traer *(trah-ehr)* (to bring; to carry) is a useful, albeit irregular, verb. You're always bringing or carrying something, and someone often brings things to you. For example, you bring a camera to photograph places you visit, and at the restaurant, a waiter brings you food and drink. Here's how you conjugate it:

Conjugation	*Pronunciation*
yo traigo	*yoh* *trahee*-goh
tú traes	*too* *trah*-ehs
él, ella, usted trae	*ehl, eh*-yah, oos-*tehd* *trah*-eh
nosotros traemos	*noh-soh*-trohs trah-*eh*-mohs
vosotros traéis	*boh-soh*-trohs trah-*eh*ees
ellos, ellas, ustedes traen	*eh*-yohs, *eh*-yahs, oos-*teh*-dehs *trah*-ehn

Practising new verbs is always a good idea. Here are some phrases for you to try:

- ✔ **Traigo una cámara digital.** *(trahee-goh oo-nah kah-mah-rah dee-Hee-tahl)* (I'm bringing a digital camera.)

- ✔ **¿Traes las fotos?** *(trah-ehs lahs foh-tohs)* (Are you bringing the photos?)

✔ **No hay problema con lo que traemos.** *(noh ah-ee proh-bleh-mah kohn loh keh trah-eh-mohs)* (There's no problem with what we're bringing.)

✔ **Traemos cosas de uso personal.** *(trah-eh-mohs koh-sahs deh oo-soh pehr-soh-nahl)* (We're carrying things for our personal use.)

Choosing Taxi or Bus

Whether you arrive in Spain by plane or train, you're going to leave the airport or station and search for a taxi, a bus or the car rental office (check out the later sections 'Addressing Driving Concerns' and 'Renting a Car'). At some airports, you pay the taxi before taking it.

These phrases help you make the necessary arrangements:

✔ **¿Dónde encuentro un taxi?** *(dohn-deh ehn-kooehn-troh oon tahk-see)* (Where do I find a taxi?)

✔ **¿Hay una parada de taxis?** *(ah-ee oo-nah pah-rah-dah deh tahk-sees)* (Is there a taxi rank?)

✔ **¿Puedo pagar el taxi con tarjeta?** *(poo-eh-doh pah-gahr ehl tahk-see kohn tahr-Heh-tah)* (Can I pay the taxi with a bank card?)

✔ **Sí, el taxi se puede pagar con tarjeta al llegar a su destino.** *(see ehl tahk-see seh poo-eh-deh pah-gahr kohn tahr-Heh-tah ahl yeh-gahr ah soo dehs-tee-noh)* (Yes, you can pay the taxi with a bank card when [we] arrive at your destination.)

Talkin' the Talk

Carla hails a taxi to get to a hotel someone recommended to her. She has the hotel's business card.

Carla: **Voy al hotel Ninotitas.**
Boh-ee ahl oh-tehl nee-noh-tee-tahs
I'm going to the Ninotitas hotel.

Taxi driver: **¿En qué calle está?**
ehn keh kah-yeh ehs-tah
What street is it on?

Carla: **Está en la calle Francisco Silvela, 67.**
ehs-tah ehn lah kah-yeh frahn-thees-koh seel-beh-lah seh-sehn-tah ee seeeh-teh
It's on Francisco Silvela Street, 67.

Taxi driver: **¿A ver la tarjeta del hotel?**
ah behr lah tahr-Heh-tah dehl oh-tehl
Can I see the hotel card?

Ah, ya sé. Vamos.
ah yah seh bah-mohs
Ah, I know. Let's go.

Here are some useful phrases for when you need to take a bus from the airport or train station:

✔ **¿Hay una parada de autobús?** *(ah-ee oo-nah pah-rah-dah deh ahoo-toh-boos)* (Is there a bus stop?)

✔ **¿Hay un bus para ir al centro?** *(ahy oon boos pah-rah eer ahl thehn-troh)* (Is there a bus to the city centre?)

✔ **¿Se compra el billete dentro?** *(seh kohm-prah elh bee-yeh-teh dehn-troh)* (Do I buy the ticket on the bus [literally: inside]?)

Talkin' the Talk

Dee is tired from her flight and can't find a taxi. She spots a bus arriving. Is it going where she needs to go? Is she going to have to walk far with her luggage? Here's how she finds out.

Dee: **¿Este autobús va al centro?**
ehs-teh ahoo-toh-boos bah ahl thehn-troh
Is this bus going to the city centre?

Bus driver: **¿A qué calle va?**
ah keh kah-yeh bah
What street are you going to? [formal]

Dee: **Avenida del Pilar.**
ah-beh-nee-dah dehl pee-lahr
del Pilar Avenue.

Bus driver: **Sí le dejo cerca. Suba.**
see leh deh-Hoh thehr-kah soo-bah
Yes, I'll leave you close. Come on up. [formal]

Words to Know

cerca	_thehr_-kah	close by
el bus	elh boos	the bus
la calle	lah _kah_-yeh	the street
la parada	lah pah-_rah_-dah	the stop
se paga	seh _pah_-gah	one pays

Addressing Driving Concerns

Fortunately, when you drive in Spain, many of the rules of the road are very similar to those in the UK, with the obvious exception that you have to drive on the opposite side of the road!

If you plan to rent a car during your trip, try to find out before you go if arranging the rental from home via the Internet holds any advantages for you. Generally, doing so is cheaper.

Carrying your driving licence

Spain accepts valid UK driving licences. In some situation, however, such as if you passed your driving test outside the European Union, you may need to carry and show an International Driving Licence.

Reading road signs

Most road signs in Spain are based on internationally standardised symbols rather than words. This system makes them very easy to understand, no matter what language you speak. Here are just a couple of the most important signs:

- A *do not enter* sign is a circle in a red background, crossed by a diagonal line.

- A *stop* sign is always an octagonal red sign with the word **stop** inside – yes, as in the English word 'stop'. Stop is used because it's internationally recognised and helps avoid any disasters!

Ask at the car rental office if you can expect to see any worded road signs that you don't understand.

Talkin' the Talk

At the car rental office, Samuel gets information about differences in road signs between the area he's used to driving in and the one he's about to explore.

Samuel Thompson:	**¿La señalización es igual que en el Reino Unido?** *lah seh-nyah-lee-thah-thee-<u>ohn</u> ehs ee-goo-<u>ahl</u> keh ehn el <u>rehee</u>-noh oo-<u>nee</u>-doh* Are the road signs the same as in the UK?
Rental office attendant:	**Son muy parecidas. Aquí tiene ejemplos.** *sohn <u>moo</u>-ee pah-reh-<u>thee</u>-dahs ah-<u>kee</u> <u>teeeh</u>-neh eh-<u>Hehm</u>-plohs* They are very similar [to those of the UK]. Here you can see some examples.
Samuel Thompson:	**¿Cómo son los reglas de tráfico?** *<u>koh</u>-moh sohn lahs <u>reh</u>-glahs deh <u>trah</u>-fee koh* What are the traffic rules like?
Rental office attendant:	**Son las mismas reglas que usa en su país.** *sohn lahs <u>mees</u>-mahs <u>reh</u>-glahs keh <u>oo</u>-sah ehn soo pah-<u>ees</u>* They are the same as in your country.
Samuel Thompson:	**¿Se puede acelerar con luz amarilla?** *seh <u>pooeh</u>-deh ah-theh-leh-<u>rahr</u> kohn looth ah-mah-<u>reh</u>-yah* Can you accelerate on a yellow [amber] light?
Rental office attendant:	**¡No, no se puede!** *noh noh seh <u>pooeh</u>-deh* No, you can't!

Catching on to kilometres

Did you know that a mile is equal to 1.6 kilometres? Perhaps not – you probably have other things to worry about! Well, you need to get to grips with kilometres, because virtually every other country – Spain included – uses them. But you can use miles with no trouble, and so you can surely use kilometres.

Here are some useful short cuts to think about when trying to figure out distances: 30 miles equals 50 kilometres (and so 50 kilometres per hour is 30 miles per hour). Also, 50 miles equals 80 kilometres. Finally, 60 miles is 96 kilometres – but you can think of it as *close* to 100.

To end your problems in conversion, your hired car displays kilometres on the dashboard and the road signs are all in kilometres! So, just go with the flow.

Renting a Car

After arriving in Spain, and depending on your plans, you may prefer to hire a car instead of taking a taxi or a bus. Whether at the airport or on the street, these two questions can come in handy:

- ✔ **¿Dónde alquilan coches?** *(dohn-deh ahl-kee-lahn koo-chehs)* (Where do they rent cars?)

- ✔ **¿Hay oficina de alquiler?** *(ah-ee oh-fee-thee-nah deh ahl-kee-lehr)* (Is there a car rental office?)

Having found a car rental office, here are some things you can say when making your inquiry:

- ✔ **Quiero alquilar un coche.** *(keeeh-roh ahl-kee-lahr oon koo-cheh)* (I want to rent a car.)

- ✔ **Me puede dar una lista de precios?** *(meh pooeh-deh dahr oo-nah lees-tah deh preh-theeohs)* (Can you give me a price list?)

- ✔ **¿Cuánto cuesta al día?** *(kooahn-toh koo-ehs-tah ahl dee-ah)* (How much is it per day?)

- ✔ **¿Cuánto cuesta por semana?** *(kooahn-toh koo-ehs-tah pohr seh-mah-nah)* (How much is it per week?)

- ✔ **¿Cuántos kilómetros puedo hacer?** *(kooahn-tohs kee-loh-meh-trohs pooeh-doh ah-thehr)* (How many kilometres may I do?)

✔ **¿Cuántos kilómetros por litro hace este coche?** *(kooahn-tohs kee-loh-meh-trohs pohr lee-tro ah-theh ehs-teh koo-cheh)* (How many kilometres per litre does this car do?)

✔ **¿Cuánto cuesta el seguro?** *(kooahn-toh kooehs-tah ehl seh-goo-roh)* (How much is the insurance?)

✔ **¿Tiene un mapa de la región?** *(teeeh-neh oon mah-pah deh lah reh-Hee-ohn)* (Do you have a map?)

✔ **¿Tiene navegador por satélite incorporado?** *(teeeh-neh nah-beh-gah-dohr pohr sah-teh-lee-the een-kohr-poh-rah-doh)* (Does it come with built-in satellite-navigation?)

✔ **¿Las instrucciones del navegador son sólo en español?** *(lahs eens-trook-thee-oh-nehs dehl nah-beh-gah-dohr sohn soh-loh ehn ehs-pah-nyohl)* (Do the satellite-navigation commands come only in Spanish?)

✔ **¿Dónde está la rueda de repuesto?** *(dohn-deh ehs-tah lah roo-eh-dah deh reh-poo-ehs-toh)* (Where's the spare tyre?)

✔ **¿Dónde tengo que devolver el coche?** *(dohn-deh tehn-goh keh deh-bohl-behr ehl koo-cheh)* (Where do I have to return the car?)

Preparing to drive

You need to know some details about the car you're renting and the driving conditions in the area you're visiting. The following phrases help you to get the necessary information:

✔ **¿El coche es manual o automático?** *(ehl koo-cheh ehs mah-noo-ahl oh ah-oo-toh-mah-tee-koh)* (Is the car manual or automatic?)

✔ **¿Es difícil conducir por la autovía?** *(ehs dee-fee-theel koon-doo-theer pohr lah ahoo-toh-bee-ah)* (Is it difficult to drive on the motorway?)

✔ **Hay que tener mucha prudencia.** *(ah-ee keh teh-nehr moo-chah proo-dehn-theeah)* (You have to be very careful.)

✔ **¿Habrá mucho tráfico por la mañana?** *(ah-brah moo-choh trah-fee-koh pohr lah mah-nyah-nah)* (Will there be much traffic in the morning?)

✔ **¿Cuál es la mejor hora para salir de la ciudad?** *(kooahl ehs lah meh-Hohr oh-rah pah-rah sah-leer deh lah theeh-oo-dahd)* (When is the best time to get out of the city?)

Hitting the road

The people at the car rental office may know something about the roads that you're about to explore. Here are some questions to ask and answers you may get while the agent and you are looking at a map:

✔ **¿Están las carreteras en buen estado?** *(ehs-tahn lahs kah-rreh-teh-rahs ehn booehn ehs-tah-doh)* (Are the roads in good condition?)

✔ **No todas. Estas son algo estrechas.** *(noh toh-dahs ehs-tahs sohn ahl-goh ehs-treh-chahs)* (Not all of them. These are a little narrow.)

✔ **Esa carretera tiene muchos baches.** *(eh-sah kah-rreh-teh-rah teeeh-nehn moo-chohs bah-chehs)* (That road has a lot of potholes.)

✔ **Estas están excelentes.** *(ehs-tahs ehs-tahn ehks-theh-lehn-tehs)* (These [roads] are excellent.)

✔ **Hay autopista.** *(ah-ee ahoo-toh-pees-tah)* (There's a motorway.)

✔ **Son de peaje.** *(sohn deh peh-ah-Heh)* (They are toll [roads].)

Words to Know

acelerar	ah-theh-leh-rahr	to accelerate
alquilan	ahl-kee-lahn	they rent
alquiler	ahl-kee-lehr	the rent/hire
conducir	koon-doo-theer	to drive
el peaje	ehl peh-ah-Heh	the toll
estrechas	ehs-treh-chahs	narrow [feminine and plural]
la autopista	lah ah-oo-toh-pees-tah	the motorway
la carretera	lah kah-rreh-teh-rah	the road
las reglas	lahs reh-glahs	the rules

Scheduling Issues: Running Late, Early or On Time

No matter what mode of transportation you use, you need to have a schedule and know if you're going to reach your destination on time. The following list contains phrases for when you want to schedule something and need to know how well the timing is being met:

- ✔ **adelantado** *(ah-deh-lahn-tah-doh)* ([it] is coming early)
- ✔ **atrasado** *(ah-trah-sah-doh)* ([it] is running late)
- ✔ **el horario** *(ehl oh-rah-reeoh)* (the schedule)
- ✔ **es temprano** *(ehs tehm-prah-noh)* (it's early) [time]
- ✔ **es tarde** *(ehs tahr-deh)* (it's late) [time]
- ✔ **la tarde** *(lah tahr-deh)* (the afternoon)
- ✔ **sin retraso** *(seen reh-trah-soh)* (on time)

The word **tarde** *(tahr-deh)* has different meanings depending on whether you use the definite article (the) before it or not. (Chapter 2 has more on article use in Spanish.)

Sometimes the posted or printed schedule for a bus, train or plane may not be up-to-date and you need to ask someone about it. Here are some responses you may hear where scheduling phrases come into play:

- ✔ **Hay que esperar, está atrasado.** *(ah-ee keh ehs-peh-rahr ehs-tah ah-trah-sah-doh)* (One has to wait; it's running late.)
- ✔ **El vuelo llegó adelantado.** *(ehl booeh-loh yeh-goh ah-deh-lahn-tah-doh)* (The flight came in late.)
- ✔ **Este reloj está adelantado.** *(ehs-teh reh-lohH ehs-tah ah-deh-lahn-tah-doh)* (The clock is fast.)
- ✔ **El bus va adelantado.** *(ehl boos bah ah-deh-lahn-tah-doh)* (The bus is running earlier [than scheduled].)
- ✔ **El tren va a llegar sin retraso.** *(ehl trehn bah ah yeh-gahr seen reh-trah-soh)* (The train will arrive on time.)
- ✔ **Espera porque va a llegar tarde.** *(ehs-peh-rah pohr-keh bah a yeh-gahr tahr-deh)* (Wait because it's going to arrive late.)
- ✔ **El bus viene tarde.** *(ehl boos beeeh-neh tahr-deh)* (The bus is coming late.)

Talkin' the Talk

Scheduling information is most important when you're trying to catch a flight. Susana tries to pick up a schedule at the last minute but hasn't time to read it, and so she asks for help from the airline information attendant.

Susana:	**Necesito el horario de los vuelos.** *neh-theh-see-toh ehl oh-rah-reeoh deh lohs* *boo-eh-lohs* I need the flight schedule.
Information attendant:	**Aquí hay uno.** *ah-kee ah-ee oo-noh* Here's one.
Susana:	**¿A qué hora sale el avión para Murcia?** *ah keh oh-rah sah-leh ehl ah-bee-ohn pah-rah* *muhr-thee-ah* When does the plane for Murcia leave?
Information attendant:	**Según el horario sale a las tres de la tarde.** *seh-goon ehl oh-rah-ree-oh sah-leh ah lahs trehs deh* *lah tahr-deh* According to the schedule, it leaves at three in the afternoon.
Susana:	**Me tengo que dar prisar, voy atrasada.** *meh tehn-goh keh darh-pree-sah bohee* *ah-trah-sah-dah* I have to hurry; I'm late.
Information attendant:	**Todavía no sale, va atrasado.** *toh-dah-beeah noh sah-leh bah ah-trah-sah-doh* It won't leave yet; it's running [going] late.

Using the Outgoing Verb: Salir

Salir (*sah-leer*) (to go out) is an irregular verb with many different uses. Here are just a few of them:

- ✔ **¿De dónde sale el bus a la plaza del Callao?** *(deh dohn-deh sah-leh ehl boos ah lah plah-thah dehl kah-yah-oh)* (Where does the Callao square bus leave from?)

- ✔ **¿Cada cuánto sale el bus?** *(kah-dah kooahn-toh sah-leh ehl boos)* (How often does the bus leave?)

- ✔ **Salimos a andar por la calle.** *(sah-lee-mohs ah ahn-dahr pohr lah kah-yeh)* (We went out to walk around the streets.)

> ✔ **Ellos salen de la estación de tren de Atocha.** (*eh-yohs sah-lehn deh lah ehs-tah-thee-ohn deh trehn deh ah-toh-chah*) (They're going from Atocha train station.)
>
> ✔ **Vamos a salir a la calle Orense.** (*bah-mohs ah sah-leer ah lah kah-yeh oh-rehn-seh*) (We'll come out at Orense street.)

Here's how you conjugate **salir** in the present tense:

Conjugation	*Pronunciation*
yo salgo	*yoh sahl-goh*
tú sales	*too sah-lehs*
él, ella, usted sale	*ehl, eh-yah, oos-tehd sah-leh*
nosotros salimos	*noh-soh-trohs sah-lee-mohs*
vosotros salís	*boh-soh-trohs sah-lees*
ellos, ellas, ustedes salen	*eh-yohs, eh-yahs, oos-teh-dehs sah-lehn*

Employing the Waiting Verb: Esperar

Esperar (*ehs-peh-rahr*) is the verb of hoping and waiting – maybe you're waiting because you're hoping. In any case, **esperar** is a regular verb and easy to handle, as you see in the following conjugation in the present tense. The root of this verb is **esper-** (*ehs-pehr*).

Conjugation	*Pronunciation*
yo espero	*yoh ehs-peh-roh*
tú esperas	*too ehs-peh-rahs*
él, ella, usted espera	*ehl, eh-yah, oos-tehd ehs-peh-rah*
nosotros esperamos	*noh-soh-trohs ehs-peh-rah-mohs*
vosotros esperáis	*boh-soh-trohs ehs-peh-rahees*
ellos, ellas, ustedes esperan	*eh-yohs, eh-yahs, oos-teh-dehs ehs-peh-rahn*

Whereas **esperar** plain and simple means waiting, **esperar que** (*ehs-peh-rahr keh*) means hoping. Here are some phrases to practise:

> ✔ **Espero que le guste mi coche.** (*ehs-peh-roh keh leh goos-teh mee koo-cheh*) (I hope she/he'll like my car.)
>
> ✔ **Esperamos en la cola.** (*ehs-peh-rah-mohs ehn lah koh-lah*) (We're waiting in the queue.)
>
> ✔ **Espero que venga el taxi.** (*ehs-peh-roh keh behn-gah ehl tahk-see*) (I hope the taxi will come.)

✔ **Espero el taxi.** *(ehs-peh-roh ehl tahk-see)* (I'm waiting for the taxi.)

✔ **No esperamos más el bus.** *(noh ehs-peh-rah-mohs mahs ehl boos)* (We won't wait for the bus any longer.)

✔ **Debes esperar el avión.** *(deh-behs ehs-peh-rahr ehl ah-bee-ohn)* (You must wait for the plane.)

✔ **Espera el bús para Cáceres.** *(ehs-peh-rah ehl boos pah-rah cah-theh-rehs)* (He/she is waiting for the bus to Cáceres)

Travelling Around in the City

Getting around a city can be fun but also confusing. Fortunately, plenty of people are willing to give directions. Just ask: most people love to help out.

The places we mention in the following list of useful phrases are in the city of Bilbao:

✔ **En esta ciudad hay buses y metro.** *(ehn ehs-tah thee-oo-dahd ah-ee boo-sehs ee meh-troh)* (There are buses and tubes in this city.)

✔ **En Bilbao hay trenes subterráneos.** *(ehn beel-bah-oh ah-ee treh-nehs soob-teh-rrah-neh-ohs)* (There are underground trains in Bilbao.)

✔ **El mapa del metro está en la estación.** *(ehl mah-pah dehl meh-troh ehs-tah ehn lah ehs-tah-thee-ohn)* (The map of the tube is at the station.)

✔ **Sale de la estación de Deusto.** *(sah-leh deh lah ehs-tah-thee-ohn deh deh-oos-toh)* (It departs from Deusto station.)

✔ **¿Aquí para el bus para el casco viejo?** *(ah-kee pah-rah ehl boos pah-rah ehl cahs-koh beeeh-Hoh)* (Does the Casco Viejo bus stop here?)

✔ **¿Este bus va para San Inazio?** *(ehs-teh boos bah pah-rah sahn ee-nah-theeoh)* (Does this bus go to San Inazio?)

✔ **Hay que hacer cola.** *(ah-ee keh ah-thehr koh-lah)* (You have to queue.)

✔ **¿Qué bus tomo para Ansio?** *(keh boos toh-moh pah-rah ahn-seeoh)* (What bus do I take for Ansio?)

✔ **¿El metro me deja en San Mamés?** *(ehl meh-troh meh deh-Hah ehn sahn mah-mehs)* (Does the tube leave me at San Mamés?)

Words to Know

el avión	ehl ah-bee-_ohn_	the plane
el metro	ehl _meh_-troh	the tube
la cola	lah _koh_-lah	the queue [literally: the tail]

Fun & Games

Any time you travel to a new place in Spain, you're going to have loads of questions. This game provides you with the start of some common questions. Unscramble the Spanish words and then find their English translations. Or use the English words to unscramble the Spanish. The book and the game are yours; don't let us dictate the rules!

Spanish	English
1 ¿omóc egoll a zalap la?	A. Where are we going?
2 ¿em vaell orp ravof la raeopeurot?	B. At what time?
3 ¿dedón eáts le naboc sám cacerno?	C. How can I go to the square?
4 ¿a nóded smoav?	D. Could you take me to the airport, please?
5 ¿a équ hoar?	E. Where can I find a bar?
6 ¿sote uéq se?	F. How much is this?
7 ¿denód countreen nu bra ?	G. What is this?
8 ¿nucoát catsue?	H. Where is the closest bank?

Turn to Appendix C for the answer key.

Chapter 15

Planning a Trip

. . . .

In This Chapter

▶ Creating your travel plans

▶ Handling passports, visas and other travel necessities

▶ Using the verbs to leave from/to arrive at

▶ Understanding the simple future tense

▶ Naming the months

. . . .

*T*his chapter is going to move you . . . no, not emotionally! Instead, you find out about moving to new worlds and new experiences, beyond your daily chores. In this chapter we take a look at holidays, visiting beaches and mountains and heading into a different climate. Get ready for an adventure.

Making Travel Plans

Spain is a wonderful country to visit. May to June and September to October are the best times to go, when the temperature isn't too cold or too hot, but just right. Much of Spain is very hot during summer, but the northern third of the country remains comfortable and the beaches are superb. Many people – Spaniards and visitors alike – head to the sunny valleys or the glittering beaches of the Mediterranean Sea or Atlantic Ocean to warm their bones, and Spain certainly has plenty of sun-filled sites to choose from.

Like the Spaniards themselves, avoid Madrid in July and August if possible – it's far too hot!

In Spain you can travel around and visit loads of diverse places, with different cultures, customs and festivals (check out Chapter 7 for more detail on Spanish arts and entertainment). This cultural diversity is partly the result of Moorish and Latino immigration, and the balance of these mixtures varies between areas. For example, a North African influence prevails in the southeast. But wherever you go in sunny Spain you find something unique, something special to take home in your hands and in your heart.

Most parts of Spain have one thing in common: they speak this wonderful language called Spanish, although three exceptions are listed below:

- In Cataluña, some people also speak a close cousin of Spanish, **Catalán** *(kah-tah-lahn)*.

- In Galicia, some people also speak **Gallego** *(gah-yeh-goh)*.

- In the País Vasco, some people alternate **Euskera** *(eh-oos-keh-rah)* with standard Spanish.

Whatever your desire, you can fulfil it in Spain:

- **Heading for beaches?** You can find hundreds of wonderful beaches all around the coast.

- **Looking for mountains?** Head for the north or southern **Andalucía** *(ahn-dah-loo-thee-ah)*, where you can find the **Sierra Nevada** *(see-eh-rrah neh-bah-dah)* range in **Granada** *(grah-nah-dah)* province. The highest and longest mountains in the Iberian Peninsula are the Pyrenees, dividing Spain from France and the little country of Andorra.

- **Searching for beautiful rivers?** Consider any of the major Spanish rivers, such as **el Duero** *(ehl doo-eh-roh)*, **el Tajo** *(ehl tah-Hoh)* or **el Guadiana** *(ehl goo-ah-dee-ah-nah)*, going farther south.

- **Fancying an ecological excursion?** Try **La Vera** *(lah beh-rah)* or **El Jerte** *(ehl Hehr-teh)* in the south-western region of **Extremadura** *(ehks-treh-mah-doo-rah)*. A real gift to your senses, this area is covered with cherry trees, crystal-clear streams and natural pools, with gorgeous country inns dotted around: highly recommended in spring time!

- **Wanting to discover ancient cultures?** You can find literally dozens of places along the Mediterranean coast and southern Spain where Arabs, Romans or Jews once settled.

If good food is your heart's desire, put on some comfortable shoes and check out these recommendations:

- **Looking for the finest paella** *(pah-eh-yah)*? Head for **Valencia** *(bah-lehn-thee-ah)* on the east coast.

- **Shopping for the best serrano ham?** **Cáceres** *(kah-theh-rehs)* and **Salamanca** *(sah-lah-mahn-kah)* are the prime locations.

- **Fancying some seafood?** Try **Galicia** *(gah-lee-theeah)*, in the northeast.

For more about dining out, make your way to Chapter 5.

Planning for the Weather

Spain has rainy areas and dry areas. The northern third of the country is the rainy part, but it does have comfortable temperatures. One characteristic of northern Spain is the higher altitude. This area is the upper plateau of the Iberian Peninsula, with plenty of mountains that make great skiing country in the winter. Here, the temperatures are warm to hot in the daytime with cool nights, mostly due to night breezes. The rest of inland Spain is very hot and dry in summer with average European temperatures during the winter season. Even then, however, you often see deep blue skies!

If you decide to visit the Mediterranean or South Atlantic coasts, you can enjoy the warmth almost all year long and bask in very hot summer temperatures. The Mediterranean, particularly around **Alicante** *(ah-lee-kahn-teh)*, provides Spain's warmest waters, which reach 27 degrees Celsius in August. At the northern end of Spain's Mediterranean coast, **Barcelona**'s *(barh-theh-loh-nah)* weather is typical of the coast – milder than in inland cities, but more humid. The northern Atlantic coast is very wet in winter and pleasurably warm in summer.

The best time to visit the interior of Spain is spring, where **Semana Santa** *(seh-mah-nah sahn-tah)* (Easter) is a big celebration in the cities. Between September and October is also a good time, thanks to the weather, when 21 degrees Celsius and clear skies are the norm.

Talkin' the Talk

Juan decides to take a bus to a Catalan beach, but first he needs some information.

Juan:	**¿A qué hora sale el bus para Pal?**
	ah keh oh-rah sah-leh ehl boos pah-rah pahl
	When does the bus for Pal leave?

Attendant:	**A cada hora desde las diez de la mañana hasta las diez de la noche.**
	ah kah-dah oh-rah dehs-deh lahs deeeth deh lah mah-nyah-nah ahs-tah lahs deeeth deh lah noh-cheh
	Every hour, from ten in the morning until ten in the evening.

Juan:	**¡Ah, hay muchos buses durante el día!**
	ah ah-ee moo-chos boo-sehs du-rahn-teh ehl deeah
	Ah, there are plenty of buses in the daytime!

¿Hay servicio todos los días?
Ah-ee sehr-bee-thee-oh toh-dohs lohs deeahs
Is there a service every day?

Attendant: **Los buses a Pal van de lunes a domingo.**
lohs boo-sehs ah pahl bahn deh loo-nehs ah doh-meen-goh
The Pal buses go from Monday to Sunday.

Timing Your Trip: Picking a month

Whether you prefer a warmer or cooler time of year to visit, you need to know the months of the year to help you plan your trip.

In Spanish, the names of the months don't begin with a capital letter, as they do in English.

- **enero** *(eh-neh-roh)* (January)
- **febrero** *(feh-breh-roh)* (February)
- **marzo** *(mahr-thoh)* (March)
- **abril** *(ah-breel)* (April)
- **mayo** *(mah-yoh)* (May)
- **junio** *(Hoo-nee-oh)* (June)
- **julio** *(Hoo-lee-oh)* (July)
- **agosto** *(ah-gohs-toh)* (August)
- **septiembre** *(sehp-tee-ehm-breh)* (September)
- **octubre** *(ohk-too-breh)* (October)
- **noviembre** *(noh-bee-ehm-breh)* (November)
- **diciembre** *(dee-thee-ehm-breh)* (December)

Take a look at the following examples to help you practise using dates for your trip:

- **En enero voy a ir a Sevilla.** *(ehn eh-neh-roh bohee ah eer a seh-bee-yah)* (In January, I'm going to go to Seville.)
- **Vuelvo de España en marzo.** *(boo-ehl-boh de ehs-pah-nyah ehn mahr-thoh)* (I return from Spain in March.)

✔ **El viaje es de julio a diciembre.** *(ehl beeah-Heh ehs deh Hoo-leeoh ah dee-thee-ehm-breh)* (The trip is from July to December.)

✔ **No llueve casi nada en Sevilla de mayo a noviembre.** *(noh yoo-eh-bee kah-see nah-dah ehn she-bee-yah deh mah-yoh ah noh-bee-ehm-breh)* (There's almost no rain in Seville from May to November.)

Talkin' the Talk

Juan wants to fly from Madrid to Málaga. He goes to a travel agency to book his flight.

Juan:	**Buenos días.**
	booeh-nohs deeahs
	Good morning.

Travel agent:	**Buenos días, señor. ¿En qué le puedo servir?**
	booeh-nohs deeahs seh-nyohr ehn keh leh pooeh-doh sehr-beer
	Good morning, sir. How may I help you?

Juan:	**Necesito un billete para Málaga.**
	neh-theh-see-to oon bee-yeeh-teh pah-rah mah-lah-gah
	I need a ticket for Málaga.

Travel agent:	**¿Qué día, por favor?**
	keh deeah pohr fah-bohr
	What day, please?

Juan:	**El viernes por la mañana.**
	ehl bee-ehr-nehs pohr lah mah-nyah-nah
	Friday morning.

Travel agent:	**Hay un vuelo a las ocho.**
	Ah-ee oon boo-eh-loh ah lahs oh-choh
	There's a flight at eight.

Juan:	**¿Un poco más tarde?**
	oon poh-koh mahs tahr-deh
	A little later?

Travel: agent:	**Sí, hay otro a las nueve.**
	see ah-ee oh-troh ah lahs noo-eh-beh
	Yes, there's another one at nine.

Juan:	**Ese está bien.** *eh-seh ehs-tah bee-ehn* That one's fine.
Travel agent:	**¿Hasta qué día?** *ahs-tah keh deeah* Until what day?
Juan:	**Hasta el domingo por la tarde.** *ahs-tah ehl doh-meen-goh pohr lah tahr-deh* Until Sunday afternoon.
Travel agent:	**Hay un vuelo a las siete de la tarde.** *Ah-ee oon boo-eh-loh ah lahs see-eh-teh deh lah tahr-deh* There's a flight at 7 p.m.
Juan:	**Es buena hora. Hágame la reserva.** *ehs boo-eh-nah oh-rah ah-gah-meh lah reh-sehr-bah* That's a good time. Book me that flight.
Travel agent:	**Aquí tiene, señor. El vuelo sale de Madrid Barajas a las 9 de la mañana. Tiene que estar en el aeropuerto una hora antes.** *ah-kee teeeh-neh seh-nyor el booeh-loh sah-leh deh mah-dreed bah-rah-Has ah lahs nooeh-beh deh lah mah-nyah-nah teeeh-neh keh ehs-tahr ehn ehl ah-eh-roh-pooehr-toh oo-nah oh-rah ahn-tehs* Here are the tickets. Your departure time from Madrid Barajas will be 9 a.m. You have to be at the airport an hour ahead of time.

Mastering Visas and Passports

To enter Spain from another country, you need to go through some formalities. The requirements for entering vary depending on which country you're coming from and what passport you hold. Our advice is to check with a travel agent or a Spanish consulate to determine the documents and medical requirements (such as vaccinations) that you need in order to enter Spain. Travelling to Spain from another European Union country, however, is normally quite straightforward.

Always carry your passport, whether or not you need to; even when you don't plan to go beyond your original destination, always be sure to keep it safe. A passport is an important document to have when dealing with banks or in emergencies.

When you're required to have a visa, you must have a passport. The passport is where your visa (a permit to visit a country) is stamped. Some countries don't require visas.

Chapter 11 contains lots of money-handling wisdom.

Talkin' the Talk

The following dialogue is relevant for citizens of the United Kingdom who want to go to a Spanish destination. Patricia, who lives in London but comes from overseas, has some questions about travelling to Palma de Mallorca.

Patricia:	**¿Es éste el Consulado de España?** *ehs ehs-teh ehs ehl kohn-soo-lah-doh deh esh-pah-nyah* Is this the Spanish Consulate?
Consulate attendant:	**Sí, ¿en qué le puedo servir?** *see ehn keh leh pooeh-doh sehr-beer* Yes, how can I help you? [formal]
Patricia:	**¿Necesito un visado para ir a Palma?** *neh-theh-see-toh oon bee-sah-doh pah-rah eer ah pahl-mah* Do I need a visa to go to Palma?
Consulate attendant:	**Depende. ¿Es ciudadana Británica?** *deh-pehn-deh ehs thee-oo-dah-dah-nah bree-tah-nee-kah* That depends. Are you a British citizen?
Patricia:	**No, no soy británica pero vivo en Londres.** *Noh noh sohy bree-tah-nee-kah peh-roh bee-boh ehn lohn-drehs* I'm not from Great Britain but I live in London.
Consulate attendant:	**¿Por cuánto tiempo va?** *pohr kooahn-toh teeehm-poh bah* How long will you be [staying] there?
Patricia:	**De noviembre a marzo.** *deh noh-bee-ehm-breh ah mahr-thoh* From November to March.
Consulate attendant:	**Son cinco meses. ¿Va como turista?** *sohn theen-koh meh-sehs bah koh-moh too-rees-tah* That's five months. Are you going as a tourist?

Patricia:	**Sí.**
	see
	Yes.

Consulate attendant:	**Va a necesitar visado de turista.**
	bah ah neh-theh-see-tahr bee-sah-doh deh too-rees-tah
	You'll need a tourist visa.

Patricia:	**¿Tengo que venir aquí por el visado?**
	tehn-goh keh beh-neer ah-kee pohr ehl bee-sah-doh
	Do I have to come here for the visa?

Consulate attendant:	**No. Se lo mandamos por correo, si quiere.**
	Noh seh loh mahn-dah-mohs pohr koh-rreh-oh see kee-eh-reh
	No. We can post it to you, if you want.

Phrases to Know

billete de ida	beeh-yeh-teh deh ee-dah	one way ticket (literally: ticket to go)
billete de ida y vuelta	bee-yeh-teh deh ee-dah ee booehl-tah	round trip ticket (literally: ticket to go and return)
el billete de vuelta	ehl beeh-yeh-teh deh boo ehl-tah	a single return-ticket (only return journey)
la fecha de llegada	lah feh-chah deh yeh-gah-dah	the arrival date
la fecha de partida	lah feh-chah deh pahr-tee-dah	the departure date
la hora de salida	lah oh-rah deh sah-lee-dah	the take-off time
vuelo con escala	boo-eh-loh kohn ehs-kah-lah	flight with an stopover
vuelo directo	boo-eh-loh dee-rehk-toh	direct flight

Talkin' the Talk

Phil Potts needs to cancel his trip to Bilbao.

Phil Potts: **Señorita, ¿por favor?**
seh-nyoh-ree-tah pohr fah-bohr
Miss, please?

Travel
agent: **Sí, ¿en qué puedo servirle?**
see ehn keh pooeh-doh sehr-beer-leh
Yes, How can I help? [formal]

Phil Potts: **Quisiera cancelar un viaje a Bilbao.**
kee-seeeh-rah kahn-theh-lahr oon bee-ah-Heh ah beel-bah-oh
I'd like to cancel a trip to Bilbao.

Travel
agent: **¿Cuándo iba a viajar?**
kooahn-doh ee-bah ah bee-ah-Hahr
When were you going?

Phil Potts: **El lunes próximo.**
ehl loo-nehs prohk-see-moh
Next Monday.

Travel
agent: **¿A qué nombre está la reserva?**
ah keh nohm-breh ehs-tah lah reh-sehr-bah
What name is the booking under?

Phil Potts: **A nombre de Phil Potts.**
ah nohm-breh deh Phil Potts
In the name of Phil Potts.

Travel
agent: **Bien, cancelado. ¿Algo más?**
beeehn kahn-theh-lah-doh ahl-goh mahs
Good! I've cancelled it. Anything else?

Phil Potts: **No, eso es todo, gracias.**
noh eh-soh ehs toh-doh grah-theeahs
No, that's all, thank you.

Using the Verb to Go: Ir

Ir *(eer)* (to go) is an irregular verb – so much so that you have to take it on faith that the following table shows the present tense conjugation of the verb. You can't tell just by looking at the words:

Conjugation	*Pronunciation*
yo voy	*yoh bohy*
tú vas	*too bahs*
él, ella, usted va	*ehl, eh-yah, oos-tehd bah*
nosotros vamos	*noh-soh-trohs bah-mohs*
vosotros váis	*boh-soh-trohs bahees*
ellos, ellas, ustedes van	*eh-yohs, eh-yahs, oos-teh-dehs bahn*

Travelling into the simple future: Ir a viajar

You can use the verb **ir** *(eer)* (go), just like the English verb *to go*, to make a kind of future tense called the simple future: it's like saying, 'I'm going to travel'. In Spanish, that phrase is **voy a viajar** *(bohy ah bee-ah-Hahr)*. So what follows is an example of the use of the verb **ir** with the infinitive of **viajar** *(bee-ah-Hahr)*, to demonstrate the simple future of the travelling verb:

Word	*Pronunciation*
yo voy a viajar	*yoh bohy ah bee-ah-Hahr*
tú vas a viajar	*too bahs ah bee-ah-Hahr*
él, ella, usted va a viajar	*ehl, eh-yah, oos-tehd bah a bee-ah-Hahr*
nosotros vamos a viajar	*noh-soh-trohs bah-mohs ah bee-ah-Hahr*
vosotros váis a viajar	*boh-soh-trohs bahees ah bee-ah-Hahr*
ellos, ellas, ustedes van a viajar	*eh-yohs, eh-yahs, oos-teh-dehs bahn a bee-ah-Hahr*

Practising using the future tense of **ir a viajar** can be fun, and so check out the following:

- ✔ **Voy a viajar en avión.** *(bohy a bee-ah-Hahr ehn ah-bee-ohn)* (I'm going to travel by plane.)

- ✔ **Ellos van a viajar en bus.** *(eh-yohs bahn ah bee-ah-Hahr ehn boos)* (They're going to travel by bus.)

✔ **Vamos a viajar en tren.** *(bah-mohs ah bee-ah-Hahr ehn trehn)* (We'll be travelling by rail.)

✔ **Tú vas a ir en avión.** *(too bahs a eer ehn ah-bee-ohn)* (You're going to go by plane.)

✔ **Voy a ir a comer.** *(bohy ah eer ah koh-mehr)* (I'm going to go to eat.)

✔ **Todos nos vamos a divertir.** *(toh-dohs nohs bah-mohs ah dee-behr-teer)* (We're all going to have fun.)

✔ **Vas a llegar cansado.** *(bahs ah yeh-gahr kahn-sah-doh)* (You'll be tired when you arrive.)

✔ **Va a querer volver.** *(bah ah keh-rehr bohl-behr)* (He/she will want to return.)

✔ **Nosotros vamos a llevar las maletas.** *(noh-soh-trohs bah-mohs ah yeh-bahr lahs mah-leh-tahs)* (We're going to carry the luggage.)

Scheduling hours and minutes

When you want to say that you're going somewhere in the present or future (or, indeed, went somewhere in the past), you're talking about time. And when you talk about time, you need to know about minutes and hours. Here you go! Right on time!

✔ **Voy a las diez de la mañana.** *(bohy ah lahs deeeth deh lah mah-nyah-nah)* (I'm going at ten o'clock in the morning.)

✔ **Llega a las nueve de la noche.** *(yeh-gah ah lahs nooeh-beh deh lah noh-cheh)* (He/she arrives at nine o'clock in the evening.)

✔ **Son las veinte horas y treinta minutos.** *(sohn lahs beh-een-teh oh-rahs ee treheen-tah mee-noo-tohs)* (It's 20:30 [literally: 20 hours and 30 minutes.])

✔ **Son las ocho cuarenta y cinco.** *(sohn lahs oh-choh koo-ah-rehn-tah ee theen-koh)* (It's 8:45.)

✔ **Vengo a la una y cuarto.** *(behn-goh ah lah oo-nah ee koo-ahr-toh)* (I'm coming at a quarter past one.)

✔ **A las dos menos cuarto llovió.** *(ah lash dohs meh-nohs koo-ahr-toh yoh-bee-oh)* (It rained at a quarter to two.)

✔ **Son las once menos diez.** *(sohn lahs ohn-theh meh-nohs deeeth)* (It's ten to eleven.)

Head over to Chapter 5 for more about numbers. In the meantime, continue to practise your scheduling phrases with the following:

✔ **¿Qué hora es?** *(keh oh-rah ehs)* (What time is it?)

✔ **Un minuto, por favor.** *(oon mee-noo-toh pohr fah-bohr)* (One minute, please.)

✔ **Un segundo, por favor.** *(ooh seh-goon-doh pohr fah-bohr)* (One second, please.)

✔ **Un momento por favor.** *(oon moh-mehn-toh pohr fah-bohr)* (One moment, please.)

Words to Know

la hora	lah oh-rah	the hour
el minuto	ehl mee-noo-toh	the minute
el segundo	ehl seh-goon-doh	the second
menos cuarto	meh-nohs koo-ahr-toh	a quarter to
y media	eeh meh-deeah	and an half
la tarde	lah tahr-deh	the afternoon
la noche	lah noh-cheh	the night

Packing For Your Visit

One of the most important things to consider when travelling is planning what to take with you.

As regards clothes, the Spanish are a bit more formal than people in the UK and pay a good deal of attention to fine clothing. You're sure to feel better walking on the city streets if you have something elegant or pleasant to wear! In addition, when chilling out in the evening in cities, you look more in style if you give the shorts and short skirts a miss.

When you're visiting religious buildings such as churches or cathedrals, plan to dress respectfully and wear longish skirts, dresses or long trousers. Shorts are great on the beach but not appropriate for churches.

Talkin' the Talk

Jane and Antonio are talking about what to pack for their upcoming trip. See how they discuss what they need.

Jane: **Falta hacer las maletas.**
fahl-tah ah-thehr lahs mah-leh-tahs
We still have to pack the luggage.

Antonio: **Mejor es llevar un pijama.**
meh-Hohr ehs yeh-bahr oon pee-Hah-mah
It's better to take pyjamas.

Y un jersey, por si hace fresco.
ee oon Her-seh-ee pohr see ah-theh frehs-koh
And a jumper, in case it's cool.

Jane: **Llevo ropa ligera de algodón.**
yeh-boh roh-pah lee-Heh-rah deh ahl-goh-dohn
I'm taking light, cotton clothes.

Antonio: **Aquí está tu traje de baño.**
ah-kee ehs-tah too trah-Heh deh bah-nyoh
Here's your swimsuit.

Jane: **Llevo zapatos para la playa.**
yeh-boh thah-pah-tohs pah-rah lah plah-yah
I'm taking shoes for the beach.

Antonio: **Estos zapatos son para la ciudad.**
ehs-tohs thah-pah-tohs sohn pah-rah lah thee-oo-dahd
These shoes are for the city.

Jane: **También llevo un vestido ligero.**
tahm-bee-ehn yeh-boh oon behs-tee-doh lee-Heh-roh
I'm also taking a light dress.

Antonio: **Aquí están mis zapatos cómodos.**
ah-kee ehs-tahn mees thah-pah-tohs koh-moh-dohs
Here are my comfortable shoes.

Jane: **Tenemos tres maletas y un bolso.**
teh-neh-mohs trehs mah-leh-tahs ee oon bohl-soh
We have three suitcases and one bag.

Taking Along Your Computer

For those hours between sightseeing and visiting, you may decide to take along your laptop. Here are some phrases that can help when talking about your computer:

- ✔ **Voy a llevar conmigo el ordenador portátil.** *(bohy ah yeh-bahr kohn-mee-goh ehl or-deh-nah-dor pohr-tah-teel)* (I'll take my laptop.)

- ✔ **No te olvides de la batería.** *(noh teh ohl-bee-dehs deh lah bah-teh-ree-ah)* (Don't forget its battery.)

- ✔ **¿Vas a llevar el adaptador?** *(bahs a yeh-bahr ehl ah-dahp-tah-dohr)* (Will you take a plug adapter?)

- ✔ **Necesitamos el adaptador para cargar la batería.** *(neh-theh-see-tah-mohs ehl ah-dahp-tah-dohr pah-rah kahr-gahr la bah-teh-ree-ah)* (We need the adaptor to charge the battery.)

Words to Know

cargar	kahr-_gahr_	to charge
el adaptador	ehl ah-dahp-tah-_doh_r	plug adaptor
el ordenador portátil	ehl ohr-deh-nah-_dor_ pohr-_tah_-teel	laptop computer
la batería	lah bah-teh-_ree_-ah	battery

Talkin' the Talk

The trip is over and these friends are talking about how it went. You can practise along with them.

Daniel: **¿Cómo fue tu viaje?**
koh-moh foo-eh-_too_ bee-ah-Heh
How was your trip?

Agustín: **¡Fabuloso!**
fah-boo-_loh_-soh
Fabulous!

Daniel: **¿dónde estuviste?**
dohn-deh ehs-too-bees-teh
Where were you?

Agustín: **Estuve en Puerto Banús.**
ehs-too-beh ehn poo-ehr-toh bah-noohs
I was in Puerto Banús.

Daniel: **¿Cómo fuiste?**
koh-moh foo-ees-teh
How did you get there?

Agustín: **Fui en avión y volví en bus.**
fooee ehn ah-bee-ohn ee bohl-bee ehn boos
I went by plane and returned by bus.

Daniel: **¿Cuánto tarda el avión?**
kooahn-toh tahr-dah ehl ah-bee-ohn
How long does the plane take?

Agustín: **Quince minutos.**
keen-theh mee-noo-tohs
15 minutes.

Daniel: **¿Y el bus?**
ee ehl boos
And the bus?

Agustín: **Seis horas.**
seh-ees oh-rahs
Six hours.

Fun & Games

Choosing the month to travel is the first part of planning any trip. The illustration below shows the four seasons. Each of the 12 months is scrambled below. Unscramble the month and then write it in the blank next to the appropriate season. (Remember, the names of the months aren't capitalised in Spanish.)

Beefror   oneer

biomnerve   oyam

breedicim   permbitees

goosta   rozam

joinu   tubecor

libra   ujoil

Chapter 16

Handling Emergencies

. . . .

In This Chapter

▶ Asking for help

▶ Communicating at the hospital

▶ Talking with doctors

▶ Dealing with the police

▶ Protecting your legal rights abroad

. . . .

*B*e prepared. That's the Boy Scout motto, and it's not a bad idea for any situation. You always need to be prepared for emergencies, especially in a country whose residents don't speak your native tongue. Language differences can complicate an emergency if no one can understand you, or if you don't understand what's being said.

This chapter looks at two main areas in which you may experience an emergency:

> ✔ **Health concerns** – for example, breaking an arm or experiencing stomach flu.
>
> ✔ **'Legal' emergencies** – for example, car accidents and other infractions that require the help of your consulate or a lawyer.

But before you start preparing for such emergencies, you need to know a few important words to get you the necessary help quickly.

Shouting for Help

If you find yourself in a situation where you need to call for help, thumbing through your dictionary isn't going to be quick enough. Therefore, you may want to memorise the words and phrases in this section.

Here are some words to use when you need to call for assistance (you can use the first two words interchangeably; the third word is the least dramatic of the three for 'help', and often is used just for asking for a hand with something):

- ✔ **¡Socorro!** *(soh-koh-rroh)* (Help!)
- ✔ **¡Auxilio!** *(ah-ook-see-lee-oh)* (Help!)
- ✔ **¡Ayúda!** *(ah-yoo-dah)* (Help!)

Here are some other basic distress-signalling words:

- ✔ **¡Cuidado!** *(kooee-dah-doh)* (Watch out! [literally: care!])
- ✔ **¡Fuego!** *(foo-eh-goh)* (Fire!)
- ✔ **¡Terremoto!** *(teh-rreh-moh-toh)* (Earthquake!)
- ✔ **¡Una inundación!** *(oo-nah ee-noon-dah-thee-ohn)* (Flooding!)
- ✔ **¡Un temblor!** *(oon tehm-blohr)* (An earth tremor!)

You can use one of the following words to speed up your request:

- ✔ **¡Aprisa!** *(ah-pree-sah)* (Hurry!)
- ✔ **¡Deprisa!** *(deh-pree-sah)* (Hurry [quickly]!)
- ✔ **¡Rápido!** *(rah-pee-doh)* (Quick!)

Handling Health Problems

When an illness or accident jeopardises your health, panicking is a common and understandable reaction. In this section, we help to guide you through these potential problems in a calm and prudent manner.

In our experience, most native Spanish speakers are caring, gentle people who are tolerant of faulty pronunciation and very ready to help a foreigner. In fact, they may even be overly helpful, leaving you with the difficult task of being firm and level-headed about your needs without damaging their feelings and being negative about their goodwill.

Here are some sentences to help you be just as caring and kind, but at the same time firm with your refusal for help, when you don't want any. Suppose the person trying to be helpful says things such as the following:

- ✔ **¡Pobrecito! ¿Le ayudo?** *(poh-breh-thee-toh leh ah-yoo-doh)* (Poor you [literally: poor little (male) you]. Can I help you?)
- ✔ **¡Venga, todos a ayudar!** *(behn-gah toh-dohs ah ah-yoo-dar)* (Come everybody, let's help!)

In which case, you can answer as follows:

- **Estoy bien, no me ayudes.** *(ehs-tohy beeen noh meh ah-yoo-dehs)* (I'm fine, don't help me [informal].)

- **Muchas gracias, prefiero estar solo.** *(moo-chahs grah-theeahs preh-feeeh-roh ehs-tahr soh-loh)* (Thank you very much, I prefer to be [left] alone.)

- **Estoy bien, gracias, no necesito ayuda.** *(ehs-tohy beeehn grah-theeahs noh neh-theh-see-toh ah-yoo-dah)* (I'm fine, thanks, I don't need help.)

- **Es muy amable, gracias.** *(ehs moo-ee ah-mah-bleh grah-theeahs)* (You're [formal, singular] very kind, thanks.)

- **Ustedes son muy amables, pero estoy bien.** *(oos-teh-dehs sohn moo ee ah-mah-blehs peh-roh ehs-tohy beeehn)* (You're [formal, plural] very kind, but I'm fine.)

If you ask for a doctor who speaks English, and you're introduced to one, try to make sure that the doctor's English is better than your Spanish before you get involved. If you're having trouble being understood in English or Spanish, ask for another doctor whose language skills more closely match your own.

Remember that if you have to speak in Spanish to the Spanish-speaking person you're addressing, things go better if you speak s-l-o-w-l-y. Another thing to keep in mind is that in an emergency generally the best part of people comes to the fore. Don't worry about money when those about you want to help. You'll have time for that when you've recovered, or are out of the mess. Also, let people help you if at all possible; helping others makes people feel good.

As to procedures relating to emergency rooms or hospitals, let those things work themselves out, and simply be a 'patient' patient. Remember that all those concerned are doing the best they can. Finally, keep in mind that procedures can vary from place to place in relation to the availability of people and equipment.

If you get sick while travelling, ask for advice at your hotel's reception desk.

Helping out: Using ayudar

The verb **ayudar** *(ah-yoo-dahr)* (to help) is, as you'd expect, a very helpful word to know. **Ayudar** is a regular verb of the **-ar** variety, and so is very easy to conjugate. Here's **ayudar** conjugated in the present tense:

Conjugation	Pronunciation
yo ayudo	*yoh ah-yoo-doh*
tú ayudas	*too ah-yoo-dahs*
él, ella, usted ayuda	*ehl, eh-yah, oos-tehd ah-yoo-dah*
nosotros ayudamos	*noh-soh-trohs ah-yoo-dah-mohs*
vosotros ayudáis	*boh-soh-trohs ah-yoo-dahees*
ellos, ellas, ustedes ayudan	*eh-yos, eh-yas, oos-teh-dehs ah-yoo-dahn*

Some helpful phrases follow for when you're talking more formally to people you haven't met before – such as doctors or passers-by. We also give you informal phrases for situations when you're closely related to the people around you, or when they're children.

We begin with some grammatically formal phrases you can use when you want to be helpful. The formal way of speech is normally used on your part and on the part of others. It shows your respect to doctors, for example, and their respect for you, because you don't share an intimate or informal relationship:

- ✔ **¿Le ayudo?** *(leh ah-yoo-doh)* (Can I help you?)

- ✔ **Sí, ayúdeme pida una ambulancia.** *(see ah-yoo-deh-meh pee-dah oo-nah ahm-boo-lahn-theeah)* (Yes, help me get an ambulance.)

- ✔ **Espere. Le van a ayudar a llevar al herido.** *(ehs-peh-reh leh bahn ah ah-yoo-dahr ah yeh-bahr ahl eh-ree-doh)* (Wait. They'll help you carry the injured person.)

- ✔ **Ayude al enfermo a bajar de la camilla.** *(ah-yoo-deh ahl ehn-fehr-moh ah bah-Hahr deh lah kah-mee-yah)* (Help the ill person get off the stretcher.)

- ✔ **¡Deprisa!** *(deh-pree-sah)* (Hurry up!)

Words to Know

el enfermo	ehl ehn-*fehr*-moh	the ill person [male]
la enferma	lah ehn-*fehr*-mah	the unwell person [female]
la camilla	lah kah-*mee*-yah	the stretcher; the trolley
llevar	yeh-*bahr*	to carry

Grammatical informality is appropriate when you talk to a child, or if the person is someone you know or who's close to you. The following phrases are for informal situations:

- ✔ **¿Te ayudo?** *(teh ah-yoo-doh)* (Can I help you?)

- ✔ **Sí, ayúdame.** *(see ah-yoo-dah-meh)* (Yes, help me.)

- ✔ **¡Te busco un médico!** *(teh boos-koh oon meh-dee-koh)* (I'll get a doctor for you!)

- ✔ **¡Deprisa!** *(deh-pree-sah)* (Hurry up!)

- ✔ **¡Sujétame!** *(soo-Heh-tah-meh)* (Hold onto me!)

Assisting yourself with reflexive pronouns

The pronouns you use when you talk about someone to whom something happened are called reflexive pronouns, and Spanish uses them quite often – much more so than English. Table 16-1 shows you which pronoun to use when the person the pronoun represents is the object of the action.

Table 16-1	Reflexive Pronouns
Pronoun	*Translation*
me *(meh)*	me
te *(teh)*	you
le *(leh)*	him, her, you (formal, singular)
nos *(nohs)*	us
os *(ohs)*	you
les *(lehs)*	them, you (formal, plural)

So how and when do you use these pronouns? Well, hang in there . . . help is on its way!

In English you say 'his leg hurts'. In Spanish, you say **le duele la pierna** *(leh-dooeh-leh lah pee-ehr-nah)* (literally: him hurts the leg). The difference between the two is that in English, the leg is supposed to feel the pain (leg is the grammatical subject of the sentence); in Spanish, the owner of the leg feels the pain. And because both the leg and the pain belong to the same person, in Spanish the pain goes back to 'him' – the owner of the leg and of the pain – which in Spanish is indicated by **le** *(leh)*. So the verb, which expresses an action, is reflected back onto the person, not the leg; the person is hurt by virtue of owning the leg. **Le** is the object of the action and a reflexive pronoun.

Expressing pain when you're hurt

When you're hurt, you want to be able to tell people so that they can help ease your pain. To do so, you use reflexive pronouns (as explained in the preceding section 'Assisting yourself with reflexive pronouns').

The following sentences tell you how to talk about pain – and, just like carrying an umbrella can prevent rain, we hope that practising talking about pain can prevent you from getting hurt (in Spanish, anyway)!

- **Me duele la espalda.** *(meh doo-eh-leh lah ehs-pahl-dah)* (My back hurts [literally: me hurts the back].)
- **¿Le duele la cabeza?** *(leh doo-eh-leh lah kah-beh-thah)* (Does your head hurt? [singular, formal])
- **Le duele todo.** *(leh doo-eh-leh toh-doh)* (He hurts all over.)
- **Nos duelen los piés.** *(nohs doo-eh-lehn lohs pee-ehs)* (Our feet hurt.)
- **¿Te duele aquí?** *(teh doo-eh-leh ah-kee)* (Does it hurt you [singular, informal] here?)

Talkin' the Talk

After a collision, Julia is taken to a hospital and is being examined to see if she's broken anything.

Doctor:	**¿Tienes dolor en la pierna?** *tee-eh-nehs doh-lohr ehn lah pee-ehr-nah* Does your leg hurt [literally: do you have any pain in the leg]?
Julia:	**Sí doctor, ¡me duele mucho!** *see dohk-tohr meh doo-eh-leh moo-choh* Yes, doctor, it hurts a lot!
Doctor:	**Vamos a sacarte unos rayos X.** *bah-mohs ah sah-kahr-teh oo-nohs rah-yohs eh-kees* We'll take some X-rays.
X-ray technician:	**Aquí, súbete a la mesa.** *ah-kee soo-beh-teh ah lah meh-sah* Here, get on the table.
	No te muevas por favor. *noh teh moo-eh-bahs pohr fah-bohr* Don't move, please.

Doctor: **Ya están las radiografías.**
          yah ehs-<u>tahn</u> lahs rah-deeoh-grah-<u>fee</u>-ahs
          The X-ray pictures are done.

          Aquí tienes una fractura.
          ah-<u>kee</u> tee<u>eh</u>-nehs <u>oo</u>-nah frahk-<u>too</u>-rah
          You have a fracture here.

          Vamos a tener que enyesarte la pierna.
          <u>bah</u>-mohs ah teh-<u>nehr</u> keh ehn-yeh-<u>sahr</u>-teh lah
          pe-<u>eehr</u>-nah
          We need to put your leg in plaster.

          Te voy a dar un analgésico.
          teh bohy a dahr oon ah-nahl-<u>Heh</u>-see-koh
          I'll give you a painkiller.

Words to Know

el analgésico	ehl ah-nahl-<u>Heh</u>-see-koh	the painkiller
el médico	<u>meh</u>-dee-koh	the doctor
el yeso	ehl <u>yeh</u>-soh	the plaster (in casts or walls)
enyesar	ehn-yeh-<u>sahr</u>	to set in a cast
la fractura	lah frahk-<u>too</u>-rah	the fracture (broken bone)
la pierna	lah pee-<u>ehr</u>-nah	the leg
la radiografía	lah rah-deeoh-grah-<u>fee</u>-ah	the X-ray

Getting help for a bleeding wound

Here are some examples of how to get medical help for someone who's bleeding:

✔ **¡Es una emergencia!** *(ehs <u>oo</u>-nah eh-mehr-<u>Hehn</u>-thee-ah)* (There's an emergency!)

✔ **¡Un médico, por favor!** *(oon <u>meh</u>-dee-koh pohr fah-<u>bohr</u>)* (A doctor, please!)

✔ **¡Una ambulancia, rápido!** *(oo-nah ahm-boo-lahn-theeah rrah-pee-doh)* ([Call] an ambulance, quickly!)

✔ **Lo más rápido posible.** *(loh mahs rah-pee-doh poh-see-bleh)* (As fast as possible.)

✔ **¡Estoy sangrando mucho!** *(ehs-tohy sahn-gran-doh moo-choh)* (I'm bleeding a lot!)

✔ **Tiene un corte.** *(teeeh-neh oon kohr-teh)* (You [formal] have a cut.)

✔ **Necesitas puntos.** *(neh-theh-see-tahs poon-tohs)* (You [informal] need stitches.)

Words to Know

el corte	ehl _kohr_-teh	the cut
la emergencia	lah eh-mehr-_Hehn_-thee-ah	the emergency
los puntos	lohs _poon_-tohs	the stitches [surgical]
sangrar	_sahn_-grahr	to bleed

Closing the wound

If you ever need to get stitches, here are some useful phrases:

✔ **Me duele mucho.** *(meh doo-eh-leh moo-choh)* (It hurts a lot.)

✔ **Le vamos a poner anestesia local.** *(leh bah-mohs a poh-nehr ah-nehs-teh-see-ah loh-kahl)* (We'll give you [formal] a local anaesthetic.)

✔ **¡Ya se pasó el dolor!** *(yah seh pah-soh ehl doh-lohr)* (The pain is gone!)

Words to Know

el dolor	ehl doh-_lohr_	the pain
la anestesia	lah ah-nehs-_teh_-see-ah	the anaesthetic
la herida	lah eh-_ree_-dah	the wound

Telling where it hurts

We now provide several phrases that may be useful in telling someone where you hurt. (In Table 16-2 in the later section 'Describing symptoms', we provide some body-part vocabulary that may also come in handy.)

- **Me sangra la nariz.** *(meh sahn-grah lah nah-reeth)* (My nose is bleeding.)

- **No puedo ver.** *(noh pooeh-doh behr)* (I can't see.)

- **Me entró algo en el ojo.** *(meh ehn-troh ahl-goh ehn ehl oh-Hoh)* (Something got into my eye.)

- **Me torcí el tobillo.** *(meh tohr-thee ehl toh-bee-yoh)* (I twisted my ankle.)

- **Se rompió el brazo derecho.** *(seh rohm-pee-oh ehl brah-thoh deh-reh-choh)* (He broke his right arm.)

- **La herida está en el antebrazo.** *(lah eh-ree-dah ehs-tah ehn ehl ahn-teh-brah-thoh)* (The wound is on the forearm.)

- **Le duele la muñeca izquierda.** *(leh doo-eh-leh lah moo-nyeh-kah eeth-kee-ehr-dah)* (Her left wrist hurts.)

- **Se cortó en el dedo índice.** *(seh kohr-toh ehn ehl deh-doh een-dee-theh)* (He has a cut on his index finger.)

- **Se torció el cuello.** *(seh tohr-thee-oh ehl koo-eh-yoh)* (He/she twisted his/her neck.)

- **Ahora ya no sale sangre.** *(ah-oh-rah yah noh sah-leh sahn-greh)* (It stopped bleeding [literally: now there's no more blood coming out].)

- **Usted tiene la presión muy alta.** *(oos-tehd teeeh-neh lah preh-see-ohn moo-ee ahl-tah)* (You have very high blood pressure.)

- **He sentido náuseas.** *(eh sehn-tee-doh nah-oo-seh-ahs)* (I felt nauseous.)

Talkin' the Talk

Julia just can't get rid of her headache, and so she decides to see her doctor. She's at her doctor's surgery, talking to the receptionist.

Julia: **¿Está el doctor Díaz?**
ehs-tah ehl dohk-tohr dee-ath
Is Dr Díaz in?

Receptionist: **Sí, ¿Tiene cita?**
see teeeh-neh thee-tah
Yes, [he's in]. Do you have an appointment?

Julia: **No tengo cita, pero necesito verle.**
*noh tehn-goh thee-tah peh-roh neh-theh-see-toh
behr-leh*
I don't have an appointment, but I need to see him.

Tengo mucho dolor de cabeza.
Tehn-goh moo-cho doh-lohr deh kah-beh-thah
I have a bad headache.

Receptionist: **Muy bien, ¿cómo se llama?**
moo-ee beeehn koh-moh seh-yah-mah
Very well, what's your name?

Julia: **Soy Julia Frank.**
sohy Hoo-lee-ah frahnk
I'm Julia Frank.

Receptionist: **Un momento, por favor. Tome asiento en la sala de espera.**
*oon moh-mehn-toh pohr fah-bohr toh-meh ah-see
ehn-toh ehn lah sah-lah deh ehs-peh-rah*
One moment, please. Take a seat in the waiting room.

Talkin' the Talk

After waiting a few minutes, Julia is ushered into the doctor's room and begins to explain her symptoms.

Julia: **Me duele la cabeza.**
meh doo-eh-leh lah kah-beh-thah
My head hurts.

Dr Díaz: **¿Desde cuándo?**
dehs-deh koo-ahn-doh
Since when?

Julia: **Desde ayer. Me golpeé la cabeza.**
dehs-deh ah-yehr meh gohl-peh-eh lah kah-beh-thah
Since yesterday. I banged my head.

Dr Díaz: **¿Cómo se golpeó?**
koh-moh seh gohl-peh-oh
How did you bang [your head]?

Julia: **Me caí en la calle.**
                meh-kah-ee ehn lah kah-yeh
                I fell in the street.

Dr Díaz: **Tiene mareos?**
                tee-eh-neh mah-reh-ohs
                Do you get dizzy?

Julia: **Sí, tengo mareos.**
                see tehn-goh mah-reh-ohs
                Yes, I get dizzy.

Dr Díaz: **Vamos a tenerla en observación durante dos días.**
                *bah-mohs ah teh-nehr-lah ehn ohb-sehr-bah-thee-
                ohn doo-rahn-teh dohs dee-ahs*
                We'll keep you under observation for two days.

Words to Know

el mareo	*ehl mah-reh-oh*	*the dizziness*
golpear	*gohl-peh-ahr*	*to hit; to bang*
la cabeza	*lah kah-beh-thah*	*the head*
la cita	*lah thee-tah*	*the appointment*
la observación	*lah ob-sehr-bah-thee-ohn*	*the observation*
ver	*behr*	*to see*

Describing symptoms

Table 16-2 lists common terms for body parts and medical problems that you may need to know when visiting the doctor.

Table 16-2	Helpful Words in a Medical Emergency	
Spanish	*Pronunciation*	*English*
Head and neck		
el ojo	*ehl oh-Hoh*	the eye
la boca	*lah boh-kah*	the mouth
la lengua	*lah lehn-gooah*	the tongue
la oreja	*lah oh-reh-Hah*	the ear
la nariz	*lah nah-reeth*	the nose
el cara	*lah kah-rah*	the face
la barbilla	*lah bahr-bee-yah*	the chin
el labio	*el lah-bee-oh*	the lip
el cuello	*ehl kooeh-yoh*	the neck
las amígdalas	*lahs ah-meeg-dah-lahs*	the tonsil
Torso		
el hombro	*ehl ohm-broh*	the shoulder
el corazón	*ehl koh-rah-thohn*	the heart
el pulmón	*el pool-mohn*	the lung
el estómago	*ehl ehs-toh-mah-goh*	the stomach
el intestino	*ehl een-tehs-tee-noh*	the bowel; intestine; gut
el hígado	*ehl ee-gah-doh*	the liver
el riñón	*ehl ree-nyohn*	the kidney
Arms and hands		
el brazo	*ehl brah-thoh*	the arm
el antebrazo	*ehl ahn-teh-brah-thoh*	the forearm
la muñeca	*lah moo-nyeh-kah*	the wrist
la mano	*lah mah-noh*	the hand
el dedo	*ehl deh-doh*	the finger
el pulgar	*ehl pool-gahr*	the thumb
el dedo índice	*ehl deh-doh een-dee-theh*	the index finger
el dedo medio	*ehl deh-doh meh-deeoh*	the middle finger
el dedo anular	*ehl deh-doh ah-noo-lahr*	the ring finger
el dedo meñique	*ehl deh-doh meh-nyee-keh*	the little finger

Spanish	Pronunciation	English
Legs and feet		
el muslo	*ehl moos-loh*	the thigh
la pierna	*lah pee-ehr-nah*	the leg
el pie	*ehl peeeh*	the foot
el dedo del pie	*ehl deh-doh dehl peeeh*	the toe
el tobillo	*ehl toh-bee-yoh*	the ankle
la pantorrilla	*lah pahn-toh-rree-yah*	the calf
la planta del pie	*lah plahn-tah dehl peeeh*	the sole of the foot
General health		
la salud	*lah sah-lood*	the health
sano	*sah-noh*	healthy
enfermo	*ehn-fehr-moh*	sick
derecho	*deh-reh-choh*	right
izquierdo	*eeth-kee-ehr-doh*	left
la cirugía	*lah thee-roo-Hee-ah*	the surgery
la herida	*lah eh-ree-dah*	the wound
la orina	*lah oh-ree-nah*	the urine
la sangre	*lah sahn-greh*	the blood
la presión sanguínea	*lah preh-see-ohn sahn-ghee-neh-ah*	the blood pressure
el estornudo	*ehl ehs-tohr-noo-doh*	the sneeze
la náusea	*lah nah-oo-seh-ah*	the nausea; sickness
el estreñimiento	*ehl ehs-treh-nyee-mee-ehn-toh*	the constipation
la evacuación	*lah eh-bah-koo-ah-thee-ohn*	the bowel movement (literally: evacuation)
la receta	*lah reh-theh-tah*	the prescription
la medicina	*lah meh-dee-thee-nah*	the medication; the medicine
la farmacia	*lah fahr-mah-theeah*	the pharmacy
el jarabe	*ehl Hah-rah-beh*	the syrup; the elixir; the mixture

When you sneeze among native Spanish-speakers, you never get a chance to excuse yourself. The moment you sneeze, someone immediately says: **¡salud!** *(sah-lood)* (health!) And you immediately answer: **¡gracias!** *(grah-theeahs)* (thanks!).

Braving the dentist

If you have a dental problem in Spain, you're going to discover that dental care is a bit less expensive than in Britain. Part of the reason is that dental surgeries in Spain are more common than in some parts of the UK; just be sure to find a dentist with a 'big smile' to take care of your problem!

You may find the following phrases helpful when you go to a Spanish-speaking dentist:

- **Necesito un dentista.** *(neh-theh-see-toh oon dehn-tees-tah)* (I need a dentist.)

- **¿Me puedes recomendar un dentista?** *(meh poo-eh-dehs reh-koh-mehn-dahr oon dehn-tees-tah)* (Can you recommend [informal] a dentist?)

- **Doctor, me duelen las muelas.** *(dohk-ohr meh dooeh-lehn lahs moo-eh-lahs)* (Doctor, I have a toothache.)

- **Tiene una caries.** *(tee-eh-neh oo-nah kah-ree-ehs)* (You have [formal] a cavity.)

- **Se me rompió una muela.** *(seh meh rohm-pee-oh oo-nah moo-eh-lah)* (I broke a molar.)

- **Le pondré anestesia local.** *(leh pohn-dreh ah-nehs-teh-see-ah loh-cahl)* (I'll give you a local anaesthetic.)

- **Te taparé la caries.** *(teh tah-pah-reh lah kah-ree-ehs)* (I'll fill [informal] the cavity.)

- **Te sacaré la muela.** *(teh sah-kah-reh lah moo-eh-lah)* (I'll pull [informal] the molar out.)

- **Le pondré un puente.** *(leh-pohn-dreh oon poo-ehn-teh)* (I'll put in [formal] a bridge.)

Words to Know

dolor de muelas	doh-*lohr* deh moo-*eh*-lahs	toothache
el dentista	ehl dehn-*tees*-tah	the dentist
el diente	ehl dee-*ehn*-teh	the tooth
la caries	lah *kah*-ree-ehs	the cavity
la muela	lah moo-*eh*-lah	the molar
romper	rohm-*pehr*	to break

'Insuring' that you get reimbursed

If you need to visit a dentist, or any other professional, while you're travelling, be sure you get a receipt to give to your insurance company back home. The following phrases are useful when dealing with insurance questions:

- ✔ **¿Tiene seguro dental?** *(teeeh-neh seh-goo-roh dehn-tahl)* (Do you have [formal] dental insurance?)

- ✔ **¿Tienes seguro médico?** *(teeeh-nehs seh-goo-roh meh-dee-koo)* (Do you have [informal] health insurance?)

- ✔ **¿Me puede dar un recibo para mi seguro?** *(meh poo-eh-deh dahr ooh reh-thee-boh pah-rah mee seh-goo-roh)* (Can you give [formal] me a receipt for my insurance?)

Getting Help with Legal Problems

Most people obey the laws and usually don't engage in activities that involve the police or other aspects of the legal system. But accidents happen, and breaking a Spanish law that you know little or nothing about is possible. If you find yourself in this situation, you need help from your consulate or a lawyer to make sure that your rights are protected.

If you have legal dealings in Spain, take into account that the legal system is likely to be a bit different from the one in your home country, and that the Spanish laws override the laws of the country in which you hold citizenship. The essential philosophy behind the legal system, however, applies in the same way as when you're at home: you're innocent until proven guilty.

In an emergency of any kind, but particularly in a situation involving legal officials, try to be patient, and above all, co-operative. Keep in mind that, just as you're unfamiliar with the practices and procedures of a foreign system, the officers and administrators of that system may well be unaware of your legal expectations.

When you become involved in the Spanish legal system, try to get someone from your consulate to help you handle the situation. That person is more likely to take your interests to heart than a local lawyer. In fact, after you set the dates for a visit to Spain, find out where your country's closest consulate is, in case you need emergency assistance.

Here are a couple of useful phrases for finding legal help:

- ✔ **¿Hay aquí cerca un Consulado británico?** (*ah-ee ah-kee ther-kah oon kohn-soo-lah-doh bree-tah-nee-koh*) (Is a British consulate nearby?)
- ✔ **¿Hay un abogado que hable inglés?** (*ah-ee oon ah-boh-gah-doh keh ah-bleh een-glehs*) (Is there a lawyer who speaks English?)

If you're in Spain and Spanish isn't your first language, ask for a lawyer who speaks English and make sure that the lawyer's English is better than your Spanish. If you have trouble making yourself understood, find another lawyer.

Talkin' the Talk

You're most unlikely to be involved in a situation like Sebastian's, but we want to cover all your bases, and so just in case these few sentences may be useful. Remember though to remain co-operative at all times.

Police officer:	**Usted está detenido.**
	oos-tehd ehs-tah deh-teh-nee-doh
	You're under arrest.

Sebastian:	**¿Por qué?**
	pohr keh
	Why?

Police officer:	**Está circulando ebrio.**
	ehs-tah theer-koo-lahn-doh eh-breeoh
	For drunk driving.

Sebastian:	**Perdone oficial, yo no bebo alcohol.**
	Pehr-doh-neh oh-fee-thee-ahl yoh noh beh-boh ahl-koh-ohl
	Sorry officer, I don't drink alcohol.

Police officer:	**Vamos a la comisaría, por favor.**
	bah-mohs ah lah koh-mee-sah-ree-ah pohr fah-bohr
	Please, let's go to the police station.

Sebastian:	**Creo que usted se equivoca.**
	kreoh keh oos-tehd seh eh-kee-boh-kah
	I believe you're mistaken.

Police officer:	**Venga conmigo.**
	Behn-gah kohn-mee-goh
	Come with me [formal].

Sebastian:	**Quiero hablar con un abogado.**
	keeeh-roh ah-blahr kohn oon ah-boh-gah-doh
	I want to talk to a lawyer.

	Quiero hablar con mi consulado.
	keeeh-roh ah-blahr kohn mee kohn-soo-lah-doh
	I want to talk to my consulate.

	Quiero hablar por teléfono.
	keeeh-roh ah-blahr pohr teh-leh-foh-noh
	I want to talk on the phone.

Sticking 'em up

In the unlikely event that someone mugs or attacks you while you're in Spain, you can attract the help you need by using these phrases:

✓ **¡Me roban!** *(meh roh-bahn)* (Thief! [literally: they're robbing me!])

✓ **¡Ayuda!** *(ah-yoo-dah)* (Help!)

✓ **¡A por el ladrón!** *(ah pohr ehl lah-drohn)* (Catch [him/her]!)

✓ **¡Policía!** *(poh-lee-thee-ah)* (Police!)

We hope you never need to use them, but if you're ever robbed or attacked in Spain, these phrases are important to know:

✔ **¡Llamen a la policía!** (_yah_-mehn ah lah poh-lee-_thee_-ah) (Call the police!)

✔ **¡Me robó la cartera!** (meh roh-_boh_ lah kahr-_teh_-rah) ([She/he] stole my wallet!)

✔ **Haga una denuncia a la policía.** (_ah_-gah _oo_-nah deh-_noon_-theeah ah la poh-lee-_thee_-ah) (Report it to the police [literally: make an allegation at the police].)

Reporting to the police

If you do have an unpleasant encounter with a thief, here are some words that can be helpful in describing the culprit to the police:

✔ **Era un hombre bajo, corpulento.** (_eh_-rah oon _ohm_-breh _bah_-Hoh kohr-poo-_lehn_-toh) (He was a short man, heavy-set.)

✔ **Tenía pelo oscuro y barba.** (teh-_neeah peh_-loh ohs-_koo_-roh ee _bahr_-bah) (He had dark hair and a beard.)

✔ **Llevaba pantalón vaquero y camisa blanca.** (yeh-_bah_-bah pahn-tah-_lohn_ bah-_keh_-roh ee kah-_mee_-sah _blahn_-kah) (He was wearing jeans and a white shirt.)

✔ **Tendrá unos cuarenta años.** (tehn-_drah oo_-nohs koo-ah-_rehn_-tah _ah_-nyos) (He's around 40.)

✔ **Iba con una mujer delgada.** (_ee_-bah kohn _oo_-nah moo-_Hehr_ dehl-_gah_-dah) (He was with a slim woman.)

✔ **Era alta, rubia, de ojos claros.** (_eh_-rah _ahl_-tah _roo_-bee-ah deh _oh_-Hohs _klah_-rohs) (She was tall, blonde, with light-coloured eyes.)

Words to Know

atacar	ah-tah-_kahr_	to attack
claro	_klah_-roh	light
la cartera	lah kahr-_teh_-rah	the wallet
la denuncia	lah deh-_noon_-thee-ah	the allegation
oscuro	ohs-_koo_-roh	dark
robar	roh-_bahr_	to steal; to rob; to mug

Talkin' the Talk

Crash! Bang! A collision. Julia doesn't need it, but here she is. What does she do?

Julia: **¡Ayúda, por favor!**
ah-yoo-dah pohr fah-bohr
Help me, please!

Eyewitness: **¿Estás bien?**
Ehs-tahs bee ehn
Are you all right?

Julia: **¡Sí, gracias!...paré porque cambiaba la luz y choqué.**
See-grah-theeahs pah-reh pohr-keh kahm-beeah-bah lah looth ee choh-keh
Yes, thank you! I stopped because the light changed and I crashed [the car].

Police officer: **¿A qué velocidad iba?**
ah keh beh-loh-thee-dahd ee-bah
How fast were you going?

Julia: **Iba lento, a menos de cuarenta [kilómetros].**
ee-bah lehn-toh ah meh-nohs deh kooah-rehn-tah [kee-loh-meh-trohs]
I was driving slowly, less than 40 [kilometres per hour].

Police officer: **¿Tiene usted seguro del coche?**
teeeh-neh oos-tehd seh-goo-roh dehl koh-cheh
Do you have car insurance?

Julia: **Sí, quiero llamar a mi seguro.**
see keeeh-roh yah-mahr ah mee seh-goo-roh
Yes, I want to phone my insurance company.

Words to Know

lento	*lehn-toh*	slow
el choque	ehl *choh-keh*	the crash
la velocidad	lah-beh-loh-thee-*dahd*	the speed
rápido	*rah-pee-doh*	fast

Talkin' the Talk

Julia and Jorge's car dies on their way to work. They're lucky enough to find a mechanic who tries to figure out what's wrong.

Julia: **Necesitamos ayuda. El coche no funciona.**
neh-theh-see-<u>tah</u>-mohs ah-<u>yoo</u>-dah ehl <u>koh</u>-cheh noh foon-thee-<u>oh</u>-nah
We need help. The car doesn't work.

Jorge: **Buscamos un mecánico.**
boos-<u>kah</u>-mohs oon meh-<u>kah</u>-nee-koh
We're looking for a mechanic.

Nino: **Yo soy mecánico.**
yoh sohy meh-<u>kah</u>-nee-koh
I'm a mechanic.

Jorge: **Hasta ahora iba bien y ahora no arranca.**
<u>ahs</u>-tah ah-<u>oh</u>-rah <u>ee</u>-bah bee-<u>ehn</u> ee ah-<u>oh</u>-rah noh ah-<u>rrahn</u>-kah
Until now it was fine, but now it won't start.

Nino: **Vamos a revisar la batería y las bujías también.**
<u>bah</u>-mohs ah reh-bee-<u>sahr</u> lah bah-teh-<u>reeah</u> ee lahs boo-<u>Hee</u>-ahs tahm-bee-<u>ehn</u>
We'll check the battery and the spark plugs too.

Words to Know

arrancar	ah-rrahn-<u>kar</u>	to start
el mecánico	ehl meh-<u>kah</u>-nee-koh	the mechanic
el motor	ehl moh-<u>tohr</u>	the engine
la batería	lah bah-teh-<u>ree</u>-ah	the battery
las bujías	lahs boo-<u>Hee</u>-ahs	the spark plugs
revisar	reh-bee-<u>sahr</u>	to check

Using the Searching Verb: Buscar

Buscar *(boos-kahr)* is a much-used regular verb with a number of meanings: to look for, to try to find or to search for. Here's how you conjugate it:

Conjugation	*Pronunciation*
yo busco	*yoh boos-koh*
tú buscas	*too boos-kahs*
él, ella, usted busca	*ehl, eh-yah, oos-tehd boos-kah*
nosotros buscamos	*noh-soh-trohs boos-kah-mohs*
vosotros buscáis	*boh-soh-trohs boos-kahees*
ellos, ellas buscan	*eh-yohs, eh-yahs boos-kahn*

Practise using **buscar** with these phrases:

- **Buscan un mecánico.** *(boos-kahn oon meh-kah-nee-koh)* (They're looking for a mechanic.)

- **[Ellos] buscan un médico.** *(boos-kahn oon meh-dee-koh)* (They're looking for a doctor.)

- **¿Buscas un lugar donde descansar?** *(boos-kahs oon loo-gahr dohn-deh dehs-kahn-sahr)* (Are you looking for a place where you can rest?)

- **[Ella] ya no busca mas, encontró un abogado.** *(yah noh boos-kah mahs ehn-kohn-troh oon ah-boh-gah-doh)* (She isn't searching any more, she found a lawyer.)

- **Buscan un sitio y no lo encuentran.** *(boos-kahn oon see-teeoh ee noh loh ehn-koo-ehn-trahn)* (They're looking for a [parking] space and can't find one.)

Fun & Games

Albert doesn't know it yet, but unfortunately he's about to have an accident on his surfboard. You see, he invited you to join him on holiday and then decided to take up surfing to impress a Spanish girl. The thing is, Albert isn't nearly as good a surfer as he thinks he is, and he's going to knock himself out.

Good friend that you are, however, you're going to accompany Albert to the doctor and explain what happened. Fill in all Albert's body parts (in Spanish) on the illustration below. That way, you can refer to the picture if you happen to get flustered at the sight of blood. (Oh, and don't worry, Albert's going to be fine – just a few bumps and bruises, and some sorely wounded pride.)

Part IV
The Part of Tens

'With your amazing knowledge of our language
señor, you will, of course, know this means good
luck to the matador–so you must wave it
when he enters the ring.'

In this part . . .

This part provides small, easily digestible pieces of information about Spanish and Spain. You can find ways to speak Spanish quickly, plenty of essential, practical Spanish expressions and some events worth travelling to Spain for.

Chapter 17

Ten Ways to Speak Spanish Quickly

In This Chapter

▶ Travelling to acquire Spanish

▶ Adding Spanish to your repertoire through the media

▶ Making a game of Spanish vocabulary

*O*ver the years you found out the best way to thread a needle, drive a nail into wood or write a letter. Just as you acquired these skills in many different ways, so you can discover the Spanish language. The following suggestions are great ways to add this beautiful language to your life.

Visiting Spain

This suggestion may seem obvious and probably comes as no surprise, but the absolute best way by far to discover and improve your Spanish is to be in an environment where everybody speaks the language and no one speaks yours. Travelling to Spain is relatively simple and inexpensive. Immersing yourself in life there and mixing with the locals is the perfect way to improve your Spanish language skills.

Mingling with Local Spanish Speakers

You may be lucky enough to have Spanish-speaking people living or working in your own area. Among these people, you may find some who are willing to spend a few hours a week with you, doing leisure or cultural activities while speaking Spanish, perhaps in exchange for you helping them with their English. This way, you can reach Spaniards, who can be great teachers, and you may also be invited to participate in parties, outings and other opportunities to practise the lingo – while having some fun, too!

Listening to Radio, TV and the Internet

Thanks to the growth of digital media, you can easily find radio stations and TV channels that offer all kinds of Spanish programming. By listening to and watching these programmes, you add new vocabulary, gain an understanding of the language and idioms of Spanish-speaking people and gain insight into their idea of fun. Also, the Internet is a vast treasure trove of Spanish-language resources.

Renting a Film

Video clubs and libraries often offer foreign-language films, among which may be an excellent selection in Spanish. (Remember to check the Internet for Spanish films, too.) To get the effect of being in Spain, choose a film that has no dubbing or subtitles. You're sure to be amazed at how much you understand even the first time you see the film, but the good thing about watching these films is that you can play the film as many times as you like.

Checking Out Your Library

Your local library may house books, DVDs and other resources about Spain and the Spanish language. Every bit of information you get helps to build up your mental Spanish library. Here are some things to look for:

✔ Atlases, maps and satellite photos of Spain and its territories.

✔ Travel guides and books.

✔ Novels that describe Spanish places (translations of Spanish texts or books originally written in English).

You can also find access to many of the above items via the Internet, where you can find an enormous amount of information and fun things related to Spanish places.

Reading Lyrics and Liner Notes

The liner notes you find with CDs often contain the song lyrics. Try buying tracks or albums by your favourite Spanish singers and then check the lyrics. Eventually, you're bound to find yourself singing along – in Spanish!

Susana's Secret Game

As a teenager, Susanna studied three languages. Ashamed of her clumsiness, she invented a Secret Game to help. In this game, you simply insert any new word or phrase you grasp in the new language into sentences and thoughts in your head.

Here's how you play: imagine any situation you like, as though you're telling a story, explaining an event or describing a dream. In your own mind, try to do so in Spanish. For any word you don't know in Spanish, insert the English word instead.

At first, you're likely to have many English words with only a sprinkling of Spanish. But as you go on – after even a few attempts – the number of Spanish words increases.

The great thing about this game is that nobody notices whether you leave something out or make a mistake. Susanna didn't use dictionaries or have the opportunity to tune into radio podcasts, language TV programmes or websites, but slowly a new world opened up in her mind and this game helped her become fluent in English, Spanish and French.

Using Stickers

You can make up a game of your own (see the later sidebar 'Susana's Secret Game' for an example of one of the authors' creations) or set yourself a daily challenge. For example, you may decide to set yourself a target of discovering a different sentence each day:

1. Put the sentence on little stickers and attach them to your fridge, next to your computer, on your bathroom mirror or any other location.

2. Read and repeat the sentence aloud every time you go near these places.

Alternatively, you can write the Spanish word for all the things in one room of your house on little stickers, and put each sticker on the correct item. Say the Spanish word aloud every time you use the object. As you feel comfortable with the words, remove the stickers, but continue saying the name aloud. If you forget the name, replace the sticker. When the majority of stickers are gone, move to another room.

Use your imagination and have fun!

Saying It Again, Sam

Imagine that you hear a Spanish phrase in a film, you sing a line in Spanish of a song or you catch a Spanish sentence in a book. These moments are treasures, and your goal is to use and polish them continually. Several times a day, repeat those words and phrases aloud. So that you know what you're repeating, consult a Spanish–English dictionary. Soon, the treasure is yours to keep.

Taking a Spanish Class

Attending a small Spanish language class at a college in your local area is one of the most economical ways to go 'live' in Spanish. These classes can be a stimulating atmosphere in which to discover Spanish alongside other people with the same goal. You can enrol in courses aimed at beginners and intermediates through to proficient speakers – whichever level you're at, you're sure to find a class nearby. Classes are usually small and focused, but good fun, and are suitable for anyone just wanting an introduction to the language, for future travellers or for those who want to become fluent.

Finding Yourself a Tutor

Private tuition can be expensive, but if you can afford a good private teacher you can benefit from the one-on-one, individual attention, especially when you're uncertain what to do at any particular stage. Try to find a tutor who you can contact in the event that a doubt or complexity arises. Tutors can also help you to organise future trips to Spain.

Chapter 18

Ten (Plus Two) Favourite Spanish Expressions

In This Chapter

▶ Showing that you're in the know

▶ Recognising phrases you hear among Spanish speakers

This chapter provides a dozen phrases or words that Spanish speakers use all the time when they meet, greet and deal with each other.

¿Qué tal?

You use the greeting **¿qué tal?** *(keh tahl)* (how are things?) when meeting someone you already know and with whom you have an informal relationship. You can even add to this phrase to ask about something in particular; for example: **¿qué tal la comida?** *(keh tahl lah koh-mee-dah)* (how is/was the meal?), **¿qué tal la película?** *(keh tahl lah peh-lee-koo-lah)* (how was the film?) and **¿qué tal tu nueva clase de español?** *(keh tahl too noo-eh-bah klah-seh deh ehs-pah-nyol)* (how is your new Spanish class?). This phrase (which we introduce in Chapter 3) is easy to pronounce and immediately gives the impression of someone speaking the language fluently.

¿Cómo estás?

¿Cómo estás? *(koh-moh ehs-tahs?)* (how do you do?) is very similar in its effect to **¿qué tal?** (see the preceding section) but is a little more formal. You can use this phrase when speaking to almost anyone. To sound like an insider, let **¿cómo estás?** just flow out of your mouth, as though you're saying one word. (We cover this greeting in more detail in Chapter 3.) **¿Cómo está?** *(koh-moh ehs-tah?)* is the most formal version of the phrase.

¿Qué pasa?

In Spain you frequently hear **¿qué pasa?** *(keh _pah_-sah)* (what's up? [literally: what happened?])

This phrase may seem funny to you at first. Someone sees another person and cries out **¿qué pasa?**, as though they've been separated just before some big event and now want to know what happened. That's what the phrase means, but its use is much broader.

Even people who barely know each other and haven't seen one another for ages use this greeting. In any case, when you use it in Spain do so with someone you've seen at least once before. You can then sound like you've been there forever. (We mention this greeting in Chapters 1 and 3.)

¿Cómo van las cosas?

Well-educated people, such as doctors, use the very gentle greeting **¿cómo van las cosas?** *(_koh_-moh bahn lahs _koh_-sahs)* (how are things going?) to express concern. People also use this phrase when they've met the other person before.

¿Cómo van las cosas? is more appropriate than **¿cómo estás?** or **¿qué pasa?** (see the previous two sections) when greeting someone older than you or someone to whom you want to show your respect. (Check out Chapter 3 for more on this phrase.)

¡De primera!

¡De primera! *(deh pree-_meh_-rah)* (first rate!) is a phrase common with older generations in Spain, but you may hear it in a variety of places and situations. Its meaning is clear, even if you haven't heard it before. A little ditty goes with this phrase:

> **'¿Cómo estamos?' dijo Ramos.** *(_koh_-moh ehs-_tah_-mohs _dee_-Hoh _rah_-mohs)* ('How are things? [literally: how are we?]', said Ramos.)

> **'¡De primera!' dijo Rivera.** *(deh pree-_meh_-rah _dee_-Hoh ree-_beh_-rah)* ('First rate!' said Rivera.)

Ramos and Rivera are just names used in the rhyme. You can sound like one of the group with this phrase.

¿Cuánto cuesta?

You ask the question **¿cuánto cuesta?** *(koo<u>ahn</u>-toh koo<u>ehs</u>-tah)* (how much does it cost?) when you're shopping and need to know the price.

¿A cuánto? *(ah-koo<u>ahn</u>-toh)* (how much?) is very similar to **¿cuánto cuesta?**, except that this phrase may imply that you're asking the price of several things grouped together, as in **¿a cuánto está la docena?** *(ah-koo<u>ahn</u>-toh ehs-<u>tah</u> lah doh-<u>theh</u>-nah)* (how much does a dozen cost?). You can seem like an expert shopper when you use this phrase. (Chapter 6 has some examples of both these phrases in use.)

¿Cómo dices?

¿Cómo dices? *(<u>koo</u>-moh <u>dee</u>-thehs)* (what are you saying?) is a good phrase to use when you don't understand something that another person says, or if you can't follow the thread of a conversation. Dropping that final letter of the verb to make **¿cómo dice?** *(<u>koo</u>-moh <u>dee</u>-theh)* gives you a more formal version to use when addressing an old or respected person, and for yet more politeness just add **usted** *(oos-<u>tehd</u>)* (you [singular], for polite address) or **por favor** *(pohr fah-<u>bohr</u>)* (please) – or both – at the end of the phrase.

¡Un atraco!

You may think that exclaiming **¡un atraco!** *(oon ah-<u>trah</u>-koh)* (a holdup!) in the middle of bargaining for a lower price is exaggerating a little. However, adding hype to your speech can be useful – a bit like using the English colloquialism 'daylight robbery'. At least the vendor knows that you're familiar with this Spanish phrase, which communicates your indignation.

¡Un atraco! is also useful if you're a victim of a genuine crime. (Flip to Chapter 6 for more on haggling over prices and Chapter 16 for getting help in emergencies.)

¡Una ganga!

Vendors often use the phrase **¡una ganga!** *(<u>oo</u>-nah <u>gahn</u>-gah)* (a bargain!) when trying to sell you an item. You can show your familiarity with the language when you use this expression to boast about a really good purchase.

¡Buen provecho!

Imagine that you're sitting at the table, spoon in hand, ready to dip into a cup of steaming soup or a fragrant paella. In order to sound like a native, you want to say – at this exact moment – **¡buen provecho!** *(booehn proh-beh-choh!)* (enjoy your meal! or bon appetit! [literally: good profit!]) before someone else does.

¡Buen provecho! is also the right thing to say when you set a tray of food in front of your guests. (Turn to Chapter 5 to see this phrase in use.)

¡Salud!

¡Salud! *(sah-lood)* (health!) has two usages:

✔ You use this word when giving a toast, as a way to say 'Cheers!', perhaps when sharing a refreshing **sangría** *(sahn-gree-ah)*.

✔ You use this word after someone sneezes – it's the Spanish equivalent of 'bless you', to which you answer **¡gracias!**

(See Chapters 5 and 16 for more details on the two different uses of **salud**.)

¡Buen viaje!

You hear the phrase **¡buen viaje!** *(booehn beeah-Heh)* (have a good trip!) in car rental offices, train stations, airports and bus terminals. Use this expression when wishing someone a safe trip. (See Chapter 15 for more information on travelling.)

If you're reading this book as part of your preparation for travel, we say **¡buen viaje!** to you.

Chapter 19

Ten Holidays to Remember

Spain celebrates many public holidays and feasts that have their origins in Christianity, pagan worship, folklore and popular culture, and people celebrate these events with gusto and enthusiasm. The varied roots contribute to the diverse modern-day culture of Spain – something that many visitors to the country find so alluring. This chapter introduces you to some of the most famous and unique events in Spain and to some of her most inviting destinations.

Año Nuevo

Throughout Spain and the Spanish-speaking world, people celebrate the **Fiesta de Año Nuevo** *(feeehs-tah deh ah-nyoh nooeh-boh)* (New Year's Eve Party). Wherever you go during the night of 31 December and into the morning of 1 January, parties and revellers surround you, helping you cheer in the New Year in Spanish. People sing and shout **¡Salud! ¡Feliz Año Nuevo!** *(sah-lood feh-leeth ah-nyoh nooeh-boh)* (Cheers! Happy New Year!).

Few details distinguish the New Year's Eve celebrations in Spain from those of other countries. At the **Plaza Mayor** *(plah-thah mah-yohr)* (Main Square) in Madrid, as all over Spain, you may be invited to celebrate by munching your way through 12 grapes. The idea is to eat them one-by-one as the clock chimes 12 times. Much hugging and rejoicing always follows, and you dance and wish each other good luck for the New Year until the wee small hours.

La Feria de Sevilla

Seville's famous April Fair is more than 150 years old. What began all those years ago as just an agricultural and trading event soon evolved into something more festive. **La Feria de Sevilla** (lah _feh_-ree-ah deh seh-_bee_-yah) (Seville's April Fair) is now one of the major Spanish celebrations and one of the main tourist attractions in Seville. Even so, the local people still trade and close deals , keeping the April Fair in touch with its roots.

La Feria, where the women dress to impress with their typical flamenco dresses, is an ideal place for cordiality and friendship among glasses of **manzanilla** (mahn-thah-_nee_-yah) (sherry), some tapas to eat and with singing couples dancing **sevillanas** (seh-bee-_yah_-nahs) (a lively version of flamenco dance). The most important reason for going to the fair is to have a good time with friends, all the while taking in the festive surroundings.

Las Fallas de Valencia

Hopefully, you've never been in a war zone, but **Las Fallas** (lash _fah_-yahs) comes pretty close to resembling one! Firecrackers and explosives go off on every street amid the smell of gunpowder, trumpeting parades and the burning of over 350 beautiful statues. With all this on offer, **Las Fallas** is exhilarating, alarming, emotional and noisy, and one of the most unforgettable experiences that you're ever likely to have in Spain.

During **Las Fallas**, some of the Valencian region cities are filled with **ninots** (nee-_nohts_) – giant statues constructed of wood and papier-mâché, which take a whole year to construct and consist of caricatures of politicians, famous people and cartoon characters. These spectacular statues get placed dangerously close to, and stand almost as tall as, multi-storey flats, and are the highlight of the final night when they get burned to a cinder among a display of fireworks and crackers. One of the finest statues is spared each year and displayed in the Fallas Museum.

Another spectacular display during **Las Fallas** is the daily **mascletá** (mahs-cleh-_tah_) – an ear bashing display of firecrackers and smoke bombs set off in the **Plaza del Ayuntamiento** (_plah_-thah dehl ah-yoon-tah-mee-_ehn_-toh) (Town Hall Square).

Carnaval

Countless places in Spain, such as **Cádiz** (_kah_-deeth) or **Santa Cruz de Tenerife** (_sahn_-tah cruth deh teh-neh-_ree_-feh) in the Canaries, celebrate **Carnaval** (kahr-nah-_bahl_) (Shrovetide or Mardi Gras). **Carnaval** is a feast of dancing, singing and excess that comes before Lent – a time of moderation and fasting. Lent begins on Ash Wednesday and **Carnaval** activities come into full swing on the Saturday, Sunday, Monday and Shrove Tuesday that precede Ash Wednesday.

One truly special **Carnaval** event takes place in Cádiz, which becomes one big party town between 11 and 21 February – a perfect time for getting to know this city and to enjoy the inventiveness and sense of fun of the city's people. Fantastic masks and outfits in procession captivate and give flight to the imagination. Huge multitudes gather to see this spectacle – definitely one of the most amazing and unbelievably colourful carnivals in the world.

Semana Santa

Semana Santa *(seh-mah-nah sahn-tah)* is the 'Spanish Easter'. Over the week of this celebration, many communities in Spain participate in exceptional ceremonies and events. Some towns stage re-enactments of the crucifixion of Jesus, in remembrance. Whole communities such as Verges (in Girona province, Cataluña) participate in this Biblical story, as if in one large play. One person is chosen to take the part of Jesus and is 'crucified', while other village actors recite the New Testament texts. People who act out this drama prepare for months and sometimes years ahead of time and do it out of religious fervour. Thousands of visitors from overseas come to witness these re-enactments every year.

Los San Fermines

The festival of **San Fermín** *(sahn fehr-meen)* (known locally as **Sanfermines**) in the northern city of Pamplona is a well-established celebration held annually from 7 July – when the opening of the fiesta is marked by setting off a single pyrotechnic **chupinazo** *(choo-pee-nah-thoh)* (a single fierce burst of fireworks) – to midnight on 14 July. Although its most famous event is the **encierro** *(ehn-theeeh-rroh)* (the running of the bulls), the biggest day of the festival is 7 July, when thousands of people accompany a replica of the statue of **San Fermín** – a locally venerated Catholic saint and martyr – along the streets of the old part of Pamplona. **San Fermín** is accompanied by dancers and street entertainers, such as the **Gigantes** *(Heeh-gahn-tehs)* (giant-sized figures) and the **Cabezudos** *(kah-beh-thoo-dohs)* (the Bigheads).

The week-long celebration involves other traditional events too, such as various music bands at the festivals, and a giant king and queens representing the four parts of the world parading through the streets. These events were central to the plot of *The Sun Also Rises* by Ernest Hemingway, which brought the event to the attention of English-speaking people.

The festival of **San Fermín** has become one of the most internationally renowned Spanish fiestas. Well over a million people come to watch this festival every year.

Las Costas en Invierno

Spain is particularly loved for sun-soaked beach holidays, but by heading to **las costas en invierno** *(lahs cohs-tahs ehn een-bee-ehr-noh)* (the coasts in winter), you can find some really stunning places. **Galicia** *(gah-lee-theeah)*, **Asturias** *(ahs-too-reeahs)* and **Cantabria** *(cahn-tah-breeah)* in autumn, or the north of the **Costa Brava** *(cos-tah brah-bah)* in winter, are wonderful holiday destinations. The best way to experience the beauty of those areas is to drive the tiny winding cliff roads.

At the heart of the Costa Brava, the coastal scenery is spectacular, the medieval towns such as **Pals** *(pahls)* and **Peratallada** *(peh-rah-tah-yah-dah)* are beautiful and the little port and fishing villages are just lovely. Many of the small countryside villages still retain their medieval cobbled streets and the robust facades of their houses and palaces. If you're fascinated by the artist **Dalí** *(dah-lee)*, you can visit the town of **Figueres** *(fee-geh-rehs)* and find his own bizarre museum, and **Cadaqués** *(kah-dah-kehs)* by the sea, where he had his main residence.

Ask Spaniards why Galicia is worth visiting, even in the off peak season, and nine times out of ten they mention its food. Almost all the Spanish (and Portuguese) visitors who visit the region in ever-increasing numbers do so because of the tremendous food and drink. Seafood is the star, and no one should miss the fabulous **percebes** *(pehr-theh-behs)* (goose barnacles).

The rural nature of Asturias makes it attractive to visitors – its beauty mostly lies on rugged shores – although a lack of accessibility has prevented tourist development in the past. The coast is populated by attractive fishing villages, from the bustling port of **Luarca** *(loo-ahr-kah)* in the west to the beautiful harbour of **Cudillero** *(koo-dee-yeh-roh)*, whose main square seems to slide gently into the sea, and from **Ribadesella** *(ree-bah-deh-seh-yah)*, where a famous canoe race ends every year, to the seaside resort of **Llanes** *(yah-nehs)* in the east.

Moving away from the coast, the rolling landscape of inland Asturias gives way to the Cantabrian Mountains, which run along the north coast of Spain and rise to their greatest heights here in the mountain range of **Picos de Europa** *(pee-kohs deh ehoo-roh-pah)*. These mountains straddle Asturias and Cantabria and are home to the last of the Iberian brown bears.

The food of Asturias naturally reflects the traditional way of life. Beef and dairy products are excellent. The most famous local dish is **Fabada** *(fah-bah-dah)*, a filling stew of large white beans with various pork products – **morcilla** *(mohr-theh-yah)* (blood pudding), **lacón** *(lah-kohn)* (shoulder of pork) and **panceta** *(pahn-theh-tah)* (a type of pork fat).

Los Paradores de Turismo en España

The **Paradores** hotels were set up by the government to encourage quality tourism and as a way of safeguarding the national and artistic heritage of Spain.

Los **Paradores de Turismo** *(pah-rah-doh-rehs deh too-reehs-moh)* means charming luxury hotels. Many **Paradores** are medieval castles, fortresses, former palaces or ancient convents, monasteries and other historic buildings. You can also stay at modern hotels, built in traditional style, in areas of outstanding beauty. Guests receive high standards of service and accommodation at prices that are very reasonable by international standards. Enjoying Spain's charm, history, culture and cuisine comes easily in the **Paradores**.

Taking a City Break

Turismo de ciudad *(too-rehs-moh deh theh-oo-dahd)* (city breaks) are great for a short break away, and ideal for practising your new-found Spanish language skills. Two of the most popular city break destinations in Spain are Madrid and Barcelona.

Madrid is a great, cheerful destination. Possibly a 'slower burn destination' compared with the bustle of Barcelona, the capital city holds a few aces up its sleeve. For example, the **Reina Sofía** *(rrehee-nah soh-fee-ah)* museum holds Picasso's masterpiece **Guernica** *(gehr-nee-kah)*, and **El Museo del Prado** *(ehl moo-sehoo dehl prah-doh)*, with one of the world's largest art collections, is known for diverse works by **Velázquez** *(beh-lath-kehth)*, **Goya** *(goh-yah)* and **El Greco** *(ehl greh-koh)*. **El Retiro** *(ehl reh-tee-roh)* park on a sunny spring day is another treasure. This 120-hectare space is a resource for the whole city. You can find all sorts of people there – drummers, dancers, cyclists, rowers and jugglers.

For food and partying, head to the many bars and cafés of **La Latina** *(lah lah-tee-nah)* that fringe the **Rastro** market. Tables, chairs and loud conversation all spill out onto the back streets, with revellers and diners enjoying ice-cold **cañas** *(kah-nyas)* (beer served in thimble-sized glasses) and a vast array of tapas. **Madrileños** *(mah-dree-leh-nyos)* are rightly proud of their street food, but they also point out that the city is no slouch when it comes to stylish high-end restaurants.

Cosmopolitan and confident, Barcelona is an irresistible destination and you can enjoy it in so many different ways: staring wide-eyed at the glorious architecture, sitting glued to a barstool, clubbing, lounging on the beach, whiling away the hours people-watching in the cafés along **La Rambla** *(lah rahm-blah)*, strolling in leafy parks or mooching around the elegant squares. This buzzing city bursts at the seams with possibilities.

You can search out your own favourites as well – such as the rooftop sculpture park at the wonky **La Pedrera** *(lah pe-dreh-rah)* building, which is like stepping into the city's surreal side. Or take a look at the city from another angle – gliding along from the harbour in one of the pleasure boats. Whatever you do, you soon discover that Barcelona swells with life. Cool bars, outlandish buildings, green spaces, old-style tapas, Picasso – Barcelona should come with a warranty attached guaranteeing that you aren't going to be bored!

Planning Your Own Holiday

Just you and a couple of Spanish-speaking friends are more than enough to drum up a wonderful holiday party. The problem comes, of course, in deciding what to do in Spain. The preceding sections in this chapter give you some suggestions, but you have lots more to choose from.

Spain has beaches – lots of good ones – and traditional summer holiday destinations such as the Balearic Islands and the Canary Islands. The country also spoils outdoor lovers for choice, with several great mountainous areas. Between Spain and France are the Pyrenees. Northern Spain has the Cantabrian Mountains and the Picos de Europa National Park; Southern Spain has the Sierra Morena and Sierra Nevada. These areas offer a variety of activities including walking, climbing and skiing.

For people who love history, Spain is littered with places worth visiting. All over Spain, but particularly in Andalucía, you can visit many fine examples of Moorish architecture. Seville, for example, has **La Giralda** *(lah Hee-rahl-dah)* (the famous tower adjoining the Cathedral), built to serve as a minaret to the main mosque of Seville. Córdoba has the **Mezquita** *(meth-kee-tah)* (the mosque). Without doubt though, the most famous historical site in Spain is located in Granada: the **Alhambra** *(ah-lahm-brah)*. This 'red house' palace and citadel was the fortified residence of the former Moorish kings of Spain in the Middle Ages.

If art is your thing, Spain can offer you some of the world's best galleries: Thyssen Bornemisza Museum in Madrid; the Guggenheim Museum in Bilbao and Museu Nacional d'Art de Catalunya in Barcelona house many important examples of art, including works by Spaniards Pablo Picasso, Salvador Dalí and Joan Miró, perhaps the country's most famous contemporary names.

Despite all this, however, perhaps the best reason to visit Spain is the people themselves. Wherever you go in Spain, you're welcomed with opened arms. And if you make a little effort before you go to get to grips with some Spanish vocabulary and a few phrases from *Spanish For Dummies*, people are going to warm to you even more!

Chapter 20

Ten Phrases That Make You Sound Fluent in Spanish

K nowing just a few words – as long as they're the right words! – can convince others that you speak Spanish fluently. Certain phrases can make a big difference, too. This chapter gives you ten Spanish phrases to use at the right moments, in the right places. You can impress your friends and also have fun.

¡Agarrar el toro por los cuernos!

The 'very Spanish' popular exclamation **¡agarrar el toro por los cuernos!** *(ah-gah-rrahr ehl toh-roh pohr lohs kooehr-nohs)* (literally: to grab/take the bull by the horns!) isn't for emboldening someone to get into the ring as a matador! Instead, you use it to encourage someone in a decision-making situation or when someone sees an opportunity but is having trouble deciding what to do. English speakers sometimes use their version of this phrase in more dramatic scenarios, such as confronting a problem head-on in a direct, brave way, and dealing with it openly. Please, *do* try this at home!

¡Esta es la mía!

The exclamation **¡esta es la mía!** *(ehs-tah ehs lah meeah)* (this is my chance! [literally: this one is mine!]) is natural when you see an opportunity and go for it.

In this phrase, **la** *(lah)* (the) refers to **una oportunidad** *(oo-nah oh-pohr-too-nee-dahd)* (an opportunity), but you can use it in the sense of 'I got it!' as well. For instance, you may be fishing, waiting for **el pez** *(ehl pehth)* (the fish). The instant the fish bites, yelling **¡este es el mío!** is appropriate. You use the same phrase when you're waiting to catch **un vuelo** *(ehl boo_eh_-loh)* (a flight) or **un bus** *(un boos)* (a bus). When you see your plane or bus arrive, you say **¡este es el mío!**

¿Y eso con qué se come?

¿Y eso con qué se come? *(ee _eh_-soh kohn _keh_ seh _koh_-meh)* (what on earth is that? [literally: and what do you eat that with?]) is a fun phrase that implies considerable knowledge of the language. The phrase is quite classical, and is common to more than one Spanish-speaking country. You say **¿y eso con qué se come?** when you run across something absurd or unknown.

Voy a ir de fiesta

When you're getting ready for a night on the town, you sound like a native when you say, **¡voy a ir de fiesta!'** *(bohy ah eer deh fee_ehs_-tah!)* (I'm going to party!). You frequently hear the word **fiesta** *(fee_ehs_-tah)* (partying; good time) in Spain. This word even has a verb form: **fiestear** *(fee_ehs_-teh-_ahr_)* (to party; to have a good time).

If **fiestas** *(fee_ehs_-tahs)* (parties) are a jolly part of your life, you're going to love this word. **Ir de fiesta** means 'going partying', 'going to have a good time' and 'going for it all the way'.

An old, unhappy saying goes, **se acabó . . . la fiesta** *(seh ah-kah-_boh_ lah fee_ehs_-tah)* (the party's over). No worse news is to be had, but someone eventually has to bring it!

Caer fatal

You use the verb phrase **caer fatal a uno** *(kah-_ehr_ fah-_tahl_ ah _oo_-noh)* (to dislike something or someone strongly) to convey that something unpleasant happened to you. You can use **caer fatal** for almost anything that you don't like or that hurts you in some way. For example:

- You can say, **sus bromas me caen fatal** *(soos _broh_-mahs meh _kah_-ehn fah-_tahl_)* (I can't stand her/his jokes) when someone's sense of humour really gets on your nerves.

- You can say, **la comida me cayó fatal** *(lah koh-_mee_-dah meh kah-_yoh_ fah-tahl)* (the food made me sick) when suffering some painful consequence of eating food that didn't agree with you.

You can also use **fatal** *(fah-tahl)* (bad; rotten; unpleasant; fatal) on its own to say that something isn't good. For example, to tell someone that you saw a really rotten movie, you say, **la película estuvo fatal** *(lah peh-lee-koo-lah ehs-too-boh fah-tahl)*.

Nos divertimos en grande

The phrase **nos divertimos en grande** *(nohs dee-behr-tee-mohs ehn grahn-deh)* means 'we had a great time'. You can use **en grande** *(ehn grahn-deh)* (a lot; much; greatly; in a big way) for many things. For instance, you can say, **comimos en grande** *(koh-mee-mohs ehn grahn-deh)* (we ate tremendously) after a feast, or **gozamos en grande** *(goh-thah-mohs ehn gran-deh)* (we really, really enjoyed ourselves) after an extraordinarily pleasant event.

The verb **divertir** *(dee-behr-teer)* means to amuse or keep amused – just like this book amuses you and diverts your attention from other, less enjoyable things (or so we hope). **Divertirse**, *(dee-behr-teer-seh)* (to amuse [oneself]) is a reflexive form of the verb. (For more on reflexive verbs, check out Chapters 3 and 16.) **Diversión** *(dee-behr-see-ohn)* is the word for fun or entertainment.

Vérselas negras para

The idiom **vérselas negras para. . .** *(behr-seh-lahs neh-grahs pah-rah)* (to have a hard time of. . . [literally: to see black to. . . , not to see a light]) followed by a verb beautifully conveys that a task is hugely difficult. Here are some examples of this phrase in action:

- ✔ **Nos las vimos negras para terminarlo.** *(nohs lahs bee-mohs neh-grahs pah-rah tehr-mee-nahr-loh)* (We had a difficult time finishing it.)
- ✔ **Los refugiados se las vieron negras para salir del área.** *(lohs reh-foo-Heeah-dohs seh lahs bee eh-rohn neh-grahs pah-rah sah-leer dehl ah-rehah)* (The refugees had a hard time leaving the area.)
- ✔ **Juan se las ve negras para aprender inglés.** *(Hooahn seh lahs bee neh-grahs pah-rah ah-prehn-dehr een-glehs)* (Juan had a hard time learning English.) That's because he had no *For Dummies* books to guide him!

Pasó sin pena ni gloria

You generally use the phrase **pasó sin pena ni gloria** *(pah-soh seen peh-nah nee gloh-reeah)* (it was neither here nor there) to talk about an event that had little resonance with you or the public.

The verb **pasar** in this case indicates the passing of time. **Pena** *(peh-nah)* is grief and **gloria** *(gloh-reeah)* is glory. Here you're saying that the event went by without pulling you down or lifting you up – it made no difference to you. Following are some examples of how to use this phrase:

- ✔ **El concierto pasó sin pena ni gloria.** *(ehl kohn-thee-ehr-toh pah-soh seen peh-nah nee gloh-reeah)* (The concert was neither here nor there.)

- ✔ **La reunión pasó sin pena ni gloria.** *(lah rehoo-neeohn pah-soh seen peh-nah nee gloh-reeah)* (The meeting was neither here nor there.)

- ✔ **La cena se acabó sin pena ni gloria.** *(lah theh-nah seh ah-kah-boh seen peh-nah nee gloh-reeah)* (Dinner was eaten, but it was just so-so.)

¡Así a secas!

¡Así a secas! *(ah-see ah seh-kahs)* (just like that!) is an idiom that conveys astonishment or disbelief. You use this phrase in many ways – often with a snap of your fingers to help show just how quickly something happened. For instance, if you happen to know someone who always seems to be borrowing your money, you may say **me pidió mil euros, ¡así a secas!** *(meh pee-deeoh meel ehoo-rohs ah-see ah seh-kahs)* (he asked me for a thousand euros, just like that!).

¡La cosa va viento en popa!

The idiom **¡la cosa va viento en popa!** *(lah koh-sah bah bee-ehn-toh ehn poh-pah)* (it's going exceedingly well [literally: it's moving with the wind from the stern]) comes from the language of sailing. The race is on and the wind is coming into the sail from the stern – nothing can go faster or better. You can also say the following:

- ✔ **¡El trabajo anduvo viento en popa!** *(ehl trah-bah-Hoh anh-doo-boh bee-ehn-toh ehn poh-pah)* (The job went exceedingly well!)

- ✔ **¡El partido salió viento en popa!** *(ehl pahr-tee-doh sah-leeoh bee-ehn-toh ehn poh-pah)* (The match [game] went exceptionally well!)

- ✔ **¡El aprendizaje del español va viento en popa!** *(ehl ah-prehn-dee-thah-Heh dehl ehs-pah-nyohl bah bee-ehn-toh ehn poh-pah)* (Learning Spanish is going extremely well!)

Part V
Appendixes

'Please tell me if I lisp in the wrong place.'

In this part . . .

This part of the book includes important reference information. We provide a mini-dictionary in both Spanish-to-English and English-to-Spanish formats: If you encounter a Spanish word that you don't understand, or you need to say something in Spanish that you can't find in the book, try looking it up here. We also include verb tables, which show you how to conjugate regular and irregular verbs. And we give you a brief idea of the importance of the Spanish language in the modern world.

Spanish-English Mini-Dictionary

A

a pie/*ah peeeh*/walking (literally: on foot)
abogado/m/*ah-boh-gah-doh*/lawyer
abril/m/*ah-breel*/April
abrir/*ah-breer*/to open
abuela/f/*ah-booeh-lah*/grandmother
abuelo/m/*ah-booeh-loh*/grandfather
actor/m/*ahk-tohr*/actor
adelante/*ah-deh-lahn-teh*/in front, ahead
adiós/*ah-deeohs*/goodbye
aduana/f/*ah-dooah-nah*/customs
agencia/f/*ah-Hehn-theeah*/agency
agosto/m/*ah-gohs-toh*/August
agua/m/*ah-gooah*/water
aguacate/m/*ah-gooah-kah-teh*/avocado
ahora/*ah-oh-rah*/now
ajo/m/*ah-Hoh*/garlic
alfombra/f/*ahl-fohm-brah*/rug
algodón/*ahl-goh-dohn*/cotton
algún/*ahl-goon*/some
alto/*ahl-toh*/tall; high
amarillo/*ah-mah-ree-yoh*/yellow
apretado/*ah-preh-tah-doh*/tight
arroz/m/*ah-rroth*/rice
ascensor/m/*ahs-thehn-sohr*/lift
asiento/m/*ah-seeehn-toh*/seat
atacar/*ah-tah-kahr*/attack

atún/m/*ah-toon*/tuna
autopista/f/*ahoo-toh-pees-tah*/motorway
avenida/f/*ah-beh-nee-dah*/avenue
ayer/*ah-yehr*/yesterday
ayudar/*ah-yoo-dahr*/to help
azul/*ah-thool*/blue

B

balcón/m/*bahl-kohn*/balcony
baño/m/*bah-nyoh*/bathroom
barrio/m/*bah-rreeoh*/neighbourhood
bastante/*bahs-tahn-teh*/quite; enough
bello/*beh-yoh*/beautiful
biblioteca/f/*bee-blee-oh-teh-kah*/library
bicicleta/f/*bee-thee-kleh-tah*/bicycle
bigote/m/*bee-goh-teh*/moustache
billete/m/*bee-yeh-teh*/ticket; note
billetera/f/*bee-yeh-teh-rah*/wallet
blanco/*blahn-koh*/white
boca/f/*boh-kah*/mouth
bolsillo/m/*bohl-see-yoh*/pocket
bonito/m/*boh-nee-toh*/pretty; beautiful
brazo/m/*brah-thoh*/arm
brillo/*bree-yoh*/shine
brócoli/m/*broh-koh-lee*/broccoli
bueno/*booeh-noh*/good
bulevar/m/*boo-leh-bahr*/boulevard
buscar/*boos-kahr*/to search, to look for

C

caballo/m/*kah-<u>bah</u>-yoh*/horse

cabeza/f/*kah-<u>beh</u>-thah*/head

café/m/*kah-<u>feh</u>*/coffee

cajero/m/*kah-<u>Heh</u>-roh*/cashier [male]; cashpoint

caliente/*kah-lee<u>ehn</u>-teh*/hot [temperature]

calle/f/*<u>kah</u>-yeh*/street

cama/f/*<u>kah</u>-mah*/bed

cámara de video/f/*<u>kah</u>-mah-rah deh bee-<u>deh</u>-oh*/video camera

camas/f/*<u>kah</u>-mahs*/beds

cambiar/*kahm-bee<u>ahr</u>*/to change

cambio/m/*<u>kahm</u>-beeoh*/change

camino/m/*kah-<u>mee</u>-noh*/path

camisa/f/*kah-<u>mee</u>-sah*/shirt

cancelar/*kah-theh-<u>lahr</u>*/to cancel

cantar/*kahn-<u>tahr</u>*/to sing

caries/f/*<u>kah</u>-reeehs*/cavity

caro/*<u>kah</u>-roh*/expensive

carrera/f/*kah-<u>rreh</u>-rah*/race; profession

carta/f/*<u>kahr</u>-tah*/letter

cartera/f/*kahr-<u>teh</u>/rah*/wallet; briefcase

casa/f/*<u>kah</u>-sah*/house

cebollas/f/*theh-<u>boh</u>-yahs*/onions

cena/f/*<u>theh</u>-nah*/supper; dinner

cerámica/f/*theh-<u>rah</u>-mee-kah*/ceramic

cereales/m/*theh-reh-<u>ah</u>-lehs*/cereals

cereza/f/*theh-<u>reh</u>-thah*/cherry

cero/*<u>theh</u>-roh*/zero

chaqueta/f/*chah-<u>keh</u>-tah*/jacket

chico/*<u>chee</u>-koh*/little; small

chofer/m/*<u>choh</u>-fehr*/driver

cine/m/*<u>thee</u>-neh*/cinema

ciruela/f/*thee-roo-<u>eh</u>-lah*/plum

cirugía/f/*thee-roo-<u>Heeah</u>*/surgery

ciudad/f/*theeoo-<u>dahd</u>*/city

claro/*<u>klah</u>-roh*/light; of course

cobre/m/*<u>koh</u>-breh*/copper

coche/m/*<u>coh</u>-cheh*/car

cocina/f/*koh-<u>thee</u>-nah*/kitchen

cocinera/f/*koh-thee-<u>neh</u>-rah*/cook [female]

coco/m/*<u>koh</u>-koh*/coconut

código postal/m/*<u>koh</u>-dee-goh pohs-<u>tahl</u>*/post code

colgar/*kohl-<u>gahr</u>*/to hang; to hang up

collar/m/*koh-<u>yahr</u>*/necklace

comida/f/*koh-<u>mee</u>-dah*/lunch

conducir/*kohn-doo-<u>theer</u>*/to drive

contar/*kohn-<u>tahr</u>*/count

contento/*kohn-<u>tehn</u>-toh*/happy; satisfied

corazón/m/*koh-rah-<u>thohn</u>*/heart

correo/m/*koh-<u>rreh</u>-oh*/mail; post

correo electrónico/m/*koh-<u>rreh</u>-oh eh-lehk-<u>troh</u>-nee-koh*/e-mail

cosa/f/*<u>koh</u>-sah*/thing

costar/*kohs-<u>tahr</u>*/to cost (as in price)

cuándo/*koo<u>ahn</u>-doh*/when

cuánto/*koo<u>ahn</u>-toh*/how much

cuarto/m/*koo<u>ahr</u>-toh*/room

cuarto/*koo<u>ahr</u>-toh*/fourth

cuarto/m/*koo<u>ahr</u>-toh*/quarter

cuchara/f/*koo-<u>chah</u>-rah*/spoon

cuello/m/*koo<u>eh</u>-yoh*/neck

cuenta/f/*koo<u>ehn</u>-tah*/account

cuñada/f/*koo-<u>nyah</u>-dah*/sister-in-law

cuñado/m/*koo-<u>nyah</u>-doh*/brother-in-law

D

débito/*<u>deh</u>-bee-toh*/debit

décimo/*<u>deh</u>-thee-moh*/tenth

dedo/f/*deh-doh*/finger

dedo del pie/m/*deh-doh dehl peeeh*/toe

dentista/m/*dehn-tees-tah*/dentist

derecha/*deh-reh-chah*/right

derecho/*deh-reh-choh*/straight

desayuno/m/*deh-sah-yoo-noh*/breakfast

día/m/*deeah*/day

diario/m/*deeah-reeoh*/daily newspaper

dibujo/m/*dee-boo-Hoh*/drawing; the pattern

diciembre/m/*dee-theeehm-breh*/ December

diente/m/*deeehn-teh*/tooth

difícil/*dee-fee-theel*/difficult

dinero/m/*dee-neh-roh*/money

dirección/f/*dee-rehk-thee-ohn*/address

disponible/*dees-poh-nee-bleh*/available

divertido/*dee-behr-tee-doh*/amusing; funny

dolor/m/*doh-lohr*/pain

dolor de muelas/m/*doh-lohr deh mooeh-lahs*/toothache

domingo/m/*doh-meen-goh*/Sunday

dulce/*dool-theh*/sweet

E

edificio/m/*eh-dee-fee-theeoh*/building

embotellada/*ehm-boh-teh-yah-dah*/bottled

empezar/*ehm-peh-thahr*/to begin; to start

empleo/m/*ehm-pleh-oh*/job

en taxi/*ehn tahk-see*/by taxi

encontrar/*ehn-kohn-trahr*/to find

enero/m/*eh-neh-roh*/January

enfermera/f/*ehn-fehr-meh-rah*/the nurse [female]

enfermo/m,f/*ehn-fehr-moh*/sick person; ill person

ensalada/f/*ehn-sah-lah-dah*/salad

entero/*ehn-teh-roh*/whole

entradas/f/*ehn-trah-dahs*/tickets [for a show or event]

enviar/*ehn-bee-ahr*/send

equipo/m/*eh-kee-poh*/team

escuchar/*ehs-koo-chahr*/to listen; to hear

escultura/f/*ehs-kool-too-rah*/sculpture

especial/*ehs-peh-theeahl*/special

esperar/*ehs-peh-rahr*/to wait

espinaca/f/*ehs-pee-nah-kah*/spinach

esquí/m/*ehs-kee*/ski [one unit]

esquina/f/*ehs-kee-nah*/corner

estación/*ehs-tah-theeohn*/station

estacionamiento/m/*ehs-tah-theeoh-nah-mee-ehn-toh*/parking

estado/m/*ehs-tah-doh*/state

éste/m/*ehs-the*/this one

estómago/m/*ehs-toh-mah-goh*/stomach

estreñimiento/m/*ehs-treh-nyee-meeehn-toh*/constipation

F

fácil/*fah-theel*/easy

falda/f/*fahl-dah*/skirt

farmacia/f/*fahr-mah-theeah*/pharmacy

febrero/m/*feh-breh-roh*/February

fecha/f/*feh-chah*/date

feliz/*feh-leeth*/happy

feo/*feh-oh*/ugly

fideo/m/*fee-de-oh*/noodle

fiebre/f/*feeeh-breh*/fever

filete/m/*feeh-leh-teh*/steak

fotógrafo/m/*foh-toh-grah-foh*/ photographer

fresa/f/*freh-sah*/strawberry

fruta/f/*froo-tah*/fruit

fuera/*fooeh-rah*/outside

G

galletas/f/*gah-yeh-tahs*/biscuits; crackers

garantía/m/*gah-rahn-teeah*/warranty

garganta/f/*gahr-gahn-tah*/throat

gerente/m/*Heh-rehn-teh*/manager

girar/*Hee-rahr*/to turn

gracias/*grah-theeahs*/thanks, thank you

grande/*grahn-deh*/big; large

gris/*grees*/grey

guerra/f/*gheh-rrah*/war

guía/m,f/*gheeah*/guide

gustar/*goos-tahr*/to like

H

hablar/*ah-blahr*/to talk

hambre/*ahm-breh*/hungry

hecho a mano/*eh-choh ah mah-noh*/ handmade

hermana/f/*ehr-mah-nah*/sister

hermano/m/*ehr-mah-noh*/brother

hígado/m/*ee-gah-doh*/liver

higo/m/*ee-goh*/fig

hija/f/*ee-Hah*/daughter

hijo/m/*ee-Hoh*/son

hombre/m/*ohm-breh*/man

hombro/m/*ohm-broh*/shoulder

hora/f/*oh-rah*/hour

hoy/*ohee*/today

hueso/m/*ooeh-soh*/bone

huevo/m/*ooeh-boh*/egg

I

identificación/f/*ee-dehn-tee-fee-kah-theeohn*/identification

idioma/m/*ee-dee-oh-mah*/language

imprimir/*eem-pree-meer*/print

incluido/*een-klooee-doh*/included

ingeniero/m/*een-Heh-neeeh-roh*/engineer

inmigración/*een-mee-grah-theeohn*/ immigration

intestino/m/*een-tehs-tee-noh*/bowel; intestine; gut

isla/f/*ees-lah*/island

izquierda/*eeth-keeehr-dah*/left

J

jardín/m/*Hahr-deen*/garden

jueves/m/*Hooeh-behs*/Thursday

julio/m/*Hoo-leeoh*/July

junio/m/*Hoo-neeoh*/June

junto/*Hoon-toh*/together

K

kilómetro/m/*kee-loh-meh-troh*/kilometre

L

lana/*lah-nah*/wool

langostino/m/*lahn-gohs-tee-noh*/king prawn; langoustine

lástima/f/*lahs-tee-mah*/pity; shame

leche/f/*leh-cheh*/milk

lechuga/f/*leh-choo-gah*/lettuce

lengua/f/*lehn-gooah*/language (literally: the tongue)

libre/*lee-breh*/free

libro/m/*lee-broh*/book

limón/m/*lee-mohn*/lemon

limpiar/*leem-pee-ahr*/to clean

línea/f/*lee-neh-ah*/line

listo/*lees-toh*/ready; clever

llamar/*yah-mahr*/to call

llave/f/_yah-beh_/key
llegar/_yeh-gahr_/to arrive
lluvia/f/_yoo-beeah_/rain
luna/f/_loo-nah_/moon
lunes/m/_loo-nehs_/Monday

M

madera/f/_mah-deh-rah_/wood
madre/f/_mah-dreh_/mother
madrina/f/_mah-dree-nah_/godmother
maleta/f/_mah-leh-tah_/luggage; suitcase
mañana/_mah-nyah-nah_/tomorrow
mañana/f/_mah-nyah-nah_/morning
manga/f/_mahn-gah_/sleeve
mango/m/_mahn-goh_/mango
manzana/f/_mahn-thah-nah_/apple
mapa/m/_mah-pah_/map
mar/m/_mahr_/sea
marcar/_mahr-kahr_/to mark; to dial
marea/f/_mah-reh-ah_/tide
mareo/m/_mah-reh-oh_/dizziness
mariposas/f/_mah-ri-poh-sahs_/butterflies
marisco/m/_mah-rees-koh_/seafood
marrón/_mah-rrohn_/brown
martes/m/_mahr-tehs_/Tuesday
marzo/m/_mahr-thoh_/March
más/_mahs_/more
mayo/m/_mah-yoh_/may
medicina/f/_meh-dee-thee-nah_/medication; medicine
médico/m/_meh-dee-koh_/physician; doctor
medio/m/_meh-deeoh_/half
mejor/_meh-Hohr_/best
melón/m/_meh-lohn_/melon
menos/_meh-nohs_/less
miércoles/m/_meeehr-koh-lehs_/Wednesday
minuto/m/_mee-noo-toh_/minute

moneda/f/_moh-neh-dah_/coin
montaña/f/_mohn-tah-nyah_/mountain
mora/f/_moh-rah_/blackberry
morado/_moh-rah-doh_/purple
mucho/_moo-choh_/a lot; much
mueble/m/_mooeh-bleh_/furniture
mujer/f/_moo-Hehr_/woman
muñeca/f/_moo-nyeh-kah_/wrist; doll
museo/m/_moo-seh-oh_/museum
muslo/m/_moos-loh_/thigh

N

naranja/_nah-rahn-Hah_/orange
nariz/f/_nah-reeth_/nose
negro/m/_neh-groh_/black
nieta/f/_neeeh-tah_/granddaughter
nieto/m/_neeeh-toh_/grandson
niña/f/_nee-nyah_/girl
ningún/_neen-goon_/none
niño/m/_nee-nyoh_/boy
noche/f/_noh-cheh_/night
novela/f/_noh-beh-lah_/novel
noveno/_noh-beh-noh_/ninth
noviembre/m/_noh-beeehm-breh_/ November
nuera/f/_nooeh-rah_/daughter-in-law
número/m/_noo-meh-roh_/number

O

octavo/_ohk-tah-boh_/eighth
octubre/m/_ohk-too-breh_/October
ocupado/_oh-koo-pah-doh_/occupied; busy
ojo/m/_oh-Hoh_/eye
olla/f/_oh-yah_/pot
once/_ohn-theh_/eleven
ordenador/m/_ohr-deh-nah-dohr_/computer

ordenador portátil/m/*ohr-deh-nah-<u>dohr</u> pohr-<u>tah</u>-teel*/laptop computer

oreja/f/*oh-<u>reh</u>-Hah*/ear

orina/f/*oh-<u>ree</u>-nah*/urine

oro/m/*<u>oh</u>-roh*/gold

oscuro/*ohs-<u>koo</u>-roh*/dark

otro/*<u>oh</u>-troh*/other; the other one

P

padre/m/*<u>pah</u>-dreh*/father

padrino/m/*pah-<u>dree</u>-noh*/godfather

pagado/*pah-<u>gah</u>-doh*/paid for

pagar/*pah-<u>gahr</u>*/pay

país/m/*pah<u>ees</u>*/country

pájaro/m/*<u>pah</u>-Hah-roh*/bird

pantalones/m/*pahn-tah-<u>loh</u>-nehs*/trousers

papaya/f/*pah-<u>pah</u>-yah*/papaya

parque/m/*<u>pahr</u>-keh*/park

pasaporte/m/*pah-sah-<u>pohr</u>-teh*/<u>passport</u>

paseo/m/*pah-<u>seh</u>-oh*/walk

pasillo/m/*pah-<u>see</u>-yoh*/aisle; corridor

patatas/m/*pah-<u>tah</u>-tahs*/potatoes

patatas fritas/m/*pah-<u>tah</u>-tahs <u>free</u>-tahs*/ crisps

patín/m/*pah-<u>teen</u>*/skate

pato/m/*<u>pah</u>-toh*/duck

peaje/m/*peh-<u>ah</u>-Heh*/toll

pecho/m/*<u>peh</u>-choh*/chest

pelea/f/*peh-<u>leh</u>-ah*/fight

pelo/m/*<u>peh</u>-loh*/hair

pensar/*pehn-<u>sahr</u>*/to think

pequeño/*peh-keh-<u>nyoh</u>*/small

pera/f/*<u>peh</u>-rah*/pear

periódico/m/*peh-ree<u>oh</u>-dee-koh*/ newspaper

perla/f/*<u>pehr</u>-lah*/pearl

pescado/m/*pehs-<u>kah</u>-doh*/fish [as in food]

picante/*pee-<u>kahn</u>-teh*/hot [flavour]

pie/m/*pee<u>eh</u>*/foot

pierna/f/*pee<u>ehr</u>-nah*/leg

piloto/m/*pee-<u>loh</u>-toh*/pilot

piña/f/*<u>pee</u>-nyah*/pineapple

pintar/*peen-<u>tahr</u>*/to paint

pintura/f/*peen-<u>too</u>-rah*/painting

piscina/f/*pees-<u>thee</u>-nah*/swimming pool

piso/m/*<u>pee</u>-soh*/floor

plátano/m/*<u>plah</u>-tah-noh*/banana

playa/f/*<u>plah</u>-yah*/beach

plaza/f/*<u>plah</u>-thah*/square

plomo/m/*<u>ploh</u>-moh*/lead

poco/m/*<u>poh</u>-koh*/a bit; a small amount

pollo/m/*<u>poh</u>-yoh*/chicken

por ciento/*pohr thee<u>ehn</u>-toh*/per cent; percentage

potable/*poh-<u>tah</u>-bleh*/drinkable

precio/m/*<u>preh</u>-theeoh*/price

precioso/*preh-thee<u>oh</u>-soh*/gorgeous; beautiful; lovely

preguntar/*preh-goon-<u>tahr</u>*/to ask (a question)

presión sanguínea/f/*preh-see<u>ohn</u> sahn-<u>ghee</u>-neh-ah*/blood pressure

prima/f/*<u>pree</u>-mah*/cousin [female]

primero/*pree-<u>meh</u>-roh*/first

primo/m/*<u>pree</u>-moh*/cousin [male]

probador/m/*ehl proh-bah-<u>dohr</u>*/fitting room

probar/*proh-<u>bahr</u>*/to try

pronto/*<u>prohn</u>-toh*/right away; soon

propio/*<u>proh</u>-peeoh*/[one's] own

pulmón/m/*pool-<u>mohn</u>*/lung

pura/*<u>poo</u>-rah*/pure

Q

qué/*keh*/what
quedarse/*keh-dahr-seh*/to stay
queso/m/*keh-soh*/cheese
quién/*keeehn*/who
quinto/*keen-toh*/fifth

R

receta/f/*reh-theh-tah*/prescription; recipe
recibo/m/*reh-thee-boh*/receipt
reembolsar/*reh-ehm-bol-sahr*/to refund
reglas/m/*reh-glahs*/rules
repetir/*reh-peh-teer*/to repeat
reserva/f/*reh-sehr-bah*/reservation
responder/*rehs-pohn-dehr*/to answer
restaurante/m/*rehs-tahoo-rahn-teh*/ restaurant
retirar/*reh-tee-rahr*/to withdraw
reunión/f/*rehoo-neeohn*/meeting
riñón/m/*ree-nyohn*/kidney
río/m/*ree-oh*/river
robar/*roh-bahr*/to steal; to rob
rojo/*roh-Hoh*/red
rosa/*roh-sah*/pink; rose
ruinas/f/*rooee-nahs*/ruins

S

sábado/m/*sah-bah-doh*/Saturday
sala/f/*sah-lah*/living room
salado/*sah-lah-doh*/salty
saldo/m/*sahl-doh*/balance
sandía/f/*sahn-deeah*/watermelon
sangre/f/*sahn-greh*/blood

seco/*seh-koh*/dry
sed/*sehd*/thirsty
seguir/*seh-gheer*/to keep going
segundo/m/*seh-goon-doh*/second
semana/f/*seh-mah-nah*/week
septiembre/m/*sehp-teeehm-breh*/ September
séptimo/*sehp-tee-moh*/seventh
sexto/*sehks-toh*/sixth
siguiente/*see-gheeehn-teh*/next
sol/m/*sohl*/sun
subterráneo/*soob-teh-rrah-neh-oh*/ underground
suelto/*sooehl-toh*/loose

T

tabla/f/*tah-blah*/board [wood]
talla/f/*tah-yah*/size
tarde/f/*tahr-deh*/afternoon
tarjeta/f/*tahr-Heh-tah*/card
teclado/m/*teh-klah-doh*/keyboard
tele/f/*teh-leh*/TV (colloquial)
tercero/*tehr-theh-roh*/third
tía/f/*teeah*/aunt
tierra/f/*teeeh-rrah*/land
tío/m/*teeoh*/uncle
típico/m/*tee-pee-koh*/typical
tobillo/m/*toh-bee-yoh*/ankle
todavía/*toh-dah-beeah*/yet; still
tomar el sol/*toh-mahr ehl sohl*/to sunbathe
tos/f/*tohs*/cough
tráfico/m/*trah-fee-koh*/traffic
tranquilo/*trahn-kee-loh*/quiet
tren/m/*trehn*/train
trucha/f/*troo-chah*/trout

U

uva/f/*oo-bah*/grape

V

vehículo/m/*beh-ee-koo-loh*/vehicle
venta/f/*behn-tah*/sale
ver/*behr*/to see
verde/*behr-deh*/green
viaje/m/*beeah-Heh*/trip
viajero/m/*beeah-Heh-roh*/traveller
vida/f/*bee-dah*/life
vidrio/m/*bee-dreeoh*/glass

viernes/m/*beeehr-nehs*/Friday
vino/m/*bee-noh*/wine
violeta/*beeoh-leh-tah*/violet; purple
violín/m/*beeoh-leen*/violin
vivir/*bee-beer*/to live
vuelta/f/*booehl-tah*/change (as in money back)

Y

yerno/m/*yehr-noh*/son-in-law

Z

zanahoria/f/*thah-nah-oh-reeah*/carrot

English-Spanish Mini-Dictionary

A

a bit; small amount/**poco**/m/_poh-koh_

a lot; much/**mucho**/_moo-choh_

account/**cuenta**/f/_kooehn-tah_

actor/**actor**/m/_ahk-tohr_

address/**dirección**/f/_dee-rehk-thee-ohn_

afternoon/**tarde**/f/_tahr-deh_

agency/**agencia**/f/_ah-Hehn-theeah_

aisle/**pasillo**/m/_pah-see-yoh_

amusing; funny/**divertido**/
   dee-behr-tee-doh

ankle/**tobillo**/m/_toh-bee-yoh_

answer/**responder**/_rehs-pohn-dehr_

apple/**manzana**/f/_mahn-thah-nah_

April/**abril**/m/_ah-breel_

arm/**brazo**/m/_brah-thoh_

arrive/**llegar**/_yeh-gahr_

ask (a question)/**preguntar**/_preh-goon-tahr_

attack/**atacar**/_ah-tah-kahr_

August/**agosto**/m/_ah-gohs-toh_

aunt/**tía**/f/_teeah_

available/**disponible**/_dees-poh-nee-bleh_

avenue/**avenida**/f/_ah-beh-nee-dah_

avocado/**aguacate**/m/_ah-gooah-kah-teh_

B

balance/**saldo**/m/_sahl-doh_

balcony/**balcón**/m/_bahl-kohn_

banana/**plátano**/m/_plah-tah-noh_

bathroom/**baño**/m/_bah-nyoh_

beach/**playa**/f/_plah-yah_

bed/**cama**/f/_kah-mah_

begin; to start/**empezar**/_ehm-peh-thahr_

best/**mejor**/_meh-Hohr_

bicycle/**bicicleta**/f/_bee-thee-kleh-tah_

big; large/**grande**/_grahn-deh_

bill/**la cuenta**/f/_lah koo-ehn-tah_

bird/**pájaro**/m/_pah-Hah-roh_

biscuits; crackers/**galletas**/f/_gah-yeh-tahs_

black/**negro**/_neh-groh_

blackberry/**mora**/f/_moh-rah_

blood/**sangre**/f/_sahn-greh_

blood pressure/**presión sanguínea**/f/_preh-
   seeohn sahn-ghee-neh-ah_

blue/**azul**/_ah-thool_

board [wood]/**tabla**/f/_tah-blah_

bone/**hueso**/m/_ooeh-soh_

book/**libro**/m/_lee-broh_

bottled/**embotellada**/_ehm-boh-teh-yah-dah_

boulevard/**bulevar**/m/*boo-leh-bahr*

bowel; intestine; gut/**intestino**/m/ *een-tehs-tee-noh*

boy/**niño**/m/*nee-nyo*

breakfast/**desayuno**/m/*deh-sah-yoo-noh*

broccoli/**brócoli**/m/*broh-koh-lee*

brother/**hermano**/m/*ehr-mah-noh*

brother-in-law/**cuñado**/m/*koo-nyah-doh*

brown/**marrón**/*mah-rrohn*

building/**edificio**/m/*eh-dee-fee-theeoh*

butterflies/**mariposas**/f/*mah-ree-poh-sahs*

by taxi/**en taxi**/*ehn tahk-see*

C

calf/**pantorrilla**/f/*pahn-toh-rree-yah*

call/**llamar**/*yah-mahr*

cancel/**cancelar**/*kahn-theh-lahr*

car/**coche**/m/*koh-cheh*

card/**tarjeta**/f/*tahr-Heh-tah*

carrot/**zanahoria**/f/*thah-nah-oh-reeah*

cashier [male]/**cajero**/m/*kah-Heh-roh*

cavity/**caries**/f/*kah-reeehs*

ceramic/**cerámica**/f/*theh-rah-mee-kah*

cereals/**cereales**/m/*theh-reh-ah-lehs*

change/**cambiar**/*kahm-beeahr*

change (as in money back)/**vuelta**/f/ *booehl-tah*

cheese/**queso**/m/*keh-soh*

cherry/**cereza**/f/*theh-reh-thah*

chest/**pecho**/m/*peh-choh*

chicken/**pollo**/m/*poh-yoh*

cinema/**cine**/m/*thee-neh*

city/**ciudad**/f/*theeoo-dahd*

clean/**limpiar**/*leem-peeahr*

coconut/**coco**/m/*koh-koh*

coffee/**café**/m/*kah-feh*

coin/**moneda**/f/*moh-neh-dah*

computer/**ordenador**/m/*ohr-deh-nah-dohr*

constipation/**estreñimiento**/m/ *ehs-treh-nyee-meeehn-toh*

content; satisfied/**feliz**/*feh-leeth*

cook [female]/**cocinera**/f/*koh-thee-neh-rah*

copper/**cobre**/m/*koh-breh*

corner/**esquina**/f/*ehs-kee-nah*

cost (as in price)/**costar**/*kohs-tahr*

cotton/**algodón**/*ahl-goh-dohn*

cough/**tos**/f/*tohs*

count/**contar**/*kohn-tahr*

country/**país**/m/*pahees*

cousin [female]/**prima**/f/*pree-mah*

cousin [male]/**primo**/m/*pree-moh*

crisps/**patatas fritas**/f/*pah-tah-tahs free-tahs*

customs/**aduana**/f/*ah-dooah-nah*

D

dark/**oscuro**/*ohs-koo-roh*

date/**fecha**/f/*feh-chah*

daughter/**hija**/f/*ee-Hah*

daughter-in-law/**nuera**/f/*nooeh-rah*

day/**día**/m/*deeah*

debit/**débito**/*deh-bee-toh*

December/**diciembre**/m/ *dee-theeehm-breh*

dentist/**dentista**/m/*dehn-tees-tah*

difficult/**difícil**/*dee-fee-theel*

dinner/**cena**/f/*theh-nah*

dizziness/**mareo**/m/*mah-reh-oh*

doctor/**médico**/m/*meh-dee-koh*

document, passport/**pasaporte**/m/ *pah-sah-pohr-teh*

drawing; the pattern/**dibujo**/m/ *dee-boo-Hoh*

drinkable/**potable**/*poh-tah-bleh*

drive [a car]/**conducir**/*kohn-doo-theer*

driver/**chófer**/m/*choh-fehr*

dry/**seco**/*seh-koh*

duck/**pato**/m/*pah-toh*

E

ear/**oreja**/f/*oh-reh-Hah*

easy/**fácil**/*fah-theel*

egg/**huevo**/m/*ooeh-boh*

eighth/**octavo**/*ohk-tah-boh*

eleven/**once**/*ohn-theh*

e-mail/**correo electrónico**/*koh-rreh-oh eh-lehk-troh-nee-koh*

engineer/**ingeniero**/m/*een-Heh-neeeh-roh*

expensive/**caro**/*kah-roh*

eye/**ojo**/m/*oh-Hoh*

F

father/**padre**/m/*pah-dreh*

February/**febrero**/m/*feh-breh-roh*

fever/**fiebre**/f/*feeeh-breh*

fifth/**quinto**/*keen-toh*

fig/**higo**/m/*ee-goh*

fight/**pelea**/f/*peh-leh-ah*

find/**encontrar**/*ehn-kohn-trahr*

finger/**dedo**/f/*deh-doh*

first/**primero**/*pree-meh-roh*

fish/**pescado**/m/*pehs-kah-doh*

fitting room/**probador**/m/*proh-bah-dohr*

floor/**piso**/m/*pee-soh*

foot/**pie**/m/*peeeh*

fourth/**cuarto**/*kooahr-toh*

free/**libre**/*lee-breh*

Friday/**viernes**/m/*beeehr-nehs*

fruit/**fruta**/f/*froo-tah*

furniture/**mueble**/m/*mooeh-bleh*

G

garden/**jardín**/m/*Hahr-deen*

garlic/**ajo**/m/*ah-Hoh*

girl/**niña**/f/*nee-nyah*

glass/**vidrio**/m/*bee-dreeoh*

godfather/**padrino**/m/*pah-dree-noh*

godmother/**madrina**/f/*mah-dree-nah*

gold/**oro**/m/*oh-roh*

good/m/**bueno**/*booeh-noh*

goodbye/**adiós**/*ah-deeohs*

gorgeous; beautiful; lovely/**precioso**/ *preh-theeoh-soh*

granddaughter/**nieta**/f/*neeeh-tah*

grandfather/**abuelo**/m/*ah-booeh-loh*

grandmother/**abuela**/f/*ah-booeh-lah*

grandson/**nieto**/m/*neeeh-toh*

grape/**uva**/f/*oo-bah*

grapefruit/**pomelo**/m/*poh-meh-loh*

green/**verde**/*behr-deh*

grey/**gris**/*grees*

guide/**guía**/m,f/*gheeah*

H

hair/**pelo**/m/*peh-loh*

half/**medio**/m/*meh-deeoh*

handmade/**hecho a mano**/*eh-choh ah mah-noh*

hang; to hang up/**colgar**/*kohl-gahr*

happy/**feliz**/*feh-leeth*

head/**cabeza**/f/*kah-beh-thah*

heart/**corazón**/m/*koh-rah-thohn*

help/**ayudar**/*ah-yoo-dahr*

horse/**caballo**/m/*kah-bah-yoh*

hot [flavour]/**picante**/*pee-kahn-teh*

hot [temperature]/**caliente**/*kah-lee ehn-teh*

hot pepper/m/**guindilla**/*gueen-deh-yah*

hour/**hora**/f/*oh-rah*

house/**casa**/f/*kah-sah*

how much/**cuánto**/*koo-ahn-toh*

hungry/**hambre**/m/*ahm-breh*

I

identification/**identificación**/f/ *ee-dehn-tee-fee-kah-theeohn*

immigration/**inmigración**/ *een-mee-grah-theeohn*

in front; ahead/**adelante**/*ah-deh-lahn-teh*

included/**incluido**/*een-klooee-doh*

island/**isla**/f/*ees-lah*

J

jacket/**chaqueta**/f/*chah-keh-tah*

January/**enero**/m/*eh-neh-roh*

job/**empleo**/m/*ehm-pleh-oh*

July/**julio**/m/*Hoo-leeoh*

June/**junio**/m/*Hoo-neeoh*

K

keep going/**seguir**/*seh-gheer*

key/**llave**/f/*yah-beh*

keyboard/**teclado**/m/*teh-klah-doh*

kidney/**riñón**/m/*ree-nyohn*

kitchen/**cocina**/f/*koh-thee-nah*

L

land/**tierra**/f/*teeeh-rrah*

language/**idioma**/m/*ee-deeoh-mah*

language (literally: tongue)/**lengua**/f/ *lehn-gooah*

laptop computer/**ordenador portátil**/f/ *ohr-deh-nah-dohr pohr-tah-teel*

lawyer/**abogado**/m/*ah-boh-gah-doh*

lead/**plomo**/m/*ploh-moh*

left/**izquierda**/*eeth-keeehr-dah*

leg/**pierna**/f/*peeehr-nah*

lemon/**limón**/m/*lee-mohn*

less/**menos**/*meh-nohs*

letter/**carta**/f/*kahr-tah*

lettuce/**lechuga**/f/*leh-choo-gah*

library/**biblioteca**/f/*bee-blee-oh-teh-kah*

life/**vida**/f/*bee-dah*

lift/**ascensor**/m/*ahs-thehn-sohr*

light/**claro**/*klah-roh*

like/**gustar**/*goos-tahr*

line/**línea**/f/*lee-neh-ah*

listen; to hear/**escuchar**/*ehs-koo-chahr*

little, small/**pequeño**/*peh-keh-nyoh*

live/**vivir**/*bee-beer*

liver/**hígado**/m/*ee-gah-doh*

living room/**sala**/f/*sah-lah*

loose/**suelto**/*sooehl-toh*

luggage; suitcase/**maleta**/f/*mah-leh-tah*

lunch/**la comida**/f/*koh-mee-dah*

lung/**pulmón**/m/*pool-mohn*

M

mail; post/**correo**/m/*koh-rreh-oh*

man/**hombre**/m/*ohm-breh*

manager/**gerente**/m/*Heh-rehn-teh*

mango/**mango**/m/<u>mahn</u>-goh

map/**mapa**/m/<u>mah</u>-pah

March/**marzo**/m/<u>mahr</u>-thoh

mark; to dial;/**marcar**/mahr-<u>kahr</u>

May/**mayo**/m/<u>mah</u>-yoh

medication; medicine/**medicina**/f/
   meh-dee-<u>thee</u>-nah

meeting/**reunión**/f/rehoo-nee<u>ohn</u>

melon/**melón**/m/meh-<u>lohn</u>

milk/**leche**/f/<u>leh</u>-cheh

minute/**minuto**/m/mee-<u>noo</u>-toh

Monday/**lunes**/m/<u>loo</u>-nehs

money/**dinero**/m/dee-<u>neh</u>-roh

moon/**luna**/f/<u>loo</u>-nah

more/**más**/mahs

morning/**mañana**/f/mah-<u>nyah</u>-nah

mother/**madre**/f/<u>mah</u>-dreh

motorway/**autopista**/f/ahoo-toh-<u>pees</u>-tah

mountain/**montaña**/f/mohn-<u>tah</u>-nyah

moustache/**bigote**/m/bee-<u>goh</u>-teh

mouth/**boca**/f/<u>boh</u>-kah

much/**mucho**/<u>moo</u>-choh

museum/**museo**/m/moo-<u>seh</u>-oh

N

neck/**cuello**/m/koo<u>eh</u>-yoh

necklace/**collar**/m/koh-<u>yahr</u>

neighbourhood/**barrio**/m/<u>bah</u>-rreeoh

newspaper/**diario**/m/dee<u>ah</u>-reeoh

next/**siguiente**/see-ghee<u>ehn</u>-teh

night/**noche**/f/<u>noh</u>-cheh

ninth/**noveno**/noh-<u>beh</u>-noh

none/**ningún**/neen-<u>goon</u>

nose/**nariz**/f/nah-<u>reeth</u>

novel/**novela**/f/noh-<u>beh</u>-lah

November/**noviembre**/m/
   noh-bee<u>ehm</u>-breh

now/**ahora**/ah-<u>oh</u>-rah

number/**número**/m/<u>noo</u>-meh-roh

O

occupied; busy/**ocupado**/oh-koo-<u>pah</u>-doh

October/**octubre**/m/ohk-<u>too</u>-breh

one's own/**propio**/<u>proh</u>-peeoh

onion/**cebolla**/f/theh-<u>boh</u>-yah

open/**abrir**/ah-<u>breer</u>

orange/**naranja**/nah-<u>rahn</u>-Hah

outside/**fuera**/foo<u>eh</u>-rah

P

paid for/**pagado**/pah-<u>gah</u>-doh

pain/**dolor**/m/doh-<u>lohr</u>

paint/**pintar**/peen-<u>tahr</u>

painting/**pintura**/f/peen-<u>too</u>-rah

papaya/**papaya**/f/pah-<u>pah</u>-yah

park/**parque**/m/<u>pahr</u>-keh

parking/**estacionamiento**/m/
   ehs-tah-theeoh-nah-mee<u>ehn</u>-toh

passport/**pasaporte**/m/pah-sah-<u>pohr</u>-teh

pay/**pagar**/pah-<u>gahr</u>

peach/**melocotón**/m/meh-loh-koh-<u>tohn</u>

pear/**pera**/f/<u>peh</u>-rah

pearl/**perla**/f/<u>pehr</u>-lah

per cent; percentage/**por ciento**/pohr
   thee<u>ehn</u>-toh

pharmacy/**farmacia**/f/fahr-<u>mah</u>-theeah

photographer/**fotógrafo**/m/
   foh-<u>toh</u>-grah-foh

pilot/**piloto**/m/pee-<u>loh</u>-toh

pineapple/**piña**/f/<u>pee</u>-nyah

pink/**rosa**/_roh_-sah

pity; shame/**lástima**/f/_lahs_-tee-mah

plum/**ciruela**/f/_thee-rooeh_-lah

pocket/**bolsillo**/m/_bohl-see_-yoh

post code/**código postal**/m/_koh_-dee-goh
pohs-_tahl_

pot/**olla**/f/_oh_-yah

potatoes/**patatas**/f/_pah-tah_-tahs

prawn/**gambas**/f/_gahm_-bahs

prescription/**receta**/f/_rreh-theh_-tah

pretty; beautiful/**bonito**/_boh-nee_-toh

price/**precio**/m/_preh_-theeoh

print/**imprimir**/_eem-pree-meer_

pure/**pura**/_poo_-rah

purple/**morado**/_moh-rah_-doh

Q

quarter/**cuarto**/m/_koo-ahr_-toh

quiet/**tranquilo**/_trahn-kee_-loh

quite; enough/**bastante**/_bahs-tahn_-teh

R

race; profession/**carrera**/f/_kah-rreh_-rah

rain/**lluvia**/f/_yoo_-beeah

receipt/**recibo**/m/_rreh-thee_-boh

red/**rojo**/_roh_-Hoh

refund/**reembolsar**/_reh-ehm-bol-sahr_

repeat/**repetir**/_reh-peh-teer_

reservation/**reserva**/f/_reh-sehr_-bah

restaurant/**restaurante**/m/
rehs-tahoo-rahn-teh

rice/**arroz**/m/_ah-rroth_

right/**derecha**/_deh-reh_-chah

right away; soon/**pronto**/_prohn_-toh

river/**río**/m/_ree_-oh

road/**carretera**/f/_kah-rre-teh_-rah

room/**cuarto**/m/_koo-ahr_-toh

rug/**alfombra**/f/_ahl-fohm_-brah

ruins/**ruinas**/f/_rooee_-nahs

rules/**reglas**/f/_reh_-glahs

S

salad/**ensalada**/f/_ehn-sah-lah_-dah

sale/**venta**/f/_behn_-tah

salty/**salado**/_sah-lah_-doh

Saturday/**sábado**/m/_sah_-bah-doh

sculpture/**escultura**/f/_ehs-kool-too_-rah

sea/**mar**/m/_mahr_

seafood/**marisco**/m/_mah-rees_-koh

search; to look for/**buscar**/_boos-kahr_

seat/**asiento**/m/_ah-seeehn_-toh

second/**segundo**/m/_seh-goon_-doh

see/**ver**/_behr_

send/**enviar**/_ehn-beeahr_

September/**septiembre**/m/
sehp-teeehm-breh

seventh/**séptimo**/_sehp_-tee-moh

shine/**brillo**/_bree_-yoh

shirt/**camisa**/f/_kah-mee_-sah

shoulder/**hombro**/m/_ohm_-broh

shrimp/**camarón**/m/_kah-mah-rohn_

sick person; ill person/**enfermo**/m,f/
ehn-fehr-moh

sing/**cantar**/_kahn-tahr_

sister/**hermana**/f/_ehr-mah_-nah

sister-in-law/**cuñada**/f/_koo-nyah_-dah

sixth/**sexto**/_sehks_-toh

size/**talla**/f/*tah-yah*

skate/**patín**/*pah-teen*

ski/**esquí**/m/*ehs-kee*

skirt/**falda**/f/*fahl-dah*

sleeve/**manga**/f/*mahn-gah*

small/**pequeño**/*peh-keh-nyoh*

small amount/**poco**/m/*poh-koh*

some/**algún**/*ahl-goon*

son/**hijo**/m/*ee-Hoh*

son-in-law/**yerno**/m/*yehr-noh*

special/**especial**/*ehs-peh-theeahl*

spinach/**espinaca**/f/*ehs-pee-nah-kah*

spoon/**cuchara**/f/*koo-chah-rah*

square/**plaza**/f/*plah-thah*

state/**estado**/m/*ehs-tah-doh*

station/**estación**/*ehs-tah-theeohn*

stay/**quedarse**/*keh-dahr-seh*

steak/**filete**/m/*feeh-leh-teh*

steal; to rob/**robar**/*roh-bahr*

stomach/**estómago**/m/*ehs-toh-mah-goh*

straight/**derecho**/*deh-reh-choh*

strawberry/**fresa**/f/*freh-sah*

street/**calle**/f/*kah-yeh*

sun/**sol**/m/*sohl*

sunbathe/**tomar el sol**/*toh-mahr ehl sohl*

Sunday/**domingo**/m/*doh-meen-goh*

supper/**cena**/f/*theh-nah*

surgery/**cirugía**/f/*thee-roo-Heeah*

sweet/**dulce**/*dool-theh*

swimming pool/**piscina**/f/*pees-thee-nah*

T

talk/**hablar**/*ah-blahr*

tall; **high**/alto/*ahl-toh*

team/**equipo**/m/*eh-kee-poh*

tenth/**décimo**/*deh-thee-moh*

thank you/**gracias**/*grah-theeahs*

the nurse [female]/**enfemera**/f/ *ehn-fehr-meh-rah*

the other one/**otro**/*oh-troh*

thigh/**muslo**/m/*moos-loh*

thing/**cosa**/f/*koh-sah*

think/**pensar**/*pehn-sahr*

third/**tercero**/*tehr-theh-roh*

thirsty/**sed**/*sehd*

this one/**este**/*ehs-teh*

throat/**garganta**/f/*gahr-gahn-tah*

Thursday/**jueves**/m/*Hooeh-behs*

ticket; note/**billete**/m/*bee-yeeeh-teh*

tide/**marea**/f/*mah-reh-ah*

tight/**apretado**/*ah-preh-tah-doh*

today/**hoy**/*ohee*

toe/**dedo del pie**/m/*deh-doh dehl peeeh*

together/**junto**/*Hoon-toh*

toll/**peaje**/m/*peh-ah-Heh*

tomorrow/**mañana**/*mah-nyah-na*

tooth/**diente**/m/*deeehn-teh*

toothache/**dolor de muelas**/m/*doh-lohr deh moo-eh-lahs*

traffic/**tráfico**/m/*trah-fee-koh*

train/**tren**/m/*trehn*

traveller/**viajero**/m/*beeah-Heh-roh*

trip/**viaje**/m/*beeah-Heh*

trousers/**pantalones**/m/*pahn-tah-loh-nehs*

trout/**trucha**/f/*troo-chah*

try/**probar**/*proh-bahr*

Tuesday/**martes**/m/*mahr-tehs*

tuna/**atún**/m/*ah-toon*

turn/**girar**/*Hee-rahr*

TV/**tele**/f/*teh-leh*

typical/**típico**/*tee-pee-koh*

U

ugly/**feo**/*feh-oh*
uncle/**tío**/m/*teeoh*
underground/**subterráneo**/
   soob-teh-rrah-neh-oh
urine/**orina**/f/*oh-ree-nah*

V

vehicle/**vehículo**/m/*beh-ee-koo-loh*
video camera/**cámara de video**/f/*kah-
   mah-rah deh bee-deh-oh*
violet; purple/**violeta**/*beeoh-leh-tah*
violin/**violín**/m/*beeoh-leen*

W

wait/**esperar**/*ehs-peh-rahr*
walk/**paseo**/m/*pah-seh-oh*
walking/**a pie**/*ah peeeh* (literally: on foot)
wallet/**billetera**/f/*bee-yeh-teh-rah*
war/**guerra**/f/*gheh-rrah*
warranty/**garantía**/m/*gah-rahn-teeah*
water/**agua**/m/*ah-gooah*

watermelon/**sandía**/f/*sahn-deeah*
Wednesday/**miércoles**/m/*meeehr-koh-lehs*
week/**semana**/f/*seh-mah-nah*
what/**qué**/*keh*
when/**cuándo**/*kooahn-doh*
white/**blanco**/*blahn-koh*
who/**quién**/*keeehn*
whole/**entero**/*ehn-teh-roh*
wine/**vino**/m/*bee-noh*
withdraw/**retirar**/*reh-tee-rahr*
woman/**mujer**/f/*moo-Hehr*
wood/**madera**/f/*mah-deh-rah*
wool/**lana**/*lah-nah*
wrist/**muñeca**/f/*moo-nyeh-kah*

Y

yellow/**amarillo**/*ah-mah-ree-yoh*
yesterday/**ayer**/*ah-yehr*
yet; still/**todavía**/*toh-dah-beeah*

Z

zero/**cero**/*theh-roh*

Appendix B
Spanish Verbs

Conjugating Spanish Verbs

In this section, we provide some tables to show you how to conjugate regular and regular reflexive Spanish verbs.

Regular Verbs Ending in -ar: *hablar* (to speak)
Past Participle: *hablado* (spoken)

	Present	Simple Past	Future
yo (I)	hablo (speak)	hablé (spoke)	hablaré (will speak)
tú (you)	hablas	hablaste	hablarás
él/ella, Ud. (he/she/ you formal)	habla	habló	hablará
nosotros (we)	hablamos	hablamos	hablaremos
vosotros (you plural)	habláis	hablasteis	hablaréis
ellos/ellas, Uds. (they, you plural formal)	hablan	hablaron	hablarán

Regular Verbs Ending in -er: *comer* (to eat)
Past Participle: *comido* (eaten)

	Present	Simple Past	Future
yo (I)	como (eat)	comí (ate)	comeré (will eat)
tú (you)	comes	comiste	comerás
él/ella, Ud. (he/she/ you formal)	come	comió	comerá
nosotros (we)	comemos	comimos	comeremos
vosotros (you plural)	coméis	comisteis	comeréis
ellos/ellas, Uds. (they, you plural formal)	comen	comieron	comerán

Regular Verbs Ending in -ir: *vivir* (to live)
Past Participle: *vivido* (lived)

	Present	Simple Past	Future
yo (I)	vivo (live)	viví (lived)	viviré (will live)
tú (you)	vives	viviste	vivirás
él/ella, Ud. (he/she/ you formal)	vive	vivió	vivirá
nosotros (we)	vivimos	vivimos	viviremos
vosotros (you plural)	vivís	vivisteis	viviréis
ellos/ellas/Uds. (they, you plural formal)	viven	vivieron	vivirán

A Regular Reflexive Verb: *lavarse* (to wash oneself)
Past Participle: *lavado* (washed)

	Present	Simple Past	Future
yo (I)	me lavo	me lavé	me lavaré
tú (you)	te lavas	te lavaste	te lavarás
él/ella/Ud. (he/she/ you formal)	se lava	se lavó	se lavará
nosotros (we)	nos lavamos	nos lavamos	nos lavaremos
vosotros (you plural)	os laváis	os lavasties	os lavaréis
ellos/ellas/Uds. (they/you plural formal)	se lavan	se lavaron	se lavarán

Figuring Out Irregular Spanish Verbs

In this section we help you get to grips with some of those stubborn irregular verbs.

		Present	**Past**	**Future**
cerrar	_yo_	cierro	cerré	cerraré
to close	_tú_	cierras	cerraste	cerrarás
	él/ella/Ud.	cierra	cerró	cerrará
gerund:	_nosotros_	cerramos	cerramos	cerraremos
cerrando	_vosotros_	cerráis	cerrasteis	cerraréis
	ellos/ellas/Uds.	cierran	cerraron	cerrarán
comprar	_yo_	compro	compré	compraré
to buy	_tú_	compras	compraste	comprarás
	él/ella/Ud.	compra	compró	comprará
gerund:	_nosotros_	compramos	compramos	compraremos
comprando	_vosotros_	compráis	comprasteis	compraréis
	ellos/ellas/Uds.	compran	compraron	comprarán
conocer	_yo_	conozco	conocí	conoceré
to know	_tú_	conoces	conociste	conocerás
	él/ella/Ud.	conoce	conoció	conocerá
gerund:	_nosotros_	conocemos	conocimos	conoceremos
conociendo	_vosotros_	conocéis	conocisteis	conoceréis
	ellos/ellas/Uds.	conocen	conocieron	conocerán
conseguir	_yo_	consigo	conseguí	conseguiré
to get	_tú_	consigues	consiguiste	conseguirás
	él/ella/Ud.	consigue	consiguió	conseguirá
gerund:	_nosotros_	conseguimos	conseguimos	conseguiremos
consiguiendo	_vosotros_	conseguís	conseguisteis	conseguiréis
	ellos/ellas/Uds.	consiguen	consiguieron	conseguirán
dar	_yo_	doy	di	daré
to give	_tú_	das	diste	darás
	él/ella/Ud.	da	dio	dará
gerund:	_nosotros_	damos	dimos	daremos
dando	_vosotros_	dais	disteis	daréis
	ellos/ellas/Uds.	dan	dieron	darán

		Present	Past	Future
empezar	*yo*	empiezo	empecé	empezaré
to begin	*tú*	empiezas	empezaste	empezarás
	él/ella/Ud.	empieza	empezó	empezará
gerund:	*nosotros*	empezamos	empezamos	empezaremos
empezando	*vosotros*	empezáis	empezasteis	empezaréis
	ellos/ellas/Uds.	empiezan	empezaron	empezarán
encontrar	*yo*	encuentro	encontré	encontraré
to find	*tú*	encuentras	encontraste	encontrarás
	él/ella/Ud.	encuentra	encontró	encontrará
gerund:	*nosotros*	encontramos	encontramos	encontraremos
encontrando	*vosotros*	encontráis	encontrasteis	encontraréis
	ellos/ellas/Uds.	encuentran	encontraron	encontrarán
entender	*yo*	entiendo	entendí	entenderé
to understand	*tú*	entiendes	entendiste	entenderás
	él/ella/Ud.	entiende	entendió	entenderá
gerund:	*nosotros*	entendemos	entendimos	entenderemos
entendiendo	*vosotros*	entendéis	entendisteis	entenderéis
	ellos/ellas/Uds.	entienden	entendieron	entenderán
estar	*yo*	estoy	estuve	estaré
to be (location,	*tú*	estás	estuviste	estarás
temporary	*él/ella/Ud.*	está	estuvo	estará
state, w/	*nosotros*	estamos	estuvimos	estaremos
compound	*vosotros*	estáis	estuvisteis	estaréis
tenses)	*ellos/ellas/Uds.*	están	estuvieron	estarán
gerund: estando				
hacer	*yo*	hago	hice	haré
to do; to make	*tú*	haces	hiciste	harás
	él/ella/Ud.	hace	hizo	hará
gerund:	*nosotros*	hacemos	hicimos	haremos
haciendo	*vosotros*	hacéis	hicisteis	haréis
	ellos/ellas/Uds.	hacen	hicieron	harán

		Present	Past	Future
ir	*yo*	voy	fui	iré
to go	*tú*	vas	fuiste	irás
	él/ella/Ud.	va	fue	irá
gerund:	*nosotros*	vamos	fuimos	iremos
yendo	*vosotros*	vais	fuisteis	iréis
	ellos/ellas/Uds.	van	fueron	irán
jugar	*yo*	juego	jugué	jugaré
to play	*tú*	juegas	jugaste	jugarás
	él/ella/Ud.	juega	jugó	jugará
gerund:	*nosotros*	jugamos	jugamos	jugaremos
jugando	*vosotros*	jugáis	jugasteis	jugaréis
	ellos/ellas/Uds.	juegan	jugaron	jugarán
leer	*yo*	leo	leí	leeré
to read	*tú*	lees	leiste	leerás
	él/ella/Ud.	lee	leyó	leerá
gerund:	*nosotros*	leemos	leimos	leeremos
leyendo	*vosotros*	leéis	leisteis	leeréis
	ellos/ellas/Uds.	leen	leyeron	leerán
mostrar	*yo*	muestro	mostré	mostraré
to show	*tú*	muestras	mostraste	mostrarás
	él/ella/Ud.	muestra	mostró	mostrará
gerund:	*nosotros*	mostramos	mostramos	mostraremos
mostrando	*vosotros*	mostráis	mostrasteis	mostraréis
	ellos/ellas/Uds.	muestran	mostraron	mostrarán
ofrecer	*yo*	ofrezco	ofrecí	ofreceré
to offer	*tú*	ofreces	ofreciste	ofrecerás
	él/ella/Ud.	ofrece	ofreció	ofrecerá
gerund:	*nosotros*	ofrecemos	ofrecimos	ofreceremos
ofreciendo	*vosotros*	ofrecéis	ofrecisteis	ofreceréis
	ellos/ellas/Uds.	ofrecen	ofrecieron	ofrecerán
oír	*yo*	oigo	oí	oiré
to hear	*tú*	oyes	oíste	oirás
	él/ella/Ud.	oye	oyó	oirá
gerund:	*nosotros*	oímos	oímos	oiremos
oyendo	*vosotros*	oís	oisteis	oiréis
	ellos/ellas/Uds.	oyen	oyeron	oirán

		Present	Past	Future
pedir to ask for *gerund:* pidiendo	yo tú él/ella/Ud. nosotros vosotros ellos/ellas/Uds.	pido pides pide pedimos pedís piden	pedí pediste pidió pedimos pedisteis pidieron	pediré pedirás pedirá pediremos pediréis pedirán
pensar to think *gerund:* pensando	yo tú él/ella/Ud. nosotros vosotros ellos/ellas/Uds.	pienso piensas piensa pensamos pensáis piensan	pensé pensaste pensó pensamos pensasteis pensaron	pensaré pensarás pensará pensaremos pensaréis pensarán
perder to lose *gerund:* perdiendo	yo tú él/ella/Ud. nosotros vosotros ellos/ellas/Uds.	pierdo pierdes pierde perdemos perdéis pierden	perdí perdiste perdió perdimos perdisteis perdieron	perderé perderás perderá perderemos perderéis perderán
poder can *gerund:* pudiendo	yo tú él/ella/Ud. nosotros vosotros ellos/ellas/Uds.	puedo puedes puede podemos podéis pueden	pude pudiste pudo pudimos pudisteis pudieron	podré podrás podrá podremos podréis podrán
poner to put *gerund:* poniendo	yo tú él/ella/Ud. nosotros vosotros ellos/ellas/Uds.	pongo pones pone ponemos ponéis ponen	puse pusiste puso pusimos pusisteis pusieron	pondré pondrás pondrá pondremos pondréis pondrán
preferir to prefer *gerund:* prefiriendo	yo tú él/ella/Ud. nosotros vosotros ellos/ellas/Uds.	prefiero prefieres prefiere preferimos preferís prefieren	preferí preferiste prefirió preferimos preferisteis prefirieron	preferiré preferirás preferirá preferiremos preferiréis preferirán

		Present	Past	Future
querer	*yo*	quiero	quise	querré
to want	*tú*	quieres	quisiste	querrás
	él/ella/Ud.	quiere	quiso	querrá
gerund:	*nosotros*	queremos	quisimos	querremos
queriendo	*vosotros*	queréis	quisisteis	querréis
	ellos/ellas/Uds.	quieren	quisieron	querrán

		Present	Past	Future
repetir	*yo*	repito	repetí	repetiré
to repeat	*tú*	repites	repetiste	repetirás
	él/ella/Ud.	repite	repitió	repetirá
gerund:	*nosotros*	repetimos	repetimos	repetiremos
repitiendo	*vosotros*	repetís	repetisteis	repetiréis
	ellos/ellas/Uds.	repiten	repitieron	repetirán

		Present	Past	Future
saber	*yo*	sé	supe	sabré
to know	*tú*	sabes	supiste	sabrás
	él/ella/Ud.	sabe	supo	sabrá
gerund:	*nosotros*	sabemos	supimos	sabremos
sabiendo	*vosotros*	sabéis	supisteis	sabréis
	ellos/ellas/Uds.	saben	supieron	sabrán

		Present	Past	Future
salir	*yo*	salgo	salí	saldré
to leave	*tú*	sales	saliste	saldrás
	él/ella/Ud.	sale	salió	saldrá
gerund:	*nosotros*	salimos	salimos	saldremos
saliendo	*vosotros*	salís	salisteis	saldréis
	ellos/ellas/Uds.	salen	salieron	saldrán

		Present	Past	Future
ser	*yo*	soy	fui	seré
to be (perma-	*tú*	eres	fuiste	serás
nent state)	*él/ella/Ud.*	es	fue	será
gerund:	*nosotros*	somos	fuimos	seremos
siendo	*vosotros*	sois	fuisteis	seréis
	ellos/ellas/Uds.	son	fueron	serán

		Present	Past	Future
servir	*yo*	sirvo	serví	serviré
to serve	*tú*	sirves	serviste	servirás
	él/ella/Ud.	sirve	sirvió	servirá
gerund:	*nosotros*	servimos	servimos	serviremos
sirviendo	*vosotros*	servís	servisteis	serviréis
	ellos/ellas/Uds.	sirven	sirvieron	servirán
tener	*yo*	tengo	tuve	tendré
to have	*tú*	tienes	tuviste	tendrás
	él/ella/Ud.	tiene	tuvo	tendrá
gerund:	*nosotros*	tenemos	tuvimos	tendremos
teniendo	*vosotros*	tenéis	tuvisteis	tendréis
	ellos/ellas/Uds.	tienen	tuvieron	tendrán
traer	*yo*	traigo	traje	traeré
to bring	*tú*	traes	trajiste	traerás
	él/ella/Ud.	trae	trajo	traerá
gerund:	*nosotros*	traemos	trajimos	traeremos
trayendo	*vosotros*	traéis	trajisteis	traeréis
	ellos/ellas/Uds.	traen	trajeron	traerán
venir	*yo*	vengo	vine	vendré
to come	*tú*	vienes	viniste	vendrás
	él/ella/Ud.	viene	vino	vendrá
gerund:	*nosotros*	venimos	vinimos	vendremos
viniendo	*vosotros*	venís	vinisteis	vendréis
	ellos/ellas/Uds.	vienen	vinieron	vendrán
ver	*yo*	veo	vi	veré
to see	*tú*	ves	viste	verás
	él/ella/Ud.	ve	vio	verá
gerund:	*nosotros*	vemos	vimos	veremos
viendo	*vosotros*	veis	visteis	veréis
	ellos/ellas/Uds.	ven	vieron	verán

		Present	**Past**	**Future**
volver	*yo*	vuelvo	volví	volveré
to turn	*tú*	vuelves	volviste	volverás
	él/ella/Ud.	vuelve	volvió	volverá
gerund:	*nosotros*	volvemos	volvimos	volveremos
volviendo	*vosotros*	volvéis	volvisteis	volveréis
	ellos/ellas/Uds.	vuelven	volvieron	volverán

Appendix C

Spanish Facts

Here are some facts about the Spanish language:

✔ Spanish was spread around the world during Spain's colonial period, when it was carried to the peoples of the Americas. As a result, Spanish is now the official language of more than 20 countries, and is widely spoken in almost 60 countries, making it one of the world's major languages.

Countries Where Spanish Is Spoken

✔ People talk remnants of Spanish in places such as the Philippines (the Islands are named in honour of a king of Spain) and Morocco.

✔ Many people speak Spanish in the United States. Most of these people come from Puerto Rico, Cuba and Mexico.

✔ Spanish is by far the most commonly spoken language in the Western hemisphere.

✔ Spanish is the third most-spoken language in the world after Mandarin Chinese and English.

✔ The number of people across the world who speak Spanish is estimated at well over 400 million.

✔ Spanish comes from the same family of languages as the Latin used by the Romans.

Answer Key to Word Search in Chapter 13

Word Search

R	Y	L	D	N	E	I	R	F	B	D
O	A	O	T	N	A	U	C	A	I	E
D	C	M	P	G	M	K	Ñ	R	Q	R
I	V	A	A	C	Y	O	E	O	U	I
U	C	V	L	C	X	C	W	I	E	R
L	U	L	W	I	C	M	F	C	D	E
C	H	F	A	I	E	Z	O	E	A	F
N	E	I	O	M	M	N	H	R	R	E
I	R	N	Z	L	B	G	T	P	S	R
F	N	I	A	T	P	A	C	E	E	P
I	C	X	E	S	R	A	H	C	U	D

BAÑO	DIRECCION	PRECIO
CALIENTE	DUCHARSE	PREFERIR
CAMA	FRIA	QUEDARSE
CUANTO	INCLUIDO	

Answers to the Word Scramble in Chapter 14

Spanish	English
1 ¿cómo llego a la plaza?	(C)
2 ¿me lleva por favor al aeropuerto?	(D)
3 ¿dónde está el banco más cercano?	(H)
4 ¿adónde vamos?	(A)
5 ¿a qué hora?	(B)
6 ¿qué es esto?	(G)
7 ¿dónde encuentro un bar?	(E)
8 ¿cuánto cuesta?	(F)

Index

Notes

Notes

Notes

Notes

Notes

Notes

Notes

FOR DUMMIES®

Making Everything Easier!™

UK editions

BUSINESS

978-0-470-74490-1

978-0-470-74381-2

978-0-470-71382-2

FINANCE

978-0-470-99280-7

978-0-470-71432-4

978-0-470-69515-9

HOBBIES

978-0-470-69960-7

978-0-470-74535-9

978-0-470-68178-7

British Sign Language
For Dummies
978-0-470-69477-0

Business NLP For Dummies
978-0-470-69757-3

Cognitive Behavioural Therapy For
Dummies
978-0-470-01838-5

Competitive Strategy For Dummies
978-0-470-77930-9

Cricket For Dummies
978-0-470-03454-5

CVs For Dummies, 2nd Edition
978-0-470-74491-8

Divorce For Dummies, 2nd Edition
978-0-470-74128-3

eBay.co.uk Business All-in-One
For Dummies
978-0-470-72125-4

Emotional Freedom Technique For
Dummies
978-0-470-75876-2

English Grammar For Dummies
978-0-470-05752-0

Flirting For Dummies
978-0-470-74259-4

Golf For Dummies
978-0-470-01811-8

Green Living For Dummies
978-0-470-06038-4

Hypnotherapy For Dummies
978-0-470-01930-6

IBS For Dummies
978-0-470-51737-6

Lean Six Sigma For Dummies
978-0-470-75626-3

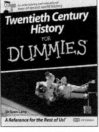
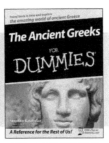

FOR DUMMIES®

The easy way to get more done and have more fun

LANGUAGES

978-0-470-51986-8

978-0-7645-5193-2

978-0-471-77270-5

MUSIC

978-0-470-48133-2

978-0-470-03275-6
UK Edition

978-0-470-49644-2

SCIENCE & MATHS

978-0-7645-5326-4

978-0-7645-5430-8

978-0-7645-5325-7

Art For Dummies
978-0-7645-5104-8

Bass Guitar For Dummies, 2nd Edition
978-0-470-53961-3

Brain Games For Dummies
978-0-470-37378-1

Christianity For Dummies
978-0-7645-4482-8

Criminology For Dummies
978-0-470-39696-4

Forensics For Dummies
978-0-7645-5580-0

German For Dummies
978-0-7645-5195-6

Hobby Farming For Dummies
978-0-470-28172-7

Index Investing For Dummies
978-0-470-29406-2

Jewelry Making & Beading
For Dummies
978-0-7645-2571-1

Knitting For Dummies, 2nd Edition
978-0-470-28747-7

Music Composition For Dummies
978-0-470-22421-2

Physics For Dummies
978-0-7645-5433-9

Schizophrenia For Dummies
978-0-470-25927-6

Sex For Dummies, 3rd Edition
978-0-470-04523-7

Sherlock Holmes For Dummies
978-0-470-48444-9

Solar Power Your Home
For Dummies, 2nd Edition
978-0-470-59678-4

The Koran For Dummies
978-0-7645-5581-7

Wine All-in-One For Dummies
978-0-470-47626-0

FOR DUMMIES®

Helping you expand your horizons and achieve your potential

COMPUTER BASICS

978-0-470-57829-2

978-0-470-46542-4

978-0-470-49743-2

DIGITAL PHOTOGRAPHY

978-0-470-25074-7

978-0-470-46606-3

978-0-470-45772-6

MAC BASICS

978-0-470-27817-8

978-0-470-46661-2

978-0-470-43543-4

Access 2007 For Dummies
978-0-470-04612-8

Adobe Creative Suite 4 Design
Premium All-in-One Desk Reference
For Dummies
978-0-470-33186-6

AutoCAD 2010 For Dummies
978-0-470-43345-4

C++ For Dummies, 6th Edition
978-0-470-31726-6

Computers For Seniors For Dummies ,
2nd Edition
978-0-470-53483-0

Dreamweaver CS4 For Dummies
978-0-470-34502-3

Excel 2007 All-In-One Desk Reference
For Dummies
978-0-470-03738-6

Green IT For Dummies
978-0-470-38688-0

Networking All-in-One Desk Reference
For Dummies, 3rd Edition
978-0-470-17915-4

Office 2007 All-in-One Desk Reference
For Dummies
978-0-471-78279-7

Photoshop CS4 For Dummies
978-0-470-32725-8

Photoshop Elements 7 For Dummies
978-0-470-39700-8

Search Engine Optimization
For Dummies, 3rd Edition
978-0-470-26270-2

The Internet For Dummies,
12th Edition
978-0-470-56095-2

Visual Studio 2008 All-In-One Desk
Reference For Dummies
978-0-470-19108-8

Web Analytics For Dummies
978-0-470-09824-0

Windows Vista For Dummies
978-0-471-75421-3

13061 p4